Oregon Wine Country

EXPLORER'S GUIDES

Oregon Wine Country

A Great Destination

SECOND EDITION

Sherry L. Moore and Jeff Welsch

The Countryman Press   Woodstock, Vermont

Explorer's Guide Oregon Wine Country: A Great Destination
Second Edition
978-1-58157-171-4

Interior photographs by the authors unless otherwise specified
Maps by Erin Greb Cartography, © The Countryman Press
Book design by Bodenweber Design
Composition by Eugenie S. Delaney

Published by The Countryman Press, P.O. Box 748, Woodstock, VT 05091
Distributed by W. W. Norton & Company, Inc., 500 Fifth Avenue, New York, NY 10110
Printed in the United States of America

10 9 8 7 6 5 4 3 2 1

For Dolores and Martin Rotto, our chauffeurs,
cheerleaders, and champions for this book.

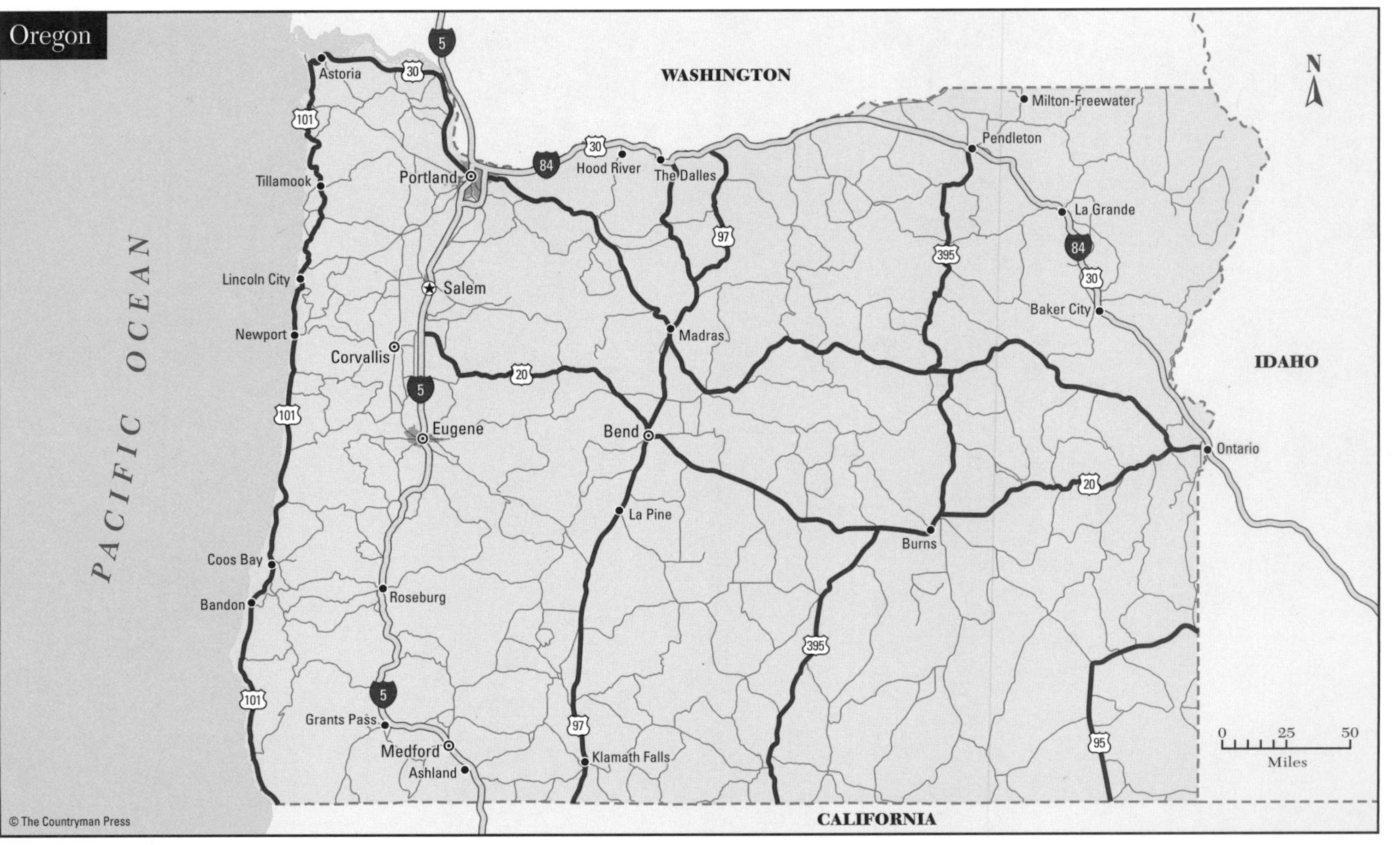
Oregon
WASHINGTON
IDAHO
CALIFORNIA
PACIFIC OCEAN
N
Astoria
Tillamook
Lincoln City
Newport
Coos Bay
Bandon
Portland
Salem
Corvallis
Eugene
Roseburg
Grants Pass
Medford
Ashland
Hood River
The Dalles
Madras
Bend
La Pine
Klamath Falls
Milton-Freewater
Pendleton
La Grande
Baker City
Burns
Ontario
5
30
101
84
97
20
395
95
0
25
50
Miles
© The Countryman Press

Contents

Acknowledgments

IT SEEMS AS IF IT TOOK A VILLAGE TO RAISE THIS BOOK. We are forever grateful to our cadre of family and friends for their support, advice, and opinions as well as to our co-workers, who put up with our absences.

This book could not have happened without the cooperation of hundreds of vintners and winemakers who were patient in answering our questions—many while in the midst of crush. Their dedication, passion, and earnest pursuit of perfection make it possible for fans like us to revel in their success and enjoy fruits of their labor, vintage after vintage.

Finally, thanks to the folks at Countryman Press—Kermit Hummel, Lisa Sacks, Doug Yeager—for their guidance and patience.

Sherry L. Moore and Jeff Welsch

Foreword

WHEN I THINK ABOUT THE EVOLUTION of Oregon's wine industry, I'm in awe. In the early 1980s, there were about 30 wineries. That's when a small group of family, friends, and college fraternity brothers had the ambitious notion of buying land in the fertile Willamette Valley and trying our hand at growing grapes.

Turns out we weren't alone. Word was getting out that Oregon was a good place for vinifera. The Willamette Valley led the way, but the Rogue, Umpqua, and Columbia Valleys were also seeing their way to vineyards.

When we harvested our first crop in 1985, we got hit right between the eyes with the old "supply and demand" adage: big supply, low demand! We couldn't get enough money for the fruit or couldn't sell it at all. Like many other growers sitting on bins of grapes with nowhere to go, we started our own winery: Eola Hills Wine Cellars.

Our timing couldn't have been better. An interesting phenomenon coincided with this early stage: Consumers started noticing Oregon wines—particularly Pinot noir. And they weren't just locals. Oregon wines were gaining worldwide recognition. It wasn't long before our "supply and demand" situation did a complete reversal.

In the years since, the Oregon wine industry has exploded. Those 30 wineries have become more than 400, with no end in sight. And Oregon's reputation as a premium wine-producing region is firmly entrenched internationally.

Only one comprehensive guidebook captures the essence of this remarkable story: *Explorer's Guide Oregon Wine Country, A Great Destination*.

Two longtime Oregonians provide the insider's knowledge you'll want for optimum winery touring. I got to know Jeff while bicycling through Oregon Wine Country. He was sports editor for the Corvallis newspaper and I figured out quickly that he writes passionately about topics that interest him.

I came to know Sherry through her work at a nearby winery. She was also a wine buyer for my local food cooperative, and she featured Eola Hills periodically at her tastings. Her knowledge and sensible approach to wine makes consumers feel comfortable and excited to taste the Oregon experience.

Having explored every corner of the state, Jeff and Sherry provide a unique perspective on our down-to-earth industry. They've gone to exhaustive lengths to include wineries with tasting rooms open to the public with regular hours. But what sets *Oregon Wine Country* apart is their insights on where to eat, sleep, play, and recreate after touring.

Whether you're an Oregonian out for the weekend or visitor on vacation in Oregon Wine Country, this is the only book you'll need.

So, welcome . . . we're glad you're here!

Tom Huggins, General Manager
Eola Hills Wine Cellars

How This Book Works

THIS BOOK IS SOLELY DEDICATED to wineries and tasting rooms in Oregon. If that seems obvious, consider most books featuring Oregon Wine Country include Washington, British Columbia, or the entire Pacific Northwest. Other guidebooks list selected wineries, usually the most renowned, and devote remaining space to photographs.

Explorer's Guide Oregon Wine Country, A Great Destination is for people who want to explore any or all wineries that offer tasting opportunities. It also includes lodging, dining, attractions, recreation, and special events we think wine tourists will find appealing and intriguing.

In some cases, we reluctantly cut well-known wineries simply because they aren't conducive to casual visits or don't operate a tasting room. Ransom Cellars, Stone Wolf, Shea Cellars, and Hawk's View, to name a few, aren't set up for the day-to-day wine tourist. Some wineries operate a semblance of a tasting rooms but were omitted because of inconsistent hours and/or difficulty in reaching them by phone; if we couldn't reach them through repeated efforts, then you probably can't, either. So, where you see a winery listed as open "by appointment," don't be deterred. It typically means it's a small operation. The owners might have other jobs or they can't consistently staff a tasting room. Think of it as calling ahead before visiting someone's home.

In our second *Oregon Wine Country* edition you'll find that details and information are pared down and more concise, to include as many listings as possible. What you won't find is critiques. Our reasoning: Wine drinkers have a wide array of subjective tastes. Personal preference prevails. We've tried to encapsulate the essence of each establishment in a few sentences, so you can choose what suits your fancy.

We've made every effort to provide current and accurate names, numbers, hours of operation, wines produced (alphabetically, followed by specialty), and icons to help guide your decisions. For space and convenience, winery websites are moved to the alphabetical Great Grape Destinations checklist section in appendix C. But be advised that the industry changes rapidly. Doors open, doors close. Hours fluctuate. Edits were made as late as March 2013.

Winery Icons

▲ = Picnic Grounds
🎁 = Gift Shop
🍴 = Food Available
🖍 = Kid Appropriate
🐾 = Dog Friendly
❖ = Rentable Event Facility

Along with licensed tasting rooms consistently open to the public, our book provides overviews of regions, AVAs, and key communities. These are places we've explored, written about, or resided in during 30 years of living in Oregon. Our insiders' knowledge will help define the optimum tour and make the most of your time in Oregon Wine Country.

Our book is arranged on the assumption that visits to the state begin in Portland. We start listings at the northern end of the Willamette Valley and continue south, concluding with the least toured—but no less interesting—regions. Although the Columbia Gorge is chapter 9, it's only 30 minutes east of Portland, so you may choose to divert for a day or two. Touring the entire Willamette Valley could easily take weeks.

We've strived to establish logical touring orders. They are intended to be in geographical order for efficiency—a bit of a trick, especially in the Willamette Valley. After all, Mother Nature didn't lay out these volcanic coastal mountains in a convenient grid. Some backtracking will be required. If at the end of the day you're still searching for that certain winery, check the alphabetical index. And, be sure to check off winery visits on our Great Grape Destinations list in appendix C. Another activity for which Oregonians have a passion is bicycling. To that end, we include sidebars on particularly appealing rides in Oregon Wine Country that feature wineries.

Lodging and dining establishments are alphabetized within each area. We chose a select, diverse few that emphasize Oregon wines. With lodging, more $ mean a premium room during peak season (Memorial Day weekend through autumn) and low $ represents a standard room, off-season rate.

Lodging

$ = $75 or less
$$ = $75–125
$$$ = $126–199
$$$$ = $200 and above

Lodging Icons

🍴 = Restaurant
🍸 = Bar
♿ = Handicapped Accessible
🐾 = Pet Friendly

Restaurants and wine bars were chosen for their emphasis of Oregon and/or Northwest wines. This is important to note because many popular and well-known places didn't make the book simply because Oregon wines are limited or nonexistent on the menu. Dining icons are based on the cost of an average single dinner entrée.

Dining

$ = 10 or less
$$ = $11–20
$$$ = $21–30
$$$$ = $30 and above

Dining Icons

B = Breakfast
L = Lunch
D = Dinner
BR = Brunch
HH = Happy Hour
LN = Late-Night Menu

A stellar lineup of Oregon wines adds to the décor at many Oregon restaurants. Courtesy Joel Palmer House

A favorite pastime in Oregon Wine Country is the festival circuit. In our Festivals and Events appendix (A), we've listed festivities by the month in which they're usually staged, including those events that have history and/or are likely to be repeated. We don't guarantee weather, but what's a little mist when your fingers are wrapped around a glass stem and your nose is warmed by fragrant esters? For more detailed information, check the Oregon Wine Advisory Board's website. Or pick up a copy of *Oregon Wine Press* before heading out.

Whether you're a dedicated oenophile or eager novice, this book will provide you with all the requisite information to help you explore a state we will forever hold near and dear. We invite you to select your destination, peruse the chapter, and follow your palate.

Then settle back into savoring all the flavors of Oregon—one winery, one restaurant, one deck view, and one celebration at a time!

Oregon Wine Country

AN INTRODUCTION

FROM THE TIME MERIWETHER LEWIS and William Clark arrived at Fort Clatsop on the Pacific Ocean in 1805, followed shortly by legions of settlers, Oregon has embodied a hardy pioneer spirit. So it is with its grape farmers and vintners.

At first blush, Oregon might not seem like wine country, even though grapes were planted as far back as the 1820s. Perhaps that's why it wasn't until two full centuries after viticulture took root in neighboring California that the wine industry became a modest contributor to Oregon's economy.

After all, it rains a lot in Oregon—at least west of the Cascade Range, where more than 80 percent of the population resides. In the western valleys and coastal areas, the steady drizzle typically starts in October and doesn't let up until the Fourth of July. As with those first Oregon Trail dreamers, fortitude and resolve are required to survive and thrive. That means a grape that doesn't mind getting ruddy, a grape that looks at the winter skies and says, "Bring it on." It means vines that like to wrap roots around rocks in uneven, inhospitable soils and mischievously threaten to run amok like undisciplined children on the long, warm days of summer.

Turns out Oregon and Pinot noir were made for each other. In the four decades since Charles Coury, David Lett, and other wine pioneers planted the fickle grape in the Dundee Hills, the state has become renowned for this complex, challenging wine that manifests differently from vineyard to vineyard.

In hindsight, the success is no surprise, given that Oregon straddles the 45th Parallel, like several famed European producing regions: France's Alsace, Bordeaux, and Burgundy, the province most aligned with the Willamette Valley. It just took savvy and raw determination to see the improbable vision through.

Pinot noir represents about 60 percent of the state's production, but Oregon's salt-of-the-earth pioneers have their share of successes with other red and white varietals—72 and counting. Although vinifera comprises the majority of vineyard space, award-winning wines are being produced from hybrids, too. Many have success with Baco noir, Maréchal Foch, and Vignoles, to name a few, because they're hardy, early

LEFT: Poppies brighten the hilltop vista at Anderson Family Vineyards in the north Willamette Valley. John Baker

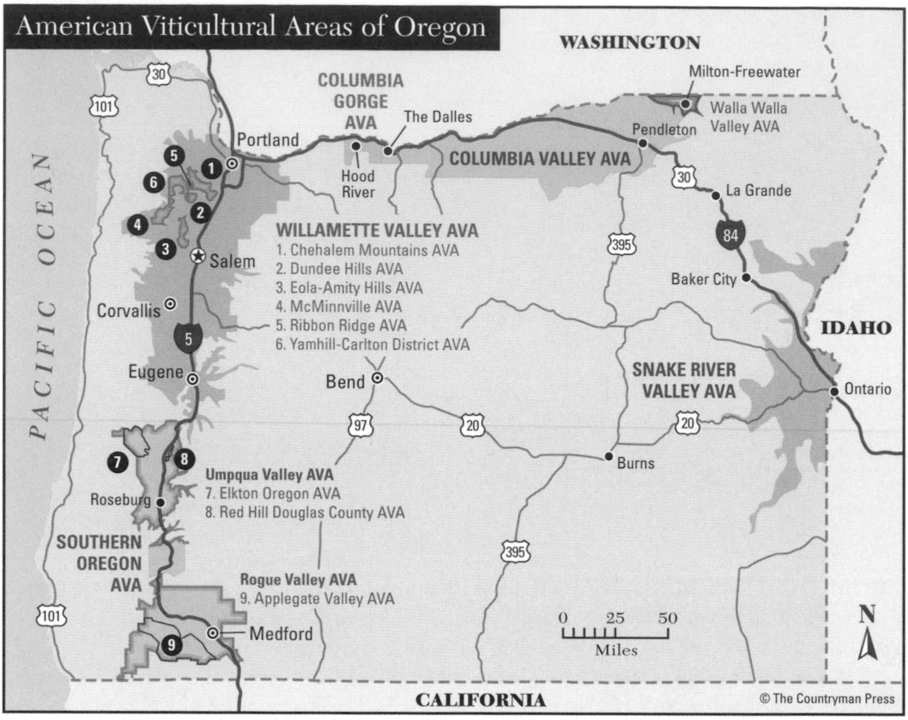

American Viticultural Areas of Oregon

WASHINGTON
COLUMBIA GORGE AVA
The Dalles
Milton-Freewater
Walla Walla Valley AVA
Portland
Hood River
Pendleton
COLUMBIA VALLEY AVA
La Grande
PACIFIC OCEAN
Salem
WILLAMETTE VALLEY AVA
1. Chehalem Mountains AVA
2. Dundee Hills AVA
3. Eola-Amity Hills AVA
4. McMinnville AVA
5. Ribbon Ridge AVA
6. Yamhill-Carlton District AVA
Baker City
Corvallis
IDAHO
Eugene
Bend
SNAKE RIVER VALLEY AVA
Ontario
Burns
Umpqua Valley AVA
7. Elkton Oregon AVA
8. Red Hill Douglas County AVA
Roseburg
SOUTHERN OREGON AVA
Rogue Valley AVA
9. Applegate Valley AVA
Medford
0 25 50
Miles
N
CALIFORNIA
© The Countryman Press

ripeners, resistant to frost—an all-too-common occurrence in late spring or early fall. Raising grapes can be a heart-stopping business.

Riches from land and sea are nonetheless abundant, and nothing stimulates the palate or imagination like Oregon foods paired with its wines. The state is a bountiful basket of epicurean and wine delights. Feast on fresh Dungeness crab paired with Old World–style Riesling, savor caught-that-day halibut matched with a Burgundian-style Chardonnay, or enjoy grilled Pacific salmon and wild mushrooms served with out-of-this-world Pinot. Finish a summer meal with juicy, hand-picked peaches drenched in Muscat ottonel, or pass the artisan farmstead cheese plate paired with sparkling Blanc de blanc or Pinot noir port. As Oregonians can readily attest, life doesn't get much better.

Newport is the Dungeness crab capital of the world. Courtesy Newport Chamber of Commerce

Part of Oregon's wine intrigue is the diversity of its regions. Within the borders of a state that's about one-third the size of France, grapes grow in the cool, damp, and rocky foothills of the Coastal Range, in the warm forests of the Rogue and Umpqua River Valleys, and in the arid high deserts of the Columbia Plateau. Within each region or AVA, conditions can be dramatically different from ridge to ridge, and even row to row.

Oregon's nearly 900 vineyards, spread among 16 approved wine-growing regions (American Viticultural Areas, or AVAs)—and likely to be 18 in 2013—are more diverse than California, which has nine times as many wineries. Oregon has more than 20,500 acres in grapes and a whopping 450 wineries. More than 1.9 million cases are produced annually, and it's a $2.7 billion industry. A record-breaking 41,500 tons of grapes were harvested in 2011, and wine tourism sweetens the state's coffers by at least $150 million annually. And all indicators in 2012 suggested the most robust harvest in the state's history, thanks to unusually warm, rainless summer days and reliably cool nights.

Despite this rarefied air, industry folks maintain their collective brand as down-to-earth neighbors. It's not unusual to find a winemaker, owner, or vineyard manager—often the same person—pouring behind the counter, ready to share his or her passion. Wine novices intimidated by the headiness of Napa and Sonoma will feel comfortable at nearly every Oregon winery. Yes, you'll find ostentatious estates with extravagant facilities and pretentious tasting rooms. But even the highest of the highbrows will be welcoming—they want to sell wine, too. The diversity makes for more interesting touring.

Oregon wine touring is a booming pastime. Buses, limos, and tour vans are available, taking the stress of finding your way to the out-of-the way and allowing maximum tasting pleasure (see appendix B). Perhaps a bittersweet sign of Oregon's emergence and loss of innocence: Nearly every winery now charges a tasting fee. Most are nominal, and a drop in the bin toward the resources poured into production.

Oregon's wine industry continues to demand transparency and ethics from itself. What you see in and on the bottle is what you get. When the label states that the vintage and fruit is from a specific appellation, such as the Columbia Gorge, at least 95

Many wineries have a designated greeter, a.k.a. the Wine Dog.

Many inviting tasting decks await your arrival. Courtesy Trinity Vineyard

percent of the wine is just that. If the label says "Pinot noir," a minimum of 90 percent of the content is just that (in recent years the state relaxed laws on 18 of the 72 varietals to allow winemakers, especially in southern Oregon, to be more competitive).

Although tasting room locations can be challenging to find, blue-and-white roadside signs usually help point the way. These days, smartphone global positioning systems (GPS) are fairly reliable, though some locales fool even modern technology. Better to point the car in your desired direction and see where you end up. By the way, in Oregon it's illegal to pump your own gas—no ruined "nose" from fuel odors here.

While on a wine tour, it's important to remember a few simple rules of etiquette. Heavy perfume or cologne can interfere with tasting and elicit frowns of disapproval. Don't feel compelled to drink an entire sample; spitting or dumping is encouraged. Too many tastes will limit your experience later in the day, especially if you're driving. It's also customary to make a purchase, especially if the tasting has been complimentary and even more so if the server has spent time with you. Groups of six or more should call ahead because some tasting rooms are small and personalized tours might be included.

Most wineries are kid- and dog-friendly, but be respectful. Children typically are welcome *if* they are supervised. Many wineries have their own dogs, and a free-wheeling visiting canine can create chaos; keep your pooch on a leash or in the car, if necessary. Remember, many tasting rooms are places of residency or living space, so respect parked equipment and hours of business. Everyone likes to "go home" after a day of work.

After a day of tasting worldly wines and meeting contagiously passionate people, you can choose among a plethora of fine eating establishments and comfortable beds in a wide array of settings. Bed and breakfasts, lodges, cabins, and chain motels are readily available—unless it's an Oregon wine holiday such as Memorial Day or Thanksgiving weekend. Crowds can get overwhelming, but the experience will be exhilarating and memorable.

Memorial Day entertainment comes in a wide variety of forms and venues. John Baker

Memorial Day weekend signals the onset of summer. New releases are ready and there's a Mardi Gras atmosphere. Wine tourists hire limos and tour buses en masse or gather in groups to caravan. Tasting rooms usually closed are open with welcome pours. The events are as diverse as the vintners, ranging from rowdy country music and Cuban dance lessons to refined classical art and barrel sampling. Wines are paired with specialty foods, from cheeses and picnic fare to the catered and exotic. Memorial Day is a time wineries put their best foot forward, and all hands are on deck to ensure a good time.

The other major celebratory season is Friday to Sunday after Thanksgiving. Crush is complete, leaves have turned, and the mood is festive but more subdued. It's a weekend for open houses, food pairing, and gift buying. It's also time for visiting family and friends to see what this wine country thing is all about. Another trend: the weekend before Thanksgiving as a preholiday opportunity to secure wines for Turkey Day dinners. In recent years, Labor Day weekend has become prime touring time as well.

A bonus to visiting Oregon wine country: no sales tax. You'll have extra dollars to indulge in more bottles or cases. An exception is lodging. Oregon tags on a "transient room tax," so figure between 8 and 10 percent added to the rate; a few towns have restaurant taxes as well.

Today, despite a sputtering economy—Oregon's unemployment remains high, though improving—optimism prevails. The number of wineries is increasing by about a dozen annually. Vineyards and wineries are popping up in places unimaginable a half-century ago. Boutique wine bars and cooperatives are budding as well.

For many dreamers of vines, wines, and quintessential tasting sessions, Oregon Wine Country truly is the Eden at the end of the trail.

History and Terroir

DOWN TO EARTH

IN 1979, A FLEDGLING OREGON VINTNER named David Lett was invited to submit a red wine for a blind tasting against the haughty French in a competition called the Gault-Millau French Wine Olympiades. Next to the aristocratic French, German, and Italian winemakers, Lett was a dirt-under-the-fingernails farmer who had this crazy notion that great wine could be made in cool, wet, blustery Oregon.

What happened next is perhaps the signature moment in what is often reverently called "the Oregon Story."

A mere three years after a California winery had stunned the French with a winning Chardonnay, Lett's wine finished among the top 10 Burgundies in a field of more than 330. He orchestrated this shocker with grapes nurtured in the unheralded northern Willamette Valley. Even more remarkable, the state had won with perhaps the world's most revered wine—made from a fickle, petulant, and occasionally ornery cool-climate grape that flummoxes some of the industry's most accomplished vintners.

Pinot noir.

This landmark success was achieved with The Eyrie Vineyards South Block Pinot less than a decade after departing his native California to start anew in Oregon. He came despite dire predictions from colleagues in the University of California–Davis oenology department. Within 15 years of the arrival of Lett and other pioneers, Oregon suddenly was a major wine player, and the industry's growth in the three decades since has been astonishing.

Where once the Willamette Valley was the sole bastion of winemaking, now vineyards have been carved out of fir forests, desert steppes, and old orchards as far south as Ashland, as far east as the Oregon-Idaho border, and in places even those early innovators never would've imagined.

Not that the very earliest vintners would have been so amazed. As far back as the 1820s, fur trappers planted grapes at French Prairie, just northeast of modern-day Salem. A half-century later, entrepreneurs Henderson Luelling and Ernest Reuter rooted vines in the Willamette Valley—the former favoring the American varietal

LEFT: Springtime in Oregon Wine Country blooms in many colors and shapes. John Baker

Concord, the latter recognizing the potential of cool-climate wine grapes. Reuter was especially interested in a grape from France's Burgundy region called—you guessed it—Pinot noir.

While Reuter also grew Pinot blanc, Riesling, and Gewürztraminer on David Hill, west of Forest Grove, other dreamers were experimenting with viticulture in the arid eastern end of the Columbia Gorge and the California-esque Umpqua, Applegate, and Rogue Valleys of southern Oregon. In fact, though the Willamette Valley is the epicenter of Oregon wine today, the state's first official winery, Valley View, was started in 1851 by Peter Britt in Jacksonville, near Medford. The state even enjoyed mild international fame—Reuter is said to have won a gold medal at the 1904 St. Louis World's Fair.

Pinot gris grapes flourish in the soils of the Willamette Valley. Bill Miller

Then, in 1914, it all ended. Prohibition forced winemakers to tear out vineyards or go broke. Many simply closed up and left their vines. Others replanted hazelnut, apple, pear, or cherry orchards. A few made legal fruit wines, and others started anew when the ban was lifted, producing wines for the military. One, Honeywood Winery just outside of Salem, began making fruit wines in 1933 and today makes both fruit- and vinifera-based wines. It's Oregon's oldest continuously operating winery.

The state's contemporary wine history really began in 1961, when another refugee from UC–Davis, Richard Sommer, planted Riesling and seven other cool-climate varietals near Roseburg. Sommer provided training for the next wave of Oregon wine pioneers and, in 1967, produced the state's first Pinot noir from his HillCrest Vineyards. Full-scale immigration began four years after that. The first were meteorologist Charles Coury and his wife, Shirley, who in 1965 planted Pinot noir and Riesling on the same Forest Grove hill where Reuter had made wine a century earlier.

And then there was Lett. Early in 1965, the 25-year-old with a pioneering spirit hopped in a modern-day Conestoga wagon—a pickup truck and trailer—and headed for his own Eden at the end of the Oregon Trail. In tow were 3,000 grapevine cuttings destined for this bold, cold new world. Lett was driven by a love for wine and a lust for a challenge. Having spent time at wineries in Burgundy, he was certain that somewhere in the hill country south of Portland awaited the perfect Pinot patch, where he would find a harmonic convergence of mild winters, warm summers, cool nights, and rich soils—a place where a hardworking, easily agitated grape would thrive.

Lett rooted his young vines in a leased rye field just outside Corvallis and continued north. He poked around both sides of the valley before settling on a 20-acre hillside site about 30 miles southwest of Portland. Lett and his new bride, Diana, paid $9,000 for their acreage. On their honeymoon, they planted the valley's first Pinot noir—though some argue the distinction belongs to Coury—the United States' first Pinot gris, and four other varietals. Thus began the story of The Eyrie Vineyards and the dedicated, congenial, and sometimes crusty man called "Papa Pinot"—a nod to his place in history and resemblance to the writer Ernest "Papa" Hemingway.

The Oregon Story is a bit of lore that wine enthusiasts here can recite at the pop of a cork. Less than a year after the 1979 Wine Olympiades, a French winemaker named Robert Drouhin orchestrated a rematch. This time, Lett's Pinot noir finished second by two-tenths of a point to Drouhin's Chambolle-Musigny.

Soon to come to Oregon were names now synonymous with the state's wine industry: Adelsheim, Ponzi, Erath, Maresh, Blosser, and many others. These accomplished folks from diverse backgrounds became self-proclaimed hippies of the dirt, bonded by a collective naiveté, adventurous spirit, and a drive to prove naysayers wrong. Farther south, in the Umpqua region, the Girardets and Troons complemented HillCrest by planting grapes, and the Wisnovsky family jump-started Peter Britt's groundbreaking winery at Valley View.

Lett's legend didn't end at great wine. He was an organic farmer before organic farming became trendy, a meticulous sort with a European ethos who finessed and massaged his wines in a tireless pursuit of quality over quantity. Along with Adelsheim, he was instrumental in the landmark land-use planning credited with saving rural Oregon lands from urban sprawl. Always there to lend a hand to those who respected the art of making beautiful wine, he was a cofounder of the Oregon Winegrowers Association and helped bring the International Pinot Noir Celebration to McMinnville. Although he never sought it, his fame grew until his death at age 69 in the autumn of 2008, after which he was eulogized by industry giants and the *New York Times*.

Seven years after the perception-altering showdown in France, the Drouhin family opened a winery in the Red Hills. With classic Oregon spirit, it was Lett and Adelsheim who helped their former competitor find his perfect Pinot patch.

TERROIR

Terroir is a French word generally meaning "sense of place." In wine terms, it's about geology, topography, and climate. Oregon's wine story really begins millions of years ago, with the evolution of the state's terroir. Of the three geologic phenomena that shaped the state, one has been a slow grind over millions of years, one a single cataclysmic moment, and the last either a lone event or a repeat covering thousands of years.

Oregon rests on the stationary Continental Plate, but just offshore under the Pacific Ocean is the restless Juan de Fuca Plate, grinding like a wheel cog at a geologic snail's pace. When the Juan de Fuca's forward motion is halted and then inevitably springs free, the result is earthquakes. When it has moved relatively smoothly, it has scraped soils off the ocean bottom and added to a coastline that once was near present-day Idaho.

This activity is all part of the tumultuous Pacific Ring of Fire, which produced a powerful series of planet-altering supervolcano eruptions about 20 million years ago in what is now eastern Oregon. The resulting Columbia River Basalt Flows covered much of the state. They are seen today in the dramatic coastal capes and the Dundee Hills.

The final piece of the geologic puzzle was placed about 15,000 years ago, when a giant ice dam on the Clark Fork of the Columbia River in western Montana burst and sent a 2,000-foot-deep wall of lake water rushing across eastern Washington, through the Columbia Gorge and up the river valleys—as far as present-day Eugene, about 130 miles from Portland in the southern end of the Willamette Valley. Whether it was one event or a series of natural dam collapses is still debated, but the result of the Missoula Floods was silt as deep as 150 feet in the north Willamette Valley. It is because of these rich soils that the valley is one of the most fertile agricultural regions in America.

As you tour the Willamette Valley, you'll hear winemakers talk reverently about two

Pinot noir clusters

Courtesy Bradley Vineyards

types of soil: Jory and Willakenzie. Jory arrived courtesy of the volcanic eruption, and Willakenzie is the result of the colliding plates. Differing soils can be a ridge apart, a vineyard apart, or even a block apart. And only the trained eye or palate can tell: With their reddish hues and clay feel, they look virtually the same. The Dundee, Salem, and Eola Hills are Jory flows, while Willakenzie soils tend to be on the west side of the valley. Yet as similar as they are in appearance, these soils produce dramatically different Pinots. Wines from Jory soils tend to be earthy and fruitier; wines from Willakenzie are darker, more intense, and tannic. Adding to further intrigue: More than a dozen other soil types are blended with the big two.

Naturally, the distinctions are not always so simple, thanks to the two other major components of terroir: climate and topography.

By and large, Oregon is known for its rain, though that's an overgeneralization. Much of the moisture falls on the coast and in the Willamette Valley, but even in the valley precipitation is relatively rare between the Fourth of July and mid-October. Southern Oregon is warmer and drier, and many grape-growing areas of eastern Oregon are as arid as Tucson, Arizona, and often require irrigation. No place epitomizes these differences more than the Columbia Gorge, which touts "a World of Wine in Forty Miles." Nearly every grape from A (Albarino) to Z (Zinfandel) is grown in this scenic chasm bisecting the Cascade Range. The west end is damp, cool, and blustery Pinot country; the east is hot and dry, the way Syrah likes it.

Farther south, the Mediterranean climes are renowned for wines familiar to California growers. The aptly named "100 Valleys of the Umpqua" region around Roseburg could easily boast "a World of Microclimates in Forty Miles" due to harmonic convergences of climate and topography. Of course, Oregon's signature grape, Pinot noir, loves the seemingly homogenous weather of the Willamette Valley, yet from ridge to ridge diverse microclimates exist. One might be a sultry Coast Range rain shadow where marine air is a nonfactor; another, the eastern end of a river corridor that brings cool Pacific breezes in the summer. One might be a south-facing slope with relentless summer sun at 1,000 feet; another, facing east with partial exposure at 500. Some parts of the Chehalem Mountains receive 60 inches of rain per year; others, 35. Small wonder that there are six American Viticulture Association (AVA) appellations in the 150-mile-long, chile-pepper-shaped Willamette Valley alone—with a seventh in the works in late 2012.

The upshot: No two wineries, no two vineyards, and no two wines of the same variety and vintage, are exactly alike. It's all part of the charm and intrigue of this fascinating place called Oregon Wine Country.

1

Portland Area

COMIN' UP ROSES

PORTLAND AREA (Willamette Valley AVA)

River City, Rose City, Stumptown, or PDX—whatever the affectionate tag, Portland is a metropolis like no other. It is a big city with a small-town persona, its soul defined not by its sprawling suburbs but by its vibrant heart. Portlanders aren't trendy; they're trendsetters. The metropolitan area's million-plus citizens are progressive, proud, and relish their individualism. Their style is casual and outdoorsy with a brush of grunge, wrapped in a layer of sophistication tinged with an air of slight indifference—friendly enough, but not overly so. Men with manicures and manbags, women in sweatshirts and heels, dogs decked in couture or mud . . . it all fits. The term *metrosexual* was probably born here. All things local, regional, sustainable, and gourmet are the norm. The whole ethos of Portlanders is that they know they have it good and they embrace every bit, sip, and bite of it. They also defend it.

A city that once allowed the Willamette River to catch on fire has become a fierce river- and land-keeper. In 1973, the state's leaders had the foresight to create urban-growth boundaries protecting rural lands just outside the city limits. Oregon also was one of the first states to require deposits on bottle returns. Going green isn't a badge of honor—it's a way of life. Thousands of cyclists commute to work, rain or shine, their task made easier by miles of bike lanes and European-style traffic signals that accommodate drivers, walkers, and pedalers.

Parks are a priority. In the West Hills above the city, Washington Park is a woodsy complex of museums, gardens, and a world-class zoo. Its extensive trail system for runners, hikers, mountain bikers, and horseback riders amid towering Douglas firs sets Portland apart from every major city in the country.

The city is defined by four quadrants of distinctive neighborhoods within districts, each with unique personality and flair: the boutique-ish Northwest, the gentrified Northeast, the old-money and alternative Southeast, and the high-density Southwest,

LEFT: Pinot noir fruit in full regalia — Bill Miller

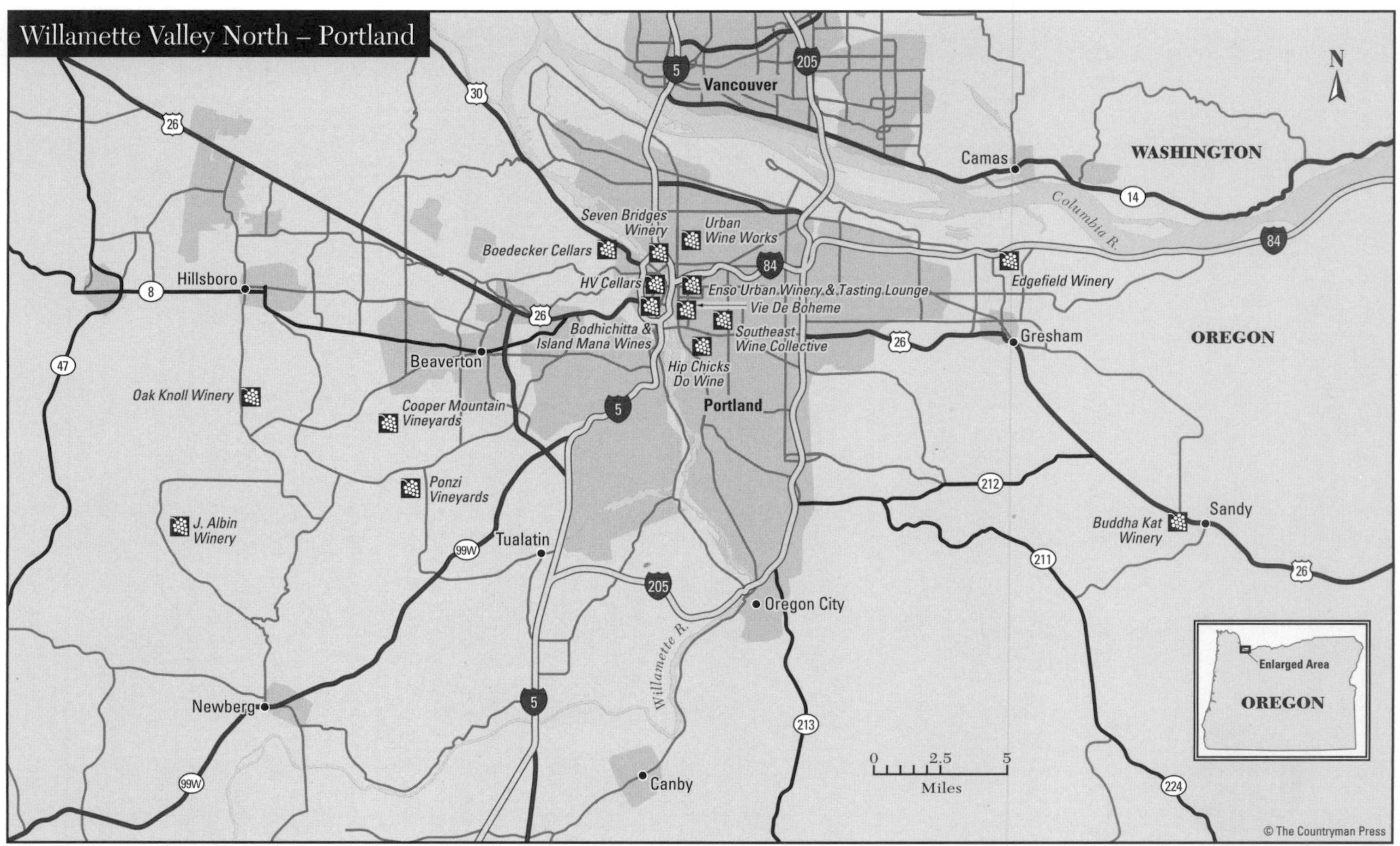
Willamette Valley North – Portland
N
WASHINGTON
OREGON
Vancouver
Camas
Columbia R.
Seven Bridges Winery
Urban Wine Works
Boedecker Cellars
Hillsboro
HV Cellars
Enso Urban Winery & Tasting Lounge
Vie De Boheme
Edgefield Winery
Bodhichitta & Island Mana Wines
Southeast Wine Collective
Gresham
Beaverton
Hip Chicks Do Wine
Oak Knoll Winery
Cooper Mountain Vineyards
Portland
Ponzi Vineyards
J. Albin Winery
Tualatin
Buddha Kat Winery
Sandy
Oregon City
Willamette R.
Enlarged Area
OREGON
Newberg
Canby
0 2.5 5
Miles
© The Countryman Press
5
205
30
26
14
84
8
47
99W
212
211
213
224

Lucky wine tasters get a tour of a vineyard in the north Willamette Valley. John Baker

where ubiquitous condos intermingle with upscale homes overlooking the city. They are divided roughly by the Willamette River flowing south–north and eclectic Burnside Avenue running east–west.

Northwest Portland is a mixture of old shabby and new chic, personified by the Pearl District and its culinary cutting edge. Once decaying, Northeast Portland now is a fashionable bastion of comfortable old homes with contemporary facelifts, an area where rusted iron rings once used to secure horses are still affixed to curbs. Southeast is a blend of cultures—and likes it that way. Southwest Portland is essentially downtown, from which the city pulse is strongest. And of late, a fifth "quadrant" has arrived: North Portland is home to the respected working class that makes the busy ports on the Willamette and Columbia Rivers hum.

Each of these communities within a community is defined by commercial cores of shopping, dining, and grocery stores that limit trips into the city—and traffic.

Portland is a food, wine, microbrew, and spirits mecca whose chefs, brewmasters, and bartenders are regionally, nationally, and internationally acclaimed. Its restaurants and nightspots are often featured in such national media as *Sunset* magazine, the Food Network, *Food & Wine*, and *Wine Spectator*. Creative chefs thrive on the abundance of fresh and locally raised, captured, or cultivated fare, ranging from berries to bovines, grains to greens, nuts to 'shrooms, seafood to spirits, artisan cheeses, pork, lamb . . . even emu. What isn't provided, they handcraft with what they have or can get in fair trade. The motto in nearly every restaurant listed below is "farm to fork"—utilizing fresh, local, seasonal, organic, and sustainable ingredients. Sysco trucks needn't apply.

Naturally, this pride of origin carries over to the area's vineyards and wine production. The city stays in tune with its "homey" wineries, making amiable connections to the food. The *Oregonian's* Food Day section (Wednesdays) lists many an event, tasting, or class with Oregon vino as its focal point. Portland's wine bars, tapas bars, bottle shops, tasting rooms, and hundreds of restaurants know how to make the most of what's nearby, meaning you won't have to travel far for a most memorable experience.

Getting Here and Around

In keeping with its fresh persona, Portland has an attractive—and busy—international airport served by 13 airlines. Four times from 2007 to 2011, **Portland International Airport** (PDX) was chosen by *Condé Nast Traveler* magazine as the best in the United States for its traveler comfort, ease of connections, security, and other touches.

For those who like to keep their feet on the ground—or at least on rails—Portland Union Station (800 NW Sixth Avenue) serves as a hub for **Amtrak**'s north–south Coast Starlight and Cascades trains, and the east-west Empire Builder. If you're behind the wheel, I-5 is the country's westernmost north–south freeway, starting on the Mexican border just south of San Diego and ending north of Seattle on the Canadian border. I-84's western terminus is Portland; it meets up with intercontinental I-80 just east of Salt Lake City. I-84's highlight is the Columbia Gorge. We recommend taking your time and stopping at the many wineries between The Dalles and Hood River.

Like all large cities, Portland's traffic is becoming more of a headache, with rush hour an issue at numerous bottlenecks. Although I-205 helps travelers skirt the city on the southeast side and I-405 provides an urban alternative to I-5 going north and south, expect slowdowns at peak travel times. Among the more common bumper-to-bumper areas are the Vista Ridge tunnels on the Sunset Highway (US 26), OR 217 between Tualatin and Beaverton, OR 99W between Beaverton and Newberg, and the I-5/I-405 junctions on the city's north and south sides.

Helping to ease the traffic is Portland's reputation as perhaps the most bicycle-friendly metropolitan area in America. Also making getting around easier is **Tri-Met's MAX Light Rail Service**, including a route to the airport. Day passes are $5 and two-hour tickets to anywhere are $2.50.

Wineries
in the Portland Area

Wine touring around Portland covers the gamut, from an urban industrial zone to classic country estates scattered throughout the hills, mostly southwest of the city. If you're starting from Portland International Airport, go downtown to the handful of wineries in two warehouse districts, and then literally head for the hills of Beaverton, Aloha, and Hillsboro. Hitting the two wineries on the east side will require some backtracking, but Buddha Kat and Edgefield are unique and worthy of exploration.

TROUTDALE

▲ 🍴 🎁 🐾 ❖ Edgefield Winery (2126 SW Halsey Street; 503-665-2992). *Tasting room:* Daily 12–10. *Fee:* $4–6. *Owners:* Mike & Brian McMenamin. *Winemaker:* Davis Palmer. *Wines:* Cabernet sauvignon, Chardonnay, Merlot, Pinot gris, Pinot noir, Riesling, Syrah, Viognier, Zinfandel, rosé, red and white blends, sparkling, dessert, port. *Cases:* 25,000–30,000. Edgefield's tasting room is a secluded hideaway from the attractions and distractions in the village complex. It feels more like a basement neighborhood bar and is typical of the McMenamin brothers' hospitality. On the property is a 3-acre vineyard of Pinot gris, which supplies the Poor Farm label—another people-pleaser. Local art, live music most evenings, and several dining options make this a definite overnight destination.

McMenamins Edgefield Manor, in Troutdale, was once the county's poor farm. Its history is painted in murals on the walls. Courtesy McMenamins

SANDY

Buddha Kat Winery (17020 Ruben Lane; 503-668-3124). *Tasting room:* Daily 9–5. *Fee:* Complimentary. *Owner:* Lorie Dilley. *Winemaker:* Josh Rude. *Wines:* Chardonnay, Gewürztraminer, Merlot, Muscat, Niagara, Pinot noir, Riesling, berry, sparkling. *Cases:* 3,500. Formerly Wasson Brothers, the oldest winery in Clackamas County continues to describe itself as "in a glass by itself." It's in orchard and nursery country between Portland and the Columbia Gorge. The winery was long known for its berry wines before selling in 2012 to Lorie Dilley, who has hired Josh Rude to add more traditional wines to the mix. At press time, Buddha Kat was turning its tasting room into a wine bar.

PORTLAND

Hip Chicks Do Wine (4510 SE 23rd Avenue; 503-234-3790). *Tasting room:* Daily 11–6. *Second location:* 602 East First Street, Newberg (503-554-5800). *Fee:* $7. *Owners/Winemakers:* Laurie Lewis & Renee Neely. *Wines:* Cabernet franc, Cabernet sauvignon, Malbec, Merlot, Muscat, Pinot gris, Pinot noir, Sangiovese, Syrah, rosé, red and white blends. *Cases:* 5,000. The original Hip Chicks label and logo are purely playful, accurately depicting the style of two fun and hip gals, Laurie and Renee. (The figures on the label resemble the team, just a tad.) The dynamic duo makes friendly, fruit-forward, and meant to drink now wines, no waiting necessary. Known for their Belly Button wine (a Pinot gris and Muscat blend), they also produce serious wines. Their target market is Gen Xers, but older folks think their wine just fine, too.

Southeast Wine Collective (2425 SE 35th Place; 503-887-8755; Wine Collective: 503-477-5511). *Tasting room:* Wed.–Fri. 3–10, Sat. & Sun. 11–11. *Owners:* Kate & Thomas Monroe. Tweaking the norm and filling a niche, Kate and Thomas Monroe, owners and founders of Division Wine Company, have created a premium custom-crush facility in the foodie-fanatical Division-Clinton neighborhood. The multipurpose venue serves as incubator for smaller winemakers with their own labels, a Euro-style

Vineyards can be found in surprising places around Portland. Courtesy McMenamins

wine bar, and retail space. Their retro-fitted building from the late '20s is enhanced by huge old-growth beams, repurposed wood, and art deco décor. Tastes, glass pours, or by the bottle mingle with light noshes. The Monroes partner with local cheese artisans for their selections, and order charcuterie from the region; plans to extend the menu are on tap.

Bow & Arrow (503-367-1306). *Owners:* Scott & Dana Frank. *Winemaker:* Scott Frank. *Wines:* Cabernet franc, Gamay noir, Melon de Bourgogne, Pinot noir. *Cases:* 1,000. Scott Frank, assistant winemaker at Cameron, enjoys making wines that reflect central France's Loire Valley.

Division Wine Making Company. *Owners:* Thomas & Kate Monroe. *Winemaker:* Thomas Monroe. *Wines:* Chardonnay, Gamay noir, Pinot noir, rosé. *Cases:* 1,000. Urbanites Tom and Kate made wine while residing in France, and caught the fever. They don't feel the need to live in the vineyard and embrace the "it takes a village concept." Their wines are balanced and elegant, with higher acidity, lower alcohol, and no reliance on modifications. Look for future experiments of Loire-type wines.

Helioterra (503-757-5881). *Owner/Winemaker:* Anne Ebenretier Hubatch. *Wines:* Mourvèdre, Pinot blanc, Pinot noir, Syrah. *Cases:* 1,500–2,000. Formerly at Apolloni, sassy cowgirl Anne likes going off the ranch by producing different varietals than the typical. Whoa Nellie, her second label, is more indicative of her personality.

Vincent (503-740-9475). *Owner/Winemaker:* Vincent Fritzsche. *Wines:* Chardonnay, Pinot noir. *Cases:* 700. Using the often-quoted philosophy, "Let the grapes do the commuting," Vincent focuses on traditionalized winemaking with his Pinot, and is a true "terroiriste."

Vie de Bohème (1530 SE Seventh Avenue; 503-360-1233). *Tasting room:* Tues.–Thurs. 4–11:30, Fri. 4–12:30, Sat. 2–12:30, Sun. 4–9. *Fee:* $12–15. *Owners:* Maison Nuvo LLC. *Winemaker:* Brad Gearhart. *Wines:* Cabernet franc, Cabernet sauvignon, Merlot, Pinot gris, Syrah, Zinfandel, red blend. *Cases:* 2,000. Vie de Bohème is a winery, wine bar, wine shop, restaurant, and nightclub all rolled into one package. Come for special tasting events or linger into the evening, when the intimate surroundings develop a nightclub atmosphere with music and dancing. If you want to explore beyond Gearhart's six wines, Vie de Bohème sells selections from around the world.

Enso Urban Winery & Tasting Lounge (1416 SE Stark Street; 503-683-3676). *Tasting room:* Tues.–Fri. 4–10, Sat. & Sun. 2–10. *Fee:* $10. *Owners/Winemakers:* Ryan Sharp & Chris Wishart. *Wines:* Müller-Thurgau, Pinot gris, Pinot noir, Riesling, red blend. *Cases:* 500. After producing small quantities of wine, Enso opened on Memorial Day Weekend in 2011 and has become a hangout for wine geeks. The evening hours suggest that Enso is more lounge than tasting room. Enjoy salami, cheese, breads, and truffles with your wine.

Urban Wine Works (1315 NE Fremont Street; 503-493-1366). *Tasting room:* Wed.–Sat. 12–7. *Fee:* $15 (includes cheese plate). *Owners:* Reuel Fish & shareholders. *Winemaker:* Jeremy Saville. *Wines:* Pinot gris, Pinot noir, red blends. *Cases:* 1,000. Urban Wine Works is the new home for Bishop Creek Cellars and a well-stocked bottle shop with wines from all over. Reuel Fish, principle shareholder, is so passionate about wine that he became a certified sommelier just for fun. The Bishop Creek brand stays focused on Pinot gris and Pinot noir—what Jeremy Saville knows best.

Seven Bridges Winery (2303 North Harding Avenue; 503-203-2583). *Tasting room:* Sat. 1–5, Apr.–Dec., and by appt. *Fee:* $5. *Owners:* Kevin & Jill Ross, & Robert Switzer. *Winemakers:* Kevin Ross & Robert Switzer. *Wines:* Cabernet franc, Cabernet sauvignon, Malbec, Merlot, Petit verdot, Sangiovese, Syrah, rosé, red blend. *Cases:* 1,000. One of Portland's newest urban wineries sits in the shadows of the Fremont Bridge, one of seven spanning the Willamette River, in the heart of an industrial area. Seven Bridges began with Malbec but has since expanded. Don't come looking for a Pinot noir; Seven Bridges is into hardy Bordeaux blends, sourcing grapes from Walla Walla and Yakima.

Boedecker Cellars (2621 NW 30th Avenue; 503-288-7752). *Tasting room:* Sat. & Sun. 1–5, Apr.–Nov., and by appt. *Fee:* $10. *Owners/Winemakers:* Stewart Boedecker & Athena Pappas. *Wines:* Pinot blanc, Pinot gris, Pinot noir. *Cases:* 6,000. Stewart and Athena, self-described as opinionated and argumentative, do everything from bin to bottle. With high acclaim from *Wine & Spirits* and *Wine Spectator*, this confident couple came onto the OWC scene like gangbusters. Their intense and big-structured wines have been well received, "making all the work worth it." They hold quarterly tasting and release parties.

HV Cellars (55 SW Ash Street; 541-294-8577). *Tasting room:* Daily 11–5. *Fee:* Complimentary. *Owners:* Terry & Evelyn Luce. *Winemaker:* Terry Luce. *Wines:* Baco noir, Chardonnay, Pinot gris, berry. The third time seems to be the charm for HV Cellars, which has tried tasting rooms on the southern Oregon coast and in Roseburg. Winemaker Terry Luce pours in a makeshift facility in a fire-station bay across from Portland's Saturday Market. The winery remains in Roseburg, where Terry continues to make his claim to fame, Baco noir. HV has also been known for blackberry, cranberry, and pomegranate wines.

Bodhichitta Winery & Island Mana Wines (526 SW Yamhill Street; 503-580-9463 or 971-229-1040). *Tasting room:* Tues.–Fri. 7–7, Sat. & Sun. 11–7. *Fee:* $3–15. *Owner/Winemaker:* Mark Proden. *Wines:* Cabernet sauvignon, Chardonnay, Chenin blanc, Pinot gris, Pinot noir, red blend, honey. *Cases:* 600. Get your New Age on at Oregon's first and only (intentionally) nonprofit winery, pronounced "bo-da-chee-ta." Mark Proden recently moved from Salem to his new location across from Pioneer Courthouse Square. His mission: Service to others comes first. Bodhichitta, Sanskrit for "inner self or soul," donates to charities close to home—and some not so close. "Passion for wine, compassion for others" seems like a noble toast.

ALOHA

▲ 🎁 ✐ **Cooper Mountain Vineyards** (9480 SW Grabhorn Road; 503-649-0027). *Tasting room:* Daily 12–5. *Fee:* $5. *Owner:* Robert J. Gross. *Winemaker:* Gilles de Domingo. *Wines:* Chardonnay, Pinot blanc, Pinot gris, Pinot noir, Tocai friulano, rosé, white blend, dessert. *Cases:* 18,000. In a state known for its eco-friendly, organic, and biodynamic winemaking, Cooper Mountain is where it began. In 1990, under the direction of Gross, a homeopath and acupuncturist, Cooper Mountain went down the natural path and changed farming methods to organic and biodynamic. It was the first winery in the Pacific Northwest to be certified biodynamic. Its wines are well known on the organic shelves, especially the NSA (no sulfites added) Pinot. Cooper Mountain also makes a barrel-aged Italian balsamic vinegar—available only in the tasting room.

HILLSBORO

▲ 🎁 ✐ 🐾 **Oak Knoll Winery** (29700 SW Burkhalter Road; 503-648-8198). *Tasting room:* Daily 11–5. *Fee:* $5. *Owner:* Kopri Inc. *Winemaker:* Jeff Herinckx. *Wines:* Cabernet sauvignon, Chardonnay, Gewürztraminer, Müller-Thurgau, Pinot gris, Pinot noir, Riesling, dessert, fruit. *Cases:* 32,000. When Ron and Marjorie Vuylsteke opened Oak Knoll in 1970, it was the third winery in the state and first in Washington County. They were famous for their fruit wines, particularly the Blak Berree (Belgian for "blackberry"), Concord, and Niagara, the hybrid some stubborn farmers grew legally during Prohibition. By the late 1970s, one out of every three bottles of wine sold in Oregon came from Oak Knoll. Today, Jeff Herinckx makes a reputable Pinot noir, and is again making Blak Berree.

▲ ✐ 🐾 **J. Albin Winery** (19495 Vista Hill Drive; 503-628-2986). *Tasting room:* Holiday weekends, and by appt. *Fee:* $10. *Owners:* John & Lynn Albin. *Winemaker:* John "J" Albin. *Wines:* Cabernet Sauvignon, Pinot gris, Pinot noir, rosé, sparkling, dessert. *Cases:* 2,000. John, nicknamed "J" in his college years, has known what he wanted to do with his life since the age of 10. He attended UC–Davis to support his vision, then followed the footsteps of wine pioneers to Oregon. This winery is a true family operation, enlisting help from J's sons to do grunt work, such as hand labeling and vineyard work.

BEAVERTON

▲ 🎁 ✐ 🐾 ❖ **Ponzi Vineyards** (14665 SW Winery Lane; 503-628-1227). *Tasting room:* Daily 10–5. *Second location:* 100 SW Seventh Street, Dundee (503-554-1500). *Fee:* $10. *Owners:* Dick & Nancy Ponzi. *Winemaker:* Luisa Ponzi. *Wines:* Arneis, Chardonnay, Dolcetto, Pinot blanc, Pinot gris, Pinot noir, Riesling, rosé, dessert. *Cases:* 11,500. The Ponzi name is synonymous with Oregon wine. The inception of the family vineyards and winery came in 1970, making Dick and Nancy among the state's original grape growers. Now daughter Luisa is winemaker, and her siblings Maria and Michel are in charge of marketing and operations. Not one to rest on his laurels, in 2008 Dick completed his dream project: a state-of-the-art winemaking facility on-site that he calls Collina del Sogno (Dream Hill). The tasting room's grandeur is highlighted by recycled old-growth timbers and stone walls meant to reflect the region's history.

Lodging
in Portland

PORTLAND

The Governor (614 SW 11th Avenue; 503-224-3400). Perhaps no Portland hotel merges history and luxury like the Governor. Built in 1909 and designed by Oregon's first state architect, it has such a presence that numerous movies have been filmed both inside and outside its ornate and dramatically lit walls. Contributing to the luxury component are remodeled rooms and penthouse suites that afford panoramic views of the city. Jake's Grill, famed for its sea-to-fork culinary delights, completes the package. $$$$

Heathman Hotel/Marble Bar (1001 SW Broadway Avenue; 503-241-4100 or 800-551-0011). The Heathman is known for exemplary guest services and high-end accoutrements, including its signature "Art of Sleep"—bed types paired with fluffy bathrobes and slippers, emulates the Euro-luxury-boutique model. The 10-story, historic (1927) building underwent a $4 million green renovation. Check into its Oregon wine-tasting package: deluxe accommodations, bottle of Oregon Pinot noir, valet parking, concierge advice for touring the Willamette Valley, and latest issue of *Wine Spectator*. The restaurant and bar share an expansive cellar of more than 600 wines leaning to Oregon and France. $$$

Hotel Lucia (400 SW Broadway; 503-225-1717). "Delivering Calm" is the motto for the lavish Lucia, which prides itself on being beyond upscale—most notably enhancements that "combine style with comfort" and impeccable service. Order an Oregon wine or bottle of bubbly when making reservations. If you're Oregon or Washington residents, check out the "staycation" rate. Under the direction of recent Iron Chef winner Vitaly Paley, the Lucia offers two memorable dining experiences—the more-formal Imperial and casual Penny Diner. Everything is made in-house at both, including the one-of-a-kind, made-from-scratch "Stanimal" hot dog at the diner and the savory "Iron Chef radish cocktail" at the Imperial. $$$$

Hotel Vintage Plaza (422 SW Broadway Avenue; 800-263-2305). A multimillion-dollar revitalization of this wine-centric hotel has uncorked a new look that blends Old World hospitality and New World luxury at affordable rates. The rooms and décor are tied to a namesake winery. Local wines are poured in the lobby from 5 to 6 PM and discounts at area wineries are offered through the concierge. You may also enjoy a glass of local fare at the highly regarded Pazzo Ristorante. $$$$

HILLSBORO

The Orenco Hotel (1457 NE Orenco Station Parkway; 503-208-5708). For a little taste of France in suburban Hillsboro, spend a night or two at the Orenco. This attractive brick boutique hotel is the hub of a village that includes a market, deli, coffee shop, wine bars, entertainment, restaurants, and a 3-acre central park modeled after a place near Versailles. Each of the 10 *de façon chic* rooms has a Jacuzzi and its own courtyard, and the fresh continental breakfast is available all day. Monthly wine-tasting events are one of the not-to-miss perks. $$$–$$$$

TROUTDALE

McMenamins Edgefield (2126 SW Halsey Avenue; 503-669-5226). Edgefield is McMenamins's signature project. Beginning in 1990, the brothers purchased 74 acres where the Multnomah County Poor Farm was built in 1911. The halls are a step back into history, with compelling murals painted by various local artists, telling the unique history of the property. Rooms in the old manor run the gamut from suites with private bath to hostel-style bunks with lockers. Of course, it's McMenamins, so there is much more than lodging: a winery, tasting room, theater pub, distillery, pool hall, menagerie of restaurants and bars, nightly music, two par-3 pitch-and-putt pub golf courses, and live outdoor concerts in the summer. $$–$$$

Dining
in Portland

Dining in Portland is a destination vacation all unto itself. Again, we've focused on the consistently cream-of-the-crop within a range of style and cuisine that emphasize Oregon wine. There are some nationally recognized and iconic establishments that didn't make the cut simply because of their wine list, not their reputation.

PORTLAND

The Bent Brick (1639 NW Marshall Street; 503-688-1655). Big changes were afoot in early 2013. Star Portland chef Scott Dolich of Park Kitchen fame has taken full culinary control of his young restaurant and fashioned a complete menu overhaul beginning on Valentine's Day. Dolich places strict emphasis on domestic-only products on his tavern-style menu—heavy on the protein. The wines, all from Oregon or Washington, are on tap—an unusual bent. D/HH $$–$$$

Bluehour (250 NW 13th Avenue; 503-226-3394). Located in the once-gritty industrial innards of the city, now revamped into the high-rent Pearl District, Bluehour is sophisticated elegance for the see-and-be-seen scene. Here you will also see one of the best happy hours in the city for diverse small plates and a not-so-small, freshly ground local beef burger on ciabatta at small prices. Fine dining from chef Thomas Boyce and co-owner Kenny Biambalvo can be spendy but splendidly satisfying, with Oregon wines by the bottle as prolific as designer-clad diners. L (Mon.–Fri.) D/HH/LN $$$$

Café Castagna (1758 SE Hawthorne Boulevard; 503-231-9959). Café Castagna is a spinoff of the grownup version (Castagna) next door. The café has an eclectic menu, mixing the usual with the unusual. Soup is always impressive and the butter-lettuce salad, which looks like an open flower blossom, is superb. Another favorite is the rail-thin-crusted pizza, dusted with creminis or tomatoes and basil. The café's famed burger served with house pickles and a stack of thin and crispy *frites* will make you steal from your neighbor's plate. Oregon and Northwest wines are well represented. D/HH/LN $$

The Farm Café (10 SE Seventh Avenue; 503-736-3276). The menu at the Farm leans distinctly to the left of meat, with sustainable, locally sourced ingredients that include wine and beer, as well as spirits. Appetizers we resist sharing: baked Brie with seasonal fruit; sweet 'n' spicy hazelnuts; and the farmhouse cheese ball spiked with horseradish. The Farm claims to serve the city's best veggie burger, and we agree. All its fare pairs well with the extensive list of Oregon wines, including no fewer than 20 Pinot noirs. Adjacent is an airy patio, a favorite place to pick up city vibes. D/HH/LN $$

Higgins Restaurant & Bar (1239 SW Broadway Avenue; 503-222-9070). Owner/chef Greg Higgins's serious commitment and relationship to Oregon purveyors is evident on his menu and in his work with Portland Chef's Collaborative. Three levels of tables and seating are accented by detailed lighting that bathes both plates and diners in a good shine. The open kitchen design allows Greg to see the pleasure of his patrons. Save room for his famed desserts. Higgins has many Oregon wines by the glass and a prolific list of Oregon whites and reds to complement a seasonal menu. L (Mon.–Fri.) D/HH/LN $$$$

Jake's Classic American Grill (611 SW Tenth Avenue; 503-220-1850). Famed for its sea-to-fork fish *and* sensational steaks, Jake's is a timeless Portland institution. The Grill is the less-pricey sister to Jake's Famous Crawfish and just one of many nationwide McCormick & Schmick's properties. Jake's caters to families (daily blue plate specials) as well as the after-work crowd with their famed happy hour. Prices are reasonable and the food consistently hits the mark. Oregon microbrews join the ranks of a vast array of Oregon and Washington wines. BR/B/L/D/HH/LN $$$

Ken's Artisan Pizza (304 SE 28th Avenue; 503-517-9951). Cofounder Ken Forkish and co-owner/chef Alan Maniscalco have what you need to fill the void especially on a gray, wet day: handcrafted pizza and local wine. The pies are fast-fired in the wood oven, dressed in seasonal and standard toppings with just the right amount of cheese on a blistered, chewy crust. Add a glass or bottle of Oregon vino and the fog is guaranteed to lift. D $$

Meriwether's (2601 NW Vaughn Street; 503-228-1250). Meriwether's is an island of casual upscale dining in a sea of industrial warehouses, with "Farm to fork" as its credo. Its 18-acre Skyline Farm grows everything from roots and legumes to eggplant and tomatoes along with the usual assortment of lettuce, herbs, and flowers. Everything else is from local suppliers: beef, pork, lamb, seafood, and fish. Meriwether's lists more than 50 Pinot noirs by the bottle, arranged according to AVA, with another 20 or so Oregon wines. The historic building was part of the 1905 Portland Expo; photos on the wall depict the grand event. L/D/HH/BR (Sat. & Sun.) $$$$

Mother's Bistro & Bar (212 SW Stark Street; 503-464-1122). When prepping for a day (and evening) of wine tasting, filling up on calorie-laden food is a good idea. Although Mother's serves healthy choices, such as a tofu portobello scramble and Bill Clinton's veggie omelet, we suggest breakfast nachos, wild salmon hash, or crunchy French toast. Even better than the choices are the prices—small wonder Mother's was chosen one of America's top restaurant bargains by *Food & Wine*. Carefully selected wines, listed by glass and bottle, are hand-picked from Oregon and Washington, and include more obscure producers. The Velvet Lounge, dressed in dangling chandeliers and gilded mirrors, offers a different menu. B/L/D/HH $$

Navarre (10 NE 28th Street; 503-232-3555). Navarre is unique even by Stumptown standards. Braving the new food front in 2001, chef and sole proprietor John Taboada sources 90 percent of his ingredients from one CSA, 47th Avenue Farms. Specials—written on a mirror hanging under the handmade oak counter—reflect morning's arrivals and the inspiration brought with them. Inside—about the size of a broom closet—mason jars full of preserved produce for future fits of culinary genius are stacked on utility shelving. Small plates of rustic Basque, Italian, and Northwest cuisine mean no fuss with presentation. Add an all-Oregon wine component and you're set for beyond-the-norm dining. B (Sat. & Sun.) D/HH $$

!Oba¡ Restaurante (555 NW 12th Avenue; 503-228-6161). Macadamia nut–encrusted swordfish. Ancho-encrusted ahi tuna. Cuban-pulled flank steak. Those are just a few of the Spanish, Portuguese, and Caribbean entrées plated at this lively restaurant on a busy Pearl District corner. The wine list has a clever rating scale and runs the international gamut, though there's plenty from the nearby Willamette Valley. On Sunday night, bottles costing at least $65 are half off—oh, boy! D/HH/LN $$$

Oregon whites pair well with the bounty of the sea. Courtesy Inn at Spanish Head

Paley's Place Bistro & Bar (1204 NW 21st Street; 503-243-2403). Chef/owner Vitaly Paley has been waving his whisk for more than 17 years in a Victorian home complete with family photos on the wall (suppliers and purveyors). Recently the winner of *Iron Chef America*, Vitaly's eco-sensitive and creative cuisine is combination Northwest and French garnished with East Coast attitude. This bistro is known for its charcuterie, hard-to-resist chocolate soufflé and the Paley burger created with ground-to-order organic beef. Paley's has a style that's intimate, homey, and yet sophisticated. It lists a healthy mix of Oregon wines, from boutique to big producer. D $$$$

Park Kitchen (422 NW Eighth Avenue; 503-223-7275). Executive chef Scott Dolich has built a solid reputation in his kitchen. Among the upper echelon of Portland dining experiences, his cuisine reflects the available bounty in this loaded state, coated in Mediterranean and American inspiration. Flavors run a full spectrum and dishes are arranged by small and large, hot or cold, allowing you to customize your meal. With an equally impressive wine list of 50 Oregon and Washington choices, your meal is complete. Look for Park's five-course wine dinners. D/HH $$$$

Pazzo Ristorante (627 SW Washington Street; 503-228-1515). Ever heard of wine salt? It's the not-so-secret ingredient chef John Eisenhart uses to give his traditional northern Italian meat, poultry, seafood, and even vegetable dishes that extra dash of distinction. Made from simmered wine, salt, sugar, and a few other seasonings, the spice is a marinade worthy of its salt. Pazzo is more than a restaurant; it's a bar and bakery as well. The wines are decidedly Oregon, especially Pinots, though naturally there's a hefty selection from Italy. B/L/D/BR $$$

Ringside Steakhouse (2165 West Burnside Avenue; 503-223-1513; second location: 14021 NE Glisan Avenue [Glendoveer Golf Course]). The original Chicago-style steakhouse, with white-shirt-and-bowtie waiters and Sinatra-style clubhouse tone, has been bustling since 1944. Back then, it was all about the steak, with maybe a chicken entrée. Today, the menu has expanded to grilled lamb, salmon, and halibut, but retains classic sides such as creamed corn and spinach casserole. The nifty 700-label wine list has many Oregon Pinots and glass pours of red or white. D/HH/LN $$$$

Veritable Quandary (1220 SW First Avenue; 503-227-7342). The VQ, a Portland landmark, and has been around at least as long as we've been old enough to drink. It's maintained its Old Town charm with polished darkwood, aged-brick interior and shoebox size—but has added enough updates to keep it as fresh as the ingredients. You'll find at least four or five red and white glass pours from Oregon producers, and 50-plus by the bottle. One tip: Order dessert first. The chocolate Nocello (hazelnut liqueur) soufflé is baked to order, and perfection takes time. BR (Sat. & Sun.) L (Mon.–Fri.) D/HH/LN $$$

Wildwood (1221 NW 21st Avenue; 503-248-9663). Wildwood is a champion for cooking from the source. Executive chef Dustin Clark has kept with the restaurant's original intent of making the most of fresh, mostly Oregon-sourced ingredients. Menus change weekly. Shellfish, fish, and wild game are a must here, as are the mushrooms. Oregon wines are still prominent on the seasonally directed list, with at least 25 Pinots always available. An open-to-viewing kitchen embraced by earthy tones and wood accents set the scene for a touch of special. L (Mon.–Sat.) D/HH (Mon.–Fri.) LN $$$$

Wine Bars

in Portland

As with our dining selections, we highlight places—from simple to complex, hip to chic, or just fun—that focus their wine pours on Oregon, or at minimum Pacific Northwest. Portland has numerous wine bars, but these are the places we like to frequent in a city that plays the game of one-upmanship like no other.

Bar Avignon (2138 SE Division Street; 503-517-0808). Wildwood's Randy Goodman and his wife, Nancy Hunt, have put together a best-of-the-best wine bar in an "everybody knows your name" setting. When you walk in, you'll sigh, drop your shoulders, and settle into re-lax-ation mode. Menu items are prepared with love—grilled panini, croquettes, and charcuterie. You'll also find more than 20 affordable wine selections by the glass, heavy on the Oregon side. We must mention the Dagoba chocolate cake with bourbon caramel sauce and *the* best crème brûlée ever. HH (Mon.–Fri.) $$

Noble Rot (1111 East Burnside, fourth floor; 503-233-1999). Noble Rot is celebrating a decade in business in its digs on the top floor of an eastside retrofitted building. Co-owner and chef Leather Storrs mixes it up with American comfort food such as cheeseburgers and fries, mac and cheese, a famous onion tart, and more typical wine fare. Local and seasonal ingredients drive the rest. The wine list is about half Oregon, half elsewhere, and the atmosphere cosmopolitan and crowded. The space is LEED Platinum and has a rooftop garden that produces herbs and veggies along with seating that highlights skyline views. D/HH/LN (Mon.–Sat.) $$$

Oregon Wines on Broadway (515 SW Broadway; 503-228-4655). A narrow, compact bar for the suits, residents, and downtown shoppers is a place to begin (or end) your thirst for knowledge of Oregon wines. With up to 30 open bottles of Pinot alone (don't ask for a list), you can compare and contrast with samples. If you settle on a fav, order a glass (served in Riedel) or purchase a bottle to share—no corkage fee. The servers pride themselves on sassy 'tudes, but don't be intimidated—you'll learn a lot and have a ton of fun. Local vintners frequently offer complimentary sampling. Mon.–Sat. $

Pour Wine Bar & Bistro (2755 NE Broadway Avenue; 503-288-7687). Robert Volz may seem quirky, but he's a man with a plan . . . or two. While cruising his neighborhood on a vintage motor scooter, he saw the empty building of his dreams and thought: wine bar! The unlikely location has lines to match the wines. The interior design is based on the work of midcentury Finnish-American architect Eero Saarinen. Small plates are prepared on an amped-up hot plate of sorts, and pair with handpicked Oregon wines by the glass. L/D/HH/LN (Mon.–Sat.) $

Thirst Bistro & Tasting Room (315 SW Montgomery Street, Suite 340; 503-295-2747). If your thirst runs to the Pacific Northwest for wine or distilled spirits, this spot has the quench for you. Almost exclusively Oregon and Washington wines by the taste, glass, or bottle, many from smaller, boutique wineries, can be enjoyed riverside, indoors or out. Thirst is dedicated to using local, organic, or natural ingredients in its regional and seasonal cuisine. Anchored on the riverfront, the bistro has large window views that give the sense of being rocked by the gentle waves of the Willamette. A new addition is the Cellar, open Wed.–Sun. 1–7 for wine tasting. D/HH (Tues.–Sun.) $$

To Do
in the Portland Area

Attractions

So much to choose from, so little time. A traveler could get lost for several days in Portland and never run out of things to do. This is a book about wine country, and so the idea is to head for the hills. But before you do, here are a few stops worth including on your itinerary.

Given that Portland has the fitting moniker "City of Roses," start with a trip to the West Hills overlooking downtown. **Washington Park** is 400 acres of woods and trails minutes from the city's heart. The centerpiece is the **Oregon Zoo** (4001 SW Canyon Road, 503-226-1561), which houses everything from regional animals to international land and sea critters. The zoo also stages a summer concert series featuring big-name entertainment. Also in Washington Park, the **International Rose Test Garden** (850 SW Rose Garden Way, 503-823-3636), the oldest of its kind in the United States, is a vivid display of more than 7,000 roses. Just a short walk from the rose gardens is the **Portland Japanese Garden** (611 SW Kingston Avenue, 503-223-1321), a verdant 5.5-acre sanctuary that paints five garden portraits of Japan. The 185-acre **Hoyt Arboretum** (4000 SW Fairview Boulevard, 503-865-8733) features more than 1,000 species of plants from every corner of the planet. Free summer concerts have been offered in the amphitheater for two weeks in August since 1908.

Down on the user-friendly Portland waterfront, take a cruise past the downtown skyline and enjoy memorable brunch, lunch, and dinner cuisine on the ***Portland Spirit*** (110 SE Caruthers Street, 503-224-3900), which plies the busy waters of the Willamette. Across from downtown on the river, you'll notice a submarine docked in front of a giant building. That's the **Oregon Museum of Science and Industry** (1945 SE Water Avenue, 503-797-4000), a.k.a. **OMSI**, which offers fascinating exhibits that appeal to young and old alike, including the submarine and a planetarium. Youngsters will enjoy the **Portland Children's Museum** (4015 SW Canyon Road, 503-223-6500), considered one of the best in the United States.

Portland is passionate about its one big-time sports franchise—the NBA's **Portland Trail Blazers** (503-797-9619). When the team is winning tickets are at a premium and the atmosphere at the Rose Garden can be much like a college game; enjoy a glass of wine from Stone Wolf Vineyards while cheering. Speaking of sports, perhaps no city in the nation is more ga-ga over professional soccer, a phenomenon reflected in sellouts of **Portland Timbers** (503-553-5400) matches at Jeld-Wen Stadium. For a different type of cultural experience, the **Laurelhurst Theater & Pub** (2735 East Burnside Street, 503-232-5511), built in 1923, has four screens and charges $4 for independent and classic films, all in digital. Watch while sipping an Oregon wine or microbrew and enjoying pizza, salad, or wrap. If you prefer a live performance in a luxurious setting, the **Portland Center for the Performing Arts** (503-248-4335) brings top-level entertainers and performers to the **Arlene Schnitzer Concert Hall** (1037 SW Broadway), **Keller Auditorium** (222 Southwest Clay Street), and three theaters within the **Antoinette Hatfield Hall** (1111 SW Broadway Avenue).

In the city's heart, **Powell's Books** (1005 West Burnside Street, 503-228-4651) has been a Portland icon since 1971. With more than one million titles, it is the largest independent new-and-used bookseller in the world. After you've made a few selections, take a brisk walk to **Pioneer Square Park** (701 SW Sixth Avenue, 503-223-1613), affectionately known as Portland's Living Room. Something is always happening there.

You can get a snapshot of a mid-1800s world with a revamped **Portland Underground** (226 NW Davis Street, 503-774-4522) tour that is both above and below ground. On this two-hour jaunt, which includes Chinatown and Old Town, you'll go underground to see where inebriated men were shanghaied into slavery and other tawdry affairs conducted. And before you take off for wine country, get a bird's-eye look at this beautiful city from the **Portland Aerial Tram** (3303 SW Bond Avenue, 503-494-8283), which connects the South Waterfront neighborhood along the Willamette River with the Oregon Health and Science University. The 3,300-foot-high ride takes three minutes.

If you make only one shopping stop downtown, it should be the **Portland Saturday Market** (108 West Burnside Street, 503-222-6072), which touts itself as the nation's largest open-air arts and crafts fair and market. The name notwithstanding, this lively and eclectic blend of vendors and performers from around the globe shows prodigious wares on Sundays as well from March through December.

Recreation

Portlanders like to spend as little time in their cars as possible, whether it's to work or play at one of the city's 700-plus parks and recreation sites. The City of Roses is surely one of the most bicycle-friendly metropolitan areas in the nation. You can rent a bike on the Eastbank Esplanade and take off in any direction for a scenic look and feel.

A favorite locale for cyclists, mountain bikers, hikers, horseback riders, and runners alike is the 30-mile **Wildwood Trail in Forest Park** (503-823-7529), an extraordinary 5,000-acre urban forest with more than 70 miles of wide single-track trails and fire roads. Forest Park is the largest natural forested area within an urban area in the United States.

Portland residents don't have to wait until winter to ski. Mount Hood, visible from nearly every nook of town, has enough snow on its glaciers for year-round schussing at **Mt. Hood Ski Bowl** (503-222-2695). It also has the largest terrain in the state for night skiing, more than 600 acres. Many skiers head to **Mt. Hood Meadows** (503-337-2217), a little farther east, for slightly better powder, smaller crowds, and the most skiable

Picnic baskets and wine touring go hand in hand. John Baker

terrain on the mountain. Smaller ski areas on the mountain include **Cooper Spur** (541-352-7803), **Timberline** (503-272-3158), and the oldest ski area on Mount Hood, **Summit** (503-272-0256), which began operations in 1927. Summit has an adjoining area called Snow Bunny for snow tubing and sledding.

Wine Shopping

Wine shops abound in Portland. Here are a few gems to look for: The **E & R Wine Shop** (6141 SW Macadam Boulevard, 503-246-6101) has made a name for itself for its vast regional selection but also for a unique deal—a handful of wines called The Critical List that you can return for half off retail if you don't like it, for any reason. **Great Wine Buys** (1515 NE Broadway Avenue, 503-287-2897) has more than 700 wines, including more than 200 from Oregon, and offers Friday and Saturday night tastings, food-pairing advice, and wine classes. At **Korkage Wine Shop** (6351 SW Capitol Highway, 503-293-3146), the mission is to sell good wine for $25 or less. Thursday night tastings (6–8 PM) are $10 and somewhat raucous. The **Vintner's Cellar** (1111 NW 16th Avenue, 503-227-3610) custom winery, in its new location in the Pearl District, has everything you need if you want wine—and if you've got a notion to see your name on a label. Labeled as Oregon's only micro-winery, this is the ultra experience for actual winemaking in four easy steps. Meanwhile, the finer things in life can be taken home for your hedonistic moods at **Pearl Specialty Market & Spirits** (900 NW Lovejoy Street, #140, 503-477-8604), where wine tastes are complemented with cheeses, chocolate, mixers, and even a good cigar. **Cork: A Bottle Shop** (2901 NE Alberta Street, 503-281-2675) has an extensive stock, and Oregon wines are a priority. **Mt. Tabor Fine Wines** (4316 SE Hawthorne Boulevard, 503-235-4444) has been a fixture in southeast Portland and offers Friday night tastings often focused on the state's wines. **CorksCru**

Wine Merchants (339 NW Broadway Avenue, 503-226-9463), the newest kid in the wine-sales business, likes to tout itself as a champion of the little guy; it has tastings every Thursday and Friday afternoon.

Information

Travel Portland Information Center, 503-275-8355 or 877-678-5263, 701 SW Sixth Avenue, www.travelportland.com

Washington County Visitors Association (Beaverton), 503-644-5555 or 800-537-3149, 11000 SW Stratus Street, suite 170, www.visitwashingtoncountyoregon.com

Winery

Willamette Valley Route 47

SIPPING HEAVEN . . . ON ROUTE 47

AFTER WATCHING THE DUNDEE and McMinnville areas steal much of the valley's wine thunder for years, exasperated vintners along a largely forgotten corridor finally waved their hands frantically and said, "Hey, over here! We make good wine too!"

Such was the genesis of the Sip 47 Wine Route, equal parts marketing tool and geographic distinction. The consortium of businesses refers to the area as "the Road Less Traveled," with good reason. Unlike the perpetual traffic jam on OR 99W, the Old Newberg Highway is classic Sunday-drive material. OR 47 in its entirety runs north–south from Clatskanie on the Columbia River through a slice of the Coast Range to the countryside northeast of McMinnville.

GETTING HERE AND AROUND

The predominant way to enjoy Sip 47 is to start on the north end in Forest Grove and head south. The fastest and easiest way to do this from Portland is to take the Sunset Highway (US 26) west past North Plains to the OR 6 exit. About 7 miles north of Forest Grove, you'll connect with OR 47. Turn left and continue into Forest Grove.

FOREST GROVE

Despite its proximity to burgeoning Portland, Forest Grove has managed to keep its literal (25 miles) and figurative distance from the state's largest city—though it is home to its fair share of commuters. Near the marshy headwaters of the Tualatin River, Forest Grove is the last town of notable size between Portland and the coast. Although orchards, nurseries, and farmlands dominate now, the large stand of oak trees for which the community is named remains on the campus of Pacific University, a private four-year liberal-arts college.

Forest Grove has done an admirable job of staying connected to its history. Ten

LEFT: Wines, vines, and views near Carlton. Courtesy Yamhill Vineyards B&B

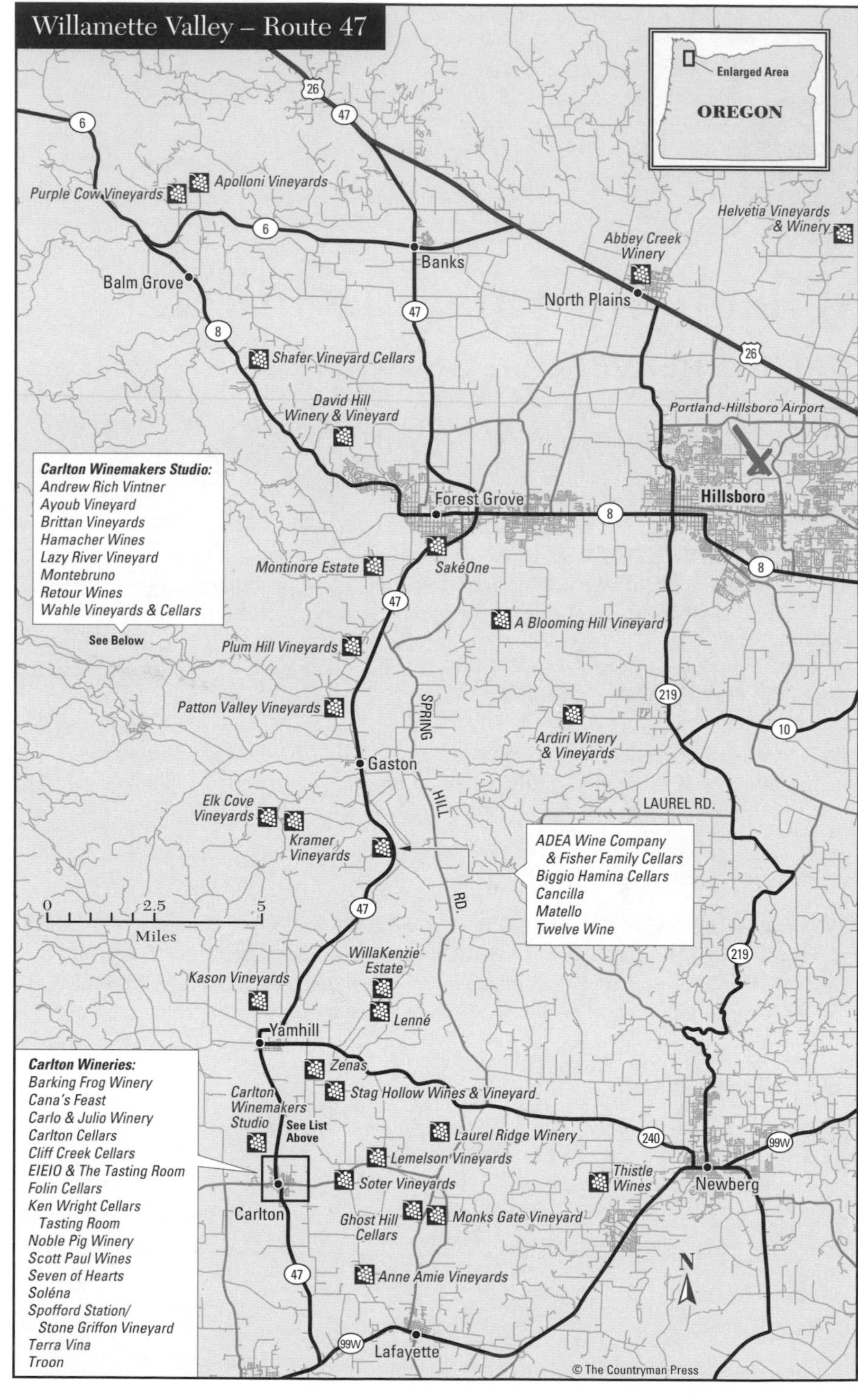
Willamette Valley – Route 47
Enlarged Area
OREGON
26
47
6
Apolloni Vineyards
Purple Cow Vineyards
Helvetia Vineyards & Winery
Abbey Creek Winery
Banks
Balm Grove
North Plains
8
Shafer Vineyard Cellars
David Hill Winery & Vineyard
Portland-Hillsboro Airport
Carlton Winemakers Studio:
Andrew Rich Vintner
Ayoub Vineyard
Brittan Vineyards
Hamacher Wines
Lazy River Vineyard
Montebruno
Retour Wines
Wahle Vineyards & Cellars
See Below
Forest Grove
Hillsboro
SakéOne
Montinore Estate
A Blooming Hill Vineyard
Plum Hill Vineyards
Patton Valley Vineyards
SPRING HILL RD.
219
10
Ardiri Winery & Vineyards
Gaston
LAUREL RD.
Elk Cove Vineyards
Kramer Vineyards
ADEA Wine Company & Fisher Family Cellars
Biggio Hamina Cellars
Cancilla
Matello
Twelve Wine
0 2.5 5
Miles
WillaKenzie Estate
Kason Vineyards
Lenné
Yamhill
Carlton Wineries:
Barking Frog Winery
Cana's Feast
Carlo & Julio Winery
Carlton Cellars
Cliff Creek Cellars
EIEIO & The Tasting Room
Folin Cellars
Ken Wright Cellars Tasting Room
Noble Pig Winery
Scott Paul Wines
Seven of Hearts
Soléna
Spofford Station/ Stone Griffon Vineyard
Terra Vina
Troon
Zenas
Stag Hollow Wines & Vineyard
Carlton Winemakers Studio
See List Above
Laurel Ridge Winery
240
99W
Lemelson Vineyards
Thistle Wines
Newberg
Soter Vineyards
Carlton
Ghost Hill Cellars
Monks Gate Vineyard
N
Anne Amie Vineyards
Lafayette
© The Countryman Press

homes are on the National Register of Historic Places. McMenamins Grand Lodge is a restored Masonic Lodge and orphanage that elicits visions of another era. More than 20 wineries call this stretch home, and despite the relative anonymity of the region, there are some big guns and historic vineyards in the Pinot noir and Chardonnay worlds.

"The Road Less Traveled" notwithstanding, Carlton is no longer a secret. Memorial Day and Thanksgiving weekends are a cluster—though it merely adds to the excitement. The community's redbrick and grain-elevator core is alive with tasting boutiques and charming restaurants; the railroad station has been retrofitted into a tasting room. The innovative Carlton Winemakers Studio was the first in the country to be registered with the U.S. Green Building Council, and the eye-catching building is LEED-certified. Friday Night Flights is a newer attraction around town that keeps doors open until 7 PM (May–October).

Wineries

in the Forest Grove Area

The Sip 47 wine route actually begins northwest of Forest Grove off OR 6, also known as NW Wilson River Highway. From Portland, take US 26 (Sunset Highway) west to Banks and the OR 6 exit. Continue west to begin your tour at Apolloni and Purple Cow wineries.

NORTH PLAINS

▲ 🖋 🐾 **Helvetia Vineyards & Winery** (22485 NW Yungen Road; 503-647-7596). *Tasting room:* Fri.–Sun. 12–5, Jan.–Oct. *Fee:* $5. *Owners:* John Platt & Elizabeth Furse. *Winemaker:* John Platt. *Wines:* Chardonnay, Gewürztraminer, Pinot gris, Pinot noir, rosé. *Cases:* 2,000. Welcome to Oregon's original Dundee Hills. Before Prohibition, the rural side of the West Hills above Portland was the hub of the state's tiny wine industry. Helvetia is the last vestige of this little-known slice of history. Swiss immigrant Jacob Yungen's century-old home is still there and serves as the winery's visitors center, where you can see his original winemaking equipment.

Abbey Creek Winery (31441 NW Commercial Street; 503-389-0619). *Tasting room:* Sat. & Sun. 12–5. *Fee:* $5. *Owner/Winemaker:* Bertony Faustin. *Wines:* Chardonnay, Gewürztraminer, Pinot gris, Pinot noir, Syrah. *Cases:* 1,000. Established in the mid-'80s, this West Hills vineyard has been given a rebirth. Bertony, originally from New York, and his father-in-law tend to the vines, but come harvest they simply get out of the grapes' way. Higher-elevation vines surrounded by dense forest give their drier-style wines a Northwest twist with hints of pine—especially in the Pinot. The tasting room is in the heart of a rural suburb that's on Portland's fringe.

FOREST GROVE

▲ **Apolloni Vineyards** (14135 NW Timmerman Road; 503-359-3606 or 503-330-5946). *Tasting room:* Daily 12–5; Fri.–Sun. 12–5, Oct.–May, and by appt. *Season:* Mar.–Dec. *Fee:* $5. *Owners:* Alfredo & Laurine Apolloni. *Winemaker:* Alfredo Apolloni. *Wines:* Chardonnay, Pinot blanc, Pinot gris, Pinot noir, rosé, Sangiovese, Viognier, red blend, dessert. *Cases:* 1,000. Alfredo Apolloni grew up in a winemaking region of northern Italy and his wine label—a 16th-century family crest—reflects his heritage. The whites, all done in stainless steel (no oak), are clean and crisp with bright acidity. The reds are masterfully crafted, including an estate Pinot barrel-aged in plenty of new oak. The affable tasting-room staff makes this a pleasurable stop for the wine and the company, and don't leave before tasting the Super Tuscan blend.

▲ ✐ 🐾 **Purple Cow Vineyards** (52720 NW Wilson School Road; 503-330-0991). *Tasting room:* Fri.–Sun. 11–5, and by appt. *Fee:* $5. *Owner/Winemaker:* Jon Armstrong. *Wines:* Muscat, Maréchal Foch, Pinot noir, Primitivo, rosé, Syrah, Tempranillo, Zinfandel, red blends, port-style. *Cases:* 1,200. In a highly competitive wine world, Purple Cow has a niche with wines that are a little different. "A winery for wine nerds" is how good-natured Jon describes his experimental vineyard. He's creating a warmer terroir for his small plot and getting big results: Syrah and Tempranillo that grow in the far north Willamette Valley. As for "different," consider the Foch-Pinot blend, a *big* red made of Lemberger, Petite sirah (Durif), and Mourvèdre that spends a teeth-staining 30 months in barrels, and the Teroldego (Italian varietal), which tastes like port without the high alcohol. He had us at dry Muscat.

▲ 🎁 **Shafer Vineyard Cellars** (6200 NW Gales Creek Road; 503-357-6604). *Tasting room:* Daily 11–5. *Fee:* Complimentary. *Owners:* Harvey & Miki Shafer. *Winemaker:* Harvey Shafer. *Wines:* Chardonnay, Gewürztraminer, Müller-Thurgau, Pinot blanc, Pinot gris, Pinot noir, Riesling, blush, port-style, sparkling. *Cases:* 20,000. The cute front entrance, with its small porch and garden furniture, doesn't prepare you for what's behind the door: a warehouse-size room loaded with enough Christmas ornaments, decorations, and tchotchkes to fill everyone's stocking. The Shafers have been making wine for more than three decades, after planting grapes on 70 acres in 1973.

▲ 🍴 ✐ 🐾 ❖ **David Hill Winery & Vineyard** (46350 NW David Hill Road; 503-992-8545). *Tasting room:* Daily 11–5. *Fee:* $5. *Owners:* Milan & Jean Stoyanov. *Winemaker:* Jason Bull. *Wines:* Chardonnay, Gewürztraminer, Merlot, Pinot blanc, Pinot gris, Pinot noir, Riesling, Tempranillo, red and white blends, dessert, port. *Cases:* 12,000. The original 1883 Reuter farmhouse serves as tasting room for David Hill Winery, which had its beginnings in 1965 when early wine entrepreneur Charles Coury planted grapes. The setting is also renowned for its splendid views of rolling landscapes; both *Sunset* and *Home & Garden* magazines have touted it as one of the finest for nuptials. Some other popular events: concerts, a bacon bash, and vineyard marathon where visitors walk a half-mile and taste wines next to vines.

🎁 ✐ ❖ **SakéOne** (820 Elm Street; 503-357-7056). *Tasting room:* Daily 11–5. *Fee:* $3–10. *Sake master:* Greg Lorenz. *Brewed on-site labels:* Momokawa: silver, diamond, ruby, and pearl; Moonstone: fruit-infused; G Label; premium. Greg Lorenz, the only American sake master, proves fermented rice wine, a.k.a. sake, isn't just for an occasional Japanese dinner, and good sake shouldn't be heated. He is definitely masterful and brews a fine assortment, all extremely food-friendly. Daily complimentary tours are led at 1, 2, and 3 PM. We suggest an indulgence of the food-pairing flight. You may also taste/purchase imported Murai Family and Yoshinogawa sake.

▲ ✐ 🐾 ❖ **Montinore Estate** (3663 SW Dilley Road; 503-359-5012). *Tasting room:* Daily 11–5. *Fee:* $5. *Owners:* Marchesi family. *Winemakers:* Stephen Webber & Ben Thomas. *Wines:* Gewürztraminer, Müller-Thurgau, Pinot gris, Pinot noir, Riesling, white blend, port-style, dessert. *Cases:* 36,000. Every winery has its branding, and at Montinore it's the size and scope of the estate's biodynamic efforts. Many wineries in this progressive state are engaged in natural farming, but the Marchesis were forerunners in an increasingly popular approach that some swear by and others deride as voodoo vineonomics. Rudy Marchesi purchased Montinore's sprawling 230 acres of grapes in 2001, and started down the natural path two years later. The grounds are plush; the architecture, stately; and the airy tasting room is elegant but homey.

▲ ❖ **Ardiri Winery & Vineyards** (35040 SW Unger Road; 503-628-6060 or 888-503-3330). *Tasting room:* Fri.–Sun. 10–5, and by appt. *Fee:* $10. *Owners/Winemakers:* Gail Lizak & John Compagno. *Wines:* Pinot blanc, Pinot gris, Pinot noir. *Cases:* 2,000. Compagno and Lizak purchased the Gypsy Dancer winery site in 2008 from renowned winemaker Gary Andrus, but the relationship began many years prior. The couple owns a 5-acre vineyard of Pinot Noir in Napa and brought their grapes north to where Lizak worked and Andrus made Ardiri's first wine. The outstanding sipping setting features benches and tables on a gorgeous patio with stone fireplace, several gas fire pits, and red fleece blankets to ward away any chill.

▲ 🎁 ✐ 🐾 ❖ **A Blooming Hill Vineyard** (5195 SW Hergert Road; 503-992-1196). *Tasting room:* Daily 11–5. *Fee:* $5. *Owners:* Jim & Holly Witte. *Winemaker:* Jim Witte. *Wines:* Chardonnay, Pinot gris, Pinot noir, Riesling, white blend. *Cases:* 2,000. A Blooming Hill's operation is small, with its tasting room in the basement of Jim and Holly's home. You'll feel as if you're in your own den, munching on Holly's homemade tapenade and crackers. The Wittes have steadfastly resisted efforts to subdivide their 40 acres in a rapidly growing bedroom community. They are fond of their location on the edge of Chehalem Mountain AVA, where the daily late-afternoon breezes cool the grapes and make it a cool place to host a small event.

Lodging
in Forest Grove

FOREST GROVE

McMenamins Grand Lodge (3505 Pacific Avenue; 503-992-9533). A grand place for sure, the 77-room lodge with groomed grounds joined the McMenamins family in 2000. The hotel and surrounding buildings come with enough stories to fill several books—you might even hear a few ghosts whispering from the walls. One of the appeals: You can have a room with a private bath, or for $40, a bunk bed with a shower down the hall. A theater and heated soaking pool are a few of the uncommon additions. With so much history to absorb, and many photos on the walls to peruse, you could lose track of time and forget why you're here—to sip on Route 47. R/B $–$$$$

The Grand Lodge in Forest Grove has enough stories to fill several books. Courtesy McMenamins

Dining
in the Forest Grove Area

GALES CREEK

Bistro Stecchino (2014 Main Street; 503-352-9921). There's plenty to love about this labor of love for owner Christian Geffrard and chef Mark Cuneo, but big hearts go out for their value pricing on food and wine. Stecchino (translation: stick) emulates an Italian cucina, with handmade noodles, sauces, and bread. Its menu isn't extensive, just focused and heavy on fresh ingredients, and local wine. D Wed.–Sun. $$

Maggie's Buns Café (2007 21st Avenue; 503-992-2231). Maggie's Buns is a breakfast and lunch spot specializing in unique salads, Thai dishes, and soups, such as B-52 chili or Hungarian mushroom. Maggie's bakes its own sandwich bread and cinnamon rolls daily. The menu varies from season to season and even day to day. Although no alcohol is served, the presence of Stumptown Coffee tells you Maggie's caters to locals as well as lucky visitors. B/L Mon.–Sat. $

1910 Main—An American Bistro (1910 Main Street, Suite A; 503-430-7014). Local-economy booster Kathy Compton has made an effort to integrate regional ingredients whenever possible in her select bistro menu. Faves and raves are: wild salmon with local honey glaze, Carlton Pork shoulder roast, and Hermiston Beef pot roast with red wine au jus. The mood is upscale casual and the wait staff welcoming. The restaurant features a local wine each week; standard are three Oregon whites and reds by the glass and more than 30 by the bottle. B (Sat. & Sun.) L/D $$

Out Aza Blue Market & Cafe (57625 NW Wilson River Highway; 503-357-2900). It's a little out-AZA-way, but don't let that deter you. The menu is Mediterranean-Southwestern-Indian inspired, with a vividly colorful interior and exterior to match. For lunch, grab a burger, wrap, or the potent Vegenator sandwich, which owner and five-star chef Gabriel claims will halt any desire to be carnivorous again. Also up for grabs: fresh-baked breads, including killer focaccia. Gabriel prides himself on supporting the small and local wineries. B (Sat.–Sun.) L/D (Wed.–Sun.) $$

Urban Decanter (2030 Main Street; 503-359-7678). Explore the wines of the region over wine-friendly appetizers, salads, or the famous panini. The vibe is casual; the staff, friendly and knowledgeable. Northwest craft brews and a short specialty cocktail list are a few minor changes new owner Becky Kramer has added. Retail sales are still focused on Northwest, with some imports. She kept the wine club, but in four variations: Northwest reds and whites, one from each, and around the world. Anticipate small changes in fun food and local wines and beers. L (Wed.–Sat.) D (Mon.–Sat.) $

To do
in the Forest Grove Area

Attractions

Few movie experiences are quite like the brew pub's independent films at **McMenamins** (3505 Pacific Avenue, 503-992-9533). If you're in the mood for something live, the **Theatre in the Grove** (2028 Pacific Avenue, 503-359-5349) offers productions throughout the year.

Recreation

For the water-minded, **Henry Hagg Lake** just southwest of Forest Grove is a popular getaway for Portlanders for boating, Jet skiing, fishing, swimming, and sailing.

Wine Shopping

The place to pick up a bottle of Oregon wine with a side of info is **The Friendly Vine Wine Shop & Tasting Room** (2004 Main Street, 503-359-1967), which also stocks selections from Europe, Australia, and South America. The Friendly Vine hosts events, private gatherings, and music with tastings every Friday evening.

GASTON TO YAMHILL

Between Forest Grove and Carlton, Gaston and Yamhill only recently have begun to ride the wine-industry coattails. With so many wineries and vineyards calling Gaston home, you'd think this town of 650 would be alive with wine events. Not so. Yet it's trying.

The town has had discussions about revamping East Main Street to be more attractive to the wine industry, à la Carlton. Meanwhile, Yamhill has retained more of its traditional agricultural aura—timber, wheat, barley, and dairy farming—than its sister city Carlton. But there is no escaping wine's grip on these communities.

Wineries

in the Gaston/Yamhill Area

GASTON

Plum Hill Vineyards (6505 SW Old Highway 47; 503-359-4706). *Tasting room:* Daily 11–5. *Fee:* Complimentary. *Owners:* R. J. & Juanita Lint. *Winemaker:* Kramer family. *Wines:* Pinot blanc, Pinot gris, Pinot noir, Riesling. *Cases:* Under 1,000. R. J. and Juanita Lint were so thrilled to be getting into the business of running their own winery in 2008 they began naming individual vines: Cork Douglas, Crush Limbaugh, Wineona Jug, and Marilyn Merlot. The Lints first got their hands grapey as volunteers during crush. They then purchased and restored a decaying farm using the old buildings for processing and a tasting room. A made-for-fun patio and grounds welcome kids and canines; in fact, they created a "pampered puppy play area" for restless dogs. The Lints are full of entertaining stories, too.

Patton Valley Vineyards (9449 SW Old Highway 47; 503-985-3445). *Tasting room:* Thurs.–Sun. 11–5. *Fee:* $10. *Owners:* Monte Pitt & Dave Chen. *Winemaker:* Derek Einberger. *Wines:* Pinot noir, rosé. *Cases:* 3,200. Patton Valley is an unassuming winery in a wealthy neighborhood. There's no artwork, lavish fixtures, high-beam ceilings, or expensive furnishings, just exquisite Pinot noir. It's not a name-dropper, just a consistent quality producer. Patton's rosé sells out quickly—grab it when you can. Patton Valley helped organize the Sip 47 marketing strategy.

Kramer Vineyards (26830 NW Olson Road; 503-662-4545). *Tasting room:* Daily 11–5, Apr.–Oct.; Thurs.–Sun., Nov.–Mar. *Fee:* $5. *Owners:* Keith & Trudy Kramer. *Winemaker:* Trudy Kramer. *Wines:* Chardonnay, Merlot, Müller-Thurgau, Pinot gris, Pinot noir,

Take a break at Kramer Vineyards on Route 47.

rosé, port-style, sparkling. *Cases:* 2,000. The Kramers' place is comfortable, easygoing, and definitely dog-friendly—you're usually greeted by one of their Labs. The tasting room is where the affable staff does its best work, generating more than 80 percent of the winery's sales. Kramer has 18 acres in production and they've just planted Pinot meunier and Grüner veltliner. Also unique at Kramer is the sale of coffees from five countries in the tasting room.

▲ ❖ **Elk Cove Vineyards** (27751 NW Olson Road; 503-985-7760). *Tasting room:* Daily 10–5. *Fee:* $5. *Owners:* Joe & Pat Campbell. *Winemaker:* Adam Godlee Campbell. *Wines:* Pinot blanc, Pinot gris, Pinot noir. *Cases:* 36,000. If you haven't seen an Elk Cove label, you don't get out much. The Campbells started in the mid-1970s and have built an empire—one of the best-known Oregon wineries in and outside the state. It took some marketing to get there, but more so outstanding wine. The tasting room is nothing short of astounding—if you can take your eyes off the trophy Roosevelt elk mount over the tasting bar, you'll enjoy sensational valley views. For the ultimate wine experience, sign up for Elk Cove's dinners.

ADEA Wine Company & Fisher Family Cellars (26421 NW Highway 47; 503-662-4509). *Tasting room:* Holiday weekends, and by appt. *Fee:* $10. *Owner:* Fisher family. *Winemaker:* Dean Fisher. *Wines:* Chardonnay, Pinot blanc, Pinot noir, rosé. *Cases:* 1,200. Ann, Dean, Erica, and Adam Fisher put their initials together and came up with ADEA. With a firm philosophy that wine is made in the vineyard, they use fruit from their own patch in the Yamhill Carlton AVA along with grapes from AVAs within 25 miles. Dean, with an assist from daughter Erica, likes to let fruit evolve into age-worthy Pinot. ADEA also serves as a custom crush facility and makes about 5,000 cases annually. The Fishers live nearby, so appointments are easy to make by phone.

YAMHILL AREA

▲ **WillaKenzie Estate** (19143 NE Laughlin Road; 503-662-3280). *Tasting room:* Daily 11–5. *Fee:* $15. *Owners:* Bernard & Ronni Lacroute. *Winemaker:* Thibaud Mandet. *Wines:* Chardonnay, Gamay noir, Pinot blanc, Pinot gris, Pinot meunier, Pinot noir. *Cases:* 20,000. WillaKenzie has an exclusive-club feel where you can imagine guests discussing lucrative mutual funds or politics while deciphering subtle nuances of the

"Dirt matters" at WillaKenzie Estates, which prides itself on sustainability. Sherry L. Moore

Lenné's hilltop perch near Yamhill offers splendid views in every direction.

vintage in their glass. One look at the walls heightens the realization you're in the upper echelon. Most notable: a presidential seal recognizing contributions to three President Clinton functions. The beautifully serene grounds are visible from a sprawling concrete patio with evenly spaced tables lending views to vineyard, forest, and wildlife serenity. Yet a down-to-earth respect for the dirt is signature for philanthropic WillaKenzie.

▲ **Lenné Estate** (18760 NE Laughlin Road; 503-956-2256). *Tasting room:* Thurs.–Sun. 12–5. *Fee:* $10. *Owners:* Steve & Karen Lutz. *Winemaker:* Steve Lutz. *Wines:* Pinot noir. *Cases:* 1,500. Lenné is easy to spot. Look for a tall, linear, all-stone, French countryside barn at the top of a vineyard that owner Steve Lutz describes as "stellar for Pinot." An iron gate beckons visitors up the steep hill to this eye-catching tasting room and winery. There is a quaint patio for drinking in views of hillside vineyards. Steve certainly likes to talk about his wines, but ask him about the New Mexico clay walls that took him years to finish. He keeps making more Pinot and has plans for expanding his production facility on-site.

Soléna (17100 NE Woodland Loop Road; 503-662-4730). *Tasting room:* Daily 11–5. *Fee:* $15. *Owners:* Laurent Montalieu & Danielle Andrus Montalieu. *Winemakers:* Laurent Montalieu & Tony Rynders. *Wines:* Cabernet sauvignon, Chardonnay, Merlot, Pinot gris, Pinot noir, Syrah, Zinfandel. *Cases:* 12,000. You can't go far in the Willamette Valley without hearing of Laurent Montalieu. His imprint is as widespread as the number of labels that list him as winemaker. Wife and business partner Danielle, daughter of the late Gary Andrus, has an impressive pedigree as well. Along with Steve and Marian Bailey, the ambitious couple also created the Grand Cru Estates, a 13,000-square-foot club outside town where members try their hands at being vintners.

Kason Vineyards (7200 Bony Road; 503-537-3070). *Tasting room:* Thurs.–Sun. 11–5, and by appt. *Fee:* Complimentary with purchase. *Owner/Winemaker:* Steve O'Neill. *Wines:* Chardonnay, Pinot noir. *Cases:* 400. Kason is one of the newest wineries in the Yamhill-Carlton AVA. Many of its grapes wind up elsewhere in Oregon and California, but some are kept on hand to produce Dijon-clone Chardonnay and Burgundian-style Pinot noir. The winery sits on a 15-acre vineyard, but the wines come from three nearby vineyards.

Zeñas (7700 NE Cooper Lane; 971-231-5128). *Tasting room:* Fri.–Sun. 12–5. *Fee:* Complimentary. *Owners:* Howard Family. *Winemakers:* Kevin & Blake Howard. *Wines:* Cabernet franc, Meritage, Merlot, Riesling, red blend. *Cases:* 1,000. The Howards are descendants of early Oregon pioneer Zenas Howard, who came west on the Oregon Trail and landed in southern Oregon. You might say the fruit for their signature blend, Meritage, as well as the Merlot and Cabernet franc, comes from "home." The Del Rio Vineyard in southern Oregon supplies the grapes for the reds, and the Riesling comes from Montinore. They opened their Carlton tasting room in 2012.

Stag Hollow Wines & Vineyard (7930 NE Blackburn Road; 503-662-5609). *Tasting room:* Holiday weekends, and by appt. Thurs.–Sun. 11–4. *Fee:* $5. *Owners:* Mark Huff & Jill Zarnowitz. *Winemaker:* Mark Huff. *Wines:* Chardonnay, Dolcetto, Muscat, Pinot noir, red blend. *Cases:* 1,500. Stag Hollow uses narrow spacing in its vineyard—3,000 plants per acre—in an effort to coax as much flavor intensity as possible out of the grapes, especially the nine clones of Pinot noir and five of Chardonnay. In doing so, Mark and Jill strive for low-input viticulture in producing "artistically crafted distinctive" wines. Part of their earth-friendly philosophy includes setting aside 10 acres of oak forest, wetlands, and creeks for the area's wild critters.

CARLTON AREA (Yamhill–Carlton District AVAs)

Carlton is one of the state's epicenters for wine touring—lively, cozy, energetic, compact, intimate, and a great place to find a bench and people-watch. For decades, this town of about 1,800 was a railroad stop on the seed-and-grain circuit. One of its top employers was a meatpacking plant. Today, it's a very different scene.

Wineries

in the Carlton Area

CARLTON

❖ **Cana's Feast** (750 West Lincoln Street; 503-852-0002). *Tasting room:* Daily 11–5. *Fee:* $10. *Owners:* Partnership of 14. *Winemaker:* Dan Duryee. *Wines:* Barbera, Counoise, Merlot, Nebbiolo, Pinot noir, Primitivo, Rosato, Sangiovese, Syrah, red blends. *Cases:* 7,500. Reminiscent of a modest Italian estate, Cana's Feast—formerly Cuneo—offers Northwest and Italian wines, an eatery with piazza seating, and bocce courts accentuated by olive and lemon trees. One of Cana's more noteworthy wines is the Sangiovese grosso, the same clone used in Brunello di Montalcino. It took some doing, but it was brought from Italy, quarantined, endured a lengthy certification process, and finally put into production in 2007.

❖ **Carlton Winemakers Studio** (801 North Scott Street; 503-852-6100). *Tasting room:* Daily 11–5, Feb.–Dec. *Fee:* $5–18/flight. All for one and one for all is the innovative and authentically cooperative spirit behind Carlton Winemakers Studio. It's the vision of Eric Hamacher and Lazy River Vineyard owner Ed Lumpkin—the latter, needing a winemaker; the former, yearning for a green winery. When the idea of a wine co-op was hatched, an alternating proprietorship was illegal in Oregon. The determined duo fought the state for years and eventually won. The stunning building opened in 2002 on the outskirts of town and, as *Food & Wine* magazine puts it, "is just plain cool." Each tenant provides their own fruit and barrels, and rotates use of the facilities.

Andrew Rich Vintner (503-852-6100) *Owner/Winemaker:* Andrew Rich. *Wines:* Cabernet franc, Malbec, Mourvèdre, Petit verdot, Pinot noir, Roussanne, Sauvignon blanc, Syrah, red and white blends, dessert. *Cases:* 8,000. Andrew Rich is a maestro with single varietals, but also has a respected reputation as a blend master. Rich, listed among the top 100 winemakers in *Wine & Spirits*, has a devoted following. Who does a Petit verdot solo? One barrel a year, it's funky, spunky, and worth the effort to attain. If you happen to catch Rich, you'll see why he's known for his dry sense of humor and quick wit.

Bachelder (905-941-3942) *Owner/Winemaker:* Thomas Bachelder. *Wines:* Chardonnay, Pinot noir. *Cases:* 750. Thomas and Mary Bachelder craft wines in

Downtown Carlton is draped in color and loaded with tasting opportunities. John Baker

three dramatically unique yet similar places: Oregon, Bourgogne (Burgundy, France), and Niagara (Ontario, Canada). The Quebec natives call it "the Bachelder Project." Their wine of choice for this experiment is Chardonnay. Their mission is to produce a Chard that with "excitement and tension"—a contrast to the sweet, oaky versions from warmer climes.

Brittan Vineyards (503-989-2507) *Owners:* Ellen & Robert Brittan. *Winemaker:* Robert Brittan. *Wines:* Chardonnay, Pinot noir, Syrah. *Cases:* 800. Robert Brittan first made wine in his dorm room at Oregon State University—a dorm-tiste, if you will. Brittan was at Stags Leap in Napa for many years, but when he couldn't make Pinot noir there, he and Ellen returned to Oregon. They have their own vineyard in the McMinnville AVA and now make their wine in Mac. Ellen continues as general manager of the studio.

Dukes Family Vineyards (503-835-0620) *Owners:* Patrick & Jackie Dukes. *Winemaker:* Kelly Kidneigh. *Wines:* Pinot noir, rosé. *Cases:* 2,000. Pursuit of perfect Pinot is the mission and passion for veterans Pat & Jackie, longtime vineyard owners who share space with their two dogs. Vineyard and production matters are left in capable hands, where all efforts are made to be "conservators of the land." They host tastings at the vineyard on occasion.

Hamacher Wines (503-852-7200) *Owner/Winemaker:* Eric Hamacher. *Wines:* Chardonnay, Pinot noir. *Cases:* 1,500. Hamacher, the brains and inspiration behind CWS, is a dad first and celebrated winemaker second. And he's married to winemaker extraordinaire Louisa Ponzi, with whom he has four children. Work starts at 5 AM so he can pick up the kids after school; Louisa works the later shift. The two could write the book on Oregon Chardonnay; they've even developed their own specialized clones.

Lazy River Vineyard (503-662-5400) *Owners:* Ned & Kirsten Lumpkin. *Winemaker:* Robert Brittan. *Wines:* Pinot gris, Pinot noir, Riesling. *Cases:* 950. There's nothing lazy about Ned and Kirsten, residents of Sun Valley, Idaho, who share equal ownership of the studio with Hamacher and Ponzi. Ed is a masters champion downhill skier and yoga enthusiast, Kirsten is a master bridge player. Both are into their grandkids and wine. People have been lining up for their Pinot noir and gris since they began bottling in 2005.

Merriman Wines (503-852-6100) *Owner/Winemaker:* Mike Merriman. *Winemaker:* Eric Braucher. *Wines:* Chenin Blanc, Pinot noir, rosé. *Cases:* 1,000. Mike Merriman purchased a vineyard in 2006 and is making his own Pinots from those vines. As for the Chenin Blanc, those grapes come from a 40-year-old vineyard in Washington's Yakima Valley.

Montebruno (503-852-6100) *Owner/Winemaker:* Joe Pedicini. *Wines:* Gewürztraminer, Pinot noir. *Cases:* 250. Vagabond chef Joe Pedicini from Brooklyn, New York, just might be the next great wine movie. He shows up for a few weeks each year to turn Willamette Valley grapes into stellar wine. He signed a contract with CWS sight unseen, and arrived in the fall of 2009 with an oak barrel in a Subaru Outback. When he's finished, he packs some bottles, leaves a few, and isn't seen until the next harvest.

Omero Cellars (503-537-2638) *Owner:* David Moore Family. *Winemaker:* Sarah Cabot. *Wines:* Pinot gris, Pinot noir. *Cases:* Under 1,000. Another small, family-owned and -run vineyard in the tiny Ribbon Ridge AVA finds a production home at the Studio. The winemaking philosophy is "be adaptable" and ready to work with fruit the harvest brings. Taste the results.

Retour Wines (971-237-4757) *Owner:* Lindsay Woodard. *Winemaker:* Eric Hamacher. *Wines:* Pinot noir. *Cases:* 900. *Food & Wine* describes Retour as a star producer. Lindsay Woodard is a sixth-generation Oregonian who lived briefly in Napa Valley before Pinot fever called her back to her native state. *Retour* is French for "back to the roots" or "a homecoming that endures."

Trout Lilly Ranch (503-852-6100) *Owners:* Peter & Carol Adams. *Winemaker:* Kelly Kidneigh. *Wines:* Pinot noir. *Cases:* 250. Peter and Carol Adams have been growing Pinot just around the bend from their friends and neighbors, the Adelsheims, since early 1970. Initially they sold their grapes, but saw their way into producing about 10 years later. Current winemaker Kidneigh makes Trout Lilly's wine as well as others' at CWS under her business name KK Wine Co.

Utopia Wines (503-298-7841) *Owner/Winemaker:* Daniel Warnshuis. *Wines:* Chardonnay, Pinot noir, Viognier, rosé, dessert. *Cases:* 1,350. Although Daniel Warnshuis makes his wine here, his tasting room is at the vineyard. (See listing in Newberg Area.)

Wahle Vineyards & Cellars (503-241-3385) *Owners:* Mark & Shaghayegh Wahle. *Winemaker:* Mark Wahle. *Wines:* Pinot noir. *Cases:* 2,000. The Wahle family lays claims to planting Yamhill-Carlton's first commercial vineyard on a 100-acre site in 1974. In a familiar story, after years of watching others produce great Pinots from their grapes, they've now entered the fray with their own label. Along the way, they've added another vineyard on Holmes Hill.

Cliff Creek Cellars' home is in southern Oregon, but its presence is well known in Carlton.
John Baker

Carlton Cellars (130 West Monroe Street; 503-474-8986). *Tasting room:* Wed.–Sun. 11–5, Mar.–Nov.; Sat. & Sun., Dec.–Feb. and by appt. *Fee:* $10. *Owners:* Dave Grooters & Robin Russell. *Winemaker:* Dave Grooters. *Wines:* Auxerrois, Pinot blanc, Pinot gris, Pinot noir, Sauvignon blanc, rosé. *Cases:* 4,000. Friendships are the story at Carlton Cellars. A longtime bond between Dave and Army buddy Nick Peirano of Nick's Italian Café sparked an interest in Oregon wine. An evolving friendship with Ken Wright led to a vineyard manager position. Another friendship, formed on a flight from Pennsylvania to Oregon, turned into a romance and eventual wedded partnership. Their Dave and Robin's labels reference another strong bond—with the Pacific Ocean.

Cliff Creek Cellars (258 North Kutch Street; 503-852-0089). *Tasting room:* Daily 12–5. *Fee:* $10. *Owner:* Garvin family. *Winemaker:* Joe Dobbes Jr. *Wines:* Cabernet franc, Cabernet sauvignon, Merlot, Syrah, red and white blends. *Cases:* 1,600. The address says Carlton, but everything else says southern Oregon—grapes are grown in the Rogue Valley. The Garvin family is spread out, explaining a tasting room nearly 300 miles from home. Daughter Ruth lives in the Portland area and oversees the Carlton location. Cliff Creek has premium, food-friendly reds and whites and its annual crop determines the blends. It's also known for its New World–style claret.

Troon (250 North Kutch Street; 503-852-3084). *Tasting room:* Daily 11–6 (closed Jan.). *Fee:* $6–8. This is a second tasting room for the renowned southern Oregon winery (see "Wineries in the Grants Pass Area"). Music in the back courtyard on summer Saturdays is a treat.

Noble Pig Winery (203 West Main Street; 503-474-2000). *Tasting room:* Daily 12–5; Fri.–Sun., Oct.–May. *Fee:* $5. *Owners:* Pollak Family. *Winemaker:* Cathy Pollak. *Wines:* Pinot blanc, Pinot gris, Pinot noir. *Cases:* 1,000. What's in a name? Nothing. And everything. "Noble Pig" had no personal connection when Cathy Pollak dreamed up the name, but it sells a lot of wine—not to mention a lot of pig paraphernalia. The winery is a small, artisan family business focused on Pinots.

Terra Vina (214 West Main Street; 503-925-0712). *Tasting room:* Daily 12–5, Dec. & Jan. by appt. *Fee:* $5. *Owners:* Karl & Carole Dinger. *Winemaker:* Karl Dinger. *Wines:* Cabernet franc, Cabernet sauvignon, Chardonnay, Malbec, Pinot noir, Riesling, Sangiovese, Syrah, Zinfandel, red blends. *Cases:* 2,000. The name has changed, but the wines haven't. The Dingers changed from "Dalla Vina Wines" for two reasons: the similarity to a California winery and an urge to be more environmentally minded. Their motto, "Respecting the Earth, Creating Great Wine," applies personally and professionally. From the vineyards they source, the focus is on high quality over high yields, and the wines reflect this intent. They also aren't shy on barrel aging, making for intense, complex, and memorable reds.

Barking Frog Winery (128 West Main Street; 503-702-5029). *Tasting room:* Fri.–Sun. 1–5, and by appt. *Fee:* $10–15. *Owners:* Ron & Cindy Helbig. *Winemaker:* Ron Helbig. *Wines:* Cabernet sauvignon, Pinot noir, Sangiovese, Syrah. *Cases:* 1,000. Ron Helbig was an amateur winemaker who won so many awards, he decided to enroll in Chemeketa Community College's oenology and viticulture program. He prefers Columbia Valley grapes over competing with the area's Pinot producers. The meaning of the winery's name is left to the imagination, but the general idea is that the frog is a symbol of prosperity and a barometer of environmental health. Barking Frog uses the Vino Seal, a glass-topped cork substitute, in a nod to sustainability.

Folin Cellars (118 West Main Street; 503-349-9616). *Tasting room:* Thurs.–Sun. 1–5, and by appt. *Fee:* $5. If you're Pinoted out, this is your stop. All the wines at Folin Cellars' second tasting room are extraordinary. (See "Wineries in the Medford Area.")

Seven of Hearts (217 West Main Street; 971-241-6548). *Tasting room:* Thurs.–Mon. 12–5, and by appt. *Fee:* $10. *Owner/Winemaker:* Byron Dooley. *Wines:* Cabernet franc, Chardonnay, Mourvèdre, Pinot gris, Pinot noir, Syrah, Viognier, red and white blends. *Cases:* 3,000. A cat named Seven stole the Dooleys' heart, and the same can be said for the heartbreak grape. Byron's Pinot is firmly Burgundian, and so is his fermented-in-neutral-oak Chardonnay. Byron, left in the rubble of the dot-com boom and bust, is constantly changing his lineup, but Pinot remains his passion. Seven of Hearts continues to share space with Honest Chocolates, owned by Byron's wife, Dana, and open Thurs.–Sun.

EIEIO & The Tasting Room (105 West Main Street; 503-852-6733). *Tasting room:* Daily 11–5; Wed.–Sun., Apr.–Dec. *Fee:* $10 (EIEIO wines), 10% of bottle price for others. *Owner/Winemaker:* Jay McDonald. *Wines:* Chardonnay, Pinot noir. *Cases:* 2,200. Plucky ol' McDonald was a New York financial wizard who found a way to buy the proverbial farm . . . er, winery. Jay is a *négociant*, meaning he buys juice from other wineries and, with a tweak, tweak here and a blend, blend there, comes up with his own wine. At EIEIO, no "swine wine" is done before its time. EIEIO also serves as tasting room for about 35 other wineries too small to have their own.

Ken Wright Cellars Tasting Room (120 North Pine Street; 503-852-7010). *Tasting room:* Daily 11–5. *Fee:* $15–20. *Owner/Winemaker:* Ken Wright. *Wines:* Cabernet franc, Malbec, Syrah, red blend. *Cases:* 11,500. Talented and iconic in the world of vineyard-specific Pinot noir, Ken Wright is a down-to-earth Oregon legend. His sophisticated country-leisure tasting room—formerly named Tyrus Evan at the Depot—is in the refurbished train station. In keeping with his commitment to supporting the community that supports him, Wright is instrumental in revitalizing Carlton's older structures, and orchestrating fundraisers. Until 2012, to get an inside look at Ken Wright Cellars you had to come to his annual Thanksgiving open house on nearby Kutch

Street. Now all of Wright's wines, including the Tyrus Evan label he introduced in 2003, are available for tasting at the stylish depot.

Scott Paul Wines (128 South Pine Street; 503-852-7300). *Tasting room:* Sat. 11–5. *Fee:* $10. *Owners:* Scott Paul & Martha Wright. *Winemaker:* Scott Paul Wright. *Wines:* Pinot noir. *Cases:* 3,000. Taking the love of Pinot to another notch, Scott Paul not only makes fine Burgundian Pinot noir, he and partner Martha started a side business of importing the French version. You reap the benefits with side-by-side tastings in their converted warehouse on the edge of town. Scott goes for what he loves, so he purchased the old building across the street for his winery. Your toughest decision: Which kind of Burgundy do you favor?

Spofford Station/Stone Griffon Vineyard (153 East Main Street; 971-237-1045). *Tasting room:* Fri. 5–7, Sat. & Sun. 12–6. *Fee:* $5. *Owner/Winemaker:* Lynne Chamberlain. *Wines:* Cabernet franc, Cabernet sauvignon, Carmenère, Malbec, Merlot, Petit Verdot, Sangiovese, Sémillon, Syrah, Tempranillo, Viognier. *Cases:* Under 1,000. "One winery, two labels, three cows" is the mantra for Lynne Chamberlain, who has opened a tasting room in Carlton to showcase her limited production from grapes grown back home in Walla Walla. Chamberlain is a one-woman show who converted a wheat and pea farm to vineyard. Her production facility is in Spofford Station, a grain elevator where wheat is still shipped to the Pacific via rail and the Columbia River system.

Carlo & Julian Winery (1000 East Main Street; 503-852-7432 or 503-550-3928). *Tasting room:* Sat. 12–5. *Fee:* Complimentary. *Owner/Winemaker:* Felix Madrid. *Wines:* Nebbiolo, Pinot noir, Tempranillo. *Cases:* Under 1,000. International is the theme. Felix, an enthusiastic organic vegetable farmer, was born in Argentina, moved to the United States as a youngster, and earned a degree in oenology at UC–Davis. He opened his winery in 1996 and produces Spanish, Italian, and French varietals. Carlo and Julian are the names of his two sons. Be sure to call ahead.

Soter Vineyards (10880 Mineral Springs Road; 503-662-5600). *Tasting room:* Daily, by appt. only at 11, 1, & 3 PM. *Fee:* $20. *Owners:* Tony & Michelle Soter. *Winemaker:* James Cahill. *Wines:* Cabernet franc, Pinot noir, sparkling. *Cases:* 1,600. Tony Soter made his name in Napa, where he founded Etude Wines. His résumé as a consultant reads like a who's who of Napa-area wineries. He continues to keep a hand in the Etude operation, but today his focus is on his Mineral Springs Ranch. Winemaker James Cahill is also a busy guy, traveling the country touting Soter's wines at dinners and opulent events.

Lemelson Vineyards (12020 NE Stag Hollow Road; 503-852-6619). *Tasting room:* Thurs.–Mon. 11–4. *Fee:* $10. *Owner:* Eric Lemelson. *Winemaker:* Anthony King. *Wines:* Chardonnay, Pinot gris, Pinot noir, Riesling, dessert. *Cases:* 10,500. No dollar was spared, no corners cut, and no compromises made at Eric Lemelson's dream winery. The building is planked with sustainable storm-damaged cedar, and its two 50-yard-long solar panels take care of about half of the electricity needs. The winery's approach to the vineyard and wines is similarly eco-friendly under the watchful eye of Anthony King, who began his winemaking career in central Texas, of all places. Tours of the organically certified facility are offered for an additional fee.

❖ **Laurel Ridge Winery** (13301 NE Kuehne Road; 503-852-7050). *Tasting room:* Daily 11–5, Jan.–Nov. *Fee:* $5. *Owner:* Susan Teppola. *Winemaker:* Chris Berg. *Wines:* Cabernet franc, Chasselas doré, Gewürztraminer, Pinot blanc, Pinot noir, Riesling, Roriz, Sauvignon blanc, Semillon, Semillon blanc, Tempranillo, Zinfandel, brut, red and white blends, sparkling, port, dessert. *Cases:* 2,500. Susan Teppola wants you to have a good time, and she loves the idea of wine geeks rubbing shoulders with novices in her recently built tasting room. The winery was incorporated in 1986 on a 240-acre farm site reputedly settled by German immigrants 100 years earlier. The state-of-the-art facility has several custom-crush clients. Laurel Ridge has unusual line-ups, most notably its Swiss Chasselas doré and French *méthode champenoise*.

Ghost Hill Cellars (12220 NE Bayliss Road; 503-852-7347). *Tasting room:* Sat. & Sun. 11–5, May–Nov., and by appt. *Fee:* $10. *Owners:* Mike & Drenda Bayliss. *Winemaker:* Rebecca Pittock-Shouldis. *Wines:* Pinot blanc, Pinot noir, rosé. *Cases:* 1,000. Savannah Ridge has seen a lot of activity in a century. It was a dairy operation in the '20s, then a sheep ranch followed by cattle and hay fields. Planting grapes began in 1972, but life intervened and it was another 27 years before 15 acres of Pinot noir were put into the rich soil. Sit in the Baylisses' tasting cabana and sip their one-of-a-kind Pinot noir blanc. Ghost Hill is named for a miner camping on the hill who was murdered for his gold more than a century ago. It is said he still looks for his killer.

Monks Gate Vineyard (9500 NE Oak Springs Farm Road; 503-852-6521). *Tasting room:* Fri.–Sun. 12–5, May–Nov., and by appt. *Fee:* $5. *Owners:* Ron & Linda Moore. *Winemaker:* Laurent Montalieu. *Wines:* Pinot noir. *Cases:* 300. Because they are a little out of the way, Ron and Linda Moore like to get up close and personal with their guests at their small, family-owned estate. They share history on their tours and explain how four different clones make for subtle differences in their small-lot Pinot. If you ask nicely, you might get Linda's Pinot noir brownie recipe.

Anne Amie Vineyards (6580 NE Mineral Springs Road; 503-864-2991). *Tasting room:* Daily 10–5, Mar.–Dec.; Fri.–Sun., Jan.–Feb. *Fee:* $10–15. *Owner:* Robert Pamplin. *Winemaker:* Thomas Houseman. *Wines:* Müller-Thurgau, Pinot blanc, Pinot gris, Pinot. noir, Riesling, Syrah, Viognier, rosé, white blends, dessert. *Cases:* 14,000. Well-known Portland-area businessman Robert Pamplin bought the Château Benoit Winery site in 1999 and did a complete transformation. The eye-popping winery sits atop certified sustainable vineyards and has splendid views of the Coast Range. The focus is on elegant and balanced wines and on 30-year-old Riesling and Müller-Thurgau vines. Anne Amie offers a bicycle tour in the area called Fête d'Été.

Lodging

in the Gaston/Yamhill/Carlton Area

YAMHILL

Lake House Vacation Rental (Address not listed for privacy; 503-476-2211). Built by an Irishman to fit his dream-house vision, this rental 5 miles north-west of Yamhill offers a Thomas Kinkade–like setting with large pond, lily pads, frogs, natural landscape, and well-equipped kitchen. High-pitched gable roofs and a red-arched entrance lend to the fairy-tale setting, with thoughtful attention to detail and comfort throughout. You might even see Tinker Bell flitting through the graceful flower gardens. If seclusion and quiet are what you're seeking, this is your Magic Kingdom. $$$$

CARLTON

Abbey Road Farm B&B (10501 NE Abbey Road; 503-852-6278). Unwind with your new favorite wine among the llamas, sheep, alpacas, and chickens on John and Judi Stuart's European-style working farm. Despite the farm exterior, the five "silo suites" are luxurious and full of creature comforts. View farm life and the famous Guadalupe Vineyard while savoring farmstead goat cheese and

Cycle Wine Country—A Taste of Sip 47

Description: Start and end at the über-cool Carlton Winemaker Studios, on a mostly flat route with a couple out-and-back side trips that traverse agricultural land southeast of town and includes the little community of Lafayette. This is classic north Willamette Valley farm and orchard country, with a few vineyards thrown in for good measure. You'll also pass by some of the more popular bed and breakfasts in the region. When finished reward yourself with stops at the many other tasting rooms in Carlton.

Wineries: Carlo & Julian Winery, Soter Vineyards, Lemelson Vineyards, Laurel Ridge Winery, Monks Gate Vineyard, Ghost Hill Cellars, Anne Amie Vineyards

Miles: 24

Elevation gain: 404

Start/Finish: Carlton Winemakers Studio

Picnic areas with views are common in Oregon Wine Country.
Courtesy Laurel Ridge Winery

- Head east on Johnson Street, then south on Kutch Street and east on Main Street. Winery stop: Carlo & Julian Winery.
- Continue straight on Hendricks Road before proceeding south on Mineral Springs Road. Winery stop: Soter Vineyards.
- Go west on Northeast Mineral Springs, then north on Johnson Road, west on Yamhill, east on Rowland Road, east on Yamhill Road, east on Hendricks Road, and then north on Stag Hollow Road. Winery stop: Lemelson Vineyards.
- Return south on Stag Hollow Road and go east on Hendricks Road, then north on Kuehne Road. Winery stop: Laurel Ridge Winery.
- Return south on Kuehne Road and continue straight on Oak Springs Farm Road. Winery stop: Monks Gate Vineyard.
- Continue on Oak Springs Farm Road and turn west on Bayliss Road. Winery stop: Ghost Hill Cellars.
- Return east on Bayliss Road, then head south on Abbey Road and go straight on Bridge Street before turning west on OR 99W and north on Mineral Springs Road. Winery stop: Anne Amie Vineyards.
- Finish the ride by continuing north on Mineral Springs Road and then west on Hendricks Road to Carlton.

fresh-baked cookies. Enjoy breakfasts enhanced by their variety of produce. A three-bedroom, two-bath vacation rental is available from June to September as well. $$$$

❖ **Brookside Inn** (8243 NE Abbey Road; 503-852-4433). Brookside's motto is "Catering to the wine & food lover's soul," and it seems to work. Wine tourists are drawn to Bruce and Susan Bandstra's 22-acre Shangri-La, with its creek, gardens, and sense of seclusion amid fir trees. Nine warmly appointed suites surround a spacious great room with stone fireplace. The Carriage House, not far from the main house, has an Egyptian tint, and sleeps up to four. Mornings are highlighted by a three-course breakfast based on a strata, frittata, or French toast. $$$–$$$$

Carlton Cottages (543 West Main Street; 503-857-8176). A 1938 English cottage in downtown Carlton can be your home for a night or a week. If you don't need the entire restored cottage, the loft above Matt and Darci Haney's design studio is a fine place for one or two guests. The 1,400-square-foot house has two downstairs bedrooms; a loft with private shower can be rented solo. $$$–$$$$

🐾 **The Carlton Inn** (648 West Main Street; 503-852-7506). Back when timber was king in Carlton, this was the baron's home. Wood floors and accents have stood the test of time, and hold turn-of-the-century character melded with modern amenities. Gourmet breakfasts made from scratch come with a nod to history as well; milk and cream are delivered by a company whose products are free of hormones and antibiotics. The B&B's three upstairs rooms are named for nearby AVAs: Dundee Hills, Eola Hills, and Yamhill-Carlton. $$$

Casa Della Valle (819 South Pine; 503-852-0180). Affable Eve and Joe Della Valle decided to open their "Home in the Valley" to guests for two good reasons: bulk up their travel fund and meet new people. Two reasonably priced, ultra-clean rooms adorned in country motif are located within a short walk to downtown Carlton. Eve happily shares tips and free tasting vouchers with new friends. A two-night minimum applies. $–$$

Lobenhaus Bed & Breakfast & Vineyard (6975 NE Abbey Road; 503-864-9173). Take your just purchased bottles of wine, settle back, and enjoy views of the woods, creek, and vineyard on the huge wraparound deck enveloping Dick and Shari Lobenstein's lodge-style, trilevel home. Emphasis is on a healthful country lifestyle, right down to an Oregon bounty breakfast; Pinot noir juice is a nice added touch. Six tasteful rooms were updated in 2012. Lobenhaus grapes are sold to A to Z Wineworks. $$$

Vacation Rentals by Owners (VRBOs). Ten properties in Carlton proper and the outskirts range from a wine producer's posh home in a Thoreau-esque setting that sleeps 15 to high-end lofts in the center of town that sleep two. All are privately owned, wine-centric, and a comfortable base while visiting an epicenter of Oregon Wine Country. www.vrbo.com/vacation-rentals/usa/oregon/willamette-valley/carlton.

Dining
in the Gaston/Yamhill/Carlton Area

GASTON

The One Horse Tavern (300 Front Street; 503-985-3273). Don't be afraid to walk in and belly up to this bar and order from the grill. While the interior matches fairly well with the exterior, food and drink are befitting the heady wineries in the 'hood. Wendy Chamberlain's pub grub is creatively above average, as is her team, but vegetarian dishes and hand-cut fries tip the scale. The down-home nature blends well with the surroundings—and newbies are treated as well as locals. L/D/HH/LN $

CARLTON

Carlton Bakery (305 West Main Street; 503-852-6687). "Quality ingredients, traditional methods" is the motto behind the madness at Carlton Bakery, formerly the Filling Station. Quality: Carlton Farms bacon and ham, local farm eggs, and freshly made whole-grain baguettes. Traditional: Reuben, ham and Swiss, turkey, and cranberry sauce. Stumptown

Coffee paired with a sweet treat will keep you humming along. B/L Wed.–Sun. $

Cielo Blu Italian Grill (119 West Main Street; 503-852-6200). Traditional and Americanized Italian cuisine pairs well with wines from the epicenter of the Willamette Valley. Antipasto (spinach dip, cheese fondue, or bleu-stuffed 'shrooms) hits the hunger zone after tasting room fatigue. If you stay for dinner, we suggest sharing the Pollo Scaloppini or adding a penne à la vodka. Cielo Blu takes pride in its house-made sauces, salad dressings, and desserts. A full bar is in the plans for owners Georgia and Greg Graven, and Retta Carl. L/D Wed.–Sun. $$

Cuvée (214 West Main Street; 503-852-6555). French cuisine in Pinot country is, of course, the quintessential pairing. An understated forefront, interior bisque walls, and black tables covered in white linens set up for special yet unfussy dining. French classics such as cassoulet and coquilles St. Jacques are expertly prepared, and the sautéed oysters are renowned, but the clams can steal the show (be prepared to find yourself sipping broth from the bowl). Add handcrafted bread, delectable desserts, and a reasonable markup on local wines—French, too—and you'll see why Cuvée is a taster's choice. The three-course prix fixe dinner Wednesday, Thursday, and Sunday for $25/person is *très bon*! D Wed.–Sun. $$$

The Horse Radish (211 West Main Street; 503-852-6656). This deli/wine bar delivers a plethora of cheeses listed by milk type, picnic salads, and antipasti to go or to stay, served family style and well matched with local wine. More than 50 Northwest wines are on the list and five to seven are typically open for tasting. In summer, settle into the back garden patio just off a small, well-landscaped parking lot. Live music on Friday and Saturday nights adds the right amount of kick. L/D (Fri. & Sat.) $

To Do

in the Gaston/Yamhill-Carlton Area

Attractions

Equestrian aficionados will appreciate the **Flying M Ranch** (23029 NW Flying M Road, 503-662-3222) 6 miles west of Yamhill. The Flying M offers camping and horseback rides from an hour to all day, including a steak-fry ride.

Recreation

Quite popular is the annual **Wine Country Half Marathon**, which begins at Stoller Vineyards and ends in downtown Carlton. Every Labor Day weekend, up to 2,000 runners ply the hills outside of Carlton. Before and after the event they celebrate, naturally, with wine poured into Riedel glasses.

More Information

Sip 47, www.sip47.com

Travel Yamhill Valley, http://travelyamhillvalley.org

Willamette Valley Wineries Association, 503-646-2985, www.willamettewines.com

Yamhill Valley Visitors Association, 503-883-7770, www.yamhillvalley.org

Yamhill-Carlton AVA, www.yamhillcarlton.org

3

Willamette Valley North

WHERE PINOT PREVAILS

MENTION OREGON WINE COUNTRY TO VINO FANS, and images of the Red Hills and undulating Chehalem Mountains invariably come to mind, along with the requisite tasting parlors and boutiques. Vineyards and wineries have sprung up seemingly everywhere since the first wave of wine pioneers arrived in the 1960s. The resulting phenomenon is a change in the rural scenery and character of small towns unlike that which any Oregonians ever would've imagined a few decades ago.

Today, the serene agricultural towns southwest of Portland have blossomed, giving other rural communities an understandable case of Pinot envy. These towns mostly embrace their newly acquired fame. The sounds of chatter and music, aroma of wine-filled barrels, and the joy and pride on vintners' faces blend into one satisfying sigh of pleasure for those lucky enough to be there.

GETTING HERE AND AROUND

Transportation begins and ends in Portland, which has a busy international airport served by every major airline. The Willamette Valley is bisected north–south by I-5, but most wineries are on two-lane roads winding through the hinterlands, adding to the charm of wine touring. A notable exception is OR 99W. Once ideal for carefree Sunday drives, 99W between Portland and McMinnville has become an all-day traffic jam. For those who want a more leisurely pace, take US 26 west through the Sunset Hills past Beaverton to the Forest Grove exit.

NEWBERG AREA (Ribbon Ridge and Chehalem Mountain AVAs)

How's this for irony: One of the wine hubs of the northern Willamette Valley was until recently a "dry" town, meaning alcohol was verboten. Newberg was founded as a Friends Church (Quaker) community in 1889 and is home to George Fox University, a four-year Christian college that still requires alcohol abstinence. Another claim to fame: President Herbert Hoover spent much of his boyhood here.

LEFT: Washington's Mount Adams rises above the vines in the Columbia Gorge. John Baker

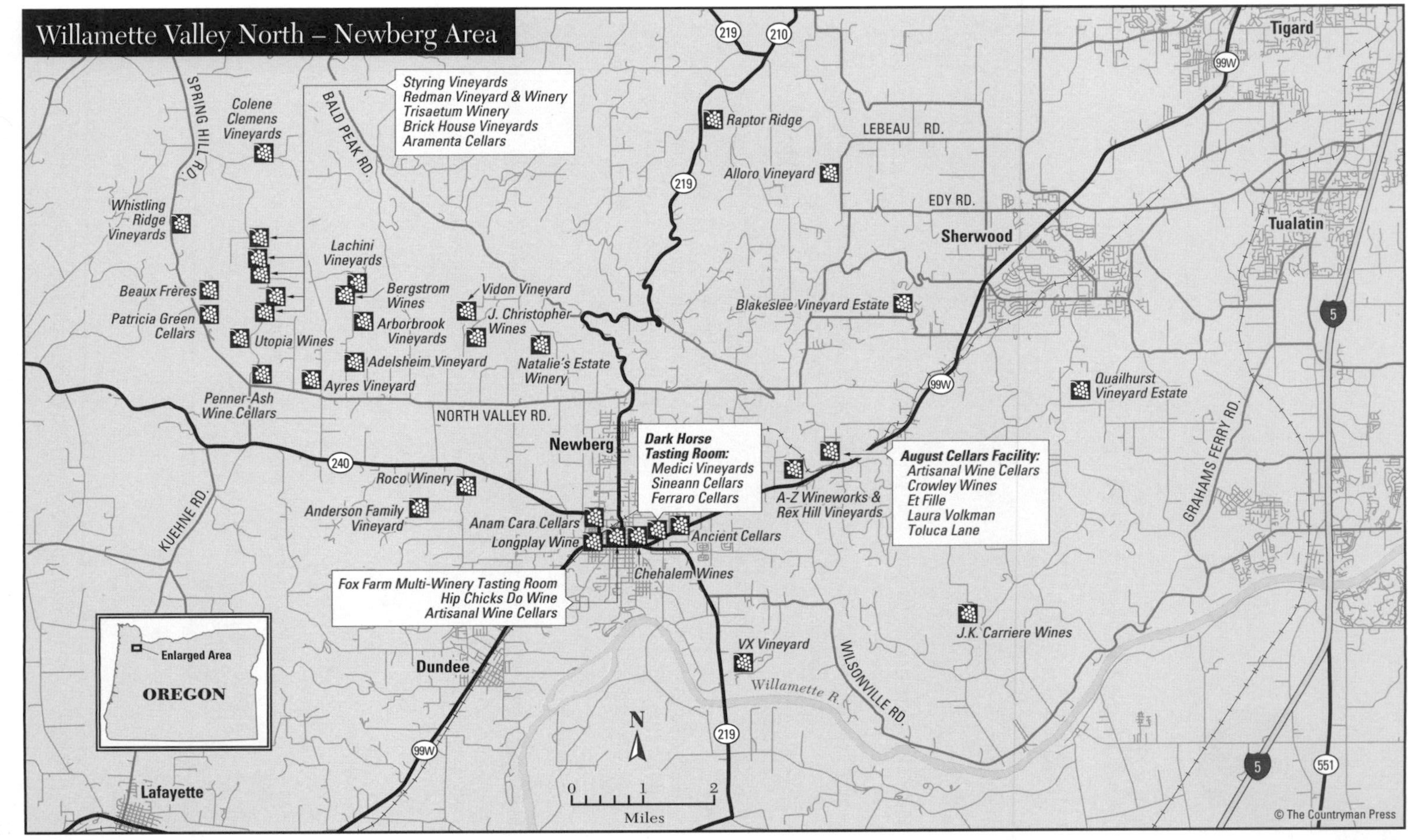
Willamette Valley North – Newberg Area
Styring Vineyards
Redman Vineyard & Winery
Trisaetum Winery
Brick House Vineyards
Aramenta Cellars
Colene Clemens Vineyards
Whistling Ridge Vineyards
SPRING HILL RD.
BALD PEAK RD.
Raptor Ridge
Alloro Vineyard
LEBEAU RD.
EDY RD.
Sherwood
Tigard
Tualatin
Lachini Vineyards
Bergstrom Wines
Vidon Vineyard
J. Christopher Wines
Beaux Frères
Patricia Green Cellars
Utopia Wines
Arborbrook Vineyards
Adelsheim Vineyard
Natalie's Estate Winery
Ayres Vineyard
Penner-Ash Wine Cellars
Blakeslee Vineyard Estate
Quailhurst Vineyard Estate
NORTH VALLEY RD.
Newberg
Dark Horse Tasting Room:
Medici Vineyards
Sineann Cellars
Ferraro Cellars
A-Z Wineworks & Rex Hill Vineyards
August Cellars Facility:
Artisanal Wine Cellars
Crowley Wines
Et Fille
Laura Volkman
Toluca Lane
GRAHAMS FERRY RD.
Roco Winery
Anderson Family Vineyard
Anam Cara Cellars
Longplay Wine
Ancient Cellars
Chehalem Wines
KUEHNE RD.
Fox Farm Multi-Winery Tasting Room
Hip Chicks Do Wine
Artisanal Wine Cellars
J.K. Carriere Wines
VX Vineyard
Willamette R.
WILSONVILLE RD.
Dundee
Lafayette
Enlarged Area
OREGON
N
0 1 2
Miles
219
210
99W
240
5
551
© The Countryman Press

Barrels share space on holiday weekends. John Baker

The town of 22,600 has loosened its mores over the years, but is still in its adolescence in terms of redefining itself as a community. Its otherwise sleepy downtown, with an old-fashioned barbershop pole and eateries, is split into one-way streets. The edge of town has the strip-mall aura that neighboring communities have avoided. In an effort to build on the wine economy, there's a visible push to liven up downtown with tasting rooms, new eateries, and art galleries.

Wineries
in the Newberg Area

On a map, Oregon's smallest appellation—less than 8 square miles—appears to be an island surrounded by three of the state's powerhouses: Dundee, Chehalem, and Yamhill-Carlton. On the ground, Ribbon Ridge is an oak- and fir-bathed peninsula protruding southward from the lush Chehalem Mountains, rising 700 feet above the green farms and pastures of the Chehalem River Valley.

Distinguishing Ribbon Ridge from its renowned neighbor appellations isn't just the fine, volcanic, marine-sediment Willakenzie soils. Nor is it merely the slightly warmer climate, which allows for an earlier growing season. Ribbon Ridge is also thought to comprise an elite club of winemakers. Pinot noir, Pinot gris, and Chardonnay are the primary crops.

The Chehalem Mountain AVA is also a subappellation of the entire Willamette Valley, yet much larger than Ribbon Ridge—20 miles long and 5 miles wide, with more than 30 wineries. The AVA has such dramatic differences in elevation, precipitation, and temperatures that harvests can be separated by as much as three weeks.

Raptor Ridge (1870 SW Hillsboro Highway; 503-628-8463). *Tasting room:* Thurs.–Mon. 11–4, May–Nov., and by appt. *Fee:* $10. *Owners:* Scott & Annie Shull. *Winemaker:* Scott Shull. *Wines:* Pinot gris, Pinot noir, rosé, dessert. *Cases:* 6,500. Raptor Ridge is named for the variety of winged predators cruising the thermals above the Chehalem foothills, mostly hawks. In summer 2010, visitors were treated to the vision at Raptor Ridge's new, full-fledged winery about 10 miles north of Newberg. Look for Raptor Ridge's special "wine events" at the new digs.

Alloro Vineyard (22075 SW Lebeau Road; 503-625-1978). *Tasting room:* Fri.–Sun. 11–5. *Fee:* $10. *Owner/Vineyard Manager:* David Nemarnik. *Winemaker:* Tom Fitzpatrick. *Wines:* Chardonnay, Muscat, Pinot noir. *Cases:* 1,500. When you turn into the driveway lined with Italian cypress, you'll feel as if you've arrived at a small Tuscan estate, complete with garden, fountain, and sheep. Owner David Nemarnik is Italian and fondly remembers his grandfather's wine press. He knew he wanted to continue the family tradition, and decided his mark would be with wine grapes. *Alloro* is Italian for "laurel"—the name of the ridge on which the vineyard sits. The setting is *bellissimo* for a gathering of friends or an afternoon of simple imbibing and wine education.

Blakeslee Vineyard Estate (20875 SW Chapman Road; 503-789-7032). *Tasting room:* Daily 11–5. *Fee:* $10. *Owners:* Bill & Sheila Blakeslee. *Winemaker:* Bill Blakeslee. *Wines:* Chardonnay, Pinot noir, Riesling, rosé. *Cases:* 2,000. What Bill Blakeslee describes as "a little boutique winery" took a new step in 2012 with the opening of a tasting room amid a 20-acre vineyard. Views of Mount Hood and the Tualatin Valley are selling points. All of Blakeslee's wines are estate reds, made in McMinnville. Look for its quarterly "pickup parties."

Quailhurst Vineyard Estate (16031 SW Pleasant Hill Road; 503-936-3633). *Tasting room:* Sat. 11–4, holiday weekends, and by appt. *Fee:* $20. *Owners:* Marvin & Deborah Hausman. *Winemaker:* Joe Dobbes. *Wines:* Pinot noir, rosé, dessert. *Cases:* 400. Coming to Quailhurst isn't just a visit, it's an event. The vineyard shares space with an equestrian facility and exquisite 1930s Japanese gardens. Chances are, you'll also get some pearls of wisdom from owner Marvin Hausman, a doctor who understands the health benefits of red wine. As a bonus, you might catch expert trainers working with horses to hone their skills for dressage competitions.

Joe Dobbes is one of Oregon's most prolific and personable winemakers.
Courtesy Joe Dobbes Wines

J. K. Carriere Wines (9995 NE Parrett Mountain Road; 503-554-0721). *Tasting room:* Fri. & Sat. 11–4, Mar.–Nov. *Fee:* $10. *Owner/Winemaker:* Jim Prosser. *Wines:* Chardonnay, Pinot noir, rosé. *Cases:* 3,000. In keeping with the philosophy "distraction is the lesser part of valor," J. K. Carriere's focus is on classic Burgundian Pinot, with sharp acidity and graceful tannins. The Prossers, now firmly entrenched on 40 acres on the southeast flanks of Parrett Mountain, have upgraded tasting facilities. Prosser tried the white-collar world before delving into the messy life of a grape grower. His label has the initials of both grandfathers; the wasp is a respectful nod to the winged devil that's almost done him in—twice.

NEWBERG AREA

▲ ✐ 🐾 ❖ VX Vineyard (8000 NE Parrish Road; 503-538-9895). *Tasting room:* Sat. & Sun. 12–5, May–Nov. *Fee:* $1 per taste. *Owners:* Hall family. *Winemaker:* John Grochau. *Wines:* Pinot blanc, Pinot gris, Pinot noir. *Cases:* 700. If you're looking for a mini wilderness retreat to fit into your touring, follow the signs to the end of Parrish Road. Keep going and you'll find yourself on Willamette Farms, a working place for the Hall family dating to the mid-1800s. Resident wildlife, nursery stock, orchards, boarded horses, and a vacation rental are on 200 acres along the Willamette River. "Vercingetorix" (pronounced "vur-sin-jet-uriks") refers to an ancient Gallic chieftain known to spare vineyards while rebelling against Caesar's Roman rule.

▲ ✐ August Cellars Facility (14000 NE Quarry Road; 503-554-6766). *Tasting room:* Daily 11–5, May–Oct. *Fee:* $5. *Owner:* Clarence Schaad family. *Winemaker:* Jim Schaad. *Wines:* Cabernet sauvignon, Chardonnay, Gewürztraminer, Maréchal Foch, Pinot noir, Riesling, rosé, port-style, dessert. *Cases:* 3,000. A stone's throw from busy OR 99W, yet worlds away from the commotion, is a working winery hosting six other small producers. Outside the green building, water gently cascades over river rock, and green leafy plants and wispy ornamental trees commune, creating a soothing wrapper for the incubating wine inside. You can see why these winemakers love to come to work. Patriarch Clarence Schaad's great-grandsons run the place. Inside, you might catch a glimpse of winemakers crafting their wares at the state-of-the-art eco-friendly winery. Call for appointments with individual wineries to taste.

Crowley Wines (971-645-3547). *Owner/Winemaker:* Tyson Crowley. *Wines:* Chardonnay, Pinot noir. *Cases:* 1,500. Grapes for Tyson Crowley's Chardonnay come from vines almost 40 years old in the famed Maresh Vineyard. Crowley is definitely in the Old World camp for his standout Pinot, yet it's reasonably priced. The keyhole on the label is a replica of one on Tyson's grandfather's cigar box.

D. P. Cellars (503-409-9541). *Owner:* Douglas Beall. *Winemaker:* Patrick Beall. *Wines:* Pinot noir. *Cases:* 1,000. The Bealls are hands-on every step of the way. Patrick pursued his passion by attending viticulture school and father Douglas used what was left of his retirement to support his dream. Barrel tastings can be arranged.

Et Fille (503-853-5836). *Owner:* Howard Mozeico. *Winemakers:* Howard Mozeico & Jessica Mozeico-Blair. *Wines:* Pinot noir, Viognier, rosé. *Cases:* 3,000. Howard, a self-taught amateur turned pro, and daughter Jessica are control freaks and close buddies—good thing, too, since they each have a hand in the work. As long as she listens, Howard says, "it works great." They do rotate music: She listens to rock and he likes classical, but they must be in tune because their wines sing. *Et fille* is French for "and daughter."

Laura Volkman (503-806-4047). *Fee:* $10. *Owner/Winemaker:* Laura Volkman. *Wines:* Chardonnay, Pinot noir. *Cases:* 500. Volkman's watercolor label of the lady in red viewing her vineyard bears a distinct likeness to Laura. Owner, grower, and winemaker, she does it all with help from her husband, kids, friends, and dog Bella. The Bella Chardonnay, with light oak treatment, is simply divine and her Pinots are indicative of the terroir from which they hail.

Toluca Lane (971-241-7728). *Owners/Winemakers:* Geoffrey & Lane Crowther. *Wines:* Pinot noir. *Cases:* 400. Geoffrey and Lane cleared scrub trees and blackberry thickets and then planted Pinot clones in their vineyard outside of Amity. Both had former careers—he, as a lawyer; she, as a Cordon Bleu–trained chef who managed the testing kitchen for *Bon Appétit*. But both wanted to live their dream. Low yields in the vineyard, with minimal intervention, define the Crowthers' style.

A to Z Wineworks & Rex Hill Vineyards (30835 North Highway 99W; 503-538-0666). *Tasting room:* Daily 10–5. *Fee:* $10. *Owners:* Bill & Debra Hatcher, Sam Tannahill & Cheryl Francis, Gregg Popovich. *Winemakers:* Michael Davies & Meredith Taggart. *Wines:* REX HILL label: Chardonnay, Pinot noir; A to Z label: Chardonnay, Pinot gris, Pinot noir, Riesling, rosé; Francis Tannahill label: Chardonnay, Gewürztraminer, Pinot noir, red blends, dessert; William Hatcher label: Pinot noir. *Cases:* 200,000. A complex family tree of owners entitles A to Z/REX HILL to the distinction of second-largest winery in Oregon. Paul Hart and Jan Jacobsen, the originators, sold the Rex Hill name, facility, and vineyards to the Hatchers (A to Z) and other investors. REX HILL led the way in pulling the Portland crowd into Willamette Valley wine country. The tasting room has enticing areas brimming with charm and many activities. Extensive cultivated gardens are perfect for impromptu or planned picnicking.

Dark Horse Tasting Room (1505 Portland Road [OR 99W]; 503-538-2427). *Tasting room:* Daily 11–5 (check for winter hours). *Fee:* $10. Dark Horse is an outlet bar of sorts for Medici, Sineann, and Ferraro Cellars. A sexy lineup of wines comes from all three producers. Peter Rosback is the winemaker for Medici and his own baby, Sineann ("shu-nay-un"). Dick Ferraro also crafts his traditional Italian line there. Dark Horse sports a European feel with warm colors, a few tables, and the obligatory long, dark wooden bar on a laurel wood floor, harvested from Medici's property. Not only are kids welcome in the side room, they'll find books, crayons, Legos . . . the works. There's a back patio for chillin' in the warmer months; food can be brought in or ordered and delivered from nearby Subterra.

Ferraro Cellars (503-758-0557). *Owners:* Dick & Mary Ferraro. *Winemaker:* Dick Ferraro. *Wines:* Cabernet sauvignon, Merlot, Zinfandel, red blend. *Cases:* 300. Dick grew up in an Italian immigrant family outside of Walla Walla, Washington. In the '40s and '50s, his grandfather was a broker of sorts for inhabitants wanting to make wine (mostly Zinfandel and Moscato). Dick remembers unloading grapes from railcars and storing them in the root cellar along with his grandmother's cured meats and pastries. All that wine imprinting lit a spark for the Ferraros.

You can sample the work of three wineries at the Dark Horse Tasting Room.

Courtesy Dark Horse Tasting Room

Medici Vineyards (503-538-9668). *Owners:* Hal & Dotty Medici. *Winemaker:* Peter Rosback. *Wines:* Pinot noir, Riesling. *Cases:* 1,000. Medici is known for old-vine vintage Pinot (planted in 1976) that has three to four years of bottle aging before release. Medici wines are a local's secret, so get them when you can.

The owners throw a great party in the vineyard on holiday weekends (28005 NE Bell Road).

Sineann Cellars (503-341-2698). *Owner/Winemaker:* Peter Rosback. *Wines:* Cabernet franc, Cabernet sauvignon, Gewürztraminer, Merlot, Pinot gris, Pinot noir, Riesling, Zinfandel, red blends, late-harvest ice-style, port-style. *Cases:* 10,000. Join the choir and sing the praises of Rosback's wines. He creates and crafts for many other well-known wineries, but these bottles are his pride and joy. His dessert wines beg for strong cheese, cozy fire, and a sublime sunset. Many of Sineann's wines are small-production and extremely popular, so stock up when you can find them.

Ancient Cellars (1505 Portland Road [Hwy 99W]; 503-312-4770 or 503-437-4827). *Tasting room:* Daily 12–5, May–Oct.; Fri.–Sun. 12–5, Nov.–Apr. *Fee:* $10. *Owners:* Chris & Craig Baker. *Winemaker:* Chris Baker. *Wines:* Cabernet franc, Cabernet sauvignon, Pinot gris, Pinot noir, Riesling, port. *Cases:* 550. The one-toed duck on the Pinot label has a story and so do the Baker brothers, who found their way home to Oregon with a purpose: find a home for good grapes. Each label is connected to a story as well as a cause. The moniker "Ancient" fits—one of the Bakers was a history major; the other, a geologist. Noteworthy: Ancient makes a port entirely from marionberries.

Longplay Wine (215 East First Street; 503-489-8466). *Tasting room:* Fri.–Sun. 11–5, Feb.–Dec.; Sat. & Sun., Dec.–Mar. *Fee:* $5. *Owner:* Todd Hansen. *Winemaker:* Jay Somers. *Wines:* Chardonnay, Pinot noir. *Cases:* 600. Todd Hansen's favorite part of growing grapes is (slowly) riding his tractor, befitting of his motto, "Analog wine for a digital world." His old-school approach means his wines aren't perfect, just full of character and meant to hold up for the long haul. *Wine Spectator* and *Wine Enthusiast* agree, dropping 90-plus points on his vineyard-specific Pinots. The colorful urban tasting room has comfy seating, meant for a long stay. The music (sometimes good, sometimes not) comes off a turntable, of course.

Fox Farm Multi-Winery Tasting Room (602 East First Street; 503-538-8466). *Tasting room:* Daily 12–8. *Fee:* $5–10. *Owners:* Thomas Ratcliff & David Fish. *Winemaker:* Joe Dobbes Jr. *Wines:* Pinot blanc, Pinot gris, Pinot noir, Syrah. *Cases:* 900. Two serious oenophiles met at Pinot Camp and said, "Let's grow grapes and make wine." Enter David's wife, Desiree, the hospitality director, and the blend was complete. Taste their small-production wines or purchase obscure and rare vintages from other producers for a fee. Flights change weekly, and private tastings or wine dinners for up to 20 take place in the back room.

Hip Chicks Do Wine (602B East First Street; 503-554-5800). *Tasting room:* Thurs.–Sun. 12–7 (check winter hours). *Fee:* $7. This is a second tasting room for Hip Chicks' Portland winery (see "Wineries in the Portland Area"), which prides itself on being a snob-free zone.

Artisanal Wine Cellars (614 East First Street; 503-537-2094). *Tasting room:* Thurs. & Fri. 4–7, Sat. & Sun. 12–7. *Owners:* Tom & Patricia Feller. *Winemaker:* Tom Feller. *Wines:* Gamay noir, Pinot blanc, Pinot noir, Tempranillo, Viognier, red and white blends. *Cases:* 1,500. The Fellers have created a welcoming tasting space that's more like a deli/wine bar/bottle shop downtown in a place once occupied by Bishop Creek Cellars. According to Patricia, Tom has been fermenting things as long as she's known him. He was a home brewer for years and decided that if he was going to live in Oregon, he should be making wine. The wines in this carefully crafted lineup have great diversity.

Chehalem Wines (106 South Center Street; 503-538-4700). *Tasting room:* Daily 11–5. *Fee:* $15. *Owners:* Harry Peterson-Nedry, Bill Stoller. *Winemakers:* Harry Peterson-Nedry and Wynne Peterson-Nedry. *Wines:* Chardonnay, Gamay noir, Grüner veltliner, Pinot blanc, Pinot gris, Pinot noir, Riesling. *Cases:* 20,000. Harry Peterson-Nedry's name and fingerprints are all over Oregon wine history. He wrote the petition that defined the tiny Ribbon Ridge AVA. Harry defines his style as a partnership with nature and technology. The tasting room—more wine bar, with large art and bistro tables—was opened to reach a broader audience and serve as anchor for a town hoping to become a wine country destination. The addition of a patio and food cart (June–Oct.) is a bonus. Chehalem's RR Pinot can be tasted and purchased by request.

Anam Cara Cellars (306 North Main Street; 503-537-9160). *Tasting room:* Daily 11–5; Sat. & Sun., Jan. & Feb. *Fee:* $10. *Owners:* Nick & Sheila Nicholas. *Winemaker:* Aron Hess. *Wines:* Chardonnay, Gewürztraminer, Pinot noir, Riesling, rosé. *Cases:* 2,500. Nick and Sheila couldn't be happier with their life in paradise, where they say they love to sit on their porch and watch the grapes grow. They also enjoy teaching others how it all works. You can find their product in wine-centric establishments throughout the state, due to Nick's 25 years in the restaurant biz. "Friend of my soul," the Celtic translation of *anam cara*, represents the sentiment of friends sharing soulful moments over wine.

Roco Winery/Cellar Door (13260 NE Red Hills Road; 503-538-7625). *Tasting room:* Thurs.–Sun. 11–5, and by appt. *Fee:* $10. *Owners:* Rollin & Corby Soles. *Winemaker:* Rollin Soles. *Wines:* Chardonnay, Pinot noir. *Cases:* 1,000. Rollin Soles has a sense of humor, a sense of history, and an even better sense of wine. He and his wife, Corby, combined the first two letters in their names to christen their winery, and labeled their vineyard "Wits' End." Rollin is also tributed for the startup and success of Argyle Winery, where he is head winemaker. His wines have been on *Wine Spectator*'s Top 100 list 11 times. ROCO's new tasting room opened in time to greet the new year in 2013.

Anderson Family Vineyard (20120 NE Herring Lane; 503-554-5541). *Tasting room:* Holiday weekends, and by appt. *Fee:* Varies. *Owners:* Cliff & Allison Anderson. *Winemaker:* Cliff Anderson. *Wines:* Chardonnay, Pinot gris, Pinot noir. *Cases:* 1,250. There are views, and then there are VIEWS. At Anderson Family Vineyard, you'll feel on top of the world, with an unobstructed 360-degree Dundee Hills panorama. Once a cow pasture on an ancient rock slide, the hill now provides "steep slopes, deep roots, and intense flavors." Many of this vineyard's organically farmed grapes are sold to a who's who list of neighbors. Cliff Anderson, who started fermenting juices under his bed at age 16, enjoys giving personalized tours of the facility and vineyard.

Natalie's Estate Winery (16825 NE Chehalem Drive; 503-807-5008). *Tasting room:* Holiday weekends, and by appt. *Fee:* $10. *Owners:* Boyd & Cassandra Teegarden. *Winemaker:* Boyd Teegarden. *Wines:* Cabernet sauvignon, Chardonnay, Merlot, Pinot noir, Sangiovese, Syrah, Viognier, Zinfandel, red blends. *Cases:* 2,000. The tasting room resembles a tree-house chalet in a vine maple and Douglas fir grove. With its antler chandelier and river-rock fireplace, it's more like a country retreat. The setting is casual, the wines serious. When Natalie's opened in 1999, Boyd worked for Ernest & Julio Gallo's wholesaler in the Portland area. The winery is named for the Teegardens' daughter.

J. Christopher Wines (17150 NE Hillside Drive; 503-554-9572). *Tasting room:* Sat. & Sun. 11–3; holiday weekends; daily by appt. 11–4. *Fee:* $10. *Owner/Winemaker:* Jay Somers. *Wines:* Chardonnay, Pinot noir, Sauvignon blanc, red blend. *Cases:* 6,000.

Barrels have many lives and purposes in wine country. John Baker

J. Christopher made headlines in 2008 when owner/winemaker Jay Somers collaborated with the famed Dr. Loosen Estate Winery in Germany to produce a transcontinental blend of Pinot noirs. That partnership is carrying over to a permanent 50-50 relationship that helped J. Christopher move into an eco-friendly $3 million facility on Chehalem Mountain. *Biodynamic* is the byword for growing grapes at J. Christopher.

▲ **Vidon Vineyard** (17425 NE Hillside Drive; 503-538-4092). *Tasting room:* Daily 11–4. *Fee:* $10. *Owners:* Don & Vicki Hagge. *Winemaker:* Don Hagge. *Wines:* Chardonnay, Pinot gris, Pinot noir. *Cases:* 1,200. Vicky and Don put their heads and names together to form the title of their vineyard (pronounced "veedon"). Don is a one-man show doing his thing, including clearing the property of debris, planting a sustainable vineyard, and making wine in his energy-efficient facility. He likes to say he picked a lot of rocks and dirt from his toenails. Vicki, now retired, handles the rest on their 20-acre property. Minimal intervention, indigenous fermentation (native yeast), and few or no additions make Vidon wines something special.

Lachini Vineyards (18225 Calkins Lane; 503-864-4553). *Tasting room:* Fri.–Sun. 11:30–4:30, May–Sept., and by appt. *Fee:* $20. *Owners:* Ron & Marianne Lachini. *Winemaker:* Laurant Montalieu. *Wines:* Cabernet sauvignon, Pinot gris, Pinot noir, dessert. *Cases:* 4,500. What began as a modest Pinot noir harvest on 45 acres in 2001 has evolved into a full-scale, ultra-premium operation producing highly regarded wines. With his Italian heritage, Ron is big on wines—and the media are big on Lachini, grant-

Lachini Vineyards began producing single-vineyard Pinot noir in 2001. John Baker

ing frequent 90s and above from *Wine Spectator* and *Wine Enthusiast*. The Lachinis' vineyard is now fully immersed in biodynamic growing practices.

Bergström Wines (18215 NE Calkins Lane; 503-554-0468 or 503-554-0463). *Tasting room:* Daily 10–4. *Fee:* $15. *Owner:* Bergström family. *Winemaker:* Josh Bergström. *Wines:* Chardonnay, Pinot noir, rosé. *Cases:* 10,000. Bergström's vineyard-specific wines are internationally acclaimed—a remarkable feat, given that the family entered the business almost by chance. Family patriarch John grew up on a small farm in Sweden, but after arriving in Oregon as a teenager studied to become a surgeon. He bought 15 acres on the flanks of the Chehalem Mountains for his retirement plan, and didn't think much about grapes until area winemakers recognized the potential. The rest, as they say, is history. Son Josh developed an affinity for wine, studied in France, and has established himself as one of the elite Pinot producers.

Arborbrook Vineyards (17770 NE Calkins Lane; 503-538-0959). *Tasting room:* Sat. & Sun. 11–5, Mon.–Fri. 11–4:30. *Fee:* $10. *Owners:* Dave & Mary Hansen. *Winemaker:* Laurent Montalieu. *Wines:* Pinot gris, Pinot noir, Sauvignon blanc, dessert. *Cases:* 2,500. Ten acres of producing vineyards surround Dave and Mary's life, and their horses. While Mary dreamed of equines, Dave dreamed of wine. They found the pasture of their dreams and converted the 1910s barn into a tasteful tasting room. In 2012, the tasting room received an upgrade, including outdoor patio and indoor bathrooms. Get your hands on their Semillon dessert wine before it sells out.

Adelsheim Vineyard (16800 NE Calkins Lane; 503-538-3652). *Tasting room:* Daily 11–4. *Fee:* $20. *Owners:* David & Ginny Adelsheim and Jack & Lynn Loacker. *Winemaker:* Dave Paige. *Wines:* Auxerrois, Chardonnay, Pinot blanc, Pinot gris, Pinot noir, Syrah, rosé. *Cases:* 45,000. When they planted their 15-acre vineyard in 1972, Ginny and David Adelsheim were forerunners in the "new wine country." A few vines and wines later, the name still resonates with pedigree and history. The carefully designed, castlelike winery and tasting room can seem intimidating, but the congenial and professional staff makes you feel comfortable. Holiday weekends are organized, educational, and full of primo tasting. Buy small-lot Pinots and Auxerrois (an Alsatian white) at the tasting room—chances are, you won't find them elsewhere.

Adelsheim has an opulent new winery and tasting room near Newberg. John Baker

Ayres Vineyard (17971 NE Lewis Rogers Lane; 503-538-7450). *Tasting room:* Holiday weekends, and by appt. *Fee:* $10. *Owners:* Don & Carol McClure, Brad & Kathleen McLeroy. *Winemaker:* Brad McLeroy. *Wines:* Pinot blanc, Pinot noir. *Cases:* 3,000. "Keep it simple, keep it real"—words befitting grapes grown in the space-limited Ribbon Ridge AVA. The McLeroys live on the property alongside Kathleen's parents and co-owners Don and Carol McClure, the designated greeters. The winery is 12 feet below the ground under the main home, making it a "cool" place to work. Ayres practices sustainable agriculture, because its three generations want to take care of where they live. Their wine has that little extra something Brad McLeroy calls "personality and soul."

Patricia Green Cellars (15225 NE North Valley Road; 503-554-0821). *Tasting room:* By appt. only, weekdays. *Fee:* $20. *Owners/Winemakers:* Jim & Patty Green. *Wines:* Pinot noir, Sauvignon blanc. *Cases:* 11,000. The Greens are known for their wine, not their sign—two wine barrels and a small sandwich board, easily missed at the entrance to their 12-acre vineyard and winery. They like it that way. Patricia Green was an early advocate of single-vineyard Pinots. Clearly focused on substance and style, their Pinots, ranging from barnyardy and mushroomy to fruit driven, spend considerable time in French oak. Expect a formal education in an informal setting with your arranged tasting.

Beaux Frères' simple tasting room belies its reputation for complex wines.

Beaux Frères (15155 NE North Valley Road; 503-537-1137). *Tasting room:* Thurs.–Mon. by appt., Mar.–Nov., and holiday weekends. *Fee:* $30. *Owners:* Michael Etzel, Robert Parker Jr., & Robert Roy. *Winemaker:* Michael Etzel. *Wines:* Pinot noir. *Cases:* 4,500. The tasting setup is unpretentious, belying the fame and origins of Beaux Frères. There's no fancy architecture or decorum here—just substantial Pinot noir. Michael Etzel convinced his brother-in-law, Robert Parker Jr. (*Wine Advocate*), to go in on a pig and dairy farm in prime Pinot country in the '80s. Michael and family planted the vines and eventually built the winery. Etzel strives for Old World wines, using natural CO_2 instead of sulfur to preserve, so be sure to decant and aerate. For the record, Parker doesn't review his wines.

▲ ✐ 🐾 **Whistling Ridge Vineyards** (14551 NE North Valley Road; 503-554-8991). *Tasting room:* Sat. & Sun. 11–4, Apr.–Nov., and by appt. *Fee:* $5. *Owners:* Richard Alvord & Patricia Gustafson. *Winemaker:* Marcus Goodfellow. *Wines:* Chardonnay, Pinot gris, Pinot noir. *Cases:* Under 1,000. "Let it be" is the philosophy at Whistling Ridge. A family affair, Richard and Patricia, with help from Chuck and Diane, their son and daughter-in-law, cultivate 15 acres. For a small vineyard, they grow many varietals. "For experimentation and fun," They have 3 acres of Gewürztraminer, Riesling, Muscat, Pinot blanc, and Schönburger, a German cousin to Pinot noir. Marcus Goodfellow, who considers himself a throwback with his old-fashioned approach, also produces his own label, Matello, Italian for "little fool."

🍴 🖋 🐾 **Colene Clemens Vineyards** (22501 NE Dopp Road; 503-662-4687). *Tasting room:* Wed.–Sun. 11–5. *Fee:* $7. *Owners:* Joe & Vicki Stark. *Winemaker:* Steve Goff. *Wines:* Pinot noir, rosé. *Cases:* 3,000. The Starks have been in Forest Grove since 1980 and run a successful cabinet manufacturing company. Fond of Pinot, they bought 120 acres in 2005 and started converting walnuts, apples, and prunes to a Pinot vineyard. They've spared the old-growth trees and saved space for a home; the 1920s barn provides yard art. Named for Vicki's mom, the winery has made a name for itself.

▲ 🖋 Styring Vineyards (19960 NE Ribbon Ridge Road; 503-866-6741). *Tasting room:* Holiday weekends, and by appt. *Fee:* $5. *Owners:* Kelley & Steve Styring. *Winemaker:* Steve Styring. *Wines:* Chardonnay, Pinot gris, Pinot noir, Riesling. *Cases:* 1,000. The Styrings make organic wines they enjoy drinking, from varietals that "love it here as much as we do." They call Pinot their passion; Riesling, their whimsy; and dessert wines, their bliss. The Styrings are Texas transplants who were bit by the Pinot bug and bought 40 acres on Ribbon Ridge. After apprenticing at neighboring wineries, they began their small-lot production in 2004.

Redman Vineyard & Winery (18975 NE Ribbon Ridge Road; 503-554-1290). *Tasting room:* Holiday weekends, and by appt. *Fee:* $15. *Owner:* Cathy Redman. *Winemaker:* Dave Paige. *Wines:* Barbera, Chardonnay, Pinot noir, Tempranillo, red blend. *Cases:* 750. Bill and Cathy Redman found their 30-acre patch of paradise on Ribbon Ridge in 2004, harvested a final batch of hazelnuts, tore out the orchard, and planted their first vineyard—a dream a quarter-century in the making. After Bill died in 2009, the area's close-knit family of wine folks helped ensure that harvest and production would go as scheduled. The winery continues to flourish, most notably with a 90 in *Wine Spectator* for a Ribbon Ridge Pinot—from the vineyard's first harvest. In Bill's honor, winemaker Dave Paige continues to make Bill's Blend, a popular Pinot and Barbera mix.

▲ 🖋 🐾 Trisaetum Winery (18401 Ribbon Ridge Road; 503-538-9898). *Tasting room:* Wed.–Mon. 11–4. *Fee:* $10. *Owners:* James & Andrea Frey. *Winemakers:* James Frey & Greg McClellan. *Wines:* Pinot noir, Riesling. *Cases:* 5,500. Were it not for a freak summer snowstorm, James and Andrea Frey might be rangers in Yosemite National Park or naturalists in Arizona. Instead, forced into Plan B on their honeymoon, they drove past snowed-in Yosemite, ended up in Napa Valley, and fell in love with wine. In 2005, they found their perfect parcel on Ribbon Ridge. Since then, they've been producing reputable selections of Pinot noir and Riesling, with a big assist from fellow winemaker Josh Bergström. The name comes from combining their children's names, Tristan and Tatum.

Brick House Vineyards (18200 Lewis Rogers Lane; 503-538-5136). *Tasting room:* Thurs.–Sat. by appt., May–Sept. *Fee:* $10. *Owners:* Doug Tunnell & Melissa Mills. *Winemaker:* Doug Tunnell. *Wines:* Chardonnay, Gamay noir, Pinot noir. *Cases:* 8,000. Set amid hazelnut orchards on Ribbon Ridge, Brick House couldn't be more starkly juxtaposed with owner Doug Tunnell's previous life as a Middle East war correspondent for CBS. The Oregon native found his calling in the vineyard, where he's one of the few in the state to grow Gamay noir—a grape he grew fond of in France. Brick House's Gamay is widely considered Oregon's best. Twenty-three acres of certified organic and biodynamic vineyard contribute to the elite status and price of the wines.

▲ Aramenta Cellars (17979 NE Lewis Rogers Lane; 503-538-7230). *Tasting room:* Daily 10:30–5. *Owners:* Ed & Darlene Looney. *Winemaker:* Ed Looney. *Wines:* Chardonnay, Pinot noir, red blend. *Cases:* 1,200. The moniker might sound a bit stuffy, but in fact Aramenta—named for Darlene's aunt—is as homespun as it gets on Ribbon

Ridge. Ed Looney, once a tool-and-die maker, knows how to handle repairs. Aside from memorable wines, you'll find a pastoral setting and atmosphere that'll lure you in for a spell. If you buy enough wine, the Looneys might invite you to cast a fly to trout in their picturesque pond. They also rent a guest studio that sleeps two ($190/night) and overlooks the pond and vineyard.

Utopia Wines (17445 NE Ribbon Ridge Road; 503-298-7841). *Tasting room:* Daily 11–6, and by appt. *Fee:* $10. *Owner/Winemaker:* Daniel Warnshuis. *Wines:* Chardonnay, Pinot noir, Viognier, rosé, dessert. *Cases:* 1,350. Truly dedicated to the site, Daniel Warnshuis ("warn-sice," rhymes with "nice") firmly believes wine begins and ends in the vineyard. His 17 acres on Ribbon Ridge have 11 clones of Pinot planted for maximum diversity—a major factor in creating complexity. Daniel happily gives tours so he can talk about a favorite subject: Pinot noir. He continues to expand with a wrap-around deck and patio built to absorb vineyard views.

Penner-Ash Wine Cellars (15771 NE Ribbon Ridge Road; 503-554-5545). *Tasting room:* Wed.–Sun. 11–5, and by appt. *Fee:* $10–15. *Owners:* Ron & Lynn Penner-Ash. *Winemaker:* Lynn Penner-Ash. *Wines:* Pinot noir, Riesling, Syrah, Viognier, red blend. *Cases:* 9,500. Lynn Penner-Ash was part of an early groundbreaking group of women winemakers, getting her start in the lead role at Rex Hill in the late 1980s. In 2001, she and her husband pursued their own label in earnest. Their winery and tasting room, built with locally sourced materials, sit atop a hill overlooking Newberg, with Mount Hood and Mount Jefferson presenting snowcapped background. Featured in *Sunset* magazine for its views and vino, Penner-Ash's impressively gorgeous grounds and patio provide a welcome respite.

Lodging

in the Newberg Area

The Allison Inn & Spa (2525 Allison Lane; 503-554-2525). Think Four Seasons on steroids. Joan and Ken Austin, owners of a highly successful dental equipment business, are well known for philanthropy. (An elementary school is named for Joan.) The Allison is just one more way the Austins are pumping energy and money into their local economy. They've created a world-class destination resort with 85 über-luxurious rooms, including 20 astounding suites. In 2011, the Allison was chosen top spa in the United States by *Travel & Leisure* magazine, and no. 12 in the world. Although opulent, the resort also strives to be green, as evidenced by its LEED Gold certification—a rarity among hotels. $$$$

Avellan Inn (16900 NE Highway 240; 503-537-9161). Patt Gheith and her Rhodesian Ridgeback, Scully, live amid 13 acres of berry and hazelnut nirvana. So it's no surprise that the results of her foraging show up in many of her "won't-leave-hungry" breakfasts. Wake up to homemade granola or seasonal fruit crepes topped with cinnamon cream, depending on Patt's mood. She also caters to vegetarian, vegan, and gluten-free needs. The inn has two comfortable rooms. $$$

Chehalem Ridge B&B (28700 NE Mountain Top Road; 503-538-3474). Perched on a hill overlooking the valley and vineyards, Chehalem Ridge is reminiscent of an ornate birdhouse. Four contemporary rooms, all with private bath, provide peace and serenity. Three have balconies with sweeping views of the valley and Coast Range. Bring more than a bird's appetite for Kristin Fintel's from-scratch breakfast highlighted by unusual homemade jams and jellies (wild carrot is a fave). She gladly accommodates special diets, especially gluten free. $$$

The DreamGiver's Inn (7150 NE Earlwood Road; 503-625-1476). Complete your vision quest in Pinot country by the staying at this dreamy property. The red-and-white colonial-style home boasts four Pottery Barn–style rooms named Trust, Grace, Courage, and Faith. Linda Kesler and Kristen Hardy formed a business with a shared dream to present pampered hospitality. They do it with heart and added touches such as plush bathrobes, window seats and reading nooks, and breakfast on the deck. You may choose a respite on one of many Adirondack chairs around the green-carpeted grounds. Touring suggestions and/or dinner reservations are part of the package. Children over age 12 are welcome. $$$–$$$$

❖ **Le Puy A Wine Valley Inn** (20300 NE Highway 240; 503-554-9528). Elegance continues to be the theme for new area lodging. Le Puy's eight rooms with views of rolling countryside plus Mount Hood and Mount Jefferson are inspired by owners Andy and Lea Duffy's trip to France's Loire Valley, where vineyards and sunflowers surround pockets of homes. Each room has a wine bar, most a balcony, and some spa tubs and gas fireplaces. All pamper and spoil. If you're lucky, Lea's baked French toast will be on your breakfast plate. *Le puy* is French for "isolated or volcanic hill"—appropriate for the setting. $$$$

Lions Gate Inn B&B (401 North Howard Street; 503-476-2211). Lions Gate, a meticulously renovated 1911 Craftsman with three bedroom suites, is within walking distance of downtown. A careful combination of earth-friendly additions (green mattresses, solar panels, tankless hot water) and restored original works (fir floors, cabinets, doors, trim) make for dramatic and distinct environs. Owner Loni Parrish feels a deep connection to community and "mature structures." Distinctive Destinations has two other rentals, part of Parrish's eco- and employee-friendly empire. $$$

University House of Newberg (401 North Meridian Street; 503-538-8438). Ever dream of that picture-perfect two-story house with a white picket fence? Leigh and David Wellikoff have it and share it enthusiastically. The three-bedroom, two-bath U House is all yours, including a fully equipped kitchen. Leigh, who claims to be chief-in-charge of bottle washing, cooking, and maintenance, loves what she does, even after 10-plus years. She can name a million things to do in Newberg, and will gladly customize your stay. Children age 12 and older are accommodated. $$$

✐ 🐾 **Vineroost** (7120 NE Earlwood Road; 503-625-2534). Vineroost is a country-charming three-bedroom B&B sleeping eight amid McKinlay Vineyards, where winemaker Matt Kinne produces about 1,000 cases of Pinot noir annually. The home, surrounded by 32 acres on Parrett Mountain, is available by the day, week, or month. An extensive vegetable garden, along with Nubian and La Manchia goats, graces the grounds. $$$

Dining
in the Newberg Area

For all the lodging options in the Newberg area, the place has been remarkably devoid of good eateries. In the recent past, people (even tasting-room staff) opted to bring their own food or head to Dundee. But the times are changing. Welcome additions will make you want to stay to satisfy those hunger pangs that heavy-duty wine touring elicit.

Jory Restaurant & Bar (2525 Allison Lane; 503-554-2526). Although the dining room and expansive terrace are glamorous and upscale, Jory avoids pretension and sets a comfortably chic tone. Easy on the eyes—if not necessarily on the wallet—it's the hottest high-end dining in these parts. Choose from entrées meant to mingle with wine accompanied by pairing suggestions. The 800-label wine list is balanced with local and world selections, and carefully crafted to be educational but not daunting. For celebratory occasions, consider the Chef's Table option, an exclusive dinner prepared by the executive chef for up to seven. BR/B/L/D $$$$

The Painted Lady (210 South College Street; 503-538-3850). Husband-and-wife team Allen Routt and Jessica Bagley combine culinary training, world travels, and experience to bring you memorable dining. Classic appetizers, salads, entrées, and desserts utilize Oregon's bounty of seafood, local meats, produce, and fruit. Oregon wines by the glass and 20 or more Pinots by the bottle head the list. "Painted lady" refers to three or more contrasting exterior colors on Victorian or Edwardian homes—a movement started in San Francisco. D Wed.–Sun. $$$$

Recipe: A Neighborhood Kitchen (115 North Washington Street; 503-487-6853). Newberg's uptick in high-quality dining continues with Recipe, which touts itself as a family place where you might be dining next to local winemakers. Owners Dustin Wyant and chef Paul Bachand separate themselves from the ordinary with gracious touches, such as an heirloom vegetable garden with 18 varieties of tomatoes. Much of the meat, seafood, and mushrooms come from area producers and foragers. The thoughtful wine list is a mix of local and international. Housed in a classic Victorian, Recipe is mostly for walk-ins, so make a reservation for parties of six or more. L/D Tues.–Sat. $$$

Subterra: A Wine Cellar Restaurant (1505 Portland Road; 503-538-6060). Martin and Janet Bleck left the demanding schedules of food-oriented lives in Florida for peace and quiet in Oregon Wine Country. They got the wine country part, but not the slower pace. Step down (below Dark Horse Tasting Room) to fine dining, linens, and soft lighting, but modest prices. Or make a meal from a vast array of tasty small plates. The inspired menu makes the most of fresh, local ingredients. Whichever way you go, you'll step into sublime dining enhanced by a plethora of local wines. L (Mon.–Fri.) D/HH $$$

To Do
in the Newberg Area

Attractions

The **Hoover-Minthorn House** (115 South River Street, 503-538-6629) is first on the list of tourist activity in Newberg. Former President Herbert Hoover lived here as a child with his uncle and aunt, John and Laura Minthorn, from 1885 to 1891. Hoover's bedroom furniture is on display in the National Register of Historic Places home.

The Willamette River draws hikers, bicyclists, historians, and picnickers to the popular **Champoeg State Heritage Area** (503-678-1649), 7 miles east of Newberg. The site of Oregon's first provisional government in 1843, Champoeg is 615 acres of forests, meadows, wetlands, trails, picnic areas, campsites, and special historical events. For a different nostalgic experience, pack a picnic (with wine) and check out what's playing at the **99W Drive-In Theatre** (3110 Portland Road, 503-538-2738) on a Friday, Saturday, or Sunday night. The drive-in, one of Oregon's few, has been showing first-run movies since 1953. If it's summer, check out Tunes on Tuesday at the **Chehalem Cultural Center** (415 East Sheridan Street, 503-537-1010), featuring terrific local bands. Also at the Cultural Center is the **Newberg Farmers' Market**, open every Tuesday afternoon from May to September.

As scenic as the Willamette Valley is, rare is the spot in wine country where you can see the Big Five volcanoes: Washington's Mount Rainier, Mount St. Helen's, and Mount Adams, and Oregon's Mount Hood and Mount Jefferson. While you're touring, be sure to take a drive up Bald Peak Road to 1,629-foot **Bald Peak State Scenic Viewpoint** (800-551-6949) and drink in the valley's best views.

Recreation

For a serene bird's-eye view, glide above the countryside in a hot-air balloon with **Vista Balloon Adventures** (503-625-7385, 23324 SW Sherk Avenue) in Sherwood or **Pacific Peaks Balloons** (503-590-5250, 16065 SW Barrington) in Tigard. Vista offers wine flights over Yamhill County vineyards that include a catered brunch. For a day on the links between winery-hopping, **Chehalem Glenn Golf Course** (4501 East Fernwood Road, 503-538-5800) in Newberg is a picturesque and reasonably challenging course.

More Information

Chehalem Valley Chamber of Commerce, 503-538-2014, 415 East Sheridan, www.chehalemvalley.org

DUNDEE/DAYTON AREA (Dundee Hills AVA)

If Yamhill County is the heart of Oregon Wine Country, then Dundee is its soul. Actually, the unassuming little town likes to think of itself as the "Heart and Soil" of the Red Hills. Named for a town in Scotland, Dundee is literally a one-stoplight blip on the highway where old buildings and rough roads show signs of its other agricultural past. Dundee was known for growing prunes and hazelnuts before David Lett arrived in 1965. In the half-century since, this rural community has become a country-chic destination of wineries, restaurants, and popular Sunday farmers' market.

Wineries

around Dundee/Dayton (Dundee Hills AVA)

The Dundee Hills are Oregon's Côte d'Or ("golden slope"). The key to the area's Pinot noir success lies in climate and southeast-facing slopes. Erosion creates ideal terrain for the finicky grape. Another factor is the Coast Range rain shadow, where moisture is limited to 35 inches annually, mostly during the winter—hopefully long after a glorious growing season and harvest. Frost is rare. About 25 wineries and 50 vineyards covering 1,200 acres are planted predominantly in Pinot noir, along with Pinot gris and a bit of Chardonnay. Many wineries have Dayton addresses but are definitely part of the Dundee AVA. The 12th & Maple Wine Company, one of the state's largest custom-crush facilities, is off the main drag and hosts periodic open houses.

DUNDEE

▲ 🎁 🖉 🐾 **Duck Pond Cellars** (23145 Highway 99W; 503-538-3199 or 800-437-3213). *Tasting room:* Daily 11–5 (10 AM summer). *Fee:* Complimentary ($5/reserves). *Owners:* Fries & Jenkins families. *Winemaker:* Mark Chargin. *Wines:* Barbera, Cabernet sauvignon, Chardonnay, Gewürztraminer, Merlot, Pinot gris, Pinot noir, Riesling, Sangiovese, Sauvignon blanc, Semillon, Syrah, Tempranillo, Viognier red, white blends,

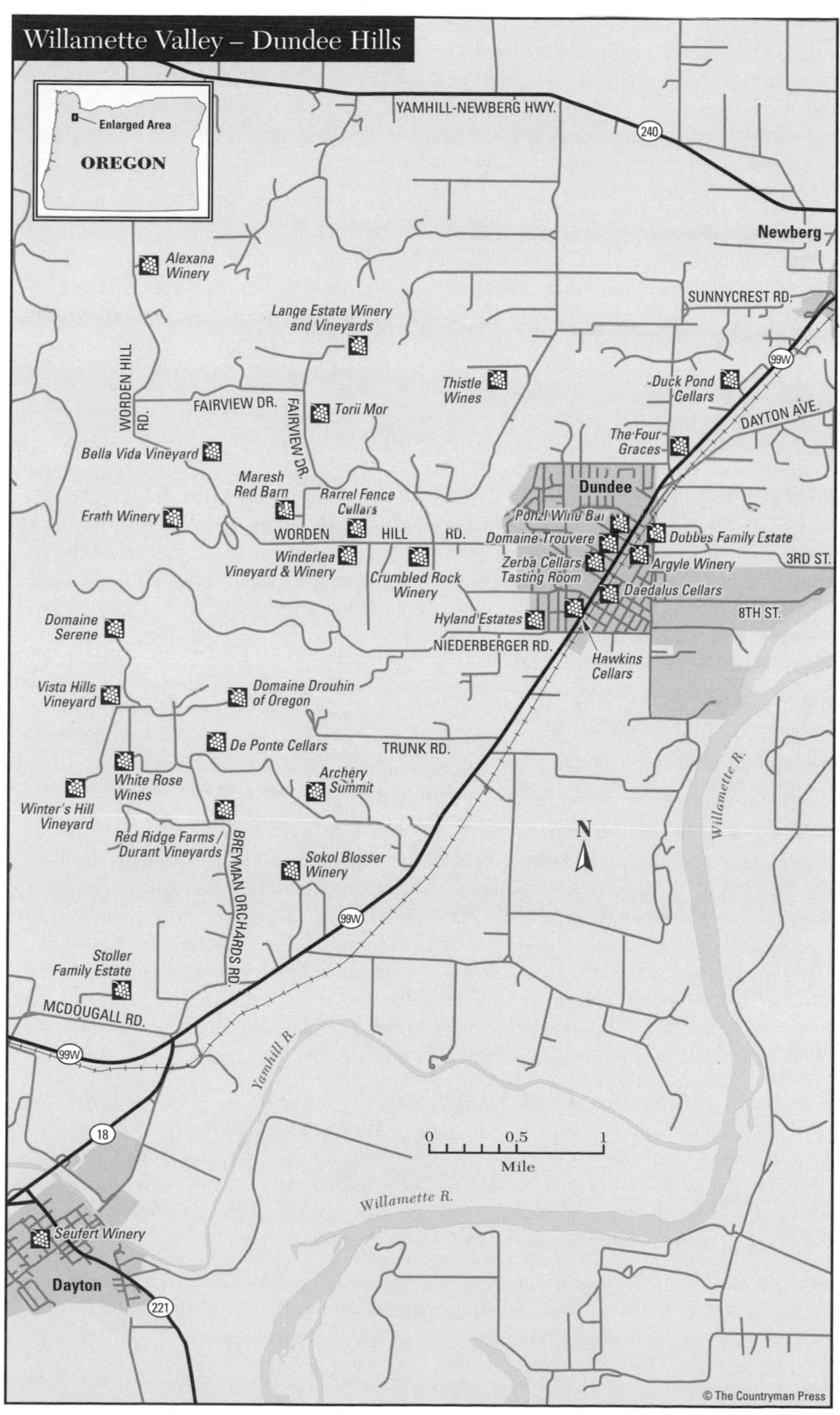
Willamette Valley – Dundee Hills
Enlarged Area
OREGON
YAMHILL-NEWBERG HWY.
240
Newberg
Alexana Winery
SUNNYCREST RD.
Lange Estate Winery and Vineyards
99W
Thistle Wines
Duck Pond Cellars
WORDEN HILL RD.
FAIRVIEW DR.
FAIRVIEW DR.
Torii Mor
DAYTON AVE.
The Four Graces
Bella Vida Vineyard
Maresh Red Barn
Dundee
Barrel Fence Cellars
Frath Winery
Ponzi Wine Bar
WORDEN HILL RD.
Domaine Trouvere
Dobbes Family Estate
Winderlea Vineyard & Winery
Crumbled Rock Winery
Zerba Cellars Tasting Room
Argyle Winery
3RD ST.
Daedalus Cellars
8TH ST.
Hyland Estates
Domaine Serene
NIEDERBERGER RD.
Hawkins Cellars
Vista Hills Vineyard
Domaine Drouhin of Oregon
De Ponte Cellars
TRUNK RD.
Archery Summit
White Rose Wines
Winter's Hill Vineyard
Red Ridge Farms / Durant Vineyards
BREYMAN ORCHARDS RD.
Sokol Blosser Winery
N
Willamette R.
99W
Stoller Family Estate
MCDOUGALL RD.
99W
Yamhill R.
18
0
0.5
1
Mile
Willamette R.
Seufert Winery
Dayton
221
© The Countryman Press

port-style, dessert. *Cases:* 120,000. Owned by the same families since 1993, Duck Pond is known for making affordable ready-to-drink wines. The production comes from 330 acres in the Willamette Valley and 540 in Washington. A family-friendly and festive tasting room is an event unto itself. The gift shop is loaded with housewares, wine accessories, apparel, gourmet food, and nonwine specialty beverages. RV and bus parking is available for tour groups (by appointment) and limited to 100.

The Four Graces (9605 NE Fox Farm Road; 800-245-2950). *Tasting room:* Daily 10–5. *Owners:* Black family. *Winemaker:* Laurent Montalieu. *Wines:* Pinot blanc, Pinot gris, Pinot noir. *Cases:* 15,000. The 110-acre Black Family Vineyard is carefully groomed and tended, and utilizes controlled yields for higher-quality grapes. The tasting room, fashioned out of the historic farmhouse, sets the mood for informative and discerning tasting. Guests are invited to detect the subtle difference between Pinots grown in Jory and Willakenzie soils as well as from biodynamic vineyards. The four graces are the Blacks' grown daughters.

Dobbes Family Estate (240 SE Fifth Street; 503-538-1141 or 800-566-8143). *Tasting room:* Daily 11–6. *Fee:* Complimentary ($10 reserves). *Owner/Winemaker:* Joe Dobbes Jr. *Wines:* Pinot gris, Pinot noir, Syrah, Viognier. *Cases:* 5,000. Joe Dobbes Jr. just might be the most prolific winemaker in Oregon. Don't let those 5,000 cases fool you—that's just for the Family Estate label. In all, Dobbes produces well beyond 60,000 cases for a stable of 11 wineries that love having his name attached. Joe makes both high-end and value wines—his top wines are balanced and sensual; the Joe brand speaks to the working folk's budget. The compact tasting room is very feng shui with a Pacific Northwest tint, and staffed by pros.

Ponzi Tasting Bar (100 SW Seventh Street; 503-554-1500). *Tasting room:* Daily 11–5. *Fee:* $2–12. At this combo tasting room and wine bar, you may sample Ponzi's line and/or other select Oregon wines by glass, flight, or bottle. A light menu is offered in this central Dundee location. Ponzi's winery is in Beaverton (see Portland wineries).

Argyle Winery (691 Highway 99W; 503-538-8520 x228 or 888-427-4953). *Tasting room:* Daily 11–5. *Fee:* 10. *Owners:* Brian Croser & Rollin Soles. *Winemaker:* Rollin Soles. *Wines:* Chardonnay, Pinot noir, Riesling, sparkling, dessert. *Cases:* 55,000. Argyle, in an old Victorian, is probably the most visited tasting room in Dundee. But that isn't what sets it apart. The winery's other claim to fame is meticulously crafted sparkling wines of Chardonnay and Pinot noir, produced by legendary winemaker Rollin Soles. Argyle also boasts two of the better labels: Nuthouse and Spirithouse, the former because the production room once stored hazelnuts and the latter for a friendly ghost that haunts the winery, at Dundee's former city hall.

Domaine Trouvère (115 SW Seventh Street; 503-487-6370). *Tasting room:* Daily 11–5. *Fee:* $10. *Owners:* Don & Wendy Lange. *Winemaker:* Don & Jesse Lange. *Wines:* Chardonnay, Pinot noir, Syrah, Tempranillo, Viognier. *Cases:* 2,500. The tasting room for Domaine Trouvère is above Red Hills Market, where the winery holds events for up to 40. This is a second label for Lange Winery, which wanted to reflect more variety with grapes sourced from other Oregon regions.

Zerba Cellars Tasting Room (810 N Highway 99W; 503-537-9463). *Tasting room:* Daily 11–5. *Fee:* $5. *Wine Press Northwest* named Zerba Winery of the Year in 2011. Find out why at the Milton-Freewater winery's zany second location.

Daedalus Cellars Company (990 North Highway 99W; 503-538-4400). *Tasting room:* Wed.–Sun. 11–5, and by appt. *Fee:* $5. *Owner/Winemaker:* Pam Walden. *Wines:*

Chardonnay, Grüner veltliner, Pinot gris, Pinot noir, Riesling, red and white blends. *Cases:* 4,000. Aron Hess and Pam Walden started the vineyard and winery under the name Daedalus, but have since gone separate ways. Pam is in the process of changing the name to "Willful Wine Company." Although she uses grapes from outside the AVA, her focus is on Dundee Hills Pinot and Grüner veltliner, a newcomer to most of the region. Her second label, Jezebel, is for a value Pinot and an eccentric white blend of varietals that play well together.

🍴 **Antica Terra Wines** (979 Southwest Alder Street; 503-244-1748). *Tasting room:* Holiday weekends, and by appt. *Fee:* $65–100 per person. *Owners:* Maggie Harrison, Scott Adelson, John Mavredakis & Michael Kramer. *Winemaker:* Maggie Harrison. *Wines:* Chardonnay, Pinot noir, rosé, red blend. *Cases:* 3,000. Few born-again winemakers have a tale as compelling as Maggie Harrison, whose epiphany came during a bout with malaria in Africa. After 10 years in Southern California, in 2005 she joined three friends who had long dreamed of owning a vineyard. The result is Antica Terra. The Pinot grapes come from older vines in an 11-acre vineyard near Amity.

Hawkins Cellars (1226 Highway 99W; 503-201-8302). *Tasting room:* Fri. & Sat. 12–5, Sun. 1–5, Feb.–Sept.; Sat. & Sun., Oct.–Dec. *Fee:* $10. *Owner/Winemaker:* Thane Hawkins. *Wines:* Cabernet sauvignon, Pinot gris, Pinot noir, Sangiovese, Syrah, Viognier, red blend. *Cases:* 600. Living the dream, the young, active, and creative Thane Hawkins, an animator who once worked for DreamWorks, makes small-lot wine from Oregon vineyards. He was a cellar rat for a few well-known wineries when he got his chance to make his own batch at Methven. On deck: an estate vineyard in the Columbia Gorge and tasting room in Hood River.

Hyland Estates (20980 NE Niederberger Road; 503-554-4200). *Tasting room:* Daily 11–5. *Fee:* $10. *Owners:* Laurent & Danielle Andrus Montalieu, and John Niemeyer. *Winemaker:* Laurent Montalieu. *Wines:* Gewürztraminer, Pinot noir, Riesling. *Cases:* 500. Laurent Montalieu has his fingers all over the Oregon wine industry. Now, after purchasing the venerable 100-acre Hyland Vineyard in 2007, the prolific winemaker and his partners have opened a tasting room to showcase wines from their oldest vines (planted in 1971). Their first releases were in 2011, and the dream continues: 55 more planted acres of Pinot. Look for seasonal "free Friday tastings."

🥖 🐾 **Thistle Wines** (10555 NE Red Hills Road; 503-200-4509). *Tasting room:* Sat. & Sun. 11–4, May–Sept. *Owners:* Jon & Laura Jennison. *Winemaker:* Jon Jennison. *Wines:* Chardonnay, Pinot blanc, Pinot gris, Pinot noir. *Cases:* 600. With the opening of a tasting room amid 27 acres of vineyards in 2012, Jon, a former banker, and Laura, a CPA, have been able to expand. The Jennisons are the epitome of a small winemaker, doing the bulk of the work themselves and selling a large portion of their crop to other wineries, save select pickings for their own bottlings.

▲ 🥖 🐾 **Crumbled Rock Winery** (9485 NE Worden Hill Road; 503-537-9682). *Tasting room:* Sat. & Sun. 11–5, Apr.–Nov., and by appt. *Fee:* $5. *Owners:* Gerard Koschal & Julia Staigers. *Winemaker:* Gerard Koschal. *Wines:* Pinot noir, Riesling. *Cases:* 500–1,000. First, the name: Gerard Koschal has a paying job as a geologist and "Crumbled Rock" references the soils in Juliard Vineyard. For 20 years his grapes served Dundee-area winemakers, before Koschal began keeping them for his own bottles. The tasting room doesn't look like much from the road, but once the vineyard unfolds with the Cascades on the horizon, you'll be glad you took the drive.

▲ 🥖 🐾 ❖ **Winderlea Vineyard & Winery** (8905 NE Worden Hill Road; 503-554-5900). *Tasting room:* Daily 11–4, May–Nov.; Thurs.–Mon., Dec.–Apr. *Fee:* $15

Cycling Wine Country—Riding the Red Hills

Description: This lovely loop showcases some of the more renowned wineries of the Dundee Hills. Starting at 200 feet above sea level at Argyle Winery in downtown Dundee, the route heads west to a maximum elevation of 873 feet in the hills west of town. You'll quickly pass through vineyards and orchards, then wind through some forest before reemerging into more farmland north of town. Because it's so short, you'll have plenty of time for visiting wineries—but pace yourself.

Wineries: Argyle Winery, Cameron Winery, Crumbled Rock Winery, Winderlea Vineyard & Winery, Maresh Red Barn, Bella Vida Vineyard, Erath Winery, Lange Estate Winery, Torii Mor, Four Graces Winery, Duck Pond Cellars, Dobbes Family Estate

Miles: 12

Elevation gain: 1,106

Start/Finish: Argyle Winery, Dundee

- Start by heading south on OR 99W, then west on County Road 12/Worden Hill Road. Winery stops: Cameron Winery, Crumbled Rock Winery, Winderlea Vineyard & Winery, Maresh Red Barn, Bella Vida Vineyard, and Erath Winery.
- Proceed east on Fairview Road, then north on Sylvan View Drive and east on Buena Vista Drive. Winery stop: Lange Estate Winery.
- Return west on Buena Vista Drive and south on Sylvan View Drive before continuing straight on Fairview Drive. Winery stop: Torii Mor Winery.
- Turn north on Red Hills Drive and east on Hidden Springs Road, then south on Fox Farms Road. Winery stop: Four Graces Winery.
- Turn north on OR 99W. Winery stop: Duck Pond Cellars.
- Return south on OR 99W and head east on 5th Street. Winery stop: Dobbes Family Estate,
- Return west on 5th Street and go south on OR 99W. Winery stop: Argyle Winery.

(donated to ¡Salud!). *Owners:* Bill Sweat & Donna Morris. *Winemaker:* Robert Brittan. *Wines:* Chardonnay, Pinot noir. *Cases:* 2,800. Bill and Donna, generous and philanthropic folks, were serious oenophiles from the East Coast who formed a crush on Pinot. Into second careers, they found the right winemaker in Brittan, who makes elegant and sensual food-friendly wines while practicing sustainable agriculture. Winderlea, whose name is a loose translation of German phrase "wind in the meadow," classifies itself as a luxury boutique winery. It uses solar and passive-solar energy, and is working toward biodynamic certification. The tasting room has a positive energy unto itself.

▲ ✐ 🐾 **Barrel Fence Cellars** (8880 Worden Hill Road; 503-538-7177). *Tasting room:* Fri.–Sun. 11–6, Apr.–Nov. *Fee:* $8. *Owners/Winemakers:* Herbert & Eleanor Sims. *Wines:* Pinot gris, Pinot noir, Sauvignon blanc. *Cases:* 100. Get a taste of the Willamette Valley and New Zealand at one of the Dundee Hills' newest wineries. The Sims family owns small vineyards in opposite hemispheres, giving visitors the opportunity to compare Pinot notes from both while sipping from the deck.

A Japanese theme flows through Torii Mor's tasting room and grounds. Courtesy Torii Mor Winery

▲ ❖ **Maresh Red Barn** (9325 NE Worden Hill Road; 503-537-1098). *Tasting room:* Wed.–Sun. 11–5, Mar.–Nov. *Fee:* $5. *Owner/Winemaker:* Jim Maresh. *Wines:* Chardonnay, Pinot gris, Pinot noir, Riesling, Sauvignon blanc. *Cases:* 500. A stroll through the family vineyard leads to the tasting room in an iconic red barn. Jim's daughter, Martha, likes to tell of Dick Erath's coming up the driveway and telling them they had the best vineyard location for Pinot noir, bar none. So, in 1969 they began planting vines. Maresh's grapes are mostly sold to several nearby wineries, save their pick for estate wines. On the grounds is a Vineyard Retreat, which can be rented by the day for groups.

▲ 🖋 🐾 **Torii Mor** (18325 NE Fairview Drive; 503-538-2279). *Tasting room:* Daily 11–5. *Fee:* $5–10. *Owners:* Donald & Margie Olson. *Winemaker:* Jacques Tardy. *Wines:* Chardonnay, Pinot blanc, Pinot gris, Pinot noir, Viognier, port-style. *Cases:* 15,000. Torii Mor's Japanese-Scandinavian name loosely translates to "gates to the earth," and Don and Margie believe that Pinot noir more than any other grape is just that. Under Jacques Tardy, a native fifth-generation Burgundian winemaker, Torii Mor's wines are heavily earthy and exquisitely crafted. A serene setting with stunning Japanese gardens and pathways lends itself to pleasant tasting.

▲ 🖋 🐾 **Lange Estate Winery & Vineyards** (18380 NE Buena Vista Drive; 503-538-6476). *Tasting room:* Daily 11–5. *Fee:* $10. *Owners:* Don & Wendy Lange. *Winemaker:* Don Lange & Jesse Lange. *Wines:* Chardonnay, Pinot gris, Pinot noir, Tempranillo. *Cases:* 19,000. The Langes have been on the scene since 1987, when they produced a barrel-fermented Pinot gris that Don labeled a "benchmark bottling." Lange started by concentrating on gris, Chardonnay, and vineyard-designate Pinots, and has stayed close to his origins. His reward: *Wine & Spirits* Winery of the Year in 2012. Don and Jesse are avid fly fishermen, which explains the prominent tribute to dry flies on most of their labels.

Alexana Winery (12001 NE Worden Hill Road; 503-537-3100). *Tasting room:* Daily 11–5. *Fee:* $20. *Owner:* Madaiah Revana. *Winemaker:* Lynn Penner-Ash & Bryan Weil. *Wines:* Chardonnay, Pinot gris, Pinot noir, Riesling. *Cases:* 6,500. Alexana has a few distinguishing traits: It's the only winery and vineyard on the west side of the Dundee Hills. Adding more uniqueness is complex soil comprising 18 types on 57 acres planted in 10 Pinot clones on four varying rootstock—all designed to work together. After producing first-rate Cabs in Napa Valley, Madaiah Revana turned to the Willamette Valley. He wasted little time making his presence known.

Bella Vida Vineyard (9380 NE Worden Hill Road; 503-538-9821). *Tasting room:* Fri.–Mon. 11–5. *Fee:* $10. *Owners:* Steven & Allison Whiteside. *Winemaker:* Jacques Tardy, Jay Somers, Brian O'Donnell, Patrick Reuter. *Wines:* Pinot noir, white blend. *Cases:* 550. Call it the Iron Chef of Winemaking. The secret ingredient is fruit from the same Red Hills vineyard: one vineyard, one vintage, multiple winemakers. Since 2002, the Whitesides have taken a scientific approach toward producing distinct Pinots. Jacques Tardy (Torii Mor) does the Burgundian thing with highly structured wines meant for laying down. Jay Somers (J. Christopher) is known for minimal intervention. Brian O'Donnell's style is New World–ish, with a balanced Pinot drinkable from the get-go. The creative and innovative Patrick Reuter (Dominio IV) lets Mother Nature take the lead. Enjoy your own taste-off on the abundant deck.

Erath Winery (9409 NE Worden Hill Road; 800-539-9463). *Tasting room:* Daily 11–5. *Fee:* $10–20. *Owner:* Ste. Michelle Wine Estates. *Winemaker:* Gary Horner. *Wines:* Dolcetto, Gewürztraminer, Pinot blanc, Pinot gris, Pinot noir, Riesling, dessert. *Cases:* 160,000. The state's largest Pinot noir producer etched its second significant marker in history by becoming the first to sell to a corporation. In 2006, publicly traded Ste. Michelle Wine Estates purchased Erath, started in 1967 by Cal Knudsen and Dick Erath, expatriates from UC–Davis. Some say it's just another step, along with palatial wineries and stiff tasting fees, in the Napa-tization of Oregon. But state vintners were gratified the winery sold to a Northwest company, and Dick Erath said he "carefully scrutinized would-be purchasers." The tasting room and comfortable venue are a must-stop for a taste of Oregon wine history.

DAYTON AREA

Archery Summit (18599 NE Archery Summit Road; 503-864-4300). *Tasting room:* Daily 10–4. *Fee:* $15. *Owner:* Crimson Wine Group. *Winemaker:* Anna Matzinger. *Wines:* Pinot noir. *Cases:* 11,000. Among revered wineries in the Red Hills, Archery Summit sits in rarefied air. Some of the mystique is history; it was founded by innovative Gary Andrus in 1993. Some of it is its cave system—so elaborate, it needed a mining permit to excavate the basalt hillside—where more than 600 oak barrels rest in natural temperatures requiring no energy use. Talented Anna Matzinger uses her intuition and science to produce sought-after Pinots. Archery's tasting room is small; groups should call ahead. Two-hour tours are offered daily by appointment.

Archery Summit offers tours through its renowned caves. Courtesy Archery Summit

De Ponte Cellars (17545 NE Archery Summit Road; 503-864-3698). *Tasting room:* Daily 11–5. *Fee:* $10. *Owners:* Fred & Shirley Baldwin. *Winemaker:* Isabelle Dutartre. *Wines:* Pinot noir. *Cases:* 3,000. De Ponte is a family-run 20-acre estate vineyard, winery, and tasting room surrounded by old-growth vines. Pull up a chair and feel like one of the family in the smart-looking tasting room, and sample Isabelle Dutartre's handiwork. There's a subtle style that emits an aura of premium quality. Isabelle might still be the only Oregon winemaker born in Burgundy. Her own brand, 1789 (a nod to the French Revolution), can be purchased in the tasting room.

Domaine Drouhin of Oregon (6750 NE Breyman Orchards Road; 503-864-2700). *Tasting room:* Daily 11–4, June–Oct. *Fee:* $10. *Owner:* Domaine Drouhin. *Winemaker:* Véronique Drouhin. *Wines:* Chardonnay, Pinot noir. *Cases:* 18,000. Maison Joseph Drouhin has been a prominent producer in Beaunne, France, since the late 1880s. It was a third-generation Drouhin, Robert, who looked at David Lett's accomplishments and determined that Oregon, not California, was the place to grow the Prince of Burgundy. His daughter, Véronique, has been winemaker since the 1988 start. The Laurène Pinot, named after Véronique's eldest daughter, is the flagship wine that's earned the most acclaim. Private tours at 10 AM and 1 PM are offered Wed.–Sun. by reservation and limited to 10 people.

Domaine Serene (6555 NE Hilltop Lane; 503-864-4600). *Tasting room:* Wed.–Mon. 11–4. *Fee:* $15. *Owners:* Ken & Grace Evenstad. *Winemaker:* Erik Kramer. *Wines:* Chardonnay, Pinot noir, Syrah. *Cases:* 20,000. The California-style complex boasts a clay tile roof over a terra-cotta stucco exterior that matches the style of its Pinot: bold, evocative, and not shy on oak. The tasting room is on the formal side, and private tasting tours can be arranged. On Serene's domaine grow Chardonnay and Pinot noir, the grape that lured the Evenstads to Oregon more than 20 years ago. If you seek the unusual, try the elegant variation on rosé—a white Pinot noir that's aged in oak with little skin contact during fermentation ($85/bottle).

Vista Hills Vineyard (6475 Hilltop Lane; 503-864-3200). *Tasting room:* Daily 12–5. *Fee:* $10. *Owners:* John & Nancy McClintock. *Winemaker:* Dave Petterson and guest winemakers. *Wines:* Pinot gris, Pinot noir. *Cases:* 2,500–3,000. On the west-facing deck overlooking the valley and Coast Range, at the appropriately named Vista Hills, you'll feel as if you're in a tree house surrounded by towering Douglas fir and white oaks. The cedar-paneled, houselike structure with floor-to-ceiling windows presents stunning views above the production facility. Instead of one winemaker, Vista Hills uses seven of the area's biggest names. Oregon's wet winters can get tiresome, so the McClintocks escape to Kona, Hawaii. Their coffee, chocolate, and bars can be purchased in the tasting room or online.

Winter's Hill Vineyard (6451 Hilltop Lane; 503-864-4538). *Tasting room:* Daily 11–5, May–Nov.; Fri.–Mon., Dec–Apr. *Fee:* $10. *Owners:* Peter & Emily Gladhart, Russell & Delphine Gladhart. *Winemaker:* Delphine Gladhart. *Wines:* Pinot blanc, Pinot gris, Pinot noir, rosé, white blend, dessert. *Cases:* 3,000. Armed with a firm belief in their vineyard and a huge work ethic, Peter and Emily started their winery in 1990. Named for Emily's parents, who tended cherry and prune orchards in the area, Winter's Hill has a significant sense of family, reflected by the addition of daughter and son-in-law to the business. Tastings are in the winery, amid the barrels and equipment, giving you a firsthand look at wine-in-the-making. The 150 acres (35 in grapes) has a birding trail and is a favored stop for horseback tours.

White Rose Estate (6250 Hilltop Lane; 503-864-2328). *Tasting room:* Daily 11–5. *Fee:* $10. *Owner:* Greg Sanders. *Winemaker:* Jesus Guillen Jr. *Wines:* Pinot noir. *Cases:* 3,500. A different approach described as "neo-classical adaptation of traditional winemaking standards" marks White Rose Pinot. Words struggle to do the setting justice. The state-of-the art winery is surrounded by terraces of lavender—not a rose in sight, white or otherwise—that provide a gentle, layered skirting and incredible views. The understated, classy tasting room was built with old-growth timber salvaged from a forest fire.

Red Ridge Farms/Durant Vineyards (5510 NE Breyman Orchard Road; 503-864-2000). *Tasting room:* Tues.–Sun. 10–5. *Fee:* $5. *Owners:* Ken & Penny Durant. *Winemakers:* Paul Durant and guest winemakers. *Wines:* Chardonnay, Pinot gris, Pinot noir. *Cases:* 400. This is a destination for the senses: exotic and native plants, herbs, trees, gardening supplies, art and trinkets, olive oil from 15 acres of Spanish olive trees, and 60 acres of grapes planted more than 30 years ago. The vineyards supply grapes for small-lot wines made by high-profile winemakers. On-site is an alluring guest suite for two, with a front deck sporting Adirondack chairs suited for sitting and sipping in the vista. Enjoy complimentary estate olive-oil tasting, too.

Sokol Blosser Winery (5000 Sokol Blosser Lane; 503-864-2282 or 800-582-6668). *Tasting room:* Daily 10–4. *Fee:* $5–15. *Owners:* Sokol Blosser family. *Winemaker:* Russ Rosner. *Wines:* Müller-Thurgau, Muscat, Pinot gris, Pinot noir, rosé, red and white blends, dessert. *Cases:* 85,000. On any list of big wine names, Sokol Blosser is at the top, and Susan continues to be a leader in the conservation arena. Sokol Blosser's 900-barrel cellar, built partially underground with wildflowers on the roof, was the first winery building in the United States to be LEED-certified. The vineyard is certified organic, and 50 percent biodiesel fuels their tractors. Susan is particularly tuned to the rhythms of the planet; she gives speeches about climate change impacts on the industry, and her goal is to be carbon-neutral. While Sokol Blosser takes stewardship seriously, it has a playful side, with concerts and festivities.

Holiday cheer fills the renovated tasting room at Sokol Blosser. Courtesy Sokol Blosser Winery

Stoller Family Estate (16161 NE McDougall Road; 503-864-3404). *Tasting room:* Daily 11–5. *Fee:* $15. *Owner:* Bill Stoller. *Winemaker:* Melissa Burr. *Wines:* Chardonnay, Pinot noir, Riesling, Syrah, Tempranillo, rosé. *Cases:* 12,000. Stoller Vineyards, once a turkey farm, is 176 acres of mostly Pinot noir set amid 373 rolling, pastoral acres, with a reclaimed tasting room. Bill and the late Cathy Stoller have always been sustainable-minded; their tasting room was built with Biscuit Fire salvaged timber and other reused materials. Natural lighting comes from a wall of windows, and the little energy required comes from solar panels. Stoller was the first winery in the country to be LEED Gold–certified. The estate also has three extraordinary rentals: a cottage, estate house, and wine farmhouse.

Seufert Winery (415 Ferry Street; 503-864-2946). *Tasting room:* Wed.–Mon. 11–5. *Fee:* $5. *Owner/Winemaker:* Jim Seufert. *Wines:* Dolcetto, Pinot noir, Syrah, white blend, dessert. *Cases:* 2,000. This is the place to test your Pinot palate. Jim Seufert makes single-vineyard Pinots from several sub-AVAs in the Willamette Valley, under varying conditions. The facility is an industrial warehouse across from Dayton's city hall where, Seufert says, "If you show up late, you won't get kicked out." Seufert, a fourth-generation Oregonian, discovered his wine passion while traveling the world, and decided his native state was an idyllic place to fulfill his destiny.

Lodging

in Dundee/Dayton

DUNDEE

❖ ♿ 🐾 **Black Walnut Inn & Vineyard** (9600 NE Worden Hill Road; 503-429-4114 or 866-429-4114). Setting the standard for luxurious lodging, the Black Walnut Inn lives up to its reputation. With nine stupendous suites, all with balcony and soaking tub accompanied by plush robes, the Tuscan-style villa has an authentically peaceful charm. Yet it remains true to its Oregon roots. After painstakingly caring for the old and forgotten walnut trees, owners Karen and Neal Utz could think of no better tribute than naming their inn after them. With a setting literally on top of 42 acres, even the worldliest of travelers will find the location spectacular. The rotating seasonal breakfast menu starts your day in a good way. The inn offers out-of-the-ordinary package deals as well. $$$$

❖ **Dundee Manor B&B** (8380 NE Worden Hill Road; 503-554-1945). Hosts Brad Cunningham and David Godfrey, two sophisticated gentlemen, share their 1908 four-square Edwardian estate and a "passion for excellence." Wine is served upon arrival and the team leaves no detail unattended. Their experienced palates and lust for fine food show on every designer breakfast plate, accompanied by candlelight and soft music. The expansive grounds are a manicured marvel, and beyond the iron-gated entrance, rocking chairs beckon from the front porch. Wine getaway packages are a regular menu item. Children age 12 and older are welcomed. $$$–$$$$

Two gentlemen on the hill offer elegant B&B accommodations at Dundee Manor.

Courtesy Dundee Manor

🍷 ❖ **Eagle Crest Wine Country Retreat** (10850 NE Eagle Crest Lane; 503-538-6072; VRBO Listing: #384832). Chris and Liz Lesieutre rent a three-bedroom, three-bath home in a convenient yet secluded hilltop location. The upstairs loft provides plenty of room for families, girls' weekends, or close friends who want an up close and personal wine country retreat. The large patio extends the living/entertaining space and hiking trails lead to at least eight wineries in the "neighborhood." Eagle Crest is part of the Home Exchange program. $$$$

🍴 🍸 ♿ 🐾 **The Inn at Red Hills** (1410 North Highway 99W; 503-538-7666). Following the European travel tradition of finding a comfortable bed, food, and gathering spot in one location, the boutique inn offers 20 units above a restaurant and wine bar. Careful planning went into retrofitting an old bank building, utilizing local labor, landscapers, supply companies, artists and food purveyors. Did we mention the individually designed rooms and serene surrounding spaces? Simply divine. Paulee restaurant and wine bar forms the base of the complex. $$$–$$$$

🍷 **Vineyard Ridge** (4000 Fairview Drive; 503-476-2211). Vineyard Ridge is one of three properties operated by Distinctive Destinations. The large, comfortable home with a fireplace sits high above town and offers a panoramic view of Pinot kingdom from the deck. If you want to be close to the Dundee action but far enough away for serenity, this is the place. $$$$

DAYTON

Martha's Cottage (101 Fifth Street; 971-241-8044). History is preserved in the form of a small, Gothic Revival–style Victorian cottage. The Morse house, built by blacksmith Benjamin Morse in 1881, has always been connected to agriculture; grapes were grown in the area pre-Prohibition. Current owner Martha Goodrich is proud to keep the history alive. Her guest house sleeps up to six and she has a serious no-smoking policy. $$$$

❖ **Wine Country Farm B&B** (6855 Breyman Orchards Road; 800-261-3446 or 503-864-3446). Joan Davenport's Wine Country Farm is a charmer squeezed between two Domaines: Drouhin and Serene. The 1910 main house has nine suites, all with panoramic views. A specialty amenity: vineyard tours on horseback. The estate vineyard provides grapes for Joan's Armonea wines, available for sampling in a casual on-site tasting room open daily 11–5. Wine Country Farm is listed in *1,000 Places to See Before You Die.* Children age 12 and older are welcomed. $$$–$$$$

Dining
in Dundee/Dayton

There's little need to mention farm-to-fork ingredients and regional cuisine in the dining options below, as that is the norm in vegetation-rich Dundee. You can't go wrong with any of them. In fact, they should exceed your expectations for dining off OR 99W.

DUNDEE

Dundee Bistro (100A SW Seventh Street; 503-554-1650). Northwest cuisine melds with Italian at this timeless and popular bistro. The menu is printed daily, and dependent on available fresh and local ingredients. Often-ordered dishes include house-made pappardelle pasta, hand-tossed pizzas, bistro burger, and white truffle fries . . . and Pinot noir berry cobbler. The wine list is heavy on regional Pinot, and selections from the 'hood. A semicovered patio area, albeit surrounded by parking, provides extra ambience. L/D $$

Paulee (1410 North Highway 99W, Suite 102; 503-538-7970). What do you create when you blend the experience of a master sommelier and an ultra-talented chef? An upscale yet casual bakery/restaurant/wine & cocktail bar befitting the valley's wine center. Cork puller Brandon Tebbe and Chef Daniel Mondok have combined synergistic energy in their redo of Farm to Fork. Naming their restaurant for the Burgundian fall festival, Brandon and Daniel, along with Sean Temple, hope to emulate with creative regional cuisine, handcrafted local brews, and wines with a preservation system that allows many glass pours. Paulee opens early (except Tuesday) for coffee and pastries. B/L (Fri.–Sun.) D (Wed.–Mon.) $$$$

Red Hills Provincial Dining (276 Highway 99W; 503-538-8224). Operated since 1992 by owner/chef team Richard and Nancy Gehrts, Red Hills has long been a favorite of the wine-and-dine crowd. Housed in a 1920s bungalow, it sits off the highway enough to miss it. Slow food is taken seriously here; don't go if you have later plans. We suggest you sit back, relax, and savor seasonal multigenerational family recipes made from scratch with a European touch. Save space for the handmade desserts, sorbets, and tortes. Wines are both local and international. D (Tue.–Sun.) $$$$

Tina's Restaurant (760 Highway 99W; 503-538-8880). For two decades, this stylish bistro is where the valley's best wines have been found, possibly accompanied by the vintners who made them. The two snug and compact rooms separated by a fireplace seat 50. Menu ingredients are farm fresh and usually organic, and now include gluten and lactose free. The self-taught chef team of Tina and David Bergen believes cuisine happens fast when working with the freshest foods. They let the food speak for itself—and speak it does! The ever-changing wine list is mostly regional. L (Tue.–Fri.) D $$$$

DAYTON

Joel Palmer House (600 Ferry Street; 503-864-2995). If you can only budget for one extravagant meal, make it Joel Palmer House. Jack and Heidi Czarnecki bought the historic two-story home with a vision for a restaurant unlike any other. The Czarneckis have always relied upon local offerings—with an international assist—but their signature ingredient is mushrooms: chanterelles, morels, porcini . . . earthy morsels in most dishes. The wild-mushroom soup is a 70-year-old family recipe. Even dessert features fungi: candy-cap mushroom crème brûlée. While Jack continues to hunt 'shrooms, son Chris is at the helm of what he describes a "freestyle" menu with inspiration ranging from Mexico to Poland. Service and ambience are friendly, impeccable, and irresistible. Particular attention is given to pairing Oregon wines. D Tue.–Sat. $$$

Oregon chanterelles pair well with earthy Pinot noir. Courtesy Joel Palmer House

To Do

in the Dundee/Dayton Area

Attractions

The Dundee Farmers' Market (Highway 99W and Seventh Street, 503-522-3206) takes place every Sunday from June to October at the Dundee Bistro/Ponzi Wine Bar parking lot. Vegetables, fruits, organic food, local specialties, and crafts are for sale.

Recreation

Combine walking and sipping with Mark DeLong's **Dundee Hills Walking Wine Tour** (503-789-7629), a 6-mile, five-winery jaunt that allows you absorb vineyards in full sensory mode; lunch is included in the $85 fee. Pick up the pace a little with the **Fueled by Wine Half Marathon** in the Dundee Hills every July. It's a challenging course that passes some well-known wineries, and the reward at the finish is a vino sampling.

More Information

Dundee Hills Winegrowers Association, 503-864-4300, www.dundeehills.org

Willamette Valley Wineries Association, 503-646-2985, www.willamettewines.com

Chehalem Mountains Winegrowers Association, www.chehalemmountains.org

Willamette Valley Central

HEAD FOR THE HILLS

BEFORE THE WILLAMETTE RIVER punches through the hills southeast of Portland and plunges over the falls at Oregon City, it serpentines through a broad valley between the Coast and Cascade Ranges, from Eugene north some 100 miles to Wilsonville. About halfway, south of Salem, the river is forced to detour to the west around another set of undulating hills.

If the countryside around Dundee and Carlton are Oregon Wine Country's A-team, then surely the Eola Hills and their neighbors between the capital city and the charming college town of McMinnville are A-1 and A-2. The heart of this region is Salem, which boasts the oldest college west of the Mississippi River in Willamette University. The soul is McMinnville, a classy place where a fraternity of winery workers gathers many evenings to sip, toast, and share tales from the vineyard. In between, along country roads, are the Petticoat Junction–esque agricultural villages of Amity, Dayton, and St. Paul.

The Willamette glides through this country almost unnoticed even though 80 percent of the state's population lives within 20 miles of its banks. This phenomenon arose more out of survival than neglect. Until the river was controlled by dams and largely straightened by engineers, it braided like so many corkscrews and frequently flooded widely, sometimes leaving steamboat-port towns permanently high and dry.

GETTING HERE AND AROUND

Although Salem is Oregon's third-largest city behind Portland and Eugene, air service is on and off. The capital city hasn't had commercial service since 2008, when Delta Airlines bailed out, following Horizon Air's departure. The **Hut Shuttle** serves Salem (503-364-4444) and Corvallis/Albany (541-926-2525) with bus service every two hours destined for Portland's airport. In addition, **Amtrak** (800-872-7245) has one Salem stop daily in each direction on the Coast Starlight between Los Angeles and Seattle.

LEFT: There's more than one way to tour Oregon Wine Country. Courtesy Eola Hills Wine Cellars

To get the full flavor of your central Willamette Valley wine tour, start in McMinnville. From the Portland airport, the best route is I-205 south to the junction of I-5. The fastest way to McMinnville from there is to head north on I-5 three miles to Exit 289, then go west through Sherwood to OR 99W. That route will take you through Newberg and Dundee to McMinnville. However, to avoid OR 99W's traffic and follow a more scenic route, go south on I-5 to Exit 283. Wilsonville Road follows the Willamette past Champoeg State Park to Newberg and a meeting with OR 99W.

McMinnville has one of Oregon's most vibrant downtowns. Courtesy McMenamins

MCMINNVILLE AREA (McMinnville AVA)

Once upon a time, McMinnville was an afterthought between Portland and Salem. Then wine happened. Give McMinnville credit: It knew what to do with a phenomenon occurring in its backyard. Few downtowns capture the essence of the new and old Oregon like this vibrant community of 32,000.

Although McMinnville has achieved a level of sophistication, it has retained some of its quirks. Most notable are the annual Turkey Rama and UFO Festival. Turkey Rama began in 1938, when turkey farms were driving the area's economic engine. Live domestic turkeys raced down Main Street, with the mayor presiding. Today, in a more sophisticated McMinnville, turkey races have given way to "Who's on Third"—a more gentrified festival on Third Street, showcasing local wineries, art, and music.

The UFO Festival's genesis is traced to 1950, when the local paper published a photo of a flying saucer hovering over an area farm. More than a half-century later, the photo's authenticity has been neither verified nor debunked, and now McMinnville hosts the country's largest gathering of UFO junkies this side of Roswell, New Mexico.

Wineries
in the McMinnville Area

McMinnville has become Oregon's wine hub, with spokes pointing north to Dundee, west to Yamhill-Carlton, and south to the Eola Hills. It's the birthplace of the world's first International Pinot Noir Celebration, first staged in 1987.

Although it isn't readily apparent, the foothills stretching for 20 miles southwest of McMinnville—where there are more than a dozen wineries and about 750 acres of vineyards—are notably different from the Red Hills of Dundee, Amity Hills, and Eola Hills just a few miles away.

The rain shadow and 1,000-foot elevation make for a warmer, drier, and more frost-free climate. Good thing, because the marine sedimentary soils are shallower here than in nearby grape-growing regions. The predominant wines are the expected Pinot noir, Pinot gris, and Pinot blanc, but their profiles are distinctly different.

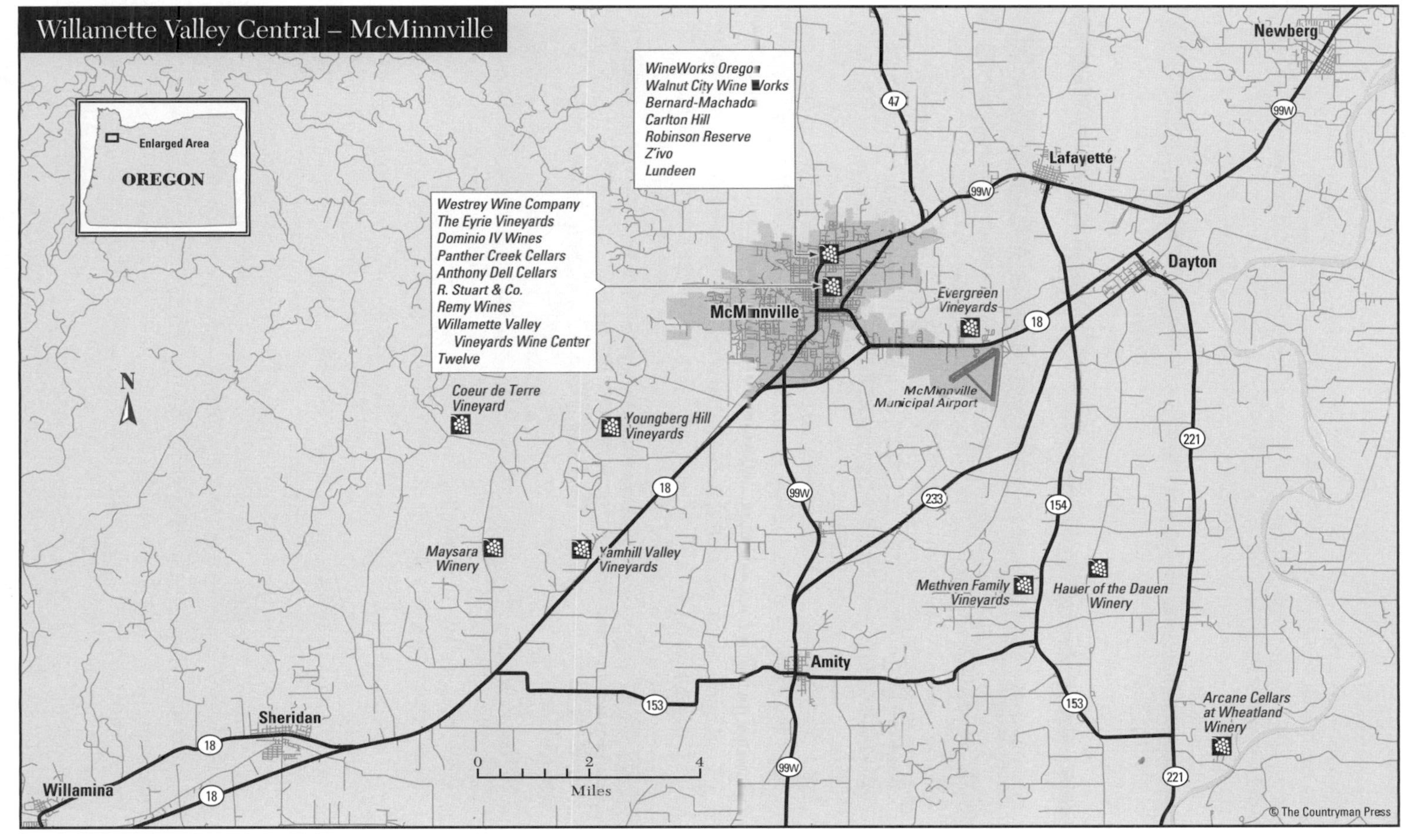
Willamette Valley Central – McMinnville
Enlarged Area
OREGON
N
WineWorks Oregon
Walnut City Wine Works
Bernard-Machado
Carlton Hill
Robinson Reserve
Z'ivo
Lundeen
Westrey Wine Company
The Eyrie Vineyards
Dominio IV Wines
Panther Creek Cellars
Anthony Dell Cellars
R. Stuart & Co.
Remy Wines
Willamette Valley Vineyards Wine Center
Twelve
Newberg
Lafayette
Dayton
McMinnville
Evergreen Vineyards
McMinnville Municipal Airport
Coeur de Terre Vineyard
Youngberg Hill Vineyards
Maysara Winery
Yamhill Valley Vineyards
Methven Family Vineyards
Hauer of the Dauen Winery
Amity
Arcane Cellars at Wheatland Winery
Sheridan
Willamina
47
99W
18
233
154
221
153
0
2
4
Miles
© The Countryman Press

Wineworks Oregon (Walnut City Wineworks) (475 NE 17th Street; 503-472-3215). *Tasting room:* Thurs.–Sun. 11–5. *Fee:* $5. *Owners:* John Gilpin & John Davidson. *Winemaker:* Michael Lundeen. *Wines:* Chardonnay, Pinot gris, Pinot noir, rosé, dessert. *Cases:* 5,000. As the name implies, there's some nutty history and yet another complicated amiable arrangement for folks who want to grow and make wine. It's a vineyard management company with long-term relationships, and it's a consortium for boutique producers. Founders John Davidson and John Gilpin formed a clubhouse of sorts for like-minded farmers and wine nerds. They formed a vertically integrated business three decades ago that includes managing orchards, vineyards, running greenhouses with rootstock, designing vineyards, and winemaking. They now oversee 200 acres of Pinot noir in the valley, including 80 of their own. Their winemaking area and tasting room, once the Willamette Valley Walnut Company, hosts the following wineries:

Bernard-Machado. *Owner/Winemaker:* John Davidson. *Wines:* Pinot noir. *Cases:* 500. Ahhh . . . Pinot noir for Burg-hounds. Davidson's private label is all about the grapes, the year, and his nearly 30 years of crafting experience. His label, named for his grandparents, is worth the $30–40 price tag.

Carlton Hill (503-852-7060). *Owners/Winemakers:* David & Dan Polite. *Wines:* Pinot noir. *Cases:* 400. Carlton Hill Vineyard (11511 NW Cummins Road) looks like a Grandma Moses painting and should be on your list of places to see before you leave Oregon. The Polites grow classic Yamhill-Carlton Pinot, with strong raspberry and earthy characteristics. Call for vineyard tours.

Lundeen Wines. *Owner/Winemaker:* Michael Lundeen. *Wines:* Pinot gris, Pinot noir, Riesling, Syrah, white blend. *Cases:* 500. Michael Lundeen was destined to become a journalist until he stumbled on a job at WillaKenzie during harvest. He was so enamored with the world of wine he nabbed a job at Domaine Serene, took viticulture courses at Chemeketa Community College under the legendary Barney Watson, and worked at wineries in Italy. *Genius Loci*, Latin for "spirit of place," is his trademark label. His white grapes come from his vineyard, Poverty Bend.

Robinson Reserve. *Winemaker:* Michael Lundeen. *Wines:* Chardonnay, Pinot noir. *Cases:* 900. The two wines produced are sourced from the picturesque Robinson Vineyard in the Willamette Valley's West Hills. Most of the production is Dijon-clone Pinot noir, with a smaller amount of Chardonnay.

Z'ivo. *Owners:* John & Katherine Zelko. *Winemaker:* John Zelko. *Wines:* Pinot noir, white blends. *Cases:* 1,500. Zelko vodka didn't want to share a name, so John took the high road and went for a multicultural patchwork for his moniker. Take "Ivo" (Johnny), add the *z*, and you get something like "life of Johnny" in Slovak. John's wines are as complicated as John's story. His Pinots are meant for cellaring and not to be rushed. Persnickety and meticulous, he once dumped 1,700 cases when a "brett bloom" appeared, because he refuses to deliver less than promised.

Westrey Wine Company (1065 NE Alpine Avenue; 503-434-6357). *Tasting room:* Thurs.–Sun. 12–5. *Fee:* $15. *Owners/Winemakers:* Amy Wesselman & David Autrey. *Wines:* Chardonnay, Pinot gris, Pinot noir. *Cases:* 4,000. "Westry" combines wife-and-husband surnames. It also suggests a team that shares the work and glory. Since 1993, Amy and David have taken a philosophical approach to making wine—no surprise given that both have philosophy degrees from Portland's progressive Reed College. Waxing philosophic, they say, helps them deal with the whims of Mother Nature.

They now own 49 acres of old vines, "Oracle," in the Dundee Hills. Their Pinot noir is one of the best for quality, consistency, and reasonable price.

The Eyrie Vineyards (935 NE 10th Avenue; 888-440-4970 or 503-472-6315). *Tasting room:* Wed.–Sun. 12–5. *Fee:* $15. *Owners:* Diana & Jason Lett. *Winemaker:* Jason Lett. *Wines:* Chardonnay, Muscat, Pinot blanc, Pinot gris, Pinot meunier, Pinot noir. *Cases:* 10,000. A trip to Oregon Wine Country isn't complete without a stop at Eyrie to "taste the history"—an apropos statement for the winery that started it all. In 1966, before it was considered a sane idea, California transplants David and Diana Lett planted Pinot and Chardonnay on their newly acquired Willamette Valley property. History took shape, the vineyard is now in the Dundee Hills AVA, and Eyrie provided affirmation that Oregon belongs on the worldwide wine map. Yet pretension is noticeably absent in the no-frills tasting room. David Lett died in 2008 but had left wine matters in the competent hands of son Jason, who worked by his dad's side since he was a tyke. As for the fitting name, an eyrie is a high, remote, and commanding place.

Remy Wines (905 NE Tenth Avenue; 503-560-2003). *Tasting room:* Fri.–Sun. 12–6. *Owner/Winemaker:* Remy Drabkin. *Fee:* Varies. *Wines:* Remy Label: Barbera, Dolcetto, Lagrein, Sangiovese, Syrah, rosé; Three Wives label: red and white blends. *Cases:* 1,400. Remy Drabkin is a one-woman dynamo. She's created two tiers for production: Her namesake wines are the premiums; the Three Wives blends are her value wines. Remy is Oregon's sole producer of Lagrein, a varietal from northern Italy near the Austrian border. It's developed a cult following. Remy's new tasting room in her winemaking facility—which also serves noshes—is named the baR (pronounced "R Bar"). It emulates Italian casualness, much like Remy herself.

Dominio IV Wines (845 NE Fifth Street; 503-474-8636). *Tasting room:* Fri. & Sat. 12–5, and by appt. *Fee:* $10. *Owners:* Patrick Reuter & Leigh Bartholomew. *Winemaker:* Patrick Reuter. *Wines:* Pinot noir, Syrah, Viognier, Tempranillo, blends. *Cases:* 4,000. Robert Louis Stevenson once said wine is poetry in a bottle—a fitting description for Patrick Reuter's wines. Reuter and his wife, Leigh Bartholomew, journeyed across the world and ultimately landed in tiny Mosier in the Columbia Gorge. Originally a friendly fixture—affectionately known as the "madman"—at the Carlton Winemakers Studio, Patrick's operations are now housed in the granary district. His terroir-driven wines are known for their age-ability.

Panther Creek Cellars (455 NE Irvine Street; 503-472-8080). *Tasting room:* Daily 12–5. *Fee:* $10. *Owner:* Chambers Communication. *Winemaker:* Michael Stevenson. *Wines:* Chardonnay, Pinot gris, Pinot noir. *Cases:* 7,500.. Three giant diesel generators at urban Panther Creek Cellars provided all of McMinnville's electricity in the late 1930s, revealing the brick building's age. Founded by Ken Wright, Panther Creek bought the facility from the city in 1989 and has retained much of its character. Winemaker Michael Stevenson started under Wright in 1992 and carries forth the tradition. The winery is certified biodynamic, organic, and recycles bottles,

Panther Creek Cellars is located in McMinnville's former power plant. Ron Kaplan

corks, and foil capsules. Chill out and sip wine on the large, underutilized, dog-friendly courtyard. At press time, the winery was in the process of being sold.

Twelve (581 NE Third Street; 503-435-1212). *Tasting room:* Thurs.–Sun. 12–6, and by appt. *Fee:* $8. *Owners:* John & Linda Lenyo. *Winemaker:* John Lenyo. *Wines:* Pinot noir, white blend. *Cases:* 900–1,200. Serious about their wine, but not too serious about themselves, "Twelve" is a reference to the irreverent movie *Spinal Tap*. Seriously, though, John makes wines that he and Linda like to drink from their sustainable vineyard: amped-up Pinots and a refreshing sipping white produced from a field blend. They opened a tasting room in 2010 and share space with Honest Chocolates. Tastings include a ganache treat infused with Twelve Pinot.

R. Stuart & Co. (528 NE Third Street; 503-472-4477). *Tasting room:* Wed.–Sat. 12–7, Sun. 12–5 (closed Sun. in winter). *Fee:* $10–12. *Owners:* Rob & Maria Stuart. *Winemaker:* Rob Stuart. *Wines:* R. Stuart Reserve label: Pinot noir, sparkling; Big Fire Label: Pinot gris, Pinot noir, rosé. *Cases:* 20,000. Approachable wines come with an approachable wine bar. In a familiar story for these parts, Rob Stuart took an old granary and converted it into a winery. He doesn't own any vineyard acreage, but buys select fruit from elsewhere and makes it downtown. The amiable wine bar ranges from quiet with few patrons to busy and raucous.

Willamette Valley Vineyards Wine Center (300 NE Third Street; 503-883-9012). *Tasting room:* Sun.–Fri. 10–5. *Fee:* $5–10. The Wine Center is a downtown satellite for Willamette Valley Vineyards, the prolific winery just south of Salem. A huge screen with an ongoing, visually stunning slide show of Oregon Wine Country provides the backdrop. Check out the all-cork floor.

Anthony Dell Cellars (250 NE Third Street; 503-910-8874). *Tasting room:* Wed.–Sun. 12–5. *Fee:* $5. *Owners/Winemakers:* Douglas Anthony Drawbond & Joy Dell Means. *Wines:* Baco noir, Pinot noir, Syrah, red blend. *Cases:* 500. "Wine will get you through times with no money better than money will get you through times with no wine"—words to live and work by for owners Douglas and Joy. The ambitious couple does everything by hand, from destemming grapes to bottling fermented juice. Their food-friendly wines show the promise of getting us through hard economic times. People of all ages are welcomed and will appreciate Abbie & Oliver's Artisan Cheeses and Tamami Chocolates, which share the space.

Evergreen Vineyards (500 NE Captain Michael King Smith Way; 503-472-9361 x4523 or 866-434-4818). Tasting Rooms: Daily 11–5. *Fee:* $5. *Owner:* Delford M. Smith. *Winemaker:* Laurent Montalieu. *Wines:* Pinot gris, Pinot noir, Riesling, nonalcoholic sparkling. *Cases:* 13,000. During crush, many a visitor has exclaimed, "This is good enough to bottle as it is," when tasting freshly pressed grapes. Under the Spruce Goose label, Evergreen sells a frizzante version, sans alcohol, which takes advantage of that intensely flavored juice. Along with wine grapes, Evergreen Agricultural Enterprises grows a few other crops in the shadows of the Spruce Goose's wings, notably the second-largest hazelnut crop in the world. Tasting rooms are in the Aviation Museum and Space Museum.

▲ ❖ **Youngberg Hill Vineyards** (10660 SW Youngberg Hill Road; 503-472-2727). *Tasting room:* Daily 11–5, Apr.–Nov.; by appt. only Dec.–Mar. *Fee:* $5. *Owner/Winemaker:* Nicolette Bailey. *Wines:* Pinot blanc, Pinot gris, Pinot noir. *Cases:* 1,800. There is no place quite like Youngberg Hill, an opulent eight-room bed & breakfast. The winery overlooks an expansive 20-year-old organic vineyard that has produced acclaimed wines. If you're into total relaxation, appreciate the essence of Oregon Wine Country

Cycle Wine Country—Over (Yam)hill and Dale

Description: This route features lots of zigging and zagging, with the promise of great wineries and restaurants waiting for you at the finish in McMinnville, which has become a wine focal point in the Willamette Valley. After pedaling in the residential outskirts of McMinnville, you'll be traversing lots of plowed land. The ride becomes more interesting once you turn on Youngberg Hill Road, site of the first winery on the route. After a few miles of scruffy timberland, you'll again arrive in farmlands. Be careful on OR 18, which is moderately busy. On Dejong Road you'll cross the Yamhill River, then recross it after you circle back amid farmlands on Bellevue Highway. With little elevation gain, novice cyclists will find this ride southwest of McMinnville manageable.

Wineries: Youngberg Hill Vineyards, Coeur de Terre Vineyards, Maysara Winery, Coleman Vineyard, Yamhill Valley Vineyards

Miles: 38

Elevation gain: 538

Start/Finish: McMinnville City Park

- Pedal west on 2nd Street, then go south on Hill Road and continue south on SW Hill Road before turning west on SW Peavine Road. Turn south again on SW Youngberg Hill Road. Winery stop: Youngberg Hill Vineyards.
- Go west on SW Masonville Road and continue straight on Eagle Point Road. Winery stop: Coeur de Terre Vineyards.
- Return east on Eagle Point Road and turn south on SW Muddy Valley Road. Winery stop: Maysara Winery.
- Proceed west on SW Latham Road. Winery stop: Coleman Vineyard.
- Head south on Grauer Road and continue south on Gopher Valley Road before turning east on OR 18 and east again on SW Christensen Road. Go south on SW Dejong Road, turn east on Ballston Road, then north on SW Broadmead Road, west on SW Bellevue Highway, north on SW Delashmutt Lane, south on OR 18, and west on SW Oldsville Road. Winery stop: Yamhill Valley Vineyards.
- Proceed west on McCabe Chapel Road, then turn east on Masonville Road and north on SW Old Sheridan Road, before heading east on SW Durham Lane. Pedal north on OR 99W to 2nd Street.

without leaving the premises—though Nicolette Bailey's feelings won't be hurt if you visit her winery neighbors. Don't be gone long or you'll miss complimentary wine tasting from 4 to 5 PM, paired with incomparable sunsets.

Coeur de Terre Vineyard (21000 SW Eagle Point Road; 503-472-3976). *Tasting room:* Wed.–Sun. 11–5. *Fee:* $5. *Owners:* Lisa & Scott Neal. *Winemaker:* Scott Neal. *Wines:* Pinot gris, Pinot noir, Riesling, dessert. *Cases:* 2,000. Lisa Neal sold vineyard real estate before she found her perfect piece of grapedom in the foothills of the Coast Range. It's a mile down an unpaved road to Coeur de Terre, but don't be deterred—the best wines are often found off dirt roads. *Coeur de terre* translates to "heart of the earth," and the Neals have put their hearts into three different soil types—Jory-like, marine-based, and a wash of the two. Each vineyard is named after a prominent female in the family. Hospitality is exemplary at this winery full of heart.

Maysara epitomizes sustainable farming and business practices. Courtesy Maysara Winery

Maysara Winery (15765 SW Muddy Valley Road; 503-843-1234). *Tasting room:* Mon.–Sat. 11–5. *Fee:* $7. *Owners:* Moe & Flora Momtazi. *Winemaker:* Tahmiene Momtazi. *Wines:* Pinot blanc, Pinot gris, Pinot noir, rosé. *Cases:* 12,000. *Maysara* is an ancient Persian term for "house of wine." At the Momtazi house you will find a true-to-the-land philosophy. You won't find a monoculture here, or chemicals, fertilizers, or other harmful additives to the natural environment. You will see biodiversity in the making. On the family's 538 acres, 250 are planted in vines. The rest is forest and pasture for sheep, beef cattle, and horses. The seeing-is-believing new winery and tasting room were constructed with an astonishing amount of rock from the property, and there's a pond full of rainbow trout to boot.

Yamhill Valley Vineyards (16250 SW Oldsville Road; 503-843-3100). *Tasting room:* Daily 11–5, Feb.–Dec. *Fee:* $5. *Owner:* Denis Burger. *Winemaker:* Stephen Cary. *Wines:* Pinot blanc, Pinot gris, Pinot noir, Riesling. *Cases:* 16,000. Yamhill devotes its energies to the three amigos of Pinot: blanc, gris, and noir, all grown on 150 acres of classic wine country landscape. The tasting room overlooks the vineyard; visitors with a good sense of timing might get a glimpse of the winemaking. Yamhill Valley has been called an "up-and-coming star" by none other than Robert Parker Jr. It's also known for a German-style drier Riesling.

▲ ✐ 🐾 **Hauer of the Dauen Winery** (16425 SE Webfoot Road; 503-868-7359). *Tasting room:* Sat. & Sun. 12–5. *Fee:* $2. *Owners:* Carl & Lores Dauenhauer. *Winemakers:* Carl Dauenhauer, Alan Dauenhauer. *Wines:* Chardonnay, Gamay noir, Gewürztraminer, Lemberger, Pinot gris, Pinot noir, Riesling, rosé. *Cases:* 5,000. Carl, a quintessential Farmer Bob, has an enthusiasm for life that bubbles forth in the form of a deep belly laugh. Hauer of Dauen has a fun roster of wine, too, all meant to be enjoyed young, with mirth and joy. New to the lineup is box-o-wines of Pinot noir, Riesling, and rosé, available only in the tasting room. The Dauenhauers are keeping it all in the family:

Grandson Alan is set to take over operations. It's a working farm; kids and dogs are always welcome, but close supervision is a must.

▲ ✐ 🐾 ❖ **Methven Family Vineyards** (11400 Westland Lane; 503-868-7259). *Tasting room:* Daily 11–5; Fri.–Sun., Oct.–June. *Fee:* $5–10. *Owners:* Allen & Jill Methven. *Winemaker:* Chris Lubberstedt. *Wines:* Chardonnay, Gamay noir, Pinot gris, Pinot noir, Riesling, rosé. *Cases:* 1,000. Methven's fabulous facilities include a full commercial kitchen that allows for fun events, including summer concerts, weddings, birthday parties, and class reunions—all frequently booked. One breathtaking look at the views of the Cascades and Mount Hood from the patio reveals why. Don't miss Methven's holiday open houses, where the food is positively potent: Joel Palmer House does the catering (think mushroom risotto).

WHEATLAND

▲ 🍴✐ 🐾 ❖ **Arcane Cellars at Wheatland Winery** (22350 Magness Road NW; 503-868-7076). *Tasting room:* Sat. & Sun. 12–4, and by appt. or chance. *Fee:* $10. *Owners:* Jeffrey Leal Silva & Jason Silva. *Winemaker:* Jason Leal Silva. *Wines:* Cabernet sauvignon, Carménère, Gewürztraminer, Merlot, Pinot blanc, Pinot gris, Pinot noir, Riesling, Semillon, Syrah, Viognier, rosé, red blend, dessert. *Cases:* 3,000. From estate grapes and select WV vineyards, the Silva family makes Pinot noir, Pinot gris, Pinot blanc, Semillon, and Riesling. The warmer weather wines are from vineyards in southern Oregon and Washington. The setting is unique in the low country on the west bank of the Willamette River, a short drive from the Wheatland Ferry.

Lodging

in the McMinnville Area

MCMINNVILLE

A'Tuscan Estate B&B (809 NE Evans Street; 503-434-9016). The name says Tuscany, but the look is American-Italian-French medley. Regardless of ethnicity, it works. A'Tuscan Estate has three lavishly decorated rooms accented by loads of Italian pottery and cloth in home-away-from-home suites. The Rollands' well-kept neighborhood property is a sensory feast with scented, mini flower and herb gardens outside, and extravagant décor of art and collectibles inside. Breakfast is the kind of exquisite you'd expect from a culinary genius; co-owner and chef Jacques Rolland is a coauthor of *The Food Encyclopedia*. $$$–$$$$

🐾 **Baker Street Inn & Vacation Rental** (129 SE Baker Street; 503-472-5575 or 800-870-5575). Centrally located in vibrant downtown "Mac," Cheryl Hockaday's comfortably stylish 1900s Craftsman exudes a welcoming aura she calls "the aloha spirit." Spirit away in one of four rooms in the main house, LeGrande Chateau. Or rent the Petite Chateau, a two-bedroom cottage on the property. Customizing your stay is Cheryl's specialty whether you seek respite, adventure and excitement, or a romantic getaway. A 10-minute walk will lead you to many dining choices. $$$

❖ **Joseph Mattey House B&B** (10221 NE Mattey Lane; 503-434-5058). The Joseph Mattey house, a registered historic Queen Anne Victorian, was built in 1870 for the Englishman Mattey. A successful butcher, he was an orphan, and after his second wife died, his estate went to his orphanage in England. Coincidentally, the current innkeepers are British. In the four wine-named rooms, all with private bath, Jack and Denise Seed have gone with comfort over décor, choosing eclectic antique furnishings to pamper rather than hinder. Denise serves up a hearty breakfast that might have you waddling to the porch, upstairs to the balcony, or into a parlor armchair. $$$

The rooftop bar at the Hotel Oregon offers a bird's-eye view of McMinnville. Courtesy McMenamins

🍸 🍴 ♿ 🐾 **McMenamins Hotel Oregon** (310 NE Evans Street; 503-472-8427). Of all the McMenamins restoration projects, the Hotel Oregon might be the closest to traditional. The four-story redbrick building with 42 European-style guest rooms was never known for its accommodations until now. In its century of existence, the building has been a Western Union office, Greyhound Bus depot, dance hall, soda fountain, and beauty salon. The artwork in the halls is one-of-a-kind and every pore of the building oozes history. A bonus: the rooftop bar, with magnificent views of downtown and the Yamhill River valley. $–$$$

Oregon Wine Cottage (515 NW Birch Street; 503-883-1974). Black leather furniture, a modern gourmet kitchen, king-size beds, and sophisticated elegance in warm earth tones are trademarks for Mike and Valerie Rogers' deceptive little brick cottage. A soaking tub for two adds to the romantic nature—or romance of nature. Bring your own food and wine. It books quickly, especially in summer. $$$

Pinot Quarters (533 NE Davis Street; 503-883-4115). Lisa and Scott Neal's 100-year-old Victorian home, handsomely restored and within blocks of downtown, puts you in the center of the action while still giving you a sense of seclusion. Two nicely furnished bedrooms overlook a lush yard bathed in colorful rhododendrons and Oregon flora. The kitchen is fully stocked if you prefer dining in. Forgot the wine? The Neals have every detail down, including an honor bar with local selections for purchase. $$$$

Red Lion Inn & Suites (2535 NE Cumulus Avenue; 503-472-1500). There's some pride at the Red Lion which shows through in its comfort-on-a-budget lodging. The 67 rooms are attractive and spacious, the beds are cushy, and the continental breakfast is a bonus. An indoor pool, spa, and fitness facility top the list of amenities. The only disadvantage: It's a bit of a hike to Mac's vibrant downtown. $$

LAFAYETTE

✐ ❖ **Kelty Estate B&B** (675 Third Street; 503-560-1512 or 800-867-3740). Manager Nicci Stokes loves everything about her family's estate of business: a classic country inn with perfect porches, century-old oak and fir trees, trim hedges, even a koi-stocked pond. Once the country home of *Oregonian* editor Paul Kelty, the property has exchanged hands at least 14 times. Since 2004, Bill and Joava Good have brought their style of generous hospitality to the graceful grounds. Five handsome guest rooms furnished with antiques—no doilies or teddy bears—make for sweet dreams. Complimentary local wine at 3 PM sets the mood for nearby wine country cuisine. $$$

Dining
in McMinnville

MCMINNVILLE

Bistro Maison (729 NE Third Street; 503-474-1888). A French bistro in Burgundy country? But of course! Chef Jean-Jacques and Deborah Chatelard transport you to Paris, sans passport and jet lag, with amazing and authentic cuisine. Classic numbers such as coq au vin, steak au poivre, and *confit de canard* are prepared and presented with experienced hands. Don't pass on the hors d'oeuvres, especially the pâtés, champignons, or truffle cheese fondue. Choose from a wide selection of "Orgundian" Pinot noirs for the pièce de résistance to a sublime meal. L/D Wed.–Sun. $$$$

Café Uncorked (19706 SW Highway 18; 503-843-4401). Café Uncorked, a garden oasis 7 miles southwest of McMinnville, has changed owners. It remains a great place for a sit-down break, takeaway lunchables for touring, or a landing spot after an exhaustive day on the wine trail. Its menu makes the most of Oregon ingredients, with crab cake salad, hazelnut-crusted salmon, and a crave-worthy grilled Dungeness crab sandwich. Or try the local beef burger. Uncork an Oregon wine, and you'll be all set. L/D $$

Crescent Café (526 NE Third Street; 503-435-2655). This fave café of visitors and residents is widely considered the best bet for breaking fast. Using fresh local ingredients is its banner and it wears it well. Carlton Farms provides pork, local farmers' eggs, and produce. Grab a cup of joe on the way—typically the wait line is long. B/L Wed.–Sun. $$

411 Eatery & Lounge (411 NE Third Street; 503-435-0880). Rick Drakeley and Maria Sachs focus with deft hands on Pacific Northwest seafood at their friendly restaurant and bar, formerly Olive You. Carrying out the theme, their wines are distinctly Oregon and Washington. Rick and Maria like to make people feel at home the old-fashioned way—no TVs. Dinner service stops at 9 PM, but apps and snacks are available until closing (11 weekends, 10 weekdays). Blackened salmon or rib eye, steamer clams, seared tuna, oyster po'boy, and house-smoked chicken are tempters. L/D/LN Wed.–Sun. $$–$$$

Nick's Italian Cafe (521 NE Third Street; 503-434-4471). Nick's was a legend before the wine phenomenon arrived. When it opened in 1977, it was one of few reasons to come downtown after dusk. Restaurant competition has increased, but the Peirano family—now daughter Carmen and her husband, Eric Ferguson—deliver flavorful Italian/Northwest fusion cuisine. Like so many in the region, they've hopped on the fresh-is-best bandwagon: pork, lamb, eggs, and produce are all local and sustainable. The Back Room (Tues.–Sat. 5 PM to closing) has a condensed menu of soup, pasta, wood-fired pizza, and light bites in a fun, informal setting. L (Tues.–Sat.) D $$–$$$

La Rambla Restaurant & Bar (238 NE Third Street; 503-435-2126). During Kathy Stoller's travels in Spain, she fell in love with tapas bars and wanted to create the same buzz in her wine-savvy town. Many dollars and several peacock feathers later, she and husband Chet have created the real deal in the oldest brick building in downtown "Mac." The light globes—custom-made with peacock patterns—are an array of fruit soaking in spigoted glass jars. Large floral arrangements, squeezed-together tables, and a long copper bar in a narrow space help emulate the bars of Barcelona. Using many farmers' market ingredients, creative and traditional tapas are served *fria* and *caliente*. More than 350 Oregon wines are yours for the choosing. L/D/HH $$–$$$

Red Fox Bakery & Café (328 NE Evans Street; 503-434-5098). Laurie and Jason

Furch start their days early, usually around 2 AM. Laurie bakes bread and Jason cooks at their specialty breakfast/lunch place. You will find fresh-baked goods, as you might expect, but lunch takes center stage at Red Fox. Soups and salads are equally fresh, creatively made with organic produce from Oak Hill Organics in Amity. If you have trouble locating the bakery, just follow your nose. B/L $

Thistle (228 NE Evans Street; 503-472-9623). Well-known chef Eric Bechard and partner Emily Howard moved out of Portland to become new kids on the burgeoning downtown restaurant block. Eric, whose reputation was honed at the Oyster Bar in Portland, uses a six-burner range to create culinary delights from foods provided mostly by local producers and fishermen. The menu changes nearly every day, and most entrées are under $20. Wines come from around the globe, with a distinctly local bent. D Tues.–Sat. $$

Wildwood Café (319 NE Baker Street; 503-435-1454). For a sure cure to a wine hangover, wander over to the Wildwood for its signature Wildwood Toast—granola-rolled French toast. You'll have plenty of company from Linfield University students who appreciate the generous portions, much-better-than-dorm-food taste, modest prices, and the flexibility to order breakfast until 2 PM. Small wonder that Wildwood draws a waiting crowd, especially on weekends. B/L $$

To Do
in the McMinnville Area

Attractions
You could easily lose track of time in McMinnville, with its seemingly endless parade of art galleries, wine shops, boutiques, restaurants, and theaters. **Fino in Fondo** (777 NE Fourth Street, 503-687-1652) "brings Italy to Oregon" in the form of exquisite charcuterie. Located in the county courthouse building, Carmen and Eric (Nick's Italian Café) have a passion for cured pork produced from heritage, free-range Berkshire and Yorkshire hogs. Stop by Thursday through Saturday from 11 to 6 for a "salumi flight" for $5. On the east edge of town is the **Evergreen Aviation Museum** (500 NE Capt. Michael King Smith Way, 503-434-4180), a massive glass building filled by the equally massive Spruce Goose, a.k.a. the Flying Boat. For a respite from wine touring, drive into the heart of the Coast Range to **Spirit Mountain Casino** (27100 SW Salmon River Hwy., 800-760-7977) in Grand Ronde. Despite the seemingly remote locale, the casino books big-name entertainment and offers dining and lodging. The **McMinnville Farmers' Market** (503-472-3605) takes place from 2:30 to 6:30 every Thursday from June to October on Cowls Street.

Recreation
Golfers will feel a little as if they're at Augusta playing in **The Masters at the Bayou Golf Course** (503-472-4651, 9301 SW Bayou Drive), a nine-hole, par-3 layout with a plantation-like mansion on the grounds.

Wine Shopping
NW Food & Gifts (445 NE Third Street, 503-434-6111) has daily tastings and everything you need for a picnic, including wines from close to 80 boutique wineries. It also has a varied selection of artisan-made gifts and treasures. **Harvest Fresh Grocery & Deli** (251 NE Third Street, 503-472-5740) has a large offering of local and regional wines, and periodic tastings.

There's always a flurry of activity at McMinnville's Farmers' Market. Courtesy Creative Commons

SALEM AREA (Eola–Amity Hills AVA)

For whatever reason—maybe government influence—when personality and charm were distributed, Oregon's capital was largely ignored. It isn't that Salem is seedy, unattractive, or unappealing. It's just, well . . . there. Maybe it's something in the water. Neither Monmouth nor Independence offers much to draw tourists, either, even though they border wine country.

Wineries
in the Amity/Salem Area

A few miles south of McMinnville, OR 99W straightens for its journey south, bordered by towering firs to the west and oak savannas of the Amity and Eola Hills to the east.

This is Pinot country with a twist. Because of a slight difference in soil composition and climate, the grapes grown in the Eola Hills are darker, spicier, and tend to bring more acidity and brightness to the wines. The wineries in this region are picturesque, many with stunning views of the Coast and/or Cascade mountains.

AMITY

▲ **Kristin Hill Winery** (3330 SE Amity-Dayton Highway; 503-835-0850). *Tasting room:* Daily 12–5; Sat. & Sun., Jan.–Mar. *Fee:* Complimentary. *Owner/Winemaker:* Eric Aberg. *Wines:* Chardonnay, Gamay nouveau, Gewürztraminer, Müller-Thurgau, Pinot gris, rosé, port-style, sparkling. *Cases:* 2,300. While serving in the armed forces in Germany and France, Eric Aberg developed an affinity for wine and bubbly. Stationed in San Francisco, he took classes at UC–Davis to learn how to make the nectar he loved. When he landed in Yamhill County and started his winery (named for a daughter) he was one of just 22. How times have changed! Eric likes to hold court in his Weinstube (tasting room) and share his labor of love along with a small dose of wine education. Fizzy Lizzy, made the traditional way (*méthode champenoise*), is always in demand, as is Generic Eric, a sweet rosé.

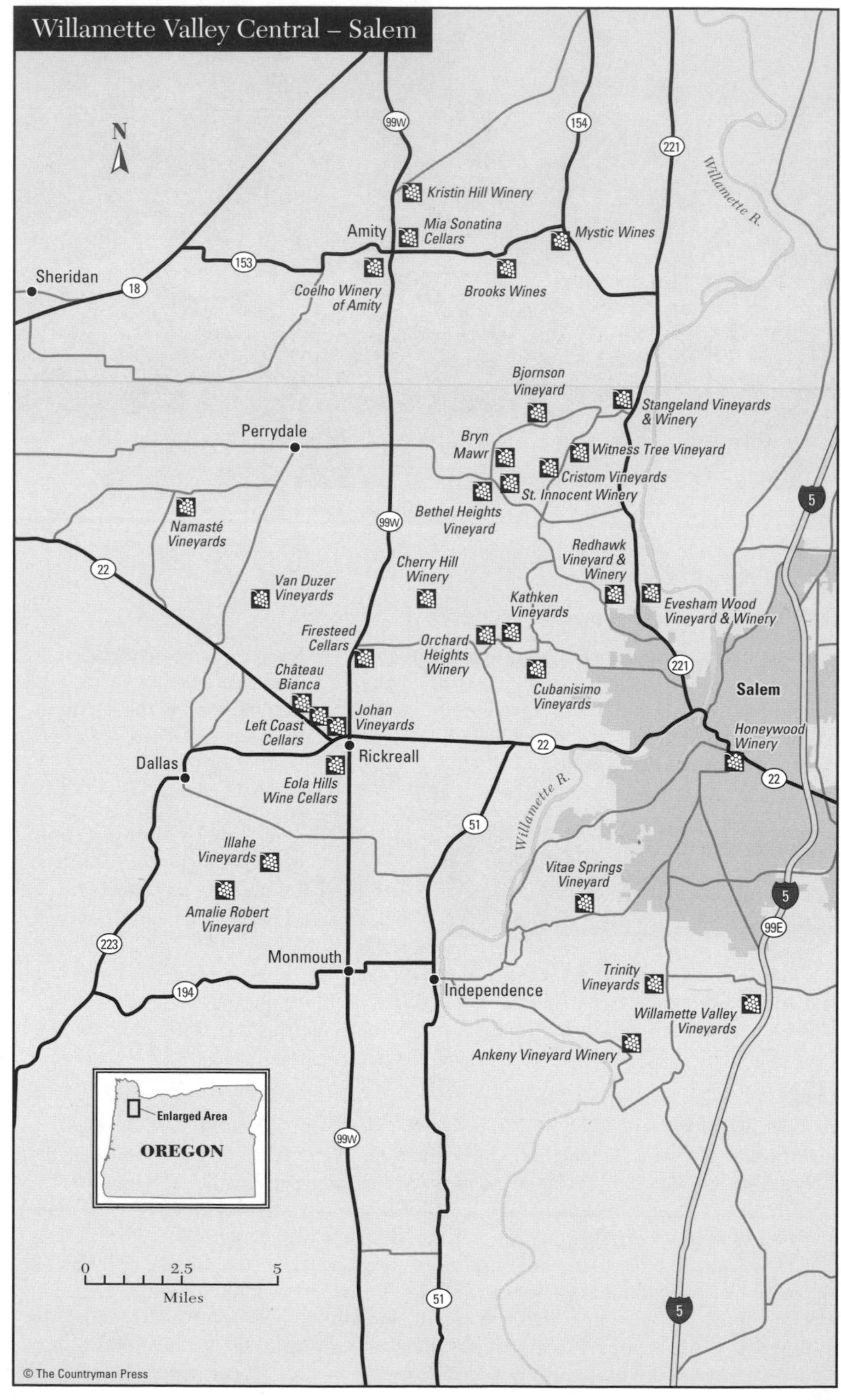

Willamette Valley Central – Salem
N
99W
154
221
Willamette R.
Kristin Hill Winery
Amity
Mia Sonatina Cellars
Mystic Wines
153
Sheridan
18
Coelho Winery of Amity
Brooks Wines
Bjornson Vineyard
Stangeland Vineyards & Winery
Perrydale
Bryn Mawr
Witness Tree Vineyard
Cristom Vineyards
St. Innocent Winery
5
Bethel Heights Vineyard
Namasté Vineyards
99W
Redhawk Vineyard & Winery
22
Cherry Hill Winery
Van Duzer Vineyards
Evesham Wood Vineyard & Winery
Kathken Vineyards
Firesteed Cellars
Orchard Heights Winery
221
Château Bianca
Cubanisimo Vineyards
Salem
Johan Vineyards
Left Coast Cellars
Honeywood Winery
22
Rickreall
Dallas
Eola Hills Wine Cellars
22
Willamette R.
51
Illahe Vineyards
Vitae Springs Vineyard
Amalie Robert Vineyard
5
99E
223
Monmouth
Trinity Vineyards
194
Independence
Willamette Valley Vineyards
Ankeny Vineyard Winery
Enlarged Area
OREGON
99W
0
2.5
5
Miles
51
5

Coelho Winery of Amity (111 Fifth Street; 503-835-9305). *Tasting room:* Daily 11–5. *Fee:* $5–15. *Owners:* Dave & Deolinda Coelho. *Winemaker:* David Coelho. *Wines:* Chardonnay, Marechel Foch, Petite sirah, Pinot gris, Pinot noir, rosé, dessert. *Cases:* 3,000. Patience is the guiding force behind the operation at Coelho, whose name is Portugeuse for "rabbit," and surname of co-owners Dave and Deolinda. Their wines are known by Portuguese monikers, too: Divertimento (fun), Renovacao (renewal), and Serinidade (serenity). The addition of Amity to the winery's name is in line with commitment to community—and you feel it in a spacious tasting room spotlighting local art and unique gifts. Iberian varietals trucked from California are used for the Portuguese wines.

Mia Sonatina Cellars (101 SE Nursery Street; 503-449-0834). *Tasting room:* Sat. & Sun. 11–5, Feb.–Dec.; and by appt. *Fee:* $5. *Owners:* Vern & Jo Spencer. *Winemaker:* Vern Spencer. *Wines:* Cabernet franc, Cabernet sauvignon, Chardonnay, Gewürztraminer, Merlot, Pinot gris, Pinot noir, Riesling, Syrah, Tempranillo, red and white blends, dessert. *Cases:* 1,500. *Mia sonatina* is Italian for "my little song," and this winery's tagline is "a song for the palate." Vern and Jo Spencer are up-and-comers with a relaxed and comfortable tasting room that matches the ambience of their quiet countryside estate. Their wines can be had for a song, with most in the $12–25 price range.

SALEM AREA

Brooks Wines (9360 SE Eola Hills Road; 503-435-1278). *Tasting room:* Tues.–Sun. 11–5. *Fee:* $5. *Owner:* Pascal Brooks. *Winemaker:* Chris Williams. *Wines:* Pinot noir, Riesling, white blend. *Cases:* 10,000. Jimi Brooks was an organic and biodynamic advocate and all-around great guy, well loved in the industry. He died of a heart attack at 34 in 2004, leaving his son, Pascal, the heir, and his sister, Janie Brooks Heuck, in charge of operations. Young Pascal is getting close to drinking age now, and the permanent winemaking facility and tasting room are in a good-vibes place. Although Brooks is famed for its Runaway label—named for a forklift accident and futile effort to move a barrel late one night—don't miss its five variations of Riesling.

Mystic Wines (11931 SE Hoodview Road; 503-581-2769). *Tasting room:* Sat. & Sun. 12–5, May–Nov. *Fee:* Negotiable. *Owner/Winemaker:* Rick Mafit. *Wines:* Barbera, Cabernet Sauvignon, Merlot, Pinot noir, Syrah, Zinfandel. *Cases:* 1,500. Take a breather in Pinot country and stop at Mafits' place to savor big reds. What's the mystique of Mystic? Sourcing the right grapes, choosing the right French oak barrels, and giving more barrel time. Rick Mafit is a very particular, hands-on guy with plenty of opinions and the experience to back them. He has production where he wants it, enough to supply his loyal fans and local restaurants. The award-winning abstract label was created by his son, Dillon.

Stangeland Vineyards & Winery (8500 Hopewell Road NW; 503-581-0355). *Tasting room:* Daily 12–5. *Fee:* $5. *Owners:* Larry & Ruth Miller. *Winemaker:* Larry Miller. *Wines:* Chardonnay, Gewürztraminer, Pinot gris, Pinot noir, Tempranillo, rosé, ice-style. *Cases:* 2,500. The Millers are gracious hosts with a mission to befriend customers and live up to their motto, "There are no strangers at Stangeland." Now a full-time winemaker, Larry has vinifera dating to 1978 and he's proud of his European awards for his Pinots. The cool—in both senses of the word—climate-controlled winery and tasting room, gracefully terraced gardens, and views of rolling hills make this a welcoming spot, especially while pedaling Bike Oregon in August. Willamette Valley Cheese and the addictive Freddy Guys Hazelnuts are available for purchase.

Witness Tree Vineyard (7111 Spring Valley Road NW; 503-585-7874). *Tasting room:* Tues.–Sun. 11–5, Mar.–Nov. *Fee:* $5. *Owners:* Dennis & Carolyn Devine. *Winemaker:* Steven Westby. *Wines:* Chardonnay, Dolcetto, Pinot blanc, Pinot gris, Pinot noir, Viognier, dessert. *Cases:* 6,000. Coming to Witness Tree feels like visiting your country cousins, right down to the entertaining goats. An attractive doublewide serves as tasting room, and a narrow wraparound porch adorned with bistro tables is a hangout for groupies. The ancient oak tree towering above the vineyard like a sentinel is a designated Oregon Heritage Tree. Every wine comes from the 51-acre vineyard surrounding the stately old tree.

The famous witness tree stands guard over the vineyard. Courtesy Witness Tree Vineyard

Cristom Vineyards (6905 Spring Valley Road NW; 503-375-3068). *Tasting room:* Tues.–Sun. 11–5; Fri.–Sun. 11–5, Jan. & Feb. *Fee:* $5–10. *Owners:* Paul & Eileen Gerrie. *Winemaker:* Steve Doerner. *Wines:* Chardonnay, Pinot gris, Pinot noir, Syrah, Viognier. *Cases:* 12,000. Walking past manicured gardens and through the antique mahogany doors makes you think of a hoity-toity tasting room—smaller, but with similar attitude. It isn't a place where smiles abound, but exquisite Pinot noirs do. Cristom grows northern Rhône varietals—Syrah and Viognier—that were some of the valley's first. "Cristom" is a combo of the Gerries' children's names, Christine and Tom, so it's pronounced "chris-tom." Vineyard blocks are named for six of the family's matriarchs; Marjorie has the oldest and most prized vines.

St. Innocent Winery (5657 Zena Road NW; 503-378-1526). *Tasting room:* Daily 11–5; Sat. & Sun., Dec.–Mar. *Fee:* $5–10. *Owner/Winemaker:* Mark Vlossak. *Wines:* Chardonnay, Pinot blanc, Pinot gris, Pinot noir, sparkling. *Cases:* 8,000–10,000. St. Innocent's name honors Mark Vlossak's father, John Innocent Vlossak, who taught his son wine appreciation early. The education included the belief that wine was meant to go with food, and Vlossak's talents shine equally as chef and winemaker. Open houses at St. Innocent are not to be missed. Exquisite wines and Mark's killer cassoulet have flavors that saints—and mere mortals—deem heavenly. And his hard-to-get sparkling wines . . . doubly divine. The winery is known for Burgundian-style single-vineyard Pinots, meant to pair with food, of course.

Bethel Heights Vineyard (6060 Bethel Heights Road NW; 503-581-2262). *Tasting room:* Tues.–Sun. 11–5. *Fee:* $5. *Owners/Winemakers:* Casteel family. *Wines:* Chardonnay, Gewürztraminer, Pinot blanc, Pinot gris, Pinot noir. *Cases:* 10,000. When Bethel Heights was established in 1977, the Casteel brothers were on the forefront of the Oregon wine scene. Today, an entire Casteel clan owns and runs the place, and remains instrumental in the industry. The affable and patient pourers like to explain subtle differences in flavor profiles depending on where grapes came from in their 51-acre vineyard (maps included). The Casteel style is to go for transparency, letting the vineyard and vintage speak for itself through the grapes.

Bryn Mawr (5955 Bethel Heights Road NW; 503-581-4286). *Tasting room:* Tues.–Sun. 11–5, May–Nov. *Fee:* $5. *Owner:* Jon & Kathy Lauer. *Winemaker:* Jon Lauer & Rachel Stary. *Wines:* Chardonnay, Dolcetto, Pinot blanc, Pinot noir, Riesling, Tempranillo, rosé. *Cases:* 1,000. You can have your wine and eat your cheese, too.

That's the case at Bryn Mawr, where you receive a complimentary cheese plate with your tasting. Spectacular views of the valley add to the experience. The Lauer family makes every effort to be earth-friendly. The vineyards are sustainable and the family raises much of its food.

▲ **Björnson Vineyard** (3635 Bethel Heights Road NW; 503-593-1584). *Tasting room:* Holiday weekends, and by appt. May–Sept. *Fee:* $5–10. *Owners:* Mark & Patricia Björnson. *Winemaker:* Patricia Björnson and guest winemakers. *Wines:* Auxerrois, Gamay noir, Pinot noir. *Cases:* 200. With three creeks, a lush forest, and hiking trails, it makes sense that Björnson is certified sustainable. In the tasting room, enjoy vineyard designate Pinots made by other winemakers, such as John Grochau (currently without tasting room). Plans are in works for more regular tasting room hours.

Evesham Wood Vineyard & Winery (3795 Wallace Road NW; 503-371-8478). *Tasting room:* Holiday weekends, and by appt. *Fee:* Varies. *Owners:* Erin & Jordan Nuccio. *Winemaker:* Erin Nuccio. *Wines:* Chardonnay, Pinot noir, rosé. *Cases:* 4,500. Erin Nuccio was making his Haden Fig wines at Evesham Wood when Russ and Mary Raney decided to retire after 25 years in the biz. He was the natural successor and the transition has been seamless. Evesham Wood still walks the walk, when it comes to being sustainable and stewards of the soil. The Nuccios don't irrigate their certified organic, 13-acre Le Puits Sec ("dry-farmed") vineyard because they believe terroir-driven wines are best expressed with little intervention. E-mail them for a tasting appointment.

▲ **Redhawk Vineyard & Winery** (2995 Michigan City Lane NW; 503-362-1596). *Tasting room:* Daily 11–5. *Fee:* $5. *Owners:* John & Betty Pataccoli. *Winemaker:* John Pataccoli. *Wines:* Cabernet sauvignon, Chardonnay, Dolcetto, Gamay noir, Pinot gris, Pinot noir, Riesling, Syrah. *Cases:* 5,000. The winery began in 1988 and was best known for a good-time Pinot called Grateful Red. The label is still there, with the same low price any Deadhead fan would appreciate, but the rest has changed dramatically. John and Betty have exploited their limitless views of the valley—who wouldn't? Enjoy their wines and a hawk's view without spending a fortune. They've gone with a more sophisticated label, but we're, uh, grateful they kept their iconic red.

▲ **Cubanisimo Vineyards** (1754 Best Road NW; 503-588-1763). *Tasting room:* Daily 11–5. *Fee:* $5. *Owner:* Mauricio Collada. *Winemaker:* Rob Stuart. *Wines:* Pinot gris, Pinot noir, rosé. *Cases:* 2,500. Transport yourself to a place far away from the green and gray of Oregon. White sands, Floridian beach colors, and Cuban music are the hallmark of Havana native Mauricio Collada's tasting room. And, there might be something extra in the Pinot that pairs better with spicy food. A dash of pepper? He's not saying. Come to one of the more unique wineries in the state for a Latin mood swing and dance lessons.

▲ ❖ **Orchard Heights Winery** (6057 Orchard Heights Road NW; 503-391-7308). *Tasting room:* Mon.–Sat. 11–5, Sun. 9–5. *Fee:* $5. *Owners:* Michael & Gwen Purdy. *Winemaker:* Shawn Dunaway. *Wines:* Cabernet sauvignon, Gewürztraminer, Merlot, Pinot gris, Pinot noir, Riesling, rosé, fruit. *Cases:* 35,000. Orchard Heights is one of those wineries that transcends the ordinary tasting experience and is a destination stop. With its popular Sunday brunch, daily lunch menu, and extensive gift shop, there is always a flurry of activity. The grounds are pretty and the location picturesque; the patio is a great spot for a picnic. This winery has fared well with traditional varietals, but especially popular are tropical specialty wines.

▲ ❖ **Kathken Vineyards** (5739 Orchard Heights Road NW; 503-316-3911). *Tasting room:* Holiday weekends, and by appt. June–Sept. *Fee:* $5. *Owners:* Ken & Kathy

Slusser. *Winemaker:* Ken Slusser. *Wines:* Chardonnay, Pinot gris, Pinot noir, Riesling, Syrah, rosé, red blend, port-style. *Cases:* 2,500. Kathken's tasting room doesn't have regular hours, but what sets it apart is its weekly concert series in the summer. From June to September, anywhere from 50 to 350 people will come to the country for food and good times. Elevations ranging from 700 to 1,000 feet ensure stressed vines and distinct tastes—most notably the "grapefruity" Pinot gris.

▲ 🍾 **Cherry Hill Winery** (7867 Crowley Road; 503-623-7867). *Tasting room:* Mon.–Fri. 10–4, Sat. & Sun. 11–5, or by appt. *Fee:* $10. *Owners:* Mike & Jan Sweeney. *Winemaker:* Ken Cook. *Wines:* Pinot gris, Pinot noir, rosé. *Cases:* 7,000. Wild cherries once were prolific on the hill—thus the name—and then the domestic variety was planted in the 1960s. Thirty years later, Pinot noir was put into the Jory soils. The owners kept the orchard, so you can buy dried Royal Ann cherries covered in dark chocolate—a treat with the Pinot noir. Cherry Hill recently opened a sparkling new winery and tasting room.

▲ 🍾 **Firesteed Cellars** (2200 North Pacific Highway West; 503-623-8683). *Tasting room:* Daily 11–5. *Fee:* $5. *Owner:* Howard Rossback. *Winemaker:* Bryan Croft. *Wines:* Chardonnay, Pinot gris, Pinot noir, Riesling. *Cases:* 80,000. Despite the large production, Firesteed is a low-key winery where the emphasis is on what it describes as "ancient agricultural practices." The staff likes to make the visit educational and fun for all, whether you're an experienced "winer" or first-time taster.

DALLAS

▲ 🎁 🍴 🍾 🐾 **Van Duzer Vineyards** (11975 Smithfield Road; 503-623-6420 or 800-884-1927). *Tasting room:* Daily 11–5. *Fee:* $10. *Owners:* Carl & Marilyn Thoma. *Winemaker:* Jerry Murray. *Wines:* Pinot gris, Pinot noir, rosé, port-style. *Cases:* 15,000. Van Duzer has one of most enticing labels for depicting a sensuous sense of place and taste, featuring Zephyr, Greek goddess of the gentle afternoon wind. She embodies what the vineyard manager and winemaker embrace—cool Pacific breezes funneling east through the Van Duzer Corridor. Take in the landscaped surroundings and neighboring wildlife sanctuary while having a taste-off between the Homestead and Flagpole Pinot noirs. Look for wine club dinners.

▲ 🍾 🐾 ❖ **Namasté Vineyards** (5600 Van Well Road; 503-623-4150). *Tasting room:* Daily 12–6. *Fee:* $10. *Owner:* Dave Masciorini. *Winemaker:* Andreas Wetzel. *Wines:* Gewürztraminer, Pinot noir, Riesling, white blend, port. *Cases:* 2,500. "The spirit of the wine honors the spirit of the vine." The motto at this winery is a twist on a Hindu greeting meaning "I honor the spirit in you." Dave Masciorini's philosophy may be simple, but his wines are not. He has strong opinions about wimpy Pinots; his are intentionally husky. Also popular is a semisweet white blend called Peace. Occasional concerts are part of the summer program.

RICKREALL

▲ 🎁 🍴 ❖ **Château Bianca** (17485 Highway 22; 503-623-6181). *Tasting room:* Daily 10–5. *Fee:* $5. *Owners:* Helmut & Liselotte Wetzel. *Winemaker:* Andreas Wetzel. *Wines:* Chardonnay, Gewürztraminer, Maréchal Foch, Pinot blanc, Pinot gris, Pinot noir, Riesling, Syrah, brut, port-style, dessert. *Cases:* 15,000. If you can't find a wine you like at Château Bianca, it might not exist. The country-casual tasting room has anywhere from 20 to 23 bottles uncorked at any one time, and not a one is a budget buster. Château Bianca trucks in tons of grapes to complement production from its own vineyard. Winemaker Andreas Wetzel is definitely Pinot-centric—Pinot noir, Pinot gris, and Pinot blanc—but the winery runs virtually the gamut of cool-climate offerings.

Cycle Wine Country—Twist And Shout

Description: Get your climbing legs moving for a ride that includes some of the prettiest country in the northern Willamette Valley, while also featuring a short ride through urban West Salem. The Eola Hills run northward from the northwest edge of Salem. After a flat warm-up on Rickreall Road, you'll begin heading uphill when you turn north on Oak Grove Road. The route twists and winds through Douglas fir forest and vineyards to some of the area's most popular wineries, at times providing wonderful views of the Cascade and Coast ranges.

Wineries: Eola Hills Wine Cellars, Orchard Heights Winery, Evesham Wood Vineyard, St. Innocent Winery, Zena Heights Vineyard, Cristom Vineyards, Witness Tree Vineyard, Stangeland Vineyards & Winery, Elton Vineyards, Mystic Wines, Brooks

Miles: 49

Elevation gain: 2,191

Start/Finish: Eola Hills Wine Cellars, Rickreall

- Start north on OR 99W, then east on Rickreall Road and north on Oak Grove Road before turning east on Orchard Heights Road. Winery stop: Orchard Heights Winery.
- Head north on Doaks Ferry Road and continue north on Wallace Road. Winery stop: Evesham Wood Vineyard.
- Proceed west on Zena Road. Winery stop: St. Innocent Winery/Zena Heights Vineyard.
- Go north on Spring Valley Road: Winery stops: Cristom Vineyards and Witness Tree Vineyard.
- Continue north on Hopewell Road. Winery stop: Stangeland Vineyards & Winery.
- Veer west on Jerusalem Hill Road, head north on Oak Road and continue straight on Ingram Lane. Winery stop: Elton Vineyards.
- Turn south on Ingram Lane, east on Oak Road, north on Hopewell Road, north on Lafayette Highway, and then west on Hood View Road. Winery stop: Mystic Wines.
- Go west on Eola Hills Road. Winery stop: Brooks Wines.
- Proceed south on Skyline Road, then west on Yampo Road, south on Oak Grove Road, west on OR 22, and south on OR 99W back to Eola Hills Wine Cellars.

Biking through Oregon Wine Country with Eola Hills Wine Cellars' support has become a popular August pastime.

Courtesy Eola Hills Wine Cellars

▲ **Left Coast Cellars** (4225 North Highway 99W; 503-831-4916). *Tasting room:* Daily 12–5, and by appt. *Fee:* $5. *Owners:* Suzanne Larson. *Winemaker:* Luke McCollom. *Wines:* Chardonnay, Pinot blanc, Pinot gris, Pinot noir, Syrah. *Cases:* 5,500. Follow the copper-sculpted arrows, make a few left turns, and be prepared for a most appealing setting among old-growth oaks. A true pride of place greets your every sense. In an effort to go green, Suzanne received a USDA grant for installation of solar panels. The signature wine is the approachable and food-friendly Cali's Cuvée, a Pinot noir blended with all barrels of the vintage. A busy kitchen puts out small gourmet plates. Plan to stay awhile and stroll the grounds.

Johan Vineyards (4285 North Highway 99W; 866-379-6029). *Tasting room:* Daily 12–5, Mar.–Dec. *Fee:* $5. *Owners:* Dag Johan Sundby & Nils Dag Sunby. *Winemaker:* Dan Rinke & Don Cooper. *Wines:* Chardonnay, Pinot gris, Pinot noir, Vin gris, rosé. *Cases:* 1,750. Johan produces Willamette Valley classics from a biodynamic vineyard that winemakers Dan and Don describe as a peaceful "worry-free zone." Norway native Dag Johan Sundby believes in high-quality fruit, and it shows. The vineyard's second label, Farmlands, is in line with its socially conscious attitude, and a portion of the profits goes to the Friends of Family Farmers. For a special taste of Norway, attend Johan's Syttende Mai (May 17) celebration.

▲ 🎁 ✐ ❖ **Eola Hills Wine Cellars** (501 South Pacific Highway [OR 99W]; 503-623-2405 or 800-291-6730). *Tasting room:* Daily 10–5. *Fee:* Complimentary. *General manager:* Tom Huggins. *Winemaker:* Steve Anderson. *Wines:* Cabernet sauvignon, Chardonnay, Gewürztraminer, Maréchal Foch, Merlot, Pinot gris, Pinot noir, Riesling, Sangiovese, Sauvignon blanc, Syrah, Viognier, Zinfandel, dessert. *Cases:* 50,000. There are as many wines to taste as there are events sponsored by Eola Hills Wine Cellars. Founder and general manager Tom Huggins, a former OSU long-distance runner, has an affinity for all things Pacific Northwest and loves to organize trips combining best-of-all-worlds good times. Sunday Brunch and winemaker dinners take place in the barrel room, where the aroma and atmosphere provide an unparalleled mix. Our favorite outing is Bike Oregon Wine Country, every weekend in August.

▲ ✐ **Illahe Vineyards & Winery** (3275 Ballard Road; 503-831-1248). *Tasting room:* Thurs.–Sat. 11–4, and by appt. May–Sept. *Fee:* $15. *Owner:* Lowell & Pauline Ford. *Winemakers:* Brad Ford. *Wines:* Grüner veltliner, Pinot gris, Pinot noir, Riesling, Viognier. *Cases:* 4,000. Lowell and Pauline Ford bring years of working with big hitters in the Oregon wine industry, so they know what they're doing in an 8,000-square-foot winery that's as eco-friendly as they come. Illahe produces nearly as much power as it uses with solar panels. Much of the winery is underground so temperatures are easily managed, rainwater is collected, and the vineyards are LIVE-certified. Illahe is especially proud of its reserve and grand reserve Pinot noirs.

Amalie Robert Vineyard (13531 Bursell Road; 503-882-8833). *Tasting room:* Holiday weekends, and by appt. *Fee:* $10. *Owners/Winemakers:* Dena Drews & Ernie Pink. *Wines:* Chardonnay, Pinot noir, Pinot meunier, Syrah, Viognier. *Cases:* 3,000. What was once a cherry orchard quickly evolved into a premium grape vineyard for some of the industry's bigger names. Today, Amalie Robert is sharing the wealth with some credible wines of its own. The first estate crush came in 2006, about a decade after technogeeks Dena and Ernie began drawing up their dreams on cocktail napkins over wine. By 2011, Amalie Robert was chosen among the nation's top 100 wineries by *Wine & Spirits*. It's known for an annual Earth Day celebration.

SALEM

🎁 🍴 🐾 **Honeywood Winery** (1350 Hines Street SE; 503-362-4111). *Tasting room:* Mon.–Fri. 9–5, Sat. 10–6, Sun. 1–5. *Fee:* Complimentary. *Owners:* Paul & Marlene Gallick. *Winemaker:* Marlene Gallick & Kyle Blair. *Wines:* Cabernet sauvignon, Chardonnay, Gewürztraminer, Maréchal Foch, Merlot, Müller-Thurgau, Pinot blanc, Pinot gris, Pinot noir, Riesling, Syrah, fruit. *Cases:* 30,000. You may have noticed a lot of "oldest this" or "oldest that" in Oregon. They're all accurate in their own way, but this is the real deal—dating back to post-Prohibition 1933, it's the oldest continuously operating winery in the state. When Ron Honeyman and John Wood formed Columbia Distillers, they made fruit brandies and liquors; when they branched into wine, they renamed their business Honeywood. Their Pinot noir and Maréchal Foch are two of the crowd-pleasers among 47 wines. A large selection of Oregon foods, from cheese to nuts, and wine accessories adds to the stop.

Vitae Springs Vineyard (3675 Vitae Springs Road South; 503-588-0896 or 503-581-3411). *Tasting room:* Fri. 5–9, and by appt. *Fee:* $5. *Owners:* Earl & Pamela Van Volkinburg. *Winemakers:* Earl & Joel Van Volkinburg. *Wines:* Grüner veltliner, Pinot noir, Riesling. *Cases:* 1,000. The elder Van Volkinburgs were stationed at Hahn Air Base in Germany's Mosel Valley when they fell in love with wine. Their son, Joel, and his wife, Michelle, carry the same passion and are an integral part of operations. Earl stumbled onto Grüner veltliner when a Hungarian friend gave him 50 plants, and for 30 years they made it for personal consumption—the first in the United States to do so. Joel began to propagate Grüner when it received international attention. They say it's great with turkey, razor clams, oysters, whitefish, chicken, pork, and even pasta dishes.

Ankeny Vineyard Winery (2565 Riverside Road South; 503-378-1498). *Tasting room:* Daily 11–5. *Fee:* $5. *Owners:* Joe Olexa. *Winemaker:* Andy Thomas. *Wines:* Chardonnay, Maréchal Foch, Pinot gris, Pinot noir, rosé, red blends, dessert. *Cases:* 2,500. Andy does what some winemakers only do in secret: Blend a small amount of another red to color the Pinot noir. He comes out of the winery closet with a Pinot noir and Maréchal Foch blend called Crimson that's friendly and approachable (Foch) with acidity for backbone (Pinot). With its warm hospitality and views of Ankeny National Wildlife Refuge's migratory birds, you may decide to stay awhile—especially for Friday "Wine Downs" on the deck in the summer.

▲ 🎁 🍴 🥖 🐾 ❖ **Trinity Vineyards** (1031 Wahl Lane South; 503-371-6977). *Tasting room:* Sat. & Sun. 12–6, and holiday weekends. *Fee:* $1 per taste. *Owners:* Steve & Cindy Parker. *Winemaker:* Steve Parker. *Wines:* Pinot gris, Pinot noir, Sangiovese,

Like most tasting rooms in Oregon Wine Country, Trinity lacks pretense. Courtesy Trinity Vineyards

Syrah, Viognier, rosé. *Cases:* 850. Starting from scratch was more than Steve and Cindy Parker bargained for when they purchased their plot of the Oregon wine dream. The native Oregonians bought an existing vineyard and fantasized about drinking their own wine. After untangling and pruning, the Parkers discovered the vines were planted east to west, the trellis system was rotted, and self-rooted Riesling and Gewürztraminer vines had taken over. It took five years of undoing before they could start doing. They built their home, replanted the vineyard, and constructed a tasting room. The completed package is nothing short of spectacular.

Pressing juice the Old World way at Willamette Valley Vineyards' Grape Stomp.

Courtesy Willamette Valley Vineyards

TURNER

❖ **Willamette Valley Vineyards** (8800 Enchanted Way SE; 503-588-9463). *Tasting room:* Daily 11–6. *Fee:* $5–10. *Owner:* Jim Bernau. *Winemaker:* Don Crank III. *Wines:* Cabernet sauvignon, Chardonnay, Gewürztraminer, Müller-Thurgau, Pinot gris, Pinot noir, Riesling, Syrah, Viognier, dessert. *Cases:* 85,000. Willamette Valley might just be Oregon's most visible winery, due to massive distribution and its location off I-5 just south of Salem. The vineyards blanket the South Salem Hills and beckon weary interstate travelers to stop and sip. One of the state's top three producers, Willamette Valley is Oregon's only publicly owned and traded winery. Despite a big-business air, it has done a creditable job of creating an entertaining tasting room. It hosts myriad events, including a popular annual grape stomp where you can get your feet squishy and purply—just like in the Old Country.

Lodging

in the Salem Area

SALEM

🍸🍴 ❖ **The Grand Hotel** (201 Liberty Street SE; 877-540-7800 or 503-540-7800). Located in the heart of downtown action, the Grand's 193 rooms and suites are a cut above in a city lacking in unique lodging. The hotel offers Oregon wine packages and a complimentary bottle of wine, along with directions for self-guided tours of wine country. Other packages: river trips, golf, and dinners. The Grand also makes every effort to go green, achieving EarthWISE certification with composting, recycling, and emphasis on the purchase of local products. $$$

MONMOUTH

Mamere's Bed & Breakfast (212 North Knox Street; 503-838-1514). MaMere's, named for owner Terri Gregory's grandmother, brings a taste of French/New Orleans hospitality to this quiet college town. Rooms in this colorfully striking century-old Queen Anne Victorian house reflect the Southern sentiment with such names as the Mardi Gras Muse and Louisiana Lair. The house is across the street from Main Street Park, a happening place in the summer. Gregory had MaMere's up for sale in early 2013, but the B&B is a Monmouth institution unlikely to change appreciably. $$

HOPEWELL

❖ **Hopewell Bed & Breakfast** (22350 Hopewell Road NW; 503-868-7848). Enjoy country solitude and relaxation in the heart of a working cattle farm, where you'll savor vegetables from the garden. Both cottages are private and each has its own entrance. Breakfast can be served in your room or on your personal deck overlooking the pond. The Country Cottage has a queen-size bed; the Lakeside, a king; both have satellite TV. Finish a day of wine touring with a soak in the hot tub. $$$$

Dining

in the Salem Area

SALEM

Bentley's Grill (291 Liberty Street SE; 503-779-1660). With its location next to Salem's Conference Center and Grand Hotel, Bentley's has become the preferred choice for downtowners. It's known for emphasis on Oregon ingredients, most notably Rogue Valley cheeses and bay shrimp. It has a clever way of delineating menu choices: turf, farm, and ocean. For the budget minded, Bentley's prepares a trio of three-course dinners for less than $30. Its wine list is proudly tilted toward Oregon. L/D/HH Tues.–Sat. $$–$$$

La Capitale (508 State Street; 503-585-1975). Jazzy notes mingle with clanking plates, tinkling glassware, and kitchen buzz. Dropped lighting and tall bistro tables dot the bar area, where you can watch chef David Rosales create his magic in an open kitchen. Rosales's affinity for French cuisine surprises and delights locals and out-of-towners. Favorites: steak bavette, tuna carpaccio, spit-roasted chicken, and *pommes frites* (the two dipping sauces are best mixed). A well-executed wine list earns favor, with local choices integrated among regional and international choices. L/D/HH Mon.–Sat. $$–$$$

Crooked House Bistro (1142 Edgewater Street; 503-385-8851). Chef Bernard Malherbe makes it his mission to prepare and present exquisitely crafted food with complementing wine in a harmonious and personalized package. His meals are French inspired and reap the benefits of Oregon ingredients. His wine menu also reflects what is near and dear, including French selections. Given its intimate and limited seating, it's a good idea to bring friends for your table companions. D Tues.–Sat. $$$

Grand Vines (195 High Street NE; 503-399-9463). Maggie Crawford and 11 close friends were simultaneously celebrating a new president and lamenting failing 401Ks when the idea of purchasing a bottle shop came up. Conversation halted and ideas started to ferment. Congenial Maggie has a small but pleasing menu to complement wines by the taste, glass, or bottle. Grand Vines is a place to catch your breath with comfy seating and banks of windows to see downtown happenings, including colorful characters. L/D Mon.–Sat. $–$$

Orupa (500 Liberty Street Southeast, Suite 150; 503-588-3639). Wine-friendly food is the order of the day at the Afshars' new place (Old Europe Inn). Their new name reflects their cuisine—a combination of Oregon and European flavors. They are persnickety (Hely) perfectionists (Hans), creating food that surpasses the presentation, served in the form of pizzas, pasta, sandwiches, and seafood. They still bake their own bread, and occasionally their sauerkraut soup makes the specials (don't miss). Oregon reds—heavy on Pinot—and whites are available by the glass and bottle. A separate, equally enticing menu is offered at the bar, along with local draft beers. L (Mon.–Fri.) D/HH $$–$$$

Roberts Crossing (3635 River Road South; 503-584-1035). "Something for everyone" is the simple yet heartfelt message from Roberts Crossing, a cheerful establishment along the railroad tracks

Rainy days are common in the Willamette Valley, but so are rainbows. Courtesy Trinity Vineyards

southwest of the city. Many items on the Northwest-focused menu are familiar, yet attention getters are the cambozola mushroom burger—$2 extra for gluten-free bun—and bourbon berry salmon. Keep your ear tuned for the rumble of trains, meaning it's time for crossing bell drink specials. The wine list is a Northwest and international fusion, with a solid injection of local. Put the winemaker dinners on your calendar. D Tues.–Sun. $$$

Wild Pear Restaurant & Catering (372 State Street; 503-378-7515). Its reputation built on catering, Wild Pear opened for lunch and dinner with soup, salads, wraps, and pizzas with flair in an artsy setting where flavors run with wild abandon. Take the starters: white-truffle sweet-potato fries, maple bleu cheese and candied pecans, mushroom-and-cheese strudel. Entrées are so satisfying you might not want dessert, but we doubt it; the Key lime tartlet will be calling your name. Only Oregon wines are served and the menu is mostly farm-to-fork. L/HH Mon.–Sat. $$

DALLAS

Latitude One (904 Main Street; 503-831-1588). The attitude at Latitude: Bring some culinary culture to a blue-collar town. Latitude One does just that with a limited yet diverse menu that ranges from steak to steamer clams to smoked chicken quesadilla. The economy minded will appreciate small plates and happy hour menu. Above all, this fun little place is trying to capitalize on the local wine rage with a laudable selection—all from Oregon, thank you. Owner Marlene Cox spices up the calendar with winemaker dinners, private afternoon winery tours, and vino-related events. D/HH/LN Thurs.–Sat. $$

FALLS CITY

The Bread Board (401 North Main Street; 503-787-5000). It's worth a country drive to find this funky little Coast

Range community for the scenery and the "Bread Boys'" remarkable food. John Volkmann and Keith Zinn make their own dough for breads, scones, and pastries they offer beginning at 7 AM Friday through Sunday mornings. Flatbread-style pizzas are prepared in the largest wood-fired oven in Oregon, beginning at 4 PM until closing at 8. Round out your meal with a market-fresh salad and bottle of local wine. D Fri.–Mon. $$

INDEPENDENCE

Ragin' River Steak Co. (154 South Main Street; 503-837-0394). "Ragin' River" is a bit of a misnomer, given that the meandering Willamette River across the street is anything but ragin'. The restaurant, in a 19th-century building in placid downtown, has a relaxed ambience. Chances are, the owner will stop by to make sure everything is prepared to your wishes. Ragin' River makes its own bread, salad dressings, and churns its own butter. The restaurant pours many Oregon wines, especially big reds to go with big steaks. L/D/HH Tues.–Sun. $$–$$$

MONMOUTH

Crush Wine Bar (105 East Main Street; 503-838-0399). Thanks to Monmouth's relatively recent decision to legally allow alcohol, Crush has added some evening spunk to town. Josh Brandt's wine bar serves light nosh of panini and pizzas. Stop by for Thursday night flights highlighting individual wine regions. The tastings run from 6 to 9 PM and are complimentary. Rotating local brews are on tap, too. Crush is just a fun place to hang, catch a game, or lounge in comfy chairs by the fire. D/LN Tues.–Sat. $–$$

To Do

in the Salem Area

Attractions

Between touring the wineries of the Amity and Eola Hills, take a brief detour at the whistle-stop community of Hopewell to cross the Willamette on the **Wheatland Ferry** (503-588-7979). Cars are $2 each way. In 1844, the ferry was the first to carry a covered wagon across the river to what is now **Willamette Mission State Park** (503-393-1172), occupied by settlers in 1834. A highlight is a 250-year-old black cottonwood tree, the country's oldest. On the west side of the river, **Wings of Wonder** (5978 Willamette Ferry Street, 503-838-0976) in Independence is a nonprofit with exhibits and live butterflies from all over the world.

Amid farmlands outside of Amity is the **Brigittine Priory of Our Lady of Consolation Monastery** (23300 SW Walker Lane, 503-835-8080), where fudge and truffles help keep the lights on. In the fall, the monks produce more than 3,600 pounds of fudge in three days. The monastery's candy shop, with free fudge samples, is open daily.

In Salem, the **Mission Mill Museum** (1313 Mill Street SE, 503-585-7012) is a tribute to an old woolen mill and the community built around it, including an original water-powered turbine. History also seeps from every creaky floorboard of the **Deepwood Estate** (1116 Mission Street SE, 503-363-1825), a 4-acre Shangri-La near the heart of downtown. The restored Victorian home features a variety of events and was once chosen by *Sunset* magazine as one of the top historic homes in the West.

For one more step into history, consider a performance at **Elsinore Theatre** (170 High Street, 503-375-3574). The Gothic Elsinore opened in 1926 with a Cecil B. DeMille silent movie and for a quarter-century was the most exquisite theater between Portland and San Francisco. Classic films, concerts, and other acts fill the calendar today.

For a watery perspective of Salem, the ***Willamette Queen*** (503-371-1103) riverboat at Riverside Park is an authentic sternwheeler in the mold of those that ran up the

Willamette as far south as Corvallis in the 1800s. Choose between a gourmet dinner or Sunday brunch cruise, or a lunch float. Just north of Salem, off the I-5 exit at Brooks, are the **Northwest Vintage Car and Motorcycle Museum, Pacific Northwest Truck Museum**, and **Oregon Electric Railway Museum**, all in the same **Western Antique Powerland** complex (503-393-2424).

If you've got the kids, **Enchanted Forest** (8462 Enchanted Way, 503-371-4242), off I-5 south of Salem, will be a hit. Open spring and summer, it's best known for a log ride and haunted house. Go for dinner and a movie at the **Northern Lights Theatre Pub** (3893 Commercial Street SE, 503-585-4232), where you're more than welcome to sip your favorite vino while you watch. Take a trip back in time at the **Dallas Motor Vu** (503-623-4449, 315 SE Fir Villa), one of four drive-in theaters in the state and the only one showing first-run movies. For $18 a carload, back up the car to one of the 437 spaces and be entertained the old-fashioned way.

It doesn't snow much in the Willamette Valley, but somehow the only museum in the western United States dedicated to the Arctic has found a home in Monmouth. The **Jensen Arctic Museum** (509 West Church Street, 503-838-8468) at Western Oregon University focuses on the indigenous peoples of that region. For more locally oriented museums, there's the **Oregon Heritage Museum** (112 South Third Street, 503-838-4989) in Independence and the **Polk County Museum** (503-623-6251) at the Polk County Fairgounds, south of the junction of OR 99W and OR 22 in Rickreall.

If you're a mountain biker, head west of Falls City to the **Black Rock Trails** at Camp Tapawingo, sometimes called Disneyland by riders who appreciate the variety of terrain and man-made challenges. Trails are open year-round. Name notwithstanding, the Salem **Saturday Farmers' Market** (503-585-8264) is open for business every Wednesday from May to October on the corner of High and Market Streets. The capital city also has year-round **Salem Public Market** (2140 Rural Street, 503-623-6605) on Saturdays; Oregon's oldest farmers' market is in a heated indoor facility between 12th and 13th Streets. The downtown **Independence Farmers' Market** (503-838-5424), open Saturdays from April to November, has local art and produce.

Recreation

If you're looking for the ideal place to hike, bike, Rollerblade, or run around Salem, try **Minto-Brown Island Park** along the Willamette. At just under 900 acres, it's a sea of tranquility on the fringe of urban hum. Golf fans won't lack for options: No fewer than 12 public courses are in the area. If the salmon are running from the Pacific to their spawning grounds, the North Santiam River is one of the best streams in Oregon to land a burly Chinook.

Wine Shopping

Santiam Wine Company (1930 Commercial Street SE, 503-589-0775) has a crammed-to-the-gills shop with more than 100 Oregon bottles. Specializing in the hard-to-find, its owner is also a pink freak, with a large section of rosés, many from Oregon producers. Under new ownership, **Papà di Vino** (1130 Royvonne Avenue SE, #104, 503-364-3009) is still Tusc-Oregon-y, with Italian-table-clothed tables, vases of sunflowers, a cozy corner with overstuffed chairs, fireplace, and small bar with three stools.

More Information

McMinnville Area Chamber of Commerce, 503-472-6196, www.mcminnville.org, 417 NW Adams Street

Salem Convention and Visitors Association, 503-581-4325 or 800-874-7012, www.travelsalem.com, 1313 Mill Street SE

Oregon Wine Country: The Willamette Valley, 866-548-5018, McMinnville AVA, wwwmcminnvilleava.org

Eola-Amity AVA, www.eolaamityhills.com/content/EA_profiles.php

McMinnville AVA, www.mcminnvilleava.org/wineries

5

Willamette Valley East

EAST OF EDEN

EAST OF INTERSTATE 5 is the oft-forgotten side of the Willamette Valley. The area between Portland's southeast suburbs and east Salem is characterized by rich farmlands rising gently to meet the forested slopes of the Cascades.

Most of the communities have no more than a few thousand residents. Economies revolve around agriculture and evolve toward timber the farther east you go. Although wineries are a relatively recent revelation, some established vineyards grow on the south- and west-facing slopes above acres of hazelnuts, loganberries, raspberries, sorghum, and noble-fir Christmas tree farms.

Of all the east valley's communities, Silverton, Aurora, and Mount Angel are the most tourist-friendly. Silverton is a leafy, manicured town astride Silver Creek, with vintage mansions and oak trees for blocks on each side of the boutique shops along Main and Water Streets. Aurora is a National Historic District with a museum, antique warehouse, and winery in a storied 1905 bank building. Another interesting community is Woodburn, east of I-5 about midway between Portland and Salem. Known mostly to Oregonians for its busy outlet mall, Woodburn has cultural diversity unlike anywhere except Portland.

GETTING HERE AND AROUND

Tours of the east Willamette Valley best begin in Portland. Start at the Oswego Hills Winery, just off I-205 in the southeast corner of the metropolitan area. From there, get back on I-205 and head east to Oregon City, where you'll take the OR 99E exit across the Willamette River. OR 99E is the highway lifeline of the east Willamette Valley's wine country, much the way OR 99W is west of the interstate.

Pull over and take a brief peek at Willamette Falls—try to ignore the industrial complex—continue south on 99E along the river into the east valley. You'll crisscross the countryside between 99E and OR 213 down to the southernmost winery, Silver Falls, and then return to Portland on I-5. Or you can cross through Salem to tour the dozens of wineries of the mid–Willamette Valley on the other of the river.

LEFT: Growing and producing Oregon wine is labor-intensive. Frank Barnett

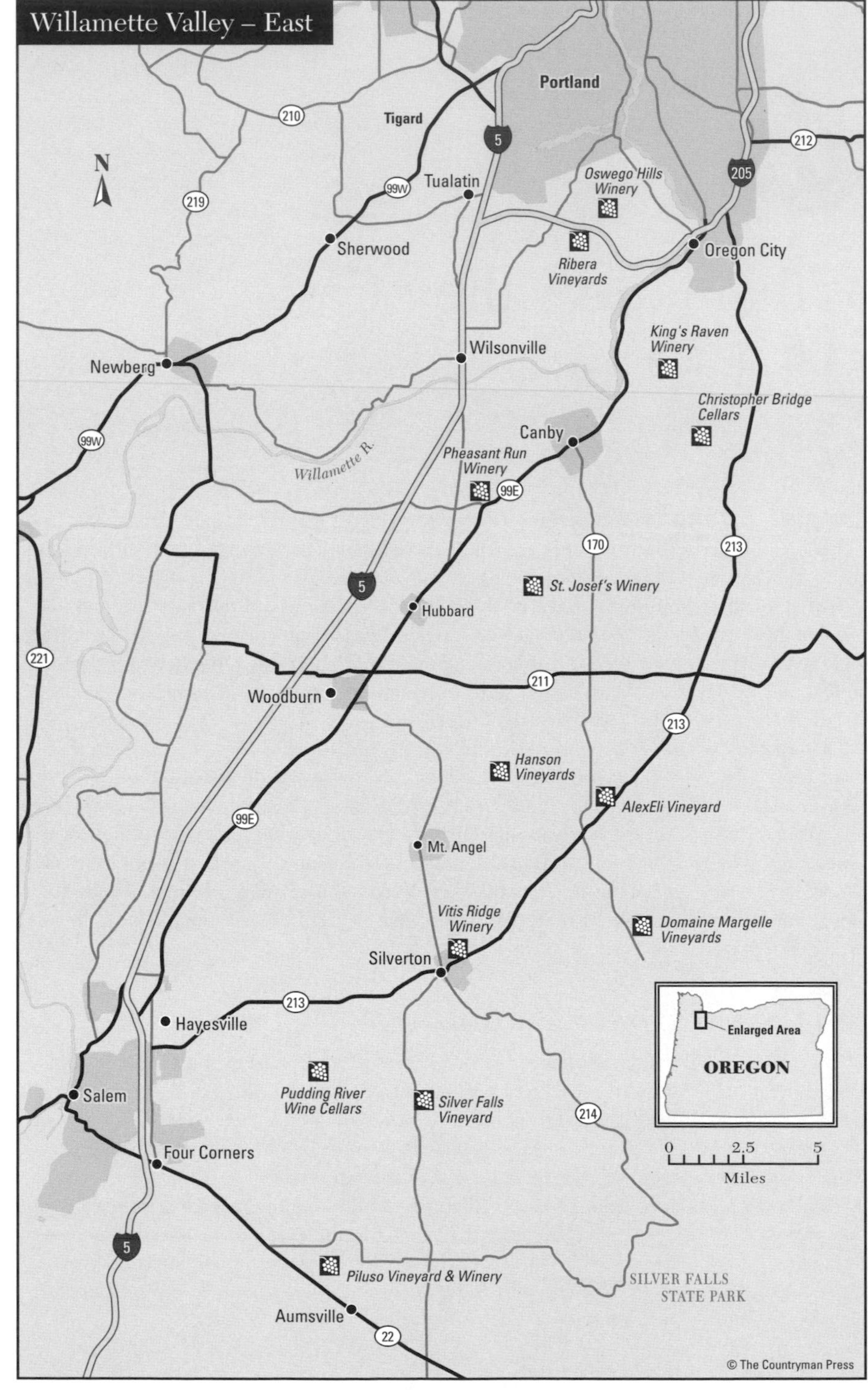
Willamette Valley – East
Portland
Tigard
N
Tualatin
Oswego Hills Winery
Sherwood
Oregon City
Ribera Vineyards
King's Raven Winery
Wilsonville
Newberg
Christopher Bridge Cellars
Canby
Pheasant Run Winery
Willamette R.
St. Josef's Winery
Hubbard
Woodburn
Hanson Vineyards
AlexEli Vineyard
Mt. Angel
Vitis Ridge Winery
Domaine Margelle Vineyards
Silverton
Hayesville
Enlarged Area
OREGON
Salem
Pudding River Wine Cellars
Silver Falls Vineyard
Four Corners
0 2.5 5
Miles
Piluso Vineyard & Winery
SILVER FALLS STATE PARK
Aumsville
© The Countryman Press

Wineries

in the East Willamette Valley

Imagine how Oregon wine history might have turned out if David Lett had found just one available hillside on which to plant Pinot back in the 1960s. The story goes that when Lett came north from California to look for the perfect Pinot plantation, he stayed in Silverton, looked for available land, and found every acre entrenched in existing agriculture—and pricey, to boot. Lett went west to Dundee, and the east valley was largely forgotten until recently. Like the Sip 47 crew on the west side, east valley wineries like to think of themselves as a separate entity.

WEST LINN

❖ **Oswego Hills Winery** (450 Rosemont Road; 503-655-2599). *Tasting room:* Sun. 12–5, holiday weekends, and by appt. *Fee:* $10. *Owner:* Jerry Marshall. *Winemaker:* Derek Lawrence. *Wines:* Cabernet sauvignon, Chardonnay, Maréchal Foch, Merlot, Petite sirah, Pinot gris, Pinot noir, Riesling, Syrah, Viognier, Zinfandel, rosé, red and white blends, port. *Cases:* 3,000. You can't get much closer to Portland and be in an actual commercial vineyard—"A smorgasbord of wines right on the urban-growth boundary," owner Jerry Marshall describes it. Jerry, a former airline pilot, rehabbed a decaying creamery, pump house, and 1938 barns to create an extraordinary rural environment between the urban hum of Lake Oswego and West Linn. Much of the facility is bathed in white, including the farm home, which is surrounded by cedar and fig trees, and a mature vineyard.

Ribera Vineyard (21775 SW Ribera Lane; 503-638-7323). *Tasting room:* Sat. & Sun. 1–5. *Season:* Apr.–Nov. *Fee:* $5. *Owner:* Darrel & Molly Roby. *Winemaker:* Darrel Roby & Marcus Goodfellow. *Wines:* Chardonnay, Counoise, Grenache, Merlot, Pinot gris, Pinot noir, Sauvignon blanc, Syrah, rosé, red blend. *Cases:* 1,000. The east valley's newest tasting room pours Pinot noir, Pinot gris, and Chardonnay from the Robys' own vineyard while also offering Rhône-style wines made with fruit from the Red Mountain and Columbia Valley AVAs. Most unique is the Counoise, a peppery grape known for its acidity but without the high tannins. Ribera makes its wines in McMinnville.

OREGON CITY

▲ ✐ ❖ **King's Raven Winery** (1512 Washington Street; 503-784-6298 or 503-656-6439). *Tasting room:* Fri.–Sun. 12–5. *Fee:* $5. *Owner:* Ingram family. *Winemaker:* Darin Ingram. *Wines:* Gewürztraminer, Léon Millot, Maréchal Foch, Pinot gris, Pinot noir, Riesling. *Cases:* 600. The King's Raven winery and vineyard is on a small hilltop south of Oregon City where grapes share space with Angus beef cattle. The Ingram family has owned the property since 1942. Although the tasting room is downtown in the Howden Art and Framing Gallery, the winery frequently stages special events at the vineyard—including movies.

▲ 🍴 🐾 ❖ **Christopher Bridge Cellars** (12770 South Casto Road; 503-263-6267). *Tasting room:* Fri. 2–5, Sat. & Sun. 12–5, Mar.–Dec., and by appt. *Fee:* $8. *Owners:* Chris & Susanne Carlberg. *Winemaker:* Chris Carlberg. *Wines:* Ehrenfelser, Muscat, Pinot gris, Pinot noir, rosé. *Cases:* 1,000. Chris and Susanne Carlberg not only appreciate what their farm brings them, they've also tuned into its rhythms. The 15-acre farm, vineyard, and winery have agriculture at its heart: grass-fed beef, chickens, and grapes. The rare Ehrenfelser, a German cross between Sylvaner and

Riesling, tastes similar to a Viognier but "with muscle," Susanne says. Speaking of muscle, a timber-framed building with a bread oven and outdoor fireplace now serves as tasting room. The Carlbergs have been working on the Castle, a large stone structure overlooking the vineyard that will host concerts, weddings, and wine dinners.

AURORA

▲ 🍴 🖉 ❖ **Pheasant Run Winery** (21690 Main Street NE; 503-678-3131). *Tasting room:* Fri.–Sun. 12–6. *Fee:* $5. *Owners:* Tara & Carl McKnight. *Winemaker:* Carl McKnight. *Wines:* Cabernet sauvignon, Merlot, Pinot gris, Pinot noir, Sangiovese, Syrah, red blend. *Cases:* 1,000. Pheasant Run's story is as much about its setting as its wines. The east valley's newest winery is in a 1905 stone building built for Portland's Lewis & Clark Exposition. Moved to Aurora—itself a National Historic District—where it became a bank, it has a sordid and colorful history culminating in a scene from the movie *Bandits*. The wines are made from some of the oldest vineyards in the Willamette Valley, as well as the Columbia Valley and Walla Walla AVAs.

CANBY

▲ 🎁 🍴 🖉 ❖ **St. Josef's Winery** (28836 South Barlow Road; 503-651-3190). *Tasting room:* Thurs.–Sun. 12–5, and by appt. *Fee:* $5. *Owners:* Josef & Lilly Fleischmann. *Winemaker:* Josef Fleischmann. *Wines:* Cabernet sauvignon, Chardonnay, Gewürztraminer, Merlot, Pinot gris, Pinot noir, Riesling, Syrah, sparkling. *Cases:* 9,000. CAUTION: WINEMAKERS AT PLAY, reads a sign at the entry to St. Josef's Winery, revealing the playful nature at this pleasant country estate. With equal slices of Italy, Switzerland, and Oregon blended into a Bavarian package amid a cypress-lined drive and acres of grapes, you have the setting for the extraordinary. After more than 30 years of producing lively and affordable wines, the Fleischmanns seem to have even more energy than ever—reflected in their many fanciful events.

WOODBURN

▲ 🐾 **Hanson Vineyards** (34948 South Barlow Road; 503-634-2348). *Tasting room:* Sat. & Sun. 12–5, Apr.–Nov, and by appt. *Fee:* $3–6. *Owners/Winemakers:* Clark Hanson & Jason Hanson. *Wines:* Chardonnay, Pinot blanc, Pinot gris, Pinot noir, Riesling. *Cases:* 500. This pastoral farm has been growing grapes since the 1920s, when Prohibition forced growers to either shut down, plant orchards, or raise such semilegal varieties as Niagara and Concord. The evolution continued when the Hansons began making berry and fruit wines in 1968, and has culminated with the planting of now-maturing French and German vinifera. The Hansons keep planting grapes with a vision for continued growth.

MOLALLA

▲ 🖉 🐾 **AlexEli Vineyard** (35803 South Highway 213; 503-829-6677). *Tasting room:* Sat. & Sun. 12–5, May–Nov., and by appt. *Fee:* $5. *Owners:* Phil Kramer & Anita Katz. *Winemaker:* Phil Kramer. *Wines:* Cabernet franc, Gewürztraminer, Malbec, Müller-Thurgau, Pinot noir, Riesling, red and white blend. *Cases:* 2,600. Anita Katz and her two sons, Philip Alexander Kramer and Anthony Eli Kramer, took over an existing winery in 2008 and renamed it, using a combination of the boys' middle names. The home, tasting room, and flagstone patio are tucked away from the highway amid a mature 18-acre vineyard. The sons have been making quantity-for-quality changes. Enjoy your wine outdoors next to AlexEli's private lake and ever-expanding gardens.

SCOTTS MILLS

❖ **Domaine Margelle Vineyards** (20159 Hazelnut Ridge Road; 503-873-0692). *Tasting room:* Holiday weekends, and by appt. *Fee:* $5. *Owners:* Steve & Marci Taylor. *Winemaker:* Sean Driggers. *Wines:* Pinot gris, Pinot noir. *Cases:* 250. Domaine Margelle is a small boutique winery amid a 50-acre vineyard on the East Valley Wine Tour map. The Taylors enjoy sharing insights about the estate and the terroir unique to eastern Willamette Valley. The bulk of the fruit goes to A to Z Wineworks, for Pinot gris, Pinot noir, Chardonnay and occasionally higher-end REX HILL wines.

SILVERTON

▲ **Vitis Ridge Winery** (990 North First Street; 503-873-9800). *Tasting room:* Fri.–Sun. 12–5, Mar.–Dec. *Fee:* Complimentary. *Owners:* Chris & Sharon Deckelmann, Bruce & Sally Eich. *Winemakers:* Chris Deckelmann & Bruce Eich. *Wines:* Cabernet franc, Cabernet sauvignon, Chardonnay, Gewürztraminer, Malbec, Maréchal Foch, Merlot, Muscat, Petit verdot, Pinot gris, Pinot noir, Riesling, Syrah, Tempranillo, red blend, dessert. *Cases:* 2,800. Vitis Ridge began as a hobby in the Deckelmanns' garage in the mid-1990s and has evolved to producing a dozen wines, about half from grapes they grow in an 80-acre vineyard. Look for the Eich family at tasting events throughout the region.

SUBLIMITY

▲ 🎁 ✐ ❖ **Silver Falls Vineyards** (4972 Cascade Hwy SE; 503-769-5056). *Tasting room:* Wed.–Sun. 11–5. *Fee:* $5. *Owners:* Duane & Gail Defree. *Winemaker:* Andreas Wetzel. *Wines:* Chardonnay, Maréchal Foch, Pinot gris, Pinot noir, Riesling, rosé, white blends, dessert, port-style, sparkling. *Cases:* 2,000. Looking for value wines? Silver Falls is your place. Of all the wines sold here, only the Reserve Pinot noir is more than $16—and it's not exactly out of sight at $25. Pinot noir is the biggest seller, although all the offerings do well.

▲ ✐ 🐾 **Pudding River Wine Cellars** (9374 Sunnyview Road NE; 503-365-0391). *Tasting room:* Daily 12–5, Apr.–Dec. *Fee:* $5. *Owners:* Sean & Stacey Driggers and John & Karen Bateman. *Winemaker:* Sean Driggers. *Wines:* Chardonnay, Pinot gris, Pinot noir, Riesling, Syrah, Viognier. *Cases:* 1,500. There are family-*owned* wineries and then there are family-*run* wineries. At Pudding River, all ages and sizes are running around, sometimes underfoot. The rooster on the label is a nod to the site's previous life as a poultry farm. A renovated tasting room on the ground floor of a small converted barn behind a 100-year-old Victorian farmhouse overlooks the meandering Pudding River. The winery has a fan base for barrel-fermented Chardonnay, but an equal number prefer the unoaked version.

AUMSVILLE

▲ **Piluso Vineyard & Winery** (6654 Shaw Highway SE; 503-749-4125). *Tasting room:* Sat. & Sun. 11–5, Apr.–Dec. *Fee:* Complimentary. *Owners:* Sandee & Pinky Piluso. *Winemaker:* Sandee Piluso. *Wines:* Dolcetto, Gamay noir, Maréchal Foch, Pinot noir, Tempranillo, white blend, dessert, port-style. *Cases:* 600. Piluso made its big intro when it scored a 90 in *Wine Spectator* for its 2006 Pinot noir. Practice makes perfect: Another winner is the Bianco dolce, a sweet dessert wine with German flair. Sandee Piluso went back to school at a ripe age to become a winemaker, and after a stint as an intern at Airlie Winery, she's running her own show.

Lodging

in theEast Willamette Valley

SILVERTON

🍴 ♿ 🐾 **Oregon Garden Resort** (895 West Main Street; 503-874-2500). The Oregon Garden has proven such a popular tourist attraction it seemed only natural to build accommodations. A state-of-the-art, eco-oriented, attractive 103-room facility with main lodge and six outbuildings blends well with lush surroundings. All rooms have fireplace and patio, and rates include admission to the Oregon Garden. The Moonstone Spa is ideal for a relaxing massage after a day of wine touring. A heated outdoor swimming pool and romance packages add even more appeal. $$

♿ 🐾 **Silverton Inn & Suites** (301 North Water Street; 503-873-1000). Filling a void, this luxury boutique hotel in the heart of downtown is a short walk to antique shops, restaurants, and other attractions. Each of the 18 rooms is decorated in a manner that depicts history—including the Clark Gable Suite. It's named for a Portlander who worked briefly in Silverton's timber industry in 1922 before he was gone with the wind to an acting career of some renown. Hang in the Heritage sitting room, with three flat-screen TVs and huge movie selection. $$–$$$$

Dining

in the East Willamette Valley

MILWAUKIE

Milwaukie Kitchen & Wine (10610 East Main Street; 503-653-3228). This suburban deli has a little bit of everything, including about 40 percent Northwest wines—especially Pinot noirs. Dinners to go, a coffee shop, pastries, groceries, and cooking classes make up the mix. Breakfast, served all day, has something for everybody—ranging from yogurt parfait to biscuits and gravy. It's all made in-house after short transportation from local producers. B/L/D $

WEST LINN

Allium Bistro (1914 Willamette Falls Drive; 503-387-5604). All ingredients are locally sourced at Allium, a cozy place offering small plates and a sharing menu. The bistro has nearly 60 wines by the glass, most from the Pacific Northwest. If you happen to be in the area on the right Sunday, try Allium's popular family-style Neighborhood Dinner, which leans toward French and Italian cuisine. D/HH $$–$$$

Five-O-Three (21900 Willamette Drive, #201; 503-607-0960). You can order a traditional burger or Spanish favorite paella at this suburban eatery. The name comes from Oregon's original area code—a nod to the state that provides the bounty. Chef John Bokman works his magic from an open kitchen slinging such favorites as pan-seared Oregon rockfish. The wine emphasis is on local and handcrafted, although a few from France and Australia make the cut. L/D/HH/LN $–$$$

AURORA

Topaz Bistro (21668 Highway 99E NE; 503-678-7770). Flexibility is the byword at Topaz, where pasta entrées come both large and small, and sharing is encouraged. The wine country quesadilla and gourmet mac and cheese are popular, along with sliders made of pork, turkey, or beef mixed with bleu cheese. The wine list is entirely Oregon and extensively from the east Willamette Valley. L/D Wed.–Sun. $–$$

SILVERTON

Silver Grille Café & Wines (206 East Main Street; 503-873-8000). Acclaimed chef Jeff Nizlek came back to the Silver Grille in August 2009 with a focus on regional fare, ranging from locally picked mushrooms and Pacific shrimp to Oregon cheeses and Northwest wines. Try the wild Oregon sturgeon entrée. The ambience is relaxed, the food a cut above anything in the east Willamette. Look for seasonal winemaker's dinners. D Wed.–Sun. $$–$$$

To Do

in the East Willamette Valley

Attractions

Most likely, you'll be starting your wine tour at the end—the End of the Oregon Trail, that is. The **End of the Oregon Trail Visitor Center** (1726 Washington Street, 503-657-9336) in Oregon City features exhibits from families that actually made the trip west in the 19th century. Along the road to wineries, take a few minutes at **Swan Island Dahlias** (995 NW 22nd Avenue, 503-266-7711) in Canby, and the **Wooden Shoe Tulip Farm** (33814 South Meridian Avenue, 503-634-2243), about 7 miles east of Woodburn. Both have massive fields of color and shops selling flowers, seeds, and bulbs.

It would be easy to spend an entire day in Aurora, an Oregon National Historic Landmark unto itself. Start at **Old Aurora Colony** (15018 Second Street NE, 503-678-5754), which in compelling text and grainy black-and-white photos tells the story of a Christian commune of Swiss and German immigrants that lasted from 1856 to 1883. Also in town is **Aurora Mills** (14971 First Street NE, 503-678-6083), an extraordinary collection of antiques from all over the country used for home décor and businesses.

If there was a single defining contemporary moment for the East Willamette Valley, it was the opening of the **Oregon Garden** (879 Main Street, 503-874-8100). The one-time lumber town was already on its way to successfully reinventing itself as a Sunday-drive destination when this 80-acre area with 20 specialty gardens began luring visitors by the thousands.

Before Oregon Garden, prime attractions were **Silver Falls State Park** (503-873-8681) and **Mount Angel Abbey** (503-845-3030) in St. Benedict. Oregon's largest state park has 11 waterfalls, ranging from the 177-foot South Falls to 27-foot Drake Falls. The Abbey is one of Oregon's most beautiful buildings, and has a famous library and a retreat home. Built in 1882, it hosts a Festival of Arts & Wine every June, three months before the raucous annual end-of-summer **Oktoberfest** (503-845-9440).

Recreation

The east side of the valley offers a bit of everything, from salmon and steelhead fishing on the Willamette and Clackamas Rivers, Class IV whitewater rafting on the Clackamas, and camping and hiking in Silver Falls State Park. For duffers, the public **Evergreen Golf Course** (11694 West Church Road NE, 503-845-9911) in Mount Angel is a modestly challenging nine holes. **Langdon Farms Golf Club** (24377 NE Airport Road, 503-678-4653) in Aurora is a popular 18-hole course, with a credible grill and happy hour.

Wine Shopping

Wine enthusiasts won't want to miss the **Howard Hinsdale Cellars Wine Bar & Bistro** (101 North Water Street, 503-873-9463) in its new location in Silverton. Hinsdale, renowned in Oregon wine circles for his work at Silvan Ridge outside of Eugene, touts the bar as a fun place to do wine. Exhibit A: Vintage TV nights.

More Information

Silverton Chamber of Commerce, 503-873-5615, www.silvertonchamber.org, 426 South Water Street

East Valley Wine Group, www.eastvalleywine.com

Vineyard
2006
OREGON
MARECHAL FOCH
WILLAMETTE VALLEY
www.wineriesoflanecounty.

6

Willamette Valley South

HEART OF THE VALLEY

WHEN YOU ARRIVE in the broad, mostly flat, U-shaped plain that is the southern Willamette Valley, you'd best choose sides. And we don't mean reds versus whites. Eugene and Corvallis also happen to be home of the state's two major universities: rivals Oregon and Oregon State. Tasting rooms can be quiet even during the autumn crush because many of the state's fans are packed into a football stadium or cloistered around a television, wearing either Oregon's green and yellow or Oregon State's black and orange.

As you drive south from Salem on either I-5 or the prettier route, OR 99W, you'll notice subtle changes. The Coast and Cascade ranges are as much as 30 miles apart, the foothills a blend of Douglas fir and oak savanna. It is drier, the summers warmer. Pinot still prevails, but grapes that don't care for the north's bluster have a fighting chance.

Eugene and Corvallis are the most diverse communities in the southern end of the valley. The table-flat fields are planted mostly with grass. The region rightly calls itself the grass-seed capital of the world and there's a decent chance the sod in your yard had its genesis here.

GETTING HERE AND AROUND

If your focus is purely the home-style wineries at this end of the valley, you can fly into Eugene's **Mahlon Sweet Field**. Typically more expensive than flying into Portland, it's served from nine western cities by Delta Connection/SkyWest (800-221-1212), United Airlines (800-241-6522), Alaska/Horizon Airlines (800-547-9308), and Allegiant Air (702-705-8888). All the major rental car agencies serve Mahlon Sweet.

If you're coming by car from the north or south, I-5 is the fastest and most direct route, but it's also the least interesting. Highways arriving from the east and west are slower but scenic. US 20 and OR 34 bisect Corvallis and Albany from both directions, and OR 126 is a beautiful drive along the McKenzie River and then to the coast.

LEFT: Saginaw Vineyard produces the French-American hybrid Maréchal Foch, an easy drinking red.
Courtesy Newport Chamber of Commerce

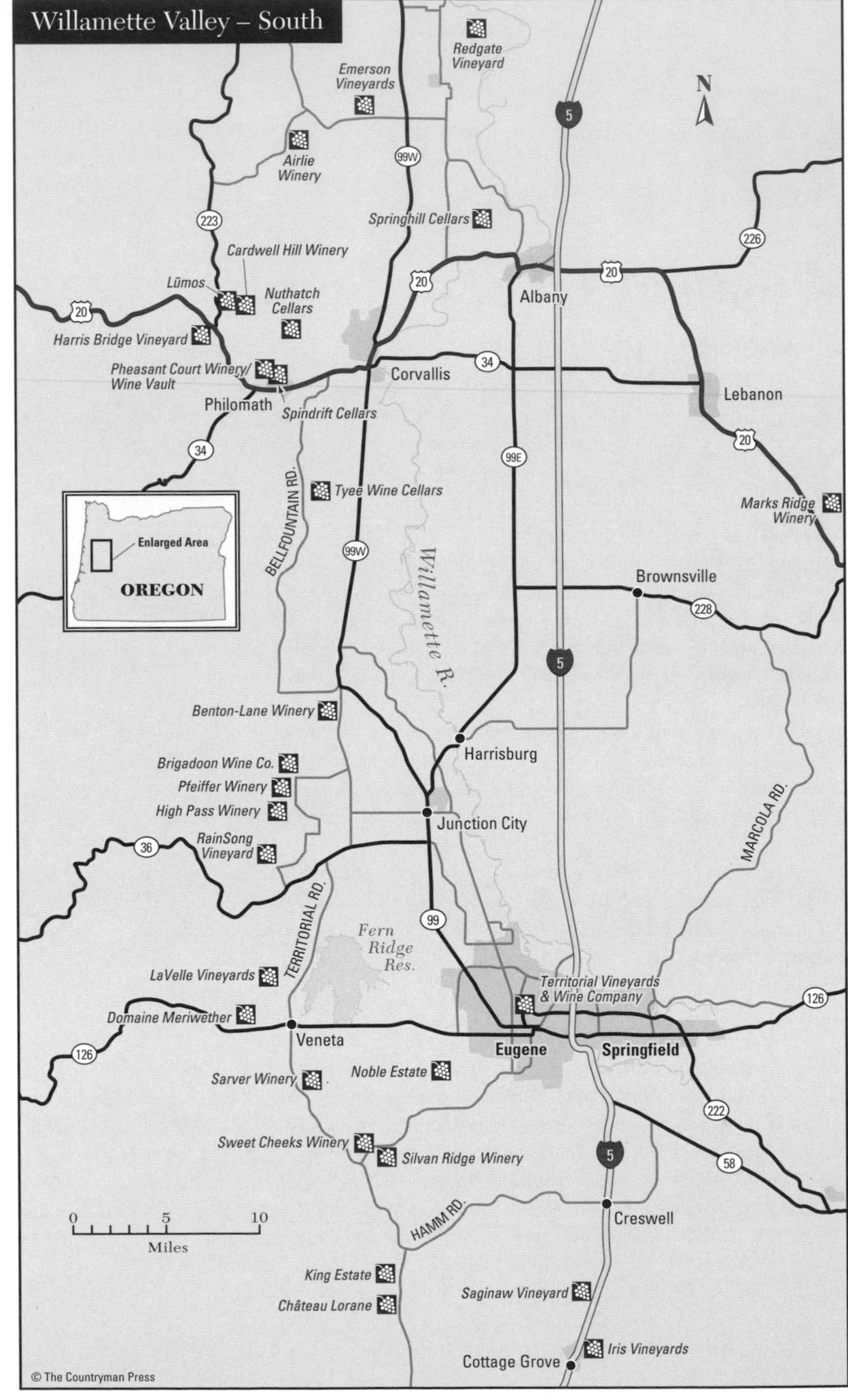
Willamette Valley – South
Redgate Vineyard
Emerson Vineyards
Airlie Winery
Springhill Cellars
Cardwell Hill Winery
Lūmos
Nuthatch Cellars
Harris Bridge Vineyard
Pheasant Court Winery/ Wine Vault
Spindrift Cellars
Philomath
Corvallis
Albany
Lebanon
Tyee Wine Cellars
BELLFOUNTAIN RD.
Marks Ridge Winery
Enlarged Area
OREGON
Willamette R.
Brownsville
Benton-Lane Winery
Harrisburg
Brigadoon Wine Co.
Pfeiffer Winery
High Pass Winery
Junction City
RainSong Vineyard
MARCOLA RD.
TERRITORIAL RD.
Fern Ridge Res.
LaVelle Vineyards
Territorial Vineyards & Wine Company
Domaine Meriwether
Veneta
Eugene
Springfield
Sarver Winery
Noble Estate
Sweet Cheeks Winery
Silvan Ridge Winery
HAMM RD.
Creswell
0 5 10
Miles
King Estate
Château Lorane
Saginaw Vineyard
Iris Vineyards
Cottage Grove
© The Countryman Press

Vineyards mesh with coastal foothills in the south Willamette Valley. John Baker

Amtrak's Coast Starlight (800-872-7245) has daily stops in Albany and Eugene. **Greyhound** (800-231-2222) has bus stations on a north–south route in Albany, Corvallis, and Eugene, and limited service on an east–west route through Albany and Corvallis that includes Philomath en route to Newport on the coast.

ALBANY/CORVALLIS AREA

The science for growing grapes in Oregon was provided by the University of California Davis, whose viticulture and oenology program celebrates more than 130 years. Today Oregon State University's Viticulture and Enology School—reared from infancy in the early 1970s by a UC–Davis graduate named Barney Watson—offers undergraduate and graduate degrees, manages its own vineyard (Woodhall), and has extension agents in the Columbia Gorge, Walla Walla region, and the Rogue and Umpqua Valleys.

Corvallis might just be the best hub for Oregon Wine Country touring. It's in easy proximity to all Willamette Valley wineries, southern Oregon is about a two-hour drive, and the coast (Newport) is over the hill an hour away. Historic Albany is equally well placed, though it doesn't have quite the same appeal. It does have nearly every style of Victorian home, some dating to the 1850s. A few miles west of Corvallis is Philomath, a onetime timber town turned bedroom community surrounded by wineries.

Wineries

in the Albany/Corvallis Area

Wineries here are places where friends like to meet and newcomers are readily welcomed into laid-back atmospheres. These are vintners who eschewed the rush of the north and prefer a farm-centric region.

ALBANY

Springhill Cellars (2920 NW Scenic Drive; 541-928-1009). *Tasting room:* Sat. & Sun. 1–5, May–Nov. *Fee:* Complimentary. *Owners:* Mike & Karen McLain. *Winemaker:* Mike McLain. *Wines:* Pinot gris, Pinot noir, rosé. *Cases:* 1,000. The McLains have been producing award-winning wines at their small family estate vineyard for years. Their Fedeweisser Festival, a German tradition, features young, still-fermenting Riesling for consumption (by the pitcher). The red and white barn is alive with music and dancing, German bratwurst, and *Zwiebelkuchen* (onion tart). Springhill's Pinot often earns high marks and is a frequent staff pick at local shops.

INDEPENDENCE

▲ Redgate Vineyard (8175 Buena Vista Road; 503-838-9883). *Tasting room:* Wed.–Sun. 11–5. *Fee:* $5. *Owner:* Steve Dunn. *Winemaker:* Steve Baron. *Wines:* Merlot, Pinot gris, Pinot noir, Syrah. *Cases:* Under 1,000. Steve Dunn thought working a vineyard and winery would be a fine way to ease into retirement. The easing part never came to fruition, thanks to the labor of love required to raise 2,400 vines on 6 acres, but the longtime home builder and carpenter isn't looking back. He and pal Steve Baron, a commodity manager for Hewlett-Packard for three decades, are in it for the long haul, producing Pinot gris and noir from their own grapes and sourcing Merlot and Syrah. Look for live music each Saturday in July.

MONMOUTH

▲ ✐ 🐾 ❖ Emerson Vineyards (11665 Airlie Road; 503-838-0944). *Tasting room:* Daily 12–5. *Fee:* $5. *Owners:* Tom & Jane Johns, Elliott & Jenny Johns. *Winemaker:* Elliott Johns. *Wines:* Chardonnay, Maréchal Foch, Pinot gris, Pinot noir, Syrah, Viognier, red blend. *Cases:* 3,500. Genuinely friendly and caring, Tom Johns is retired—on paper, anyway—from his day job as a biotech executive. He works days and nights keeping the vineyard, winery, and business duties in line. Son Elliott has a degree from OSU in fermentation science and did a stint at Elk Cove. At his family's winery, he crafts the wine and experiments with such hybrids as Baco noir, Léon Millot, and Oberlin noir. Concerts on the grounds are an added bonus every Friday during the summer season.

▲ ✐ 🐾 Airlie Winery (15305 Dunn Forest Road; 503-838-6013). *Tasting room:* Sat. & Sun. 12–5, by chance and by appt. *Season:* Mar.–Dec. *Fee:* Complimentary (donations to Food Bank). *Owner:* Mary Olson. *Winemaker:* Elizabeth Clark. *Wines:* Chardonnay, Gewürztraminer, Maréchal Foch, Müller-Thurgau, Pinot gris, Pinot noir, Riesling, white blend, sparkling dessert. *Cases:* 8,000. Airlie embodies the essence of Oregon wineries: raw determination. Mary Olson long dreamed of owning a winery and went for it in 1996. Pooling her resources, she bought her 32 acres of heaven and hard work. Not one to rely on others, she quickly learned how to operate a John Deere, manage a vineyard, and run a winery. Suzy Gagné, her first winemaker, took the wines to award-winning levels. Elizabeth Clark carries on the tradition while adding her own imprint. The Pinot gris has been a *Wine & Spirits* Top 10 of the Year several times, and Dunn Forest Pinot is one of the best-priced "Oregundian" Pinots.

Homespun fun at Lūmos, just outside of Philomath John Baker

▲ ✐ 🐾 ❖ Lūmos (24000 Cardwell Hill Road; 541-929-3519). *Tasting room:* Holiday weekends, and by appt. *Fee:* $5. *Owners:* Dai Crisp & PK McCoy. *Winemaker:* Dai Crisp & Julia Cattrall. *Wines:* Gewürztraminer, Müller-Thurgau, Pinot gris, Pinot noir. *Cases:* 2,000. If you're lucky enough to be in this neck of the woods on a wine holiday weekend, plan to hang with Dai and PK. Their retreatlike cabin on a 100-acre family farm surrounding their Wren vineyard serves as tasting room. Friends gather, imbibe, converse, and linger, usually with local musicians playing. Dai, manager of the highly regarded Temperance Hill, has made the leap to his own label and hasn't looked back. With a country-style picnic area, goats, croquet, volleyball, and badminton, it's fun for kids of all ages.

Cardwell Hill Winery (24241 Cardwell Hill Road; 541-929-9463). *Tasting room:* Sat. & Sun. 12–5, and by appt. Mar.–Nov. *Fee:* $5. *Owners:* Dan & Nancy Chapel. *Winemaker:* Dan Chapel. *Wines:* Pinot gris, Pinot noir, rosé. *Cases:* 5,000. Sit and sip on the deck at vineyard level in a relaxed, classic Douglas fir–clad setting and reflect upon days gone by. The Chapels, California transplants, learned through a few hard knocks and bumps in the road what it takes to run with the big dogs. Dan loves to show off his estate facility, where everything happens on-site, including bottling and labeling. Speaking of showing off, Cardwell had a Pinot that made *Wine Spectator*'s 100 list—quite a coup for a small producer in the southern Willamette Valley.

Harris Bridge Vineyard (22937 Harris Road; 541-929-3053). *Tasting room:* Sat. & Sun. 12–5, May–Nov. *Fee:* $5–10. *Owners/Winemakers:* Nathan Warren & Amanda Sever. *Wines:* Dessert. *Cases:* 400. Nathan and Amy have filled a niche with their sensuous and scintillating dessert wines. The winery, vineyard, and farm near Wren is adjacent to a covered bridge over the Mary's River. Nathan is the visionary and writer of the short stories encapsulated and attached to the top of each elegant bottle; Amanda does the rest. Near the overflow parking you'll see a 300-year-old section of a Douglas fir; try counting those rings after tasting Harris's sweet treats.

The Harris Covered Bridge over the Mary's River is just outside the Harris Bridge Winery's front door. John Baker

PHILOMATH

Pheasant Court Winery & Wine Vault (1301 Main Street; 541-929-7715). *Tasting room:* Sat. & Sun. 12–6. *Fee:* Complimentary ($5/reserves). *Owners/Winemakers:* Charlie & Marcia Gilson. *Wines:* Chardonnay, Maréchal Foch, Merlot, Pinot gris, Pinot noir, Syrah, red blend, port, ice-style, dessert. *Cases:* 750. The Wine Vault, a century-old retrofitted bank building, serves as tasting room for Charlie and Marcia. They're quick to entertain with a friendly greeting, complimentary flight to contemplate, and reserve lineup (for a fee). The dynamic husband-and-wife team is hard working, but recently acquired help in the form of students interested in viticulture. Their wines are crowd-pleasers, especially the Foch. Pheasant Court also produces Mary's Peak wine—tasted and purchased only at the Vault.

Spindrift Cellars (810 Applegate Street; 541-929-6555). *Tasting room:* Fri.–Sun. 12–5, May–Nov. *Fee:* $4–6. *Owners/Winemakers:* Matt & Tabitha Compton. *Wines:* Gewürztraminer, Pinot blanc, Pinot gris, Pinot noir, rosé, red and white blends.

Cases: 3,500. The ambitious Comptons made the most of their city space by creating a splashy tasting room full of warmth inside a warehouse turned green winery. Their enviro-friendly philosophy extends to their bottle closure. Sensitive to the plight and low sustainability of cork trees, they chose the spendier path—screw caps. Out of the gate, Spindrift earned media attention from *Wine Spectator* and *Wine Enthusiast*, but prices remain reasonable.

CORVALLIS

Nuthatch Cellars (8792 NW Chaparral Drive; 541-754-8483). *Tasting room:* Holiday weekends, and by appt. *Fee:* $10. *Owners:* John Bacon & Jane Smith. *Winemaker:* John Bacon. *Wines:* Carménère, Malbec, Syrah, Tempranillo, red blend. *Cases:* 350. A nuthatch is a small passerine, or perching songbird, an appropriate name for the tiny winery perched on the edge of sweet success. It's also the avian friend with whom John and Jane share their country home. Although production is limited, there's nothing small about their red wines. Full-bodied reds with grapes from southern Oregon and Columbia Valley are blended with the help of many hands, barn-raising style. Hand-bottled wines are available in area shops and restaurants.

BELLFOUNTAIN

Tyee Wine Cellars (26335 Greenberry Road; 541-753-8754). *Tasting room:* Fri.–Mon, 12–5, Apr.–Dec. *Fee:* $5. *Owners:* David & Margy Buchanan, Merrilee Buchanan Benson. *Winemaker:* Merrilee Buchanan Benson. *Wines:* Chardonnay, Gewürztraminer, Pinot gris, Pinot noir. *Cases:* 1,500. You can learn a lot about a winery through its labels. Tyee, an Indian name for "chief," has Haida art symbols such as the raven, on its bottles. It's a tribute to those who came before and served as stewards of the land. The Buchanan Family Century Farm has been recognized for land-stewardship leadership by the Oregon Wildlife Society. A visit is similar to communing with nature, especially while walking the trail with a glass of Gewürztraminer.

SWEET HOME

Marks Ridge Winery (29255 Berlin Road; 541-367-3292). *Tasting room:* Thurs.–Sun. 12–5, and by appt. *Fee:* $5. *Owners:* Jay & Janet Westly. *Winemaker:* Jay Westly. *Wines:* Gewürztraminer, Pinot noir, Riesling. *Cases:* 1,000. Marks Ridge is definitely out of the way, but the Westlys make it work and worth your while. They purchased an established vineyard at 1,200 feet and took over nurturing planted vines. Then they enrolled in vineyard-management classes at Chemeketa while simultaneously pulling in fruit. Best known for their Gewürztraminer, Jay and Janet invite you to enjoy the gorgeous grounds or take in Friday night summer concerts.

Lodging

in the Albany/Corvallis Area

ALBANY

The Pfeiffer Cottage Inn (530 Ferry Street SW; 541-971-9557). Albany's blossoming historic district received a boost when Ray and Debbie Lusk bought the 1908 Charles Pfeiffer bungalow. Two rooms are named after prominent volcanoes in the Cascades—one, a small single room; the other, a two-bedroom suite. The inn is an ideal stop for bicyclists pedaling between Salem and Eugene. If you don't get your fill wine tasting, the Lusks open at least one bottle per evening for guests. Local, organic, and farmers' market goods are used in their delicious breakfasts. $$$

CORVALLIS

At Home in Oregon, Inc. (5060 SW Philomath Boulevard; 541-929-3059). If you want to make centrally located

Corvallis your base, talk to the Ohlen family. When they started 20 years ago as a B&B, guests didn't want to leave. One property led to another and now, with 20 unique accommodations, they'll find you "your own little cave"—whether it's a modern condo, a country cottage, or expansive executive home. The Ohlens believe in full disclosure and undersell their guest housing, preferring to see the "thrilled responses," Ruth says. $$

❖ 🐾 **Hanson Country Inn** (795 SW Hanson Street; 541-752-2919). Four guest rooms in an authentic country home (circa 1928) on the edge of town are filled with personal treasures and antiques belonging to owner Pat Covey. The inn is perfectly situated for quiet or romance, and it is within walking distance of Oregon State. A hearty country breakfast sets you up for a day of nearby wine imbibing. Choose between antique-adorned rooms with private bath, or a furnished two-bedroom cottage with a fully stocked kitchen. $$$

Harrison House B&B (2310 NW Harrison Boulevard; 541-752-6248 or 800-233-6248) Located near campus in the fraternity district, Allen Goodman and Hilarie Phelps's Harrison House has an Ivy League feel to it. Four rooms each have a private bath, or for a little extra privacy rent Hannah's Cottage. The couple is known for breakfast, which rotates between savory and sweet, and made to order. Book early if you're planning a stay during a busy OSU weekend. $$$

Dining

in the Albany/Corvallis Area

BUENA VISTA

Buena Vista House (11265 Riverview Street; 503-838-6364). You'll rarely find more customized culinary selections. Claudia finds her inspiration from her own garden as well as local farms and wineries. Hours are at her whimsy, too, though you can count on weekend breakfasts from 9 to 11 and single-seating suppers beginning at 6:30. Buena Vista rancheros and homemade biscuits and gravy are signature sunrisers. Continental breakfast is complimentary if you spend the night ($65) in one of the two comfortable upstairs rooms enhanced by views of the gardens. B/D $$

ALBANY

Clemenza's Italian American Café (236 First Avenue West; 541-926-3353). Although it doesn't list Oregon wines exclusively, this clever café has a northern Italy menu and welcoming style meant to emulate the bounty of nearby fields. Clemenza's motto: "In the simple tomato we trust." The name translates to "merciful," a definition of hospitality that in turn translates to "inclusive and warmly accepting." Don't forget a cannoli or chocolate hazelnut tart—especially delicious paired with a local Pinot. D Tues.–Sat. $$

Sybaris (442 First Avenue SW; 541-928-8157). Innovative, inspired, and indulgent cuisine that heightens your senses is the intent behind Matt and Janel Bennett's successful bistro. Their menu changes monthly with the crops and is a treat to read. Matt has been nominated more than once for a James Beard Award and was a semifinalist in 2011. His wine list is Northwest-centered, and thoughtfully conceived. The culinary duo has a strong commitment to community and is so well received they opened a second restaurant (Clemenza's). Check out their wine dinners, charitable events, and rotating marquee artists. D Tues.–Sat. $$$

CORVALLIS

Aqua Seafood (151 NW Monroe Avenue [Water Street Market]; 541-752-0262). Bringing island tastes to fresh seafood, Iain and Tonya Duncan have created a destination dining oasis with aloha spirit.

Located on "Restaurant Row" along the riverfront esplanade, Aqua has a gentle motif. Aquariums of pet tropical fish swim for your enjoyment while seemingly imploring, "Make up your mind!" Faves and raves are fish & *frites*, Kahlúa pork sliders, and ahi tartare. Not so hungry? Order the coconut- and lemongrass-infused clam chowder—Yum-a-lo-ha! D/HH Tues.–Sat. $$$

Big River Restaurant & Bar (101 NW Jackson Street; 541-757-0694). For many years, Big River was the go-to restaurant in a town that, until recently, offered little more than pizza and Mexican. It's fair to say it started the food scene in a university city that should have been more culinary-current. Nuevo Italian is served under a tall ceiling of exposed pipes and beams, on a concrete floor. It can get a tad noisy, but clambor aside, the pasta and pizza are well above average; the desserts, supreme; and the baked bread from a steam-injected oven, first-rate. Our advice: Share an appetizer, salad, or entrée, but order two or three desserts. L (Mon.–Fri.) D/HH (Mon.–Sat.) $$$

Cloud & Kellys Public House (126 SW First Street; 541-753-9900). Cloud Davidson turned his bistro-style Cloud 9 into an Irish pub in 2012. Filling a cuisine void, he serves fish-and-chips, corned beef and cabbage, and traditional Irish breakfasts of rice, beans, and mushrooms topped with eggs. The wines are about half local because, as Davidson puts it, "I like to be able to throw a rock and hit the winery from my restaurant." Cloud & Kellys gets going around 2 PM, when happy hour starts. L/D/HH $$–$$$

PHILOMATH

Gathering Together Farm (25159 Grange Hall Road; 541-929-4270). John Eveland and Sally Brewer, organic farmers since 1987, have expanded with their helping-hands crew to include farm-to-fork eating in a thrown-together dining room, once a vegetable-sorting area and loading dock. Great flavors are gently coaxed from organic produce and local natural meats by chef J. C. Mersmann. Roasted meats and thin-crust, wood-fired pizzas are baked in an earth oven. Get grab-and-go from the farm stand (Tues.–Fri. 9 AM–6 PM) stocked with seasonal produce, eggs, pastries, their signature potato doughnuts, and frozen organic, hormone-free meats. They also host quarterly wine dinners with local producers. They're open April to October. B (Sat.) L (Tues.–Fri.) D (Thurs. & Fri.) $$

To Do

in the Albany/Corvallis Area

Attractions

In Albany, the **Oregon Covered Bridge Festival** (541-752-8269) every August celebrates the eight bridges in the area with timber competitions, arts, crafts, and food booths. For a pleasant summer evening on a grassy riverfront, the **River Rhythms** (541-917-7772) concert series, at the confluence of the Willamette and Calapooia Rivers, lures nationally renowned bands to Albany's Monteith Riverpark every Thursday evening in July and August.

The **Northwest Art and Air Festival** (541-917-7772) fills the Albany skies with hot-air balloons and draws 40,000 people to Timber Linn Park each August. Albany also is justifiably proud of its two historic districts. Stop at the 1849 **Monteith House Museum** (518 Second Avenue SW, 541-967-8699) from June to September to see perhaps the most authentic example of Oregon's pioneer-era history. Two festivals not to miss in Corvallis are the annual **Da Vinci Days** (541-757-6363), an event for the science- and art-minded in July, and **Corvallis Fall Festival** (541-752-9655), full of regional artisan booths in Central Park.

In Corvallis, take in an **Oregon State Beavers** (541-737-4455) football game in the fall, or just wander the pastoral campus. The men's basketball coach in 2012–13 was Craig Robinson, President Obama's brother-in-law. For the moviegoer seeking the off-beat, try the **Darkside Theater** (215 SW Fourth Street, 541-752-4161 and its independent films in a casual setting. Philomath has the **Benton County Historical Museum** (1101 Main Street, 541-929-6230) displaying the area's culture and history.

Corvallis and Albany have **farmers' markets** (541-752-1510) from April to November, each offering home-grown goods from 9 to 1 every Saturday—at First and Jackson in Corvallis and at SW Ellsworth and Fourth Street in Albany. The Corvallis market also opens from 3 to 7 every Wednesday at Second and B Streets and at the **Benton County Fairgrounds** (110 SW 53rd Street, 541-752-1510) from 8 to 1 every Wednesday from April to November.

Recreation

Corvallis-ites love hiking, biking, and paddling. The **McDonald-Dunn Research Forest** (541-737-4452) on the northwest edge of town is a favorite for hikers and mountain bikers. Walkers might enjoy the easy trails in the **William L. Finley National Wildlife Refuge** (503-588-2701) about 10 miles south of Corvallis off OR 99W.

Between them, Corvallis and Albany have three full-size public golf courses: Oregon State University's home 18 holes at **Trysting Tree** (34028 NE Electric Road, Corvallis, 541-752-3332), the family-oriented nine-hole **Marysville** (2020 SW Allen, Corvallis, 541-753-3421) and tree-lined **Golf Club of Oregon** (905 NW Springhill Drive, Albany 541-928-8338). **Golf City Par-3** (2115 NE Highway 20, Corvallis, 541-753-6213) is a fun little nine-hole chip-and-putt course.

Fishing is another favored pastime, though most ignore the placid Willamette and head for the salmon runs on the nearby Alsea, Santiam, and Siletz Rivers. Foster and Green Peter Reservoirs east of Albany in the Cascade foothills offer boating, swimming, and fishing. Skiing enthusiasts appreciate the intimate **Hoodoo Ski Bowl** (541-822-3799) on US 20 in the Cascades, about an hour east of Albany.

Wine Shopping

Jean Yates started **Avalon** (201 SW Second Street, Corvallis, 541-752-7418) as a small gourmet food gift shop before she saw the way to wine retail. The next step was to build her online store, tagged one of the "10 Best Online Wine Shops" by *Food & Wine*. Shelves are filled with "cherry-picked" selections from hard-to-find Oregon boutique producers. **Wineopolis** (151 NW Monroe Avenue, Corvallis, 541-738-1600) is a snappy bottle shop owned by self-taught wine geek Jerry Larson. You're bound to take home new knowledge with your purchase. Complimentary tastings are Saturdays, sometimes Sundays. Corvallis's **First Alternative Cooperative**'s two locations (2855 NW Grant Avenue/541-452-3115 and 1007 SE Third Street/541-753-3115) have regular samplings and solid selections of Oregon wines. **Corvallis Brewing Supply** (119 SW Fourth Street, 541-758-1674) is more into suds, but sells wine and conducts regular tastings.

More Information

Corvallis Chamber of Commerce, 541-757-1505, www.corvallischamber.com, 420 NW Second Street

Philomath Area Chamber of Commerce, 541-929-2454, www.pioneer.net, 2395 Main Street

Albany Area Chamber of Commerce, 541-926-1517, www.albanychamber.com, 435 First Avenue NW

Benton County Wineries Association, www.bentoncountywineries.com

Corvallis Tourism, 541-757-1544 or 800-334-8118, www.visitcorvallis.com

EUGENE AREA

Situated at the confluence of the workmanlike Willamette and pristine McKenzie rivers, Eugene is the Berkeley or Madison of the Pacific Northwest, with sandal-clad students in dreadlocks and refugees from the '60s protesting anything and everything. Eugene seemingly has natural foods on every corner, its Saturday Market was the first of its kind in America, and still has an all-volunteer food-buying club. This older Eugene is epitomized by the annual Oregon Country Fair in nearby Veneta, an unvarnished and uninhibited display of arts, crafts, music, and bodies.

The state's second largest city (156,000), Eugene is an active place that has always had a high opinion of itself while being self-deprecating. The Emerald City calls itself the "World's Greatest City of the Arts and Outdoors." At times it's been dubbed, with justification, both "Track Town USA" and "Gymnastics Capital of the World." Yet the town's denizens also freely admit Eugene is the planet's allergy capital, and an exasperated mayor once called it the "Anarchist Capital of the United States."

Wineries
in the Eugene Area

The wine scene around Eugene is a microcosm of the city itself. It has the rich and opulent, husband-and-wife duos, and the downright exotic and eclectic. The first vineyard in the area was planted on Silvan Ridge in 1979 in a low-elevation soil called Bellpine.

Reflecting these extremes, King Estate has all the aura of royalty the name implies, and Territorial Vineyards and Wine Company's tasting room is a warehouse on a busy city street in a neighborhood known for tie-dye and dreadlocks. Whatever your preference, be prepared for a taste of the unusual and plenty of hospitality. During summers, wineries in and around Eugene stay open as late as 9 PM.

MONROE

▲ 🧪 🐾 **Benton-Lane Winery** (23924 Territorial Highway; 541-847-5792). *Tasting room:* Daily 12–5. *Fee:* $7. *Owners:* Steve & Carol Girard. *Winemakers:* Steve Girard & Chris Mazepink. *Wines:* Chardonnay, Pinot blanc, Pinot gris, Pinot noir, rosé. *Cases:* 30,000. While making Cabernet in California, the lure of Pinot called to Steve Girard. He found his ideal place: a sheep farm in the valley. A wine pioneer in the southern Willamette Valley, Girard is proud of his LIVE certification. Although initially not a believer, using sustainable farming practices he noticed dramatic improvements in his vines and wines. Benton-Lane wines have

Steve Girard's biodynamic vineyard at Benton-Lane is full of surprises. John Baker

since made top-100 lists more than once. Its quintessential bucolic setting makes this a gotta-stop spot in the southern Willamette Valley.

JUNCTION CITY

Brigadoon Wine Co. (25166 Ferguson Road; 541-998-2600). *Tasting room:* Wed.–Sun. 12–5, Apr.–Dec. *Fee:* $5. *Owners:* Chris & Sheree Shown. *Winemaker:* Matt Shown. *Wines:* Pinot blanc, Pinot noir, Riesling. *Cases:* 1,500. It was son Matt who came up with the idea of making wine from the family's 15-acre vineyard. All that the OSU horticulture graduate had to do was learn how. Matt spent three years traveling back and forth from Oregon to New Zealand, took classes at Chemeketa Community College, and helped open the family business with an eye on limiting production to about 2,000 cases annually. So far, so good.

Pfeiffer Winery (25040 Jaeg Road; 541-998-2828). *Tasting room:* Sun.–Thurs. 11–5, Fri. & Sat. 11–9. *Fee:* $10–20 (includes Riedel glass). *Owners:* Robin & Danuta Pfeiffer. *Winemaker:* Robin Pfeiffer. *Wines:* Chardonnay, Merlot, Muscat, Pinot gris, Pinot noir, Viognier, port, red blend, white blends. *Cases:* 1,200. Tunneling into this tasting room feels like entering a catacomb, candle-lit altars enhancing the sensation. The Pfeiffers have one of the state's few solar-powered wineries, with panels that supply the entire property. Their lovely picnic grounds have expanded to include water gardens, ponds, streams, and fountains, all accentuated by LED colored lights at night. In the tasting room you'll be treated to a rave-worthy Gorgonzola torte so popular it's available for take-home. Friday through Sunday nights enjoy food cart specials such as smoked chicken sliders or fish tacos. Pfeiffer wines are only available in the tasting room.

Vinophiles enjoy sipping and sunshine on the lawn at Pfeiffer Vineyards near Eugene.

Courtesy Pfeiffer Vineyards

High Pass Winery (24757 Lavell Road; 541-998-1447). *Tasting room:* Fri.–Sun. 12–5, May–Nov. *Fee:* Complimentary. *Owner/Winemaker:* Dieter Boehm. *Wines:* Huxelrebe, Pinot gris, Pinot noir, Riesling, Sauvignon blanc, rosé, dessert. *Cases:* 2,000. Dieter Boehm's heritage is German, so it makes sense that he's known for his Germanic-style varietals—and that his Pinot is *sehr gut.* Another rarity: His wines are mostly priced at $20 or less—$30–35 for vineyard designates. Boehm alternates vintages between two dessert wines, made with Huxelrebe or Scheurebe grapes. He makes just enough wine to supply local retail markets and his tasting room—and that's how he likes it.

CHESHIRE

RainSong Vineyard (92989 Templeton Road; 541-998-1786). *Tasting room:* Holiday weekends, and by appt. *Fee:* Complimentary. *Owners:* Mike & Merry Fix. *Winemakers:* Mike Fix & Marc Hall. *Wines:* Chardonnay, Pinot meunier, Pinot noir, rosé, sparkling. *Cases:* 1,500. Let's say a group of your closest friends, 30 or so, want to buy a barrel of wine and bottle it yourselves—even affix your own clever label. For $1,500 a barrel (about $5 a bottle) or $2,500 for an estate barrel ($8.60 a bottle), RainSong will make it happen. It's a popular program, with 90 percent of the vineyard's wines sold this way, and most weekends are spent catering to the hands-on crowd.

With remaining barrels the Fix family makes small lots of the listed wines. RainSong is one of the state's few wineries to grow and bottle Pinot meunier ("MOO-nee-ay"), a cousin of Pinot noir.

ELMIRA

▲ ✐ ❖ **LaVelle Vineyards** (89697 Sheffler Road; 541-935-9406). *Tasting room:* Daily 12–5. *Fee:* Complimentary. *Owners:* Doug & Matthew LaVelle. *Winemaker:* Matthew LaVelle. *Wines:* Cabernet sauvignon, Chardonnay, Gamay noir, Gewürztraminer, Merlot, Pinot gris, Pinot noir, Riesling, Syrah, Viognier, rosé. *Cases:* 10,000. Originally LaVelle did custom crushing for clients. Today, it's busy enough just making its own. Stellar estate wines earn their share of awards, but LaVelle's Riesling, both dry and sweet, rises above. BYOP (bring your own picnic) and hike to the deck overlooking the vineyards and beyond. LaVelle's second tasting room is on the second floor of the Fifth Street Market next to Marché Restaurant (541-338-9875, Mon.–Sat. 11–9 and Sun. 11–6) in downtown Eugene.

VENETA

▲ 🍴 ✐ 🐾 ❖ **Domaine Meriwether** (88324 Vineyard Lane; 541-935-9711). *Tasting room:* Daily 11–5, later on Fridays. *Fee:* Complimentary. *Owner:* Ed "Buzz" Kawders. *Winemaker:* Ray Walsh. *Wines:* Pinot gris, Pinot meunier, Pinot noir, rosé, sparkling, dessert, ice-style. *Cases:* 1,000. "O! The Joy!"—of bubbles, that is. Explorer William Clark's famous Oregon utterance seems fitting at Meriwether, one of few wineries in these parts that makes sparkling (*méthode champenoise*) wines. Now Ray Walsh (King Estate) is bringing the label to even higher levels. After many years at Carlton Winemaker Studios, Buzz Kawders is enjoying a permanent home, improving the grounds and renovating the facilities to be more upscale, yet informal and friendly. Taste among the barrels, at the bar, or at one of the cute bistro tables. Friday late hours make for good date nights.

▲ 🍴 ✐ 🐾 **Sarver Winery** (25600 Mayola Lane; 541-935-2979). *Tasting room:* Daily 12–6 (Fri.–Sun. winter). *Fee:* $5. *Owners:* Chris & Erin Sarver. *Winemaker:* Chris Sarver. *Wines:* Gewürztraminer, Pinot gris, Pinot noir, Petite sirah, Riesling, Syrah, rosé, red blend, dessert. *Cases:* 2,000. Sarver is a laid-back, new winery with exceptional views of the Cascade Range. Chris and Erin found Michigan a difficult place to grow vinifera, so they started looking for the perfect place in Oregon and fell in love with the established Elhanan Vineyard. They began making wine in 2011 and converted a woodshed into their tasting room. Sarver made a splash with its Friday Night Fetes, serving gourmet pizzas or steak Caesar salad. About 10 people fit in the tasting room, but 100 to 150 squeeze together for live music in the summer.

EUGENE AREA

▲ 🍴 🎁 ✐ 🐾 ❖ **Sweet Cheeks Winery** (27007 Briggs Hill Road; 541-349-9463). *Tasting room:* Daily 12–6. *Fee:* Complimentary. *Owner:* Daniel Smith. *Winemaker:* Mark Nicholl. *Wines:* Chardonnay, Pinot gris, Pinot noir, Riesling, Syrah, Tempranillo, red blends, sparkling. *Cases:* 15,000. Dan Smith is a resourceful guy. The longtime grape grower (since 1978) rescued a doomed building in Junction City, dragged it home, and reassembled it for his winery. He only needed a winemaker. Fond of Australian wines, he looked Down Under for his master and came up with ambitious Mark Nicholl. Now for what to call it. Hmmm. Seems the road between the rounded vineyard hills presents itself as the name implies, at least in Dan's mind. Sumptuous views from the patio create a spectacular setting. Enjoy Friday twilight tastings or other fun events such as the October Masquerade Ball.

Silvan Ridge was one of the first wineries near Eugene. Courtesy Silvan Ridge Vineyards

Silvan Ridge Winery (27012 Briggs Hill Road; 541-345-1945). *Tasting room:* Daily 12–5. *Fee:* Complimentary ($2/taste reserve wines). *Owner:* Liz Chambers. *Winemakers:* Jonathan Oberlander & Juan-Pablo Valot. *Wines:* Cabernet sauvignon, Chardonnay, Malbec, Merlot, Muscat, Pinot gris, Pinot noir, Syrah, Viognier, rosé, red blend, dessert. *Cases:* 30,000. Silvan Ridge has been around since 1979, making it the oldest winery in Lane County. Dotted by rhododendrons and mature landscaping that give a European feel, it's the kind of place you feel special just for visiting. Bring your own lunch or snacks for various picnic settings: a fireside nook, a large room with small tables, and a vineyard-level patio with terraced gardens. Movie nights are popular in the summer. From June to December, Silvan Ridge serves pizza and cheese plates.

❖ **Noble Estate** (29210 Gimpl Hill Road; 541-338-3007). *Tasting room:* Daily 12–5. *Fee:* $5. *Owners:* Mark & Marie Jurasevich. *Winemaker:* Mark Jurasevich. *Wines:* Cabernet sauvignon, Chardonnay, Merlot, Muscat, Pinot gris, Pinot noir, Riesling, Syrah, rosé, sparkling, dessert. *Cases:* 2,000. Mark may be the winemaker, but Marie is in charge of such important matters as "capturing the sun" in the vineyard. The lion's share of the work at this intimate winery is done by the couple—growing, picking, destemming, even bottling and labeling so that they can ensure the utmost quality. The usually not-too-crowded tasting room emits a relaxing aura. A picnic area is built around a blue-tiled, Mediterranean-style soaking pool complete with pergola.

❖ **Territorial Vineyards & Wine Company** (907 West Third Avenue; 541-684-9463). *Tasting room:* Thurs.–Sat. 5–9 (or later). *Fee:* $7. *Owners:* Alan & April Mitchell, Jeff Wilson & Victoria Charles. *Winemaker:* John Jarboe. *Wines:* Chardonnay, Pinot gris, Pinot noir, Riesling, rosé. *Cases:* 5,000. Centered in the eclectic Whiteaker neighborhood, and dressed in warm colors, Territorial Wine Bar is city-funk meets Burgundy. Tradition at Territorial is live music every Thursday with free munchies. According to Lisa, the minister of hospitality, a smashing good time is the Whitaker block party the first Saturday in August, when up to 10,000 people pass by the Winery Stage. We're

Cycle Wine Country—King of The Hills

Description: Test your quads early on a ride through the Douglas fir hill country southwest and south of Eugene. The full day ride is full of twists and turns, particularly on Briggs Hill Road en route to Silvan Ridge Winery. Check out the country McCulloch Cemetery on the way to Sweet Cheeks Winery. Territorial Road is a rolling straight shot to King Estate, Oregon's largest producer, and Chateau Lorane, both worth lengthy rest stops. The little community of Lorane is quintessential Oregon. After Chateau Lorane, you'll head east on winding Cottage Grove–Lorane Road through more Coast Range fir forest before reaching more level countryside at Cottage Grove and Saginaw. Save your strength for the serpentine muscle twister en route back to Eugene. Give yourself a good part of a day to complete this one or consider an overnight.

Wineries: Silvan Ridge, Sweet Cheeks, King Estate, Chateau Lorane, Iris, Saginaw

Miles: 65

Elevation gain: 2,516

Start/Finish: Amazon City Park, Eugene

- Start south on Willamette Street, then turn west on Crest Drive and continue straight on Lorane Highway. Go west on Spencer Creek Road and south on Briggs Hill Road. Winery stops: Silvan Ridge Winery and Sweet Cheeks Winery.
- Proceed,south on Territorial Highway. Winery stop: King Estate.
- Head west on Lorane West Road. Winery stop: Chateau Lorane.
- Return east on Lorane West Road and continue east on Cottage Grove–Lorane Road and then on East Main Street and East Whiteaker Avenue. Turn north on Thornton Lane, then east on Row River Cutoff Road and north on Palmer Road. Winery stop: Iris Vineyards.
- Return south on Palmer Road, then turn east on Row River Cutoff Road, north on Sears Road, west on East Saginaw Road, and north on Delight Valley School Road. Winery stop: Saginaw Vineyard.
- Return south on Delight Valley Road and east on East Saginaw Road, then go north on Sears Road, west on East Cloverdale Road, straight on Oregon Avenue, north on OR 99, west on Dillard Road, straight on East Amazon Drive, and straight on Hilyard Street back to Amazon City Park.

fond of all Territorial's estate wines, but the rosé is a fave. Its first release was served at a James Beard dinner—not a bad intro.

LORANE

▲ 🎁 🍴 ✐ ❖ **King Estate** (80854 Territorial Road; 541-942-9874). *Tasting room:* Daily 11–9. *Fee:* Complimentary ($5/6 estate wines). *Owners:* King family. *Winemaker:* Jeff Kandarian. *Wines:* Cabernet sauvignon, Chardonnay, Pinot gris, Pinot noir, Riesling, Syrah, rosé, dessert. *Cases:* 200,000. A hillside estate fit for a king is owned by a family of Kings. The late Ed King Jr., founder of King Radio, and his wife, Caroline, wanted to grow organic hay for a stable of horses. Their son, Ed King III, lived in Oregon and owned two small vineyards. After buying their 1,033-acre ranch in the Lorane Valley, they couldn't help but notice the quality soil, hillside exposure, and neighbor who grew wine grapes. The estate vineyard now grows 470 acres of organic grapes. An additional

Visitors enjoy a sunny day on the patio at King Estate. Courtesy King Estate Winery

45 acres are orchards, organic vegetables, flower, and herb gardens that supply minutes-old ingredients for the restaurant. Reservations recommended for dining (541-685-5819).

▲ ✐ ❖ **Chateau Lorane** (27415 Siuslaw River Road; 541-942-8028). *Tasting room:* Daily 12–5, May–Sept.; Sat. & Sun., Oct.–Apr. *Fee:* $2. *Owners:* Linde & Sharon Kester. *Winemaker:* Dave Gruber. *Wines:* Baco noir, Cabernet sauvignon, Chardonnay, Gamay noir, Gewürztraminer, Huxelrebe, Malbec, Maréchal Foch, Merlot, Melon de Bourgogne, Petite sirah, Pinot gris, Pinot noir, Sauvignon blanc, Syrah, Tempranillo, Viognier, Zinfandel, dessert, fruit. *Cases:* 5,000. Linde Kester never met a grape he didn't like—or couldn't ferment into wine. In fact, Chateau Lorane might lead the state in types of wine, specializing in small lots of the unusual. Output ranges from the traditional to fruit wines. New to the winery, but not to winemaking, is Dave Gruber, a willing accomplice. Chateau Lorane has picture-perfect grounds, so plan to sip awhile.

COTTAGE GROVE

▲ 🎁 ✐ **Saginaw Vineyard** (80247 Delight Valley Road; 541-942-1364). *Tasting room:* Daily 11–5. *Fee:* Complimentary. *Owners:* Scott & Cheryl Byler. *Winemaker:* Scott Byler. *Wines:* Chardonnay, Maréchal Foch, Müller-Thurgau, Pinot gris, Pinot noir, Riesling, rosé, fruit. *Cases:* 1,750. Saginaw's century-old barn serves as the tasting room and center of authentic country ambience, with an assist from pastured sheep. Scott and Cheryl provide the homespun hospitality. Their Maréchal Foch and rosé of Pinot noir typically sell out. The Bylers also have a following for their fruit wines, including one made from blueberries grown on the farm. They enjoy hosting the different personalities that come through their doors.

Iris Vineyards (195 Palmer Avenue; 541-942-5993). *Tasting room:* Mon.–Sat. 11–4, and by appt. *Fee:* $3 (includes wineglass). *Owner:* Pamela Frye & Richard Boyles. *Winemaker:* Aaron Lieberman. *Wines:* Chardonnay, Pinot gris, Pinot noir. *Cases:* 8,000. Iris Vineyards—formerly Iris Hill—has a fresh, hip look and label. Iris Hill once had its wine custom crushed, but when that proved too costly the owners bought new digs in Cottage Grove. Now it's simply Iris, with an eye-catching label—an eye followed by the letters *ris*. The wines get attention, especially the Pinot, and can be sampled in the newly fashioned tasting room.

Lodging

in the Eugene Area

EUGENE

🍴 🍸 ❖ ♿ **Excelsior Inn & Lounge** (754 East 13th Avenue; 541-342-6963). Old World ambience and European touches in 14 rooms named for classical composers—Beethoven, Bach, and Brahms, to name a few—give the Excelsior its flair. You might stay for the restaurant, which is committed to the slow-food movement and specializes in Italian cuisine with Northwest influence. The organic fruits vegetables, eggs from free-range hens, and even the flowers come from Maurizio Paparo's farm, a CSA in rural Dexter, about 30 minutes south. You'll be glad to know breakfast is included. $$$

🍴 🍸 ❖ ♿ 🐾 **Hilton Eugene & Conference Center** (66 East Sixth Avenue; 541-342-2000 or 800-937-6660). The Hilton has long been a bellwether of Eugene's cityscape, and though there's competition for high-end lodging, it remains a player. One advantage is SHARE Wine Lounge, which spotlights Willamette Valley Pinot noir and Pinot gris, and Skinner's Restaurant, which sources local meat, poultry, and seafood. Along with standard guest rooms, there are nine junior suites. The Hilton is adjacent to the Hult Center for the Performing Arts and a short walk to prime shopping and dining. $$$

🍴 🍸 ♿ 🐾 **Inn at the 5th** (205 East Sixth Avenue; 541-743-4099 or 855-446-6285). Eugene waited three decades for a new downtown hotel, and the patient city received luxury and intimacy wrapped into a neat little boutique package. The visionary 70-room inn was hatched by Brian Obie after a visit to the Inn at the Market at Seattle's famous Pike Place. For the Inn at the 5th, the devil is in such clever details as a "butler closet" for room service, preset room temps based on request, refrigerators stocked with your selections, and much, much, more. Adjacent to Marché and attached to LaVelle's tasting room/wine bar, there's no need to travel. Just valet park and stroll. $$$$

🍴 🍸 ♿ 🐾 **Valley River Inn** (1000 Valley River Way; 541-743-1000). Valley River Inn asks you to "re-imagine" what it has to offer, and it lives up to the hype. Its 245 rooms and 12 suites have been given a facelift befitting the Northwest and the iconic setting. Balconies overlooking a lazy stretch of the Willamette River extend your space, while the earthy interior colors bring the outdoors in. Sensitive to location, the inn also provides allergen-free rooms. On-site is the RiverWalk Bakery for morning treats and specialty desserts, as well as SweetWaters, a top-rated restaurant. $$$$

SPRINGFIELD

♿ 🐾 **McKenzie Orchards Bed & Breakfast** (34694 McKenzie View Drive; 541-515-8153). Seclusion and serenity with close-in proximity are the prime features of Karen Reid's B&B along the banks of the McKenzie River. Five substantial rooms, all with river views, are named for prominent watercourses. They're spread out among three floors, topping out with the Sahalie Falls room. After a day of touring, wine down with hors d'oeuvres paired with southern Willamette Valley vino. $$$

Dining

in the Eugene Area

EUGENE

b² Wine Bar (2794 Shadow View Drive; 541-505-8909). *B*'s run rampant in the Beihl family. Founder Bruce Beihl, former wife Bettina, and brother Brad formed Eugene Wine Cellars. Upon Brad's death in 2007, sister Beverly, a retired teacher with plenty of work left in her, joined the team. Together they opened b squared—or b². The metro-chic warehouse environs aren't good for acoustics or conversation, but the tapas, dinners, and wine atone. b[2] serves as tasting room for Eugene Wine Cellars (255 Madison Street), which produces around 10,000 cases annually. L/D/HH/LN $$–$$$

Marché (296 East Fifth Avenue; 541-342-3612). Locally raised and gathered foods are the mantra at Marché. Most ingredients are free-range, organic, or sustainable. As the name implies, there's a French tint, and if you sit outside, you'll be surrounded by herb gardens. Owner Stephanie Pearl Kimmel has a wine pedigree—she wrote both the *King Estate Pinot Gris Cookbook* and *Pinot Noir Cookbook*. A bar menu is available at any time, making it a foodie and wine lover's urban paradise and respite from a day of heavy touring. B/L/D/LN $$

Oregon Electric Station (27 East Fifth Avenue; 541-485-4444). Billed as Eugene's finest continental dining, the Station is more predictable than ingenious, a quintessential steak-and-seafood kind of place. Meals have been well prepared under executive chef Tom Smith's watchful eye for more than 20 years. Slide your fork and knife into the choice prime rib eye, crab and rock shrimp cakes, or legendary seafood fettuccine. As the name implies, the restaurant's vintage brick building was once an electric train power station. Some 250-plus wines are cellared in a train car and all of the Pinot noir and gris on board is from Oregon. L (Mon.–Fri.) D/HH $$$–$$$$

Ox & Fin (105 Oakway Center; 541-302-3000). The owners of the former Osteria Sfizio decided to change the name and beef up the menu in the summer of 2012. Literally. Ox & Fin is retaining hints of its Italian roots, but has evolved into a steakhouse that focuses on sustainable and seasonal ingredients. It isn't just the menu that's more meaty, though. The wine list has expanded, too, emphasizing Oregon, Washington, and some other states as well. L (Mon.–Sat.) D/HH $$–$$$

VENETA

Our Daily Bread Restaurant (88170 Territorial Road; 541-935-4921). You might think of eating and sipping as a holy experience after dining at Our Daily Bread, housed in a renovated country church. The menu is heavy Pacific Northwest—Pacific halibut, ocean-caught salmon, oysters, and shrimp, along with organic locally raised beef. Five separate sections afford privacy to small clusters or groups. We confess, we partake in the wine service, exclusively produced in Oregon. B/L/D (Wed.–Sun.) BR (Sun.) $$

To Do

in the Eugene Area

Attractions

Once a bastion of alternative-lifestyle folks, the **Oregon Country Fair** (541-343-4298) in Veneta every July now draws people of all stripes and has been a local staple for 40 years. **University of Oregon** (541-346-4461) football games are an autumn spectacle as well; get your tickets early. Learn how the Ducks' empire all began, as well as how Eugene became known as Track Town USA, at the **Nike Store and Museum** (135 Oakway Road, 541-686-4131).

The **Lane County Historical Museum** (740 West 13th Avenue, 541-682-4242) traces the state's roots to the first arrivals on the Oregon Trail. If you want to dig deeper into regional history, visit the **University of Oregon Museum of Natural and Cultural History** (1680 East 15th Avenue, 541-346-3024), which has a 9,000-year-old pair of sandals. Art aficionados will appreciate the **Jordan Schnitzer Museum of Art** (541-346-3027), a collection of more than 12,500 primarily Pacific Northwest and Asian pieces. The **Oregon Air and Space Museum** (90773 Boeing Drive, 541-461-1101) near the airport has a remarkable collection of military fighter jets.

For the flora-minded, **Owen Rose Garden** along the Willamette River has more than 4,500 varieties and a 150-year-old black cherry tree. Lane County is renowned for its 20 covered bridges, more than in any county west of the Mississippi. A major event each summer is the **Oregon Bach Festival** (541-457-1486), which brings more than 40 concerts to the downtown Hult Center and the Beall Concert Hall. In Cottage Grove, the **Bohemia Gold Mining Museum** (737 Main Street, 541-942-5022) has a noteworthy collection of old mining equipment and photographs.

Shoppers will quickly discover there's no **Saturday Market** (541-686-8885) quite like Lane County's, located in the downtown Eugene Park Blocks. Open Saturdays from April to November, the diverse and bustling collection of about 150 booths is more celebration than market. The **Fifth Street Public Market** (541-484-0383, 296 East Fifth Street) is a place to shop, cruise on foot, and people-watch in a historic part of town. And **Sundance Natural Foods** (748 East 24th Avenue, 541-343-9142), affiliated with nearby Sundance Wine Cellars, has been offering organic, local, and wildcrafted foods at the same site since 1971; also at the store is an all-vegetarian and mostly vegan deli.

Recreation

Eugene might get an argument when it proclaims itself the Outdoor Capital of the World, but there's no question it's ideally suited for active folks. The **Adidas Amazon Running Trail** is a well-marked wood-chip course where you could easily share turf with a world-class distance runner doing interval training. Eugene is rather modest about its bicycling opportunities—it merely rates among the top 10 nationally in this category. Mountain biking trails crisscross the hills in three directions and road cyclists will find miles of lonely pavement.

When not in running shoes, locals can be found on the water. The crystal-clear and cold McKenzie River is home to exhilarating whitewater rafting and trout fishing. A more placid experience can be had on Fern Ridge Reservoir, 15 miles west of Eugene, the best place for sailing, boarding, and other boating thanks to reliable northerly winds.

Skiers go for the credible powder at **Willamette Pass Resort** (541-393-1436), about 70 miles southeast of Eugene on OR 58. One of the best mountain biking and hiking experiences anywhere is on the **McKenzie River National Recreation Trail**. Its 26 miles hug the river and its upper reaches are a challenge for even the best fat-tire riders. If you like it hot, try a soothing soak in one of the many hot springs in the Cascades. After a ride or a hike, soothe sore muscles in **Belknap Hot Springs** (541-822-3512), with two hot pools, camping, comfortable lodging, and serene gardens along the banks of the McKenzie, about 60 miles east of Eugene on OR 126.

Wine Shopping

Oenophiles can get their regional wine needs met at **Sundance Wine Cellars** (2441 Hilyard Street, 541-687-9463), which claims to have the world's largest collection of Pinot noirs. Sundance has themed tastings from 5 to 7 PM every Friday and Saturday. **The Broadway Wine Merchants** (17 Oakway Center, 541-685-0790) emphasizes Oregon and Washington vino, though you'll find outsiders, too. Complimentary wines are poured from 5 to 7 PM every Friday.

More Information

Eugene Chamber of Commerce, 541-484-1314, www.eugenechamber.com, 1401 Willamette Street

Eugene Visitor and Convention Bureau, 541-484-5307 or 800-547-5445, www.travellanecounty.org, 115 West Eighth, Suite 190

Springfield Chamber of Commerce, 541-746-1651, www.springfield-chamber.org, 101 South A Street

Eugene, Cascades and Coast Travel Center, 541-484-5307, www.travellanecounty.org, 3312 Gateway Street, Springfield

Wineries of Lane County, www.wineriesoflanecounty.com

Heart of Willamette Wineries, www.heartofwillamette.com

South Willamette Wineries Association, www.southwillamettewineries.com/wineries

Umpqua Region

LAND OF THE 100 VALLEYS

FEW PLACES BETTER EPITOMIZE Oregon's evolution than the wooded valleys where the North and South Umpqua Rivers join for their serpentine 70-mile roll through the Coast Range to the sea. The "100 Valleys of the Umpqua," once prime timber country, has long bred bruising football players and leathery men as tough as their hickory shirts. Sawmills hummed by day, the taverns of Roseburg, Myrtle Creek, and Yoncalla rumbled by night, and Roseburg was mainly an I-5 refueling stop between Portland and California.

Today, the sawmills are quieter, and steep hills and lush valleys covered in fir, sugar pine, and Pacific madrone are also leafing out in a wide range of grapevines. It's become a way Douglas County's one-sawhorse towns create economic diversification. There are two AVAs, and a third, the Elkton Oregon AVA, was set to come online in 2013.

GETTING HERE AND AROUND

Roseburg doesn't have a commercial airport, so I-5 is the way to arrive in this region. As you may already know, wine touring requires back roads. The Umpqua and Red Hill Douglas County wineries around Roseburg are roughly in the I-5 corridor, but off the beaten path.

Start your tour by exiting I-5 onto OR 38 toward Elkton. To continue to Roseburg's wineries, double-back on OR 38 to Drain and head south on OR 99 to Yoncalla. Heading south toward Roseburg stop and visit the wineries in historic Oakland.

Wineries

in the Umpqua Region (Umpqua and Red Hill Douglas County AVAs)

The rolling hills and pastures are where the state's modern-day wine industry truly began a half-century ago, and yet it remains, as vintners wistfully and optimistically put it, "the last great

LEFT: Pinot grapes bask in summer warmth, southern Oregon style. Courtesy Bradley Vineyards

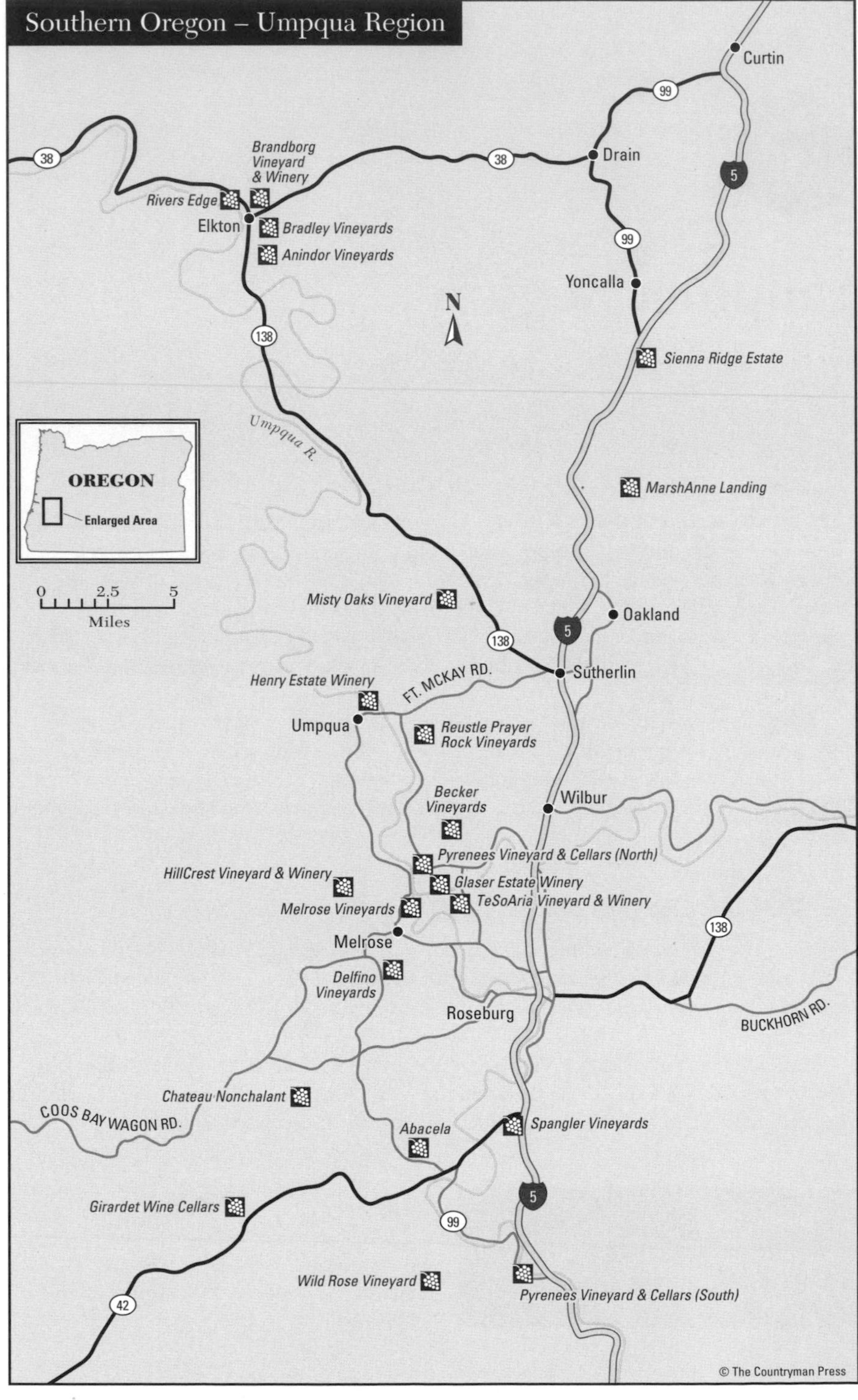
Southern Oregon – Umpqua Region
Curtin
99
38
Brandborg Vineyard & Winery
38
Drain
5
Rivers Edge
Elkton
Bradley Vineyards
Anindor Vineyards
99
Yoncalla
N
138
Sienna Ridge Estate
Umpqua R.
OREGON
Enlarged Area
MarshAnne Landing
0
2.5
5
Miles
Misty Oaks Vineyard
Oakland
5
138
Sutherlin
FT. MCKAY RD.
Henry Estate Winery
Umpqua
Reustle Prayer Rock Vineyards
Becker Vineyards
Wilbur
Pyrenees Vineyard & Cellars (North)
HillCrest Vineyard & Winery
Glaser Estate Winery
TeSoAria Vineyard & Winery
Melrose Vineyards
138
Melrose
Delfino Vineyards
Roseburg
BUCKHORN RD.
Chateau Nonchalant
COOS BAY WAGON RD.
Abacela
Spangler Vineyards
5
Girardet Wine Cellars
99
Wild Rose Vineyard
Pyrenees Vineyard & Cellars (South)
42
© The Countryman Press

undiscovered wine region in America." Oregon's first bonded winery, HillCrest, is here, founded by Richard Sommers. He was the one who planted 35 varieties of grapes northwest of Roseburg beginning in 1961, and later advised others on this crazy notion of growing grapes in the Beaver State. Sommers even produced the state's first Pinot noir at his fledgling winery northwest of Roseburg.

ELKTON

Anindor Vineyards (1171 Vintage Drive; 541-584-2637). *Tasting room:* Wed.–Sun. 11–5, May–Nov. *Fee:* Complimentary. *Owners:* Rod & Nina Pace. *Winemaker:* Rod Pace. *Wines:* Gewürztraminer, Pinot gris, Pinot noir. Riesling, dessert. *Cases:* 550. Anindor moved into the hills after a year in downtown Elkton, but the Paces like to think it's worth the trip for adventurous sorts. Its new tasting room is a 30-foot Mongolian yurt. Outside is a deck with pretty views of the vineyard. Rod's focus is on high-quality white wines, but his Pinot Noir has a twist—it ages longer than most.

Bradley Vineyards (1000 Azalea Drive; 541-584-2888). *Tasting room:* Wed.–Sun. 11–5, May–Nov., and by appt. *Second location:* Umpqua Valley Tasting Room in Jacksonville (with Rivers Edge). *Fee:* Complimentary. *Owners:* John & Bonnie Bradley. *Winemaker:* John Bradley. *Wines:* Baco noir, Pinot noir, Riesling, rosé, dessert. *Cases:* 500. "Down home and comfy" best describes the Bradleys' little farm and winery. Signage along the drive leads the way to their equipment shed turned tasting room. HERE ARE THE VINES and ROW AFTER ROW shows their fun-loving attitude. Small production and the fact that 95 percent of their grapes are sold means get their wines when you can. No need for a hard sell, especially for the Riesling and Baco noir. Bradley's sweet venue includes a yurt and sipping deck amid the forest.

Bradley Vineyards cover 25 acres near Elkton. Courtesy Bradley Vineyards

Brandborg Vineyard & Winery (345 First Street; 541-584-2870). *Tasting room:* Daily 11–5. *Fee:* $5. *Owners:* Terry & Sue Brandborg. *Winemaker:* Terry Brandborg. *Wines:* Gewürztraminer, Pinot blanc, Pinot gris, Pinot noir, Riesling, Syrah. *Cases:* 8,500. The light and airy tasting room in downtown Elkton has a U-shaped bar and a sprinkling of tables and chairs. Street-side patio seating, occasional live music, art for sale, and toys for kids are a few added amenities. Brandborg's tagline is "the coolest" because its vineyard is notably cooler than elsewhere in southern Oregon—hence its Pinot noir. Look for brick-oven pizza on weekends.

River's Edge (1395 River Drive; 541-584-2357). *Tasting room:* Daily 11–5; Wed.–Sun., Oct.–May. *Fee:* Complimentary. *Owners/Winemakers:* Michael & Vonnie Landt. *Wines:* Gewürztraminer, Pinot gris, Pinot noir. *Cases:* 3,400. Mike and Lavonne farm two of the northernmost vineyards in the Umpqua region, and the rest of the grapes come from within 3 miles of their place on the Umpqua River. Tastings are conducted in the production/storage building on a makeshift table supported by three used barrels. No need for anything fancier; the wines speak for themselves and to old ways.

OAKLAND

Sienna Ridge Estate (1876 John Long Road; 541-849-3300). *Tasting room:* Daily 12–6. *Fee:* $5–10. *Owner:* Wayne Hitchings. *Winemaker:* Terry Brandborg. *Wines:* Cabernet sauvignon, Gewürztraminer, Merlot, Pinot blanc, Pinot gris, Riesling, Pinot noir, dessert. *Cases:* 2,000. Sienna Ridge is so unusual it has its own AVA. The south-facing slopes and rich, volcanic Jory soils east of I-5 are unique to the area. The Red Hill Douglas County AVA is one of four in the entire country comprised of one vineyard—in this case the 300-plus-acre Red Hill Vineyard. The owners are proud of the designation and renovation of their 1906 outbuilding into a tasting room. Most notable among the wine lineup is their "ice vine," a dessert-style blend of Riesling and Gewürztraminer.

❖ **MarshAnne Landing** (381 Hogan Road; 541-459-7998). *Tasting room:* Wed.–Sun. 11–5, May–Sept.; Sat. & Sun., Oct.–Apr.; and by appt. *Fee:* $5. *Owners:* Greg Marsh Cramer & Frances Anne Cramer. *Winemaker:* Greg Cramer. *Wines:* Cabernet franc, Cabernet sauvignon, Chardonnay, Grenache, Merlot, Pinot noir, Syrah, Tempranillo, Viognier, rosé, red blends. *Cases:* 1,200. When you're off the beaten wine path, you need clever marketing. The UFO on an I- 5 billboard is MarshAnne Landing's first attempt to coax drivers to its hidden gem. In the tasting room, you'll be captivated by the setting, art exhibits, and wines. In the summer, you'll be amazed to find events that might include the Eugene Opera, jazz musicians, or an Elvis impersonator. "A cultural mecca in the wilderness," Fran Cramer calls it. When you say the name quickly, it sounds like . . . Martian. Hence, the Red Planet wine. The real story is the owners combined parts of their middle names.

❖ **Misty Oaks Vineyard** (1310 Misty Oaks Lane; 541-459-3558). *Tasting room:* Wed.–Sun. 11–5, Mar.–Dec., and by appt. *Fee:* $4. *Owners/Winemakers:* Steve & Christy Simmons. *Wines:* Cabernet franc, Gewürztraminer, Malbec, Pinot blanc, Pinot gris, Pinot noir, rosé, red blends. *Cases:* 1,200. This is a winery on the way up, literally and figuratively. The dryness and hilly terrain are apparent as you make your way through madrones, oaks, and layers of tall grasses to the tranquility of Steve and Christy's spot on the rise. The setting is simple, the wines not so much. Be sure to ask about the stories behind the labels—Julio's Hill is about vines that arrived before the equipment, so Julio planted all 2,100 by hand. The signature wine is a blend of Cab sauv, Cab franc, and Malbec.

▲ 🎁 ✐ 🐾 ❖ **Henry Estate Winery** (687 Hubbard Creek Road; 541-459-5120 or 800-782-2686). *Tasting room:* Daily 11–5. *Fee:* Complimentary. *Owner:* Scott Henry III. *Winemaker:* Calvin Scott Henry IV. *Wines:* Chardonnay, Gewürztraminer, Merlot, Müller-Thurgau, Pinot gris, Pinot noir, Riesling. *Cases:* 16,000. Henry Estate might be southern Oregon's best-known winery, in part for its wide distribution and because Scott Henry III created one of the industry's best-known modern-day inventions. Their first vineyards were planted on 12 acres in 1972, but the winery didn't earn international acclaim until Henry developed a two-tiered trellis system. Near the confluence of the North and South Umpqua Rivers, the estate has been in the family through three generations. The spacious grounds and tasting room are usually an event-in-the-making, so plan to stay and sip awhile.

▲ 🍴 ✐ 🐾 ❖ **Reustle Prayer Rock Vineyards** (960 Cal Henry Road; 541-459-6060). *Tasting room:* Tues.–Sat. 10–5. *Fee:* $10. *Owners:* Stephen & Gloria Reustle. *Winemaker:* Stephen Reustle. *Wines:* Grenache, Grüner veltliner, Merlot, Malbec, Pinot gris, Pinot noir, Riesling, Sauvignon blanc, Semillon, Syrah, Tempranillo, Viognier, rosé, red blend. *Cases:* 5,500. The Reustles' mammoth carved cement and cedar planked structure will leave you rubbing your eyes in disbelief. Paths lined with engraved benches and rocks are inscribed with Bible phrases and lead to the heavy, wood-carved doors. Anticipation builds as you pass miniature bonsai forest, sculptures, and large urns. Inside, the fantasy continues as you are led through chandelier-clad caves, passing barrels, and frescoed walls adorned with scripture and angels. The sit-down tasting includes nibbles to enhance the experience. An outdoor amphitheater with stadium seating completes the extravagant complex.

▲ ✐ 🐾 **Becker Vineyards** (360 Klahowya Lane; 541-677-0288). *Tasting room:* Daily 11–5. *Fee:* Complimentary. *Owners:* Charles & Peggy Becker. *Winemaker:* Charles Becker. *Wines:* Baco noir, Cabernet sauvignon, Grenache, Maréchal Foch, Müller-Thurgau, Pinot gris, Pinot noir, Syrah, rosé, red blends. *Cases:* 900. Becker is as mom-and-pop as it gets, down to Peggy's answering the business phone with a friendly "Hello." Both are retired into full-time vineyard and winery work on a pretty ridge above the Umpqua River. The Beckers are consummate do-it-yourselfers; they dry farm and don't hire help. Come harvest, they uncork a few bottles, prepare good food, and invite friends and neighbors over for crush. Dog's Drool, their popular red blend, is only available here—like all the wines.

▲ ✐ 🐾 ❖ **Pyrenees Vineyard & Cellars (North)** (707 Hess Lane; 541-672-8060). *Tasting room:* Fri.–Sun. 11–6, May–Sept. *Fee:* $5. The Pyrenees North tasting room, winery, and vineyard is the former Julianna site. Drink in the views of the South Umpqua River from a long platform deck. Live music on Sundays and food cart fare brings out the locals and lucky tourists. See the Pyrenees South location at Myrtle Creek (page 156) for more information.

▲ ✐ 🐾 ❖ **Glaser Estate Winery** (213 Independence Lane; 541-580-4867). *Tasting room:* Wed.–Sun. 12–6, May–Sept.; Fri.–Sun. 11–5, Oct.–Apr. (closed Jan.). *Fee:* $5. *Owners:* David, Sandra & Leon Glaser. *Winemakers:* Leon & Sandra Glaser. *Wines:* Baco noir, Cabernet franc, Cabernet sauvignon, Dolcetto, Grenache, Malbec, Merlot, Muscat, Pinot gris, Pinot noir, Riesling, Sangiovese, Sauvignon blanc, Syrah. *Cases:* 1,500. Take your wine—or your whiskey—to the river at Glaser, located between two rapids on the emerald waters of the North Umpqua River. The rustic cottage, with its fireplace and concrete deck with gas lanterns, matches the woodsy surroundings well.

Glaser has plenty of wines, but for a change of pace, its newly opened distillery presents vodka, white rum, limoncello, and butterscotch liqueur.

▲ ✐ 🐾 **TeSoAria Vineyard & Winery** (512 North Curry Road; 541-464-0032). *Tasting room:* Daily 11–5. *Fee:* $3. *Owners:* John & Joy Olson. *Winemaker:* John Olson. *Wines:* Chardonnay, Dolcetto, Pinot noir, Riesling, Sangiovese, Syrah, Vermentino, red and white blends, port-style. *Cases:* 5,000. After eight years at the Palotai site made famous by the gregarious Gabor, the Olsons have opened a new winery/tasting room across the North Umpqua River. The name is a condensed version of terra (soil), sol (sun), and aria (air and music). TeSoAria produces many of the classics, and John says the carefully handcrafted wines taste "like a home-cooked meal." The Palotai legacy continues: John still produces Bull's Blood, a Hungarian red blend table wine, so popular it's tough to keep in stock.

▲ 🎁 ❖ **Melrose Vineyards** (885 Melqua Road; 541-672-6080). *Tasting room:* Daily 10–5. *Fee:* Comp/3 & $10/6 (includes glass). *Owner:* Wayne Parker. *Winemaker:* Cody Parker. *Wines:* Baco noir, Chardonnay, Dolcetto, Merlot, Pinotage, Pinot gris, Pinot noir, Riesling, Sauvignon blanc, Syrah, Tempranillo, Viognier, rosé, red blend, port-style. *Cases:* 4,000. Wayne and Deedy Parker arrived from California in 1996 and proceeded to plant vines on 82 acres along the South Umpqua. After a massive winter flood in which they lost 5 acres, Wayne floodproofed the property and turned to the 100-year-old barn. In those rickety old timbers, he saw a tasting room. Rebuilding virtually beam by beam, the Parkers created a sensational setting for tastings, gatherings, and special events. Deedy passed away in 2011, but Melrose is forging ahead. Although it's a bit remote, you won't regret the effort to get here.

▲ ✐ 🐾 **HillCrest Vineyard & Winery** (240 Vineyard Lane; 541-673-3709). *Tasting room:* Daily 11–5, Mar.–Dec. *Fee:* $5. *Owners:* Dyson & Susan DeMara. *Winemaker:* Dyson DeMara. *Wines:* Cabernet sauvignon, Pinot noir, Riesling, Syrah, Tempranillo, Valdiguie, Zinfandel, ice dessert. *Cases:* 1,400. Only one winery in the state gets to say it is number one, and HillCrest was the first legally bonded operation in Oregon. The first grapes were planted in 1888, and in 1961 Richard Sommers planted 35 varieties in this soil. The DeMaras have brought fresh legs and hands to the historic winery and vineyard. While proud of their history, they're equally pleased with current efforts. It is strictly a family affair, but one with extensive wine history—and winery work in 17 countries. The number 44 on the barn references HillCrest's ranking as the nation's 44th bonded alcohol producer post-Prohibition.

▲ 🎁 ✐ 🐾 ❖ **Delfino Vineyards** (3829 Colonial Road; 541-673-7575). *Tasting room:* Daily: 11–5. *Fee:* $5. *Owners:* Jim & Terri Delfino. *Winemaker:* Jim Delfino. *Wines:* Merlot, Müller-Thurgau, Syrah, Zinfandel, rosé, dessert. *Cases:* 500. Delfino proudly opened its tasting room in 2009 after tending 18 acres of grapes for eight years. The 160-acre farm is pleasing to the eye as you wind through the vineyard to the dressed-up utilitarian tasting room. After your sipping, you can work off the calories on hiking trails that lace the estate, then pop a cork and watch the sun settle from the deck. If you stay at the guest cottage B&B ($175–200), with its lap pool and hot tub, you'll enjoy fresh eggs from the resident hens for breakfast.

▲ 🎁 ✐ 🐾 ❖ **Chateau Nonchalant** (1329 Larson Road; 541-679-2394). *Tasting room:* Fri.–Sun. 11–5, June–Sept. *Fee:* Complimentary. *Owners:* Weldon & Vicki Manning. *Winemaker:* Scott Henry Jr. *Wines:* Pinot gris, Pinot noir, Syrah, Tempranillo. *Cases:* 1,000. After providing grapes for other wineries in the region, the Mannings decided to raise the stakes and create their own product. When it came to choosing a winemaker,

Cycle Wine Country—Timber Trails & Wine Lines

Description: Take a ride back in history in the picturesque Umpqua Valley on a route that features Oregon's first bonded winery—HillCrest. Also included on this country excursion is Henry Estate, a southern Oregon icon on the North Umpqua River. Starting in Roseburg, you'll eventually cross the Umpqua, North Umpqua, and South Umpqua Rivers while pedaling through forest and agricultural land for visits to some spectacular wineries. On Melqua Road, you'll enjoy a ride along the Umpqua after the North and South forks have converged.

Wineries: HillCrest Vineyard & Winery, Melrose Vineyards, Henry Estate Winery, Reustle Prayer Rock Vineyards, Becker Vineyards, Pyrenees Vineyards

Miles: 49

Elevation gain: 1,857

Start/Finish: Riverfront Park, Roseburg

- Start by heading west on Garden Valley Road and continuing west on Melrose Road and then west on Doerner Road. Turn north on Elgarose Road and back west on Elgarose Road, then south on Vineyard Lane. Winery stop: HillCrest Vineyard & Winery.
- Proceed east on Elgarose Road and continue east on Orchard Lane, then south on Cleveland Hill Road, east on Melrose Road, and north on Melqua Road. Winery stop: Melrose Vineyards.
- Head east on Hubbard Creek Road. Winery stop: Henry Estate Winery.
- Go south on Garden Valley Road, then east on Cal Henry Road. Winery stop: Reustle Prayer Rock Vineyards.
- Return west on Cal Henry Road, then south on Garden Valley Road, east on Upper Cleveland Rapids Road, and east on Klahowya Lane. Winery stop: Becker Vineyards.
- Proceed west on Klahowya Lane and continue west on Upper Cleveland Rapids Road, then south on Garden Valley Road and south on Old Garden Valley Road, then west on Hess Lane. Winery stop: Pyrenees Vineyards.
- Return east on Hess Lane, then south on Old Garden Valley Road and south on Garden Valley back to Roseburg.

they didn't fool around and secured good friend Scott Henry Jr. Nonchalant's beautifully crafted, space-efficient tasting room was built by Vicki's brother. The gorgeous wooden deck and gardens make the most inviting setting to enjoy easy-drinking wines available only in the tasting room.

▲ 🎁 **Girardet Wine Cellars** (895 Reston Road; 541-679-7252). *Tasting room:* Daily 11–5. *Fee:* Complimentary. *Owners:* Philippe & Bonnie Girardet. *Winemaker:* Marc Girardet. *Wines:* Baco noir, Cabernet sauvignon, Chardonnay, Pinot gris, Pinot noir, Riesling, red and white blends, dessert. *Cases:* 12,000. The Girardets are from Switzerland, which doesn't explain their passion for Baco noir—a hybrid developed by Frenchman François Baco in hopes of finding a phylloxera-resistant grape. Baco thrives in the Umpqua, and the Girardets, first Philippe and now son Marc, have been producing the smooth, spicy red since 1991. It's the vineyard's signature wine, and it's fair to say that if David Lett is Oregon's "Papa Pinot," then Philippe Girardet is "Uncle Baco."

Abacela (12500 Lookingglass Road; 541-679-6642). *Tasting room:* Daily 11–5. *Fee:* $5. *Owners:* Earl & Hilda Jones. *Winemaker:* Andrew Wenzel. *Wines:* Albarino, Cabernet franc, Dolcetto, Garnacha, Malbec, Merlot, Rosada, Syrah, Tempranillo, Viognier, red and white blends, port-style. *Cases:* 11,000. Hilda and Earl searched the world to find the right terroir for their beloved Spanish varietals. They found it on an early 19th-century homestead in the Umpqua Valley, where the climate matched the famed Ribera del Duero region. They were the first in Oregon to plant Tempranillo and have been winning barrels of awards ever since first bottling. Abacela was also a trendsetter with varietals Dolcetto and Albarino, both now grown in other Oregon vineyards. The new Vine and Wine education center—including interpretive signage in the vineyard—is nothing short of phenomenal.

Abacela's rolling vineyards produce Spanish varietals, such as Garnacha and Albariño. M. Kim Lewis

▲ 🎁 ❖ ✐ **Spangler Vineyards** (491 Winery Lane; 541-679-9654). *Tasting room:* Daily 11–5. *Fee:* Complimentary. *Owners:* Pat & Loree Spangler. *Winemaker:* Pat Spangler. *Wines:* Cabernet franc, Cabernet sauvignon, Chardonnay, Merlot, Petite sirah, Sauvignon blanc, Syrah, Viognier, claret, red blend, sparkling. *Cases:* 3,000. Spangler's forte is big reds—Pat is especially proud of his claret and Petite sirah. The signature grape is Cabernet sauvignon, dry-farmed in the valley since 1968 and a potent piece of the claret. The fun tasting room has a well-stocked menagerie of gifts, and Spangler's wall of awards is mighty impressive. Spangler has a second tasting room in Newberg (203 Villa Road, 503-538-1146, next to Mike's Pharmacy).

MYRTLE CREEK

▲ 🎁 ✐ 🐾 ❖ **Pyrenees Vineyard & Cellars (South)** (15332 Old Highway 99 South; 541-863-7797). *Tasting room:* Daily 11–5. *Fee:* $5. *Owners:* Apodaca family. *Winemaker:* Thomas Shook. *Wines:* Cabernet franc, Cabernet sauvignon, Chenin blanc, Gewürztraminer, Maréchal Foch, Merlot, Pinot gris, Pinot noir, Riesling, Sauvignon blanc, Semillon, red blend. *Cases:* 8,000. This location is where the majority of Pyrenees' activities take place—on a one-time dairy farm renovated by the Apodaca family to match its Basque roots (hence Pyrenees). Girls' night out moves here after the north location closes for the season, and fun is always on the docket.

WINSTON

▲ **Wild Rose Vineyard** (375 Porter Creek Road; 541-580-5488). *Tasting room:* Daily 11–5. *Fee:* Complimentary. *Owners:* Denise & Carlos Figueroa. *Winemaker:* Carlos Figueroa. *Wines:* Cabernet sauvignon, Merlot, Pinot gris, Pinot noir, port-style, dessert. *Cases:* 500. Carlos Figueroa is a chemistry and biology instructor at Umpqua Community College, and his skills have come in handy at his humble 9-acre vineyard and spartan garage tasting room at the very end of a narrow country road. Wild Rose is fully organic, LIVE-certified, and Salmon-Safe—the whole green gamut. And Carlos is continually upgrading the homey grounds in the serene valley location.

Lodging
in the Umpqua Region

ELKTON

The Big K Guest Ranch (20029 Highway 138 West; 541-584-2295 or 800-390-2445). "Big" accurately describes 2,500 acres of outdoor wonders and 10 miles of Umpqua River frontage. In the family for more than a century, the place remains a working cattle ranch. Alvin Kesterson (a.k.a. Big K), built guest quarters to offset rising agriculture costs. Your all-inclusive stay, by the day or week, is in one of 20 quiet, log-sided cabins near the big, beautiful lodge. Oregon wines are poured at dinner, and attentive staff will point you in the direction of wineries. Fishing and hunting trips keeps the ranch open in the winter. Drive 4 miles on a gravel road for "real people, real food, and real time!" $$$$

ROSEBURG

C. H. Bailey House B&B (121 Melton Road; 541-672-1500). Even in 1909, the Bailey House was considered unique for its architecture. More than a century later, Sherry & Jay Couron have gone green while exuding the same sophisticated rural charm. Once surrounded by orchards, the impressive grounds still revel in organic fruit trees and gardens and serve as a top-notch getaway for wine tourists and anglers. Four guest rooms are bathed in warm overtones and filled with earth-friendly touches. Unwind in the country quiet with a game of bocce or just sit a spell with complimentary local wine and beer. $$$

CANYONVILLE

Seven Feathers Casino Resort (541-839-1111 or 800-548-8461). The Cow Creek Indians, first to bring gaming to Oregon, did a great job of creating a 232,500-square-foot luxury resort with a little bit of everything, from RV spots to spacious higher-end rooms. Feeling lucky? Check into a suite. A full-service day spa, indoor pool, sauna and fitness room, live entertainment, cabaret lounge, and video arcade are just a few ways to keep busy while not gambling. In March, the resort hosts the Greatest of the Grape, the longest-running wine festival in Oregon. $–$$

STEAMBOAT

Steamboat Inn (42705 North Umpqua Highway; 541-498-2230 or 800-840-8825). Fall asleep to the sound of the North Umpqua River splashing over boulders, content after savoring some of the best wine cuisine ever. The Steamboat Inn, a longtime favorite of wine fans and fishermen, begins dinner by serving hors d'oeuvres about 30 minutes after rods are put away for the day. The exquisite three-course meal is served family style on a long sugar-pine table that lends itself to meeting new folks, swapping fish tales, and sharing Oregon wine. By popular demand, Sharon and Pat Lee have published their recipes in *Thyme and the River* and its sequel, *Thyme and the River Too.* $$$$

Dining
in the Umpqua Region

ELKTON

Tomaselli's Pastry Mill and Café (14836 Highway 38; 541-584-2855). Owners Marty and Dayna Tomaselli have been serving "good food, not fast food" with a side sense of humor and congeniality in their crowded quarters for more than 30 years. Breakfast and lunches depart from the ordinary, whereas dinner entrées lean toward Italian (no surprise), with fresh handmade pasta. Plan to stay awhile for a sit-down meal, or do as we did: Order food to go, visit a winery, and come back for pickup. Tomaselli's also makes fabulous pizzas and baked goods from scratch. B/L/D Tues.–Sat. $$–$$$

ROSEBURG

Mark V Grill & Bar (563 SE Main Street; 541-229-6275). Gaining favor with visitors and locals, the Mark V pours more than 30 Oregon wines by the glass. Tapas and full dinners with made-from-scratch soups, dressings, and sauces meld well with local vino. Recent suggested pairings: TeSoAria's Bianca Blanco with Parm-encrusted halibut, Henry's Estate gris with chicken pasta, and Abacela Malbec with New York strip. Open daily, Mark's is a reliable, go-to kind of diner. B/L/D $$$–$$$$

Roseburg Station Pub & Brewery (700 SE Sheridan Street; 541-672-1934). The McMenamin arms have reached from Portland to Roseburg. And that's a good thing. The entrepreneurial and mercurial brothers have converted the old Southern Pacific railroad depot into a lively nightspot serving their wine and microbrews. The menu is classic pub fare, but thoughtful touches such as the natural and hormone-free beef raise the bar. Don't forget to indulge in a side of hand-cut fries. L/D $–$$$

OAKLAND

Tolly's Grill & Soda Fountain (115 Locust Street; 541-459-3796). Tolly's, a calling card for a town once known for turkeys, is an anchor business for this agricultural community of about 1,000. Rescued one more time from permanent closure, the historic building and menu have a facelift from new owners Tim Mitchell and Doug Longfellow. Creative lunch and dinner specials are posted daily on their Facebook page and show chef ingenuity. Regional wines are prominent on the list. L/D/HH Tues.–Sun. $$$–$$$$

Take a spin on the bar stools at Tolly's 1910 soda fountain. Courtesy Tolly's Grill & Soda Fountain

CANYONVILLE

Camas Room at Seven Feathers (146 Chief Miwaleta Lane; 800-548-8461). If you're like us, acres of blacktop parking, windowless buildings, and smoke filters are not calling you to "eat here." But it's easy to overlook these deterrents and find a pleasurable dining experience at the Camas Room. Under new identity, the menu is still loaded with Oregon ingredients—lamb, salmon, beef—but it's gentler on the pocketbook and has a more laid-back 'tude. Friday nights bring out Umpqua vintners for complimentary tastings in the lobby. Odds are, whatever you're dealt, you'll be satisfied. B/L/D/BR $$$

To Do
in the Umpqua Region

Attractions

The **Douglas County Museum** (123 Museum Drive, 541-957-7007) in Roseburg explores the 150-year history of the Umpqua region through more than 7,500 items—most in the state. Fifteen miles north of Roseburg, the town of **Oakland** was the first in Oregon to establish a historic district. With more than 80 structures at least 130 years old, the entire community is on the National Register of Historic Places. A good place to get lost on a backcountry road is the 1875 **Lookingglass Store** (541-679-

5651), the oldest building in Douglas County and once the terminus of a stage route from Oakland. Located 9 miles southwest of Roseburg, the general store once had a two-horse parking meter and was the site of an NBC Nightly News broadcast. The valley got its name from the bright sun's reflection on lush grasses.

Lions and tigers and bears in Douglas County? Oh, my! **Wildlife Safari** (1790 Safari Road, 541-679-6761) in Winston is a 600-acre drive-through wild-animal park with more than 500 exotic critters from around the globe. Like much of western Oregon, the area has covered bridges—seven of them. Get a map from the **Roseburg Visitors and Convention Bureau** (541-672-9731, 410 SE Spruce Street) for a self-guided tour. In Canyonville, the **Pioneer-Indian Museum** (421 West Fifth Street, 541-839-4845) features Indian history in the South Umpqua Valley. Relax after a day of winery hopping at the free **Summer Concert Series** (541-677-1708) at 6 PM every Tuesday in Roseburg's Stewart Park. Past performers have included the Dixie Chicks and Lyle Lovett.

Recreation

This is hook-and-bullet country, famed for its salmon, steelhead, trout, and smallmouth bass fishing on the Umpqua River. The North Umpqua is a blue-ribbon trout stream, but for diversity, try casting a dry fly to ravenous smallmouth bass on the Umpqua near Elkton. Fishermen have learned to share the North Umpqua with white-water rafters who covet the challenging but forgiving Class III rapids. Nine commercial outfitters offer one-day trips on a stream protected in the National Wild & Scenic Rivers system.

For the consummate hiking, mountain biking, or horseback riding experience, check out the 79-mile **North Umpqua Trail** (541-440-4930) on the Umpqua National Forest. This gorgeous path follows the river starting at Stillwater east of Roseburg and is broken into segments. If you'd like to include some wine tasting in a bicycling adventure, the **Cycle Umpqua Vineyard Tour** every September offers a choice of five routes ranging from 15 to 100 miles and includes three to five wineries.

Kruse Farms (541-672-5697, 532 Melrose Road, April–October) is a Roseburg shopping extravaganza, with bushels of produce, dried fruits, nuts, bakery treats, plants, local meats, and a plethora of gifts; October means pumpkins and wagon rides. The **Melrose Country Store**, (3737 Melrose Road) is the place to fill 'er up with more than gasoline. It has better than you'd expect made-to-order sandwiches and grab-n-go eats, including "Mom's potato salad." Across the road is **Larry's Little Trees** (3738 Melrose Road), a tiny forest of Japanese bonzais for gardening and landscaping indulgence.

Bring your sticks for year-round golfing at one of the Roseburg area's three public courses: the woodsy **Myrtle Creek** (1316 Fairway Drive, 888-869-7863), **Umpqua** (1919 Recreation Lane, Sutherlin, 541-459-4422), or the city's course at **Stewart Park** (900 SE Douglas Avenue, 541-672-7701).

More Information

Roseburg Visitors and Convention Bureau, 541-672-9731 or 800-444-9584, 410 SE Spruce Street, www.visitroseburg.com

Roseburg Area Chamber of Commerce, 541-672-2648, 410 SE Spruce Street, www.roseburgareachamber.org

Umpqua National Forest, 541-672-6601, 2900 NW Stewart Parkway

Oregon Wine Country Tours, 541-677-1906, 5043 Melqua Road, www.oregonwinecountrytours.com

Southern Oregon

FLY OVER NO MORE . . .

TAKE THE WILLAMETTE VALLEY and the Napa/Sonoma region, mix vigorously, then toss the ingredients onto a jumbled landscape—that's Southern Oregon Wine Country. As Interstate 5 winds through mountainous country toward Grants Pass and then the broad Rogue River Valley at Medford, it turns east to avoid the wild Klamath Mountains, taking it 30 significant miles farther from the Pacific's moist marine influence.

For many years, exasperated winery and vineyard owners referred to southern Oregon as the "Fly Over" zone—one winery even has a "Fly Over Red"—because of the legions of wine aficionados who flew over the region between California wine country and the Willamette Valley. But no more. Southern Oregon is rapidly earning a reputation for producing some of the state's finest wines.

Grants Pass is a former timber-industry giant recognizing its opportunities with wine. It has the tourism benefit of being the gateway to the mighty Rogue River of Zane Grey fame, with its splashy white-water rafting and salmon fishing. The mild Applegate Valley is named for pioneer settler Jesse Applegate.

Blue-collar Medford is the region's hub and Oregon's hottest city, with temperatures rising above 100 in the summer. Fortunately, wine tourists don't have to go far to beat the heat. Next door is Jacksonville, a National Historic Landmark and delightful foothills village. The artsy outdoors community of Ashland is 10 miles and a world away to the south at the foot of the Siskiyou Summit, sparing it from the summer sizzle.

Ashland is renowned for its acclaimed annual Shakespeare Festival, the powdery Mt. Ashland Ski and Snowboard Area, and a vibrant city center.

GETTING HERE AND AROUND

Medford has one of two commercial airports in the long 480 miles between Eugene and Sacramento, and is third busiest in the state behind Portland and Eugene. Some 60 flights a day come and go on four airlines from **Rogue Valley International-Medford**

LEFT: Valley View, near Jacksonville, has deep roots in southern Oregon's wine history.

Courtesy M. Kim Lewis

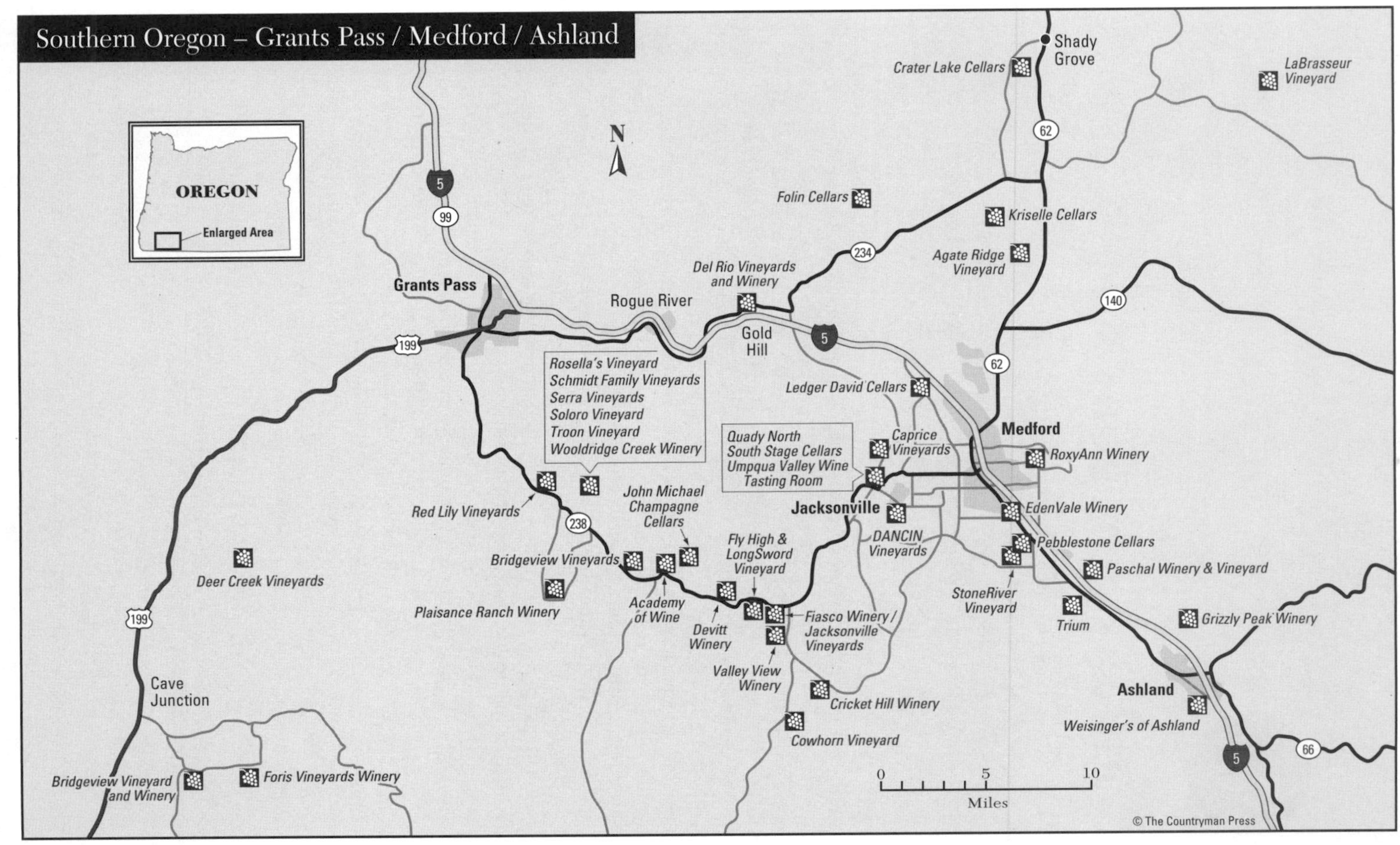
Southern Oregon – Grants Pass / Medford / Ashland
OREGON
Enlarged Area
N
Shady Grove
Crater Lake Cellars
LaBrasseur Vineyard
62
5
99
Folin Cellars
Kriselle Cellars
Agate Ridge Vineyard
234
Del Rio Vineyards and Winery
Grants Pass
Rogue River
140
199
Gold Hill
62
Ledger David Cellars
Rosella's Vineyard
Schmidt Family Vineyards
Serra Vineyards
Soloro Vineyard
Troon Vineyard
Wooldridge Creek Winery
Quady North
South Stage Cellars
Umpqua Valley Wine
Tasting Room
Caprice Vineyards
Medford
RoxyAnn Winery
Red Lily Vineyards
John Michael Champagne Cellars
Jacksonville
EdenVale Winery
238
Fly High & LongSword Vineyard
DANCIN Vineyards
Pebblestone Cellars
Bridgeview Vineyards
Paschal Winery & Vineyard
Deer Creek Vineyards
StoneRiver Vineyard
Plaisance Ranch Winery
Academy of Wine
Fiasco Winery / Jacksonville Vineyards
Trium
Grizzly Peak Winery
Devitt Winery
Valley View Winery
Cave Junction
Ashland
Cricket Hill Winery
Weisinger's of Ashland
Cowhorn Vineyard
66
0
5
10
Miles
Bridgeview Vineyard and Winery
Foris Vineyards Winery
© The Countryman Press

Airport, all coming from western hubs. Delta Connection (800-221-1212) serves Salt Lake City; United Express (800-241-6522) departs to Portland, San Francisco, and Denver; Horizon Air (800-252-7522) connects to Eugene, Portland, Los Angeles, and Seattle; and Allegiant Air (702-505-8888) arrives from Las Vegas, Los Angeles, and Phoenix.

The romance of train travel is alive and rolling with **Amtrak** (800-872-7245), which roughly follows I-5 from the north but veers over the Cascade Range southeast of Eugene and stops in Klamath Falls. A chartered bus takes passengers from Amtrak's Front Street Transfer Station in Medford to Klamath Falls. **Greyhound** (800-231-2222) has stops in Medford, Jacksonville, and Ashland.

For those behind the wheel, I-5 is the primary artery, bisecting Grants Pass, Medford, and Ashland. OR 238 connects Medford with Grants Pass and includes Jacksonville plus the pastoral Applegate Valley. To reach the Illinois Valley, take US 199 southwest from Grants Pass toward Cave Junction.

THE GRANTS PASS AND ILLINOIS VALLEY AREA

(Applegate Valley and Illinois Valley AVAs)

The catch phrase for Grants Pass—named for the former Civil War general and president—is, "It's the Climate." Today, tourism is the predominant industry, thanks not only to the Rogue River but also to the wineries that have risen from the rich soils. The Illinois Valley is in the heart of the rugged Siskiyou Mountains, carved by one of Oregon's most remote and wild rivers.

Wineries

in the Grants Pass Area (Applegate Valley AVA)

One of Oregon's newer AVAs is also home to the state's oldest winery. It was here in 1860 that an adventurous photographer named Peter Britt opened Valley View Winery in Jacksonville, just west of Medford in the Siskiyou Mountain foothills. For 59 years, virtually right up until his death, Britt produced wines in the moderate climes of the Applegate, a 50-mile south–north valley that starts near the California border.

Prohibition put a halt to further development of the industry in Oregon and elsewhere, but Valley View reopened for business in the early 1970s, when 26 acres were planted in Pinot noir, Chardonnay, Gewürztraminer, Merlot, and Cabernet sauvignon, including 14 acres on the old winery site. The route begins just south of Grants Pass on the Applegate Trail. Follow OR 238 toward Jacksonville and Medford.

GRANTS PASS

▲ 🎁 🍴 ✐ 🐾 ❖ **Red Lily Vineyards** (11777 Highway 238; 541-846-0601). *Tasting room:* Daily 11–5 (summer), Thurs.–Sun. 11–5. *Fee:* $5. *Owners:* Les & Rachael Martin. *Winemaker:* Rachael Martin. *Wines:* Tempranillo, Verdejo, rosé, red blends. *Cases:* 2,000. Les and Rachael Martin like to think of their new winery as "upscale casual," starting with their welcoming and knowledgeable staff. The focus of the Martins' constantly evolving vision is 18 acres of grapes, including Verdejo, a Spanish varietal. Pull up a lawn chair and enjoy the Applegate River's cadence. You can't go wrong sipping a glass of wine on 8,000 feet of sand along the river.

▲ 🍴 ✐ 🐾 ❖ **Schmidt Family Vineyards** (320 Kubli Road; 541-846-9985). *Tasting room:* Daily 12–5. *Fee:* $5. *Owners:* Cal & Judy Schmidt. *Winemaker:* Cal Schmidt. *Wines:*

Albarino, Cabernet franc, Cabernet sauvignon, Chardonnay, Gewürztraminer, Malbec, Merlot, Pinot Gris, Riesling, Sauvignon blanc, Syrah, Tempranillo, Viognier, Zinfandel, red blends. *Cases:* 3,200. Picture Steinbeck's *Grapes of Wrath*, only with wheelbarrows of money. An architecturally stunning, California-meets-Northwest tasting room beckons you to relax and linger awhile at the 26-acre Schmidt Family Farm. A large patio, thoughtful landscaping with dozens of trees surrounding a pond, and Siskiyou Mountain views extend the reasons to visit. Farm laborers are depicted in wall murals—no surprise, given Cal grew up on a Kansas wheat farm. It's such a popular place, the Schmidts now have two tasting rooms, one for events and one for sampling.

Serra Vineyards (222 Missouri Flats Road; 541-846-9223). *Tasting room:* Daily 11–5. *Fee:* $5. *Owners:* Braden & Fernandes families. *Winemaker:* Greg Paneitz & Kara Olmo. *Wines:* Chardonnay, Pinot noir, Syrah, rosé, red blend. *Cases:* 900. The funky Applegate Red Winery—known for Sicilian donkeys, squawking birds, and a Hawaiian theme—was left wanting after the colorful Frank Ferreira died in 2008. Then Dick Braden came to the rescue. The winery has reopened under a new name with ambitious plans that include a hilltop tasting room. Braden and Co. have added 17 acres of grapes, with more in the plan. They've modernized the vineyard with an extensive irrigation system—a 180-degree shift from the naturalist Ferreira.

Rosella's Vineyard (184 Missouri Flats Road; 541-846-6372). *Tasting room:* Thurs.–Mon. 11–5, and by appt. *Fee:* Complimentary. *Owners:* Rex & Sandi Garoutte. *Winemaker:* Rex Garoutte. *Wines:* Cabernet sauvignon, Chardonnay, Merlot, Zinfandel, red and white blends. *Cases:* 800. In a well-worn beach-style house that looks as if it came from Santa Cruz—where owner Rex Garoutte once took college oenology courses—you'll find Rex or Sandi pouring their grog and spinning a yarn or two. Rex is a chatty sort who describes himself as the "chief cook and bottle washer," and takes pride in his product.

Troon offers a fountain of afternoon tasting delights. M. Kim Lewis

Troon Vineyard (1475 Kubli Road; 541-846-9900). *Tasting room:* Daily 11–5. *Fee:* $5. *Owner:* Martin family. *Winemaker:* Herb Quady. *Wines:* Cabernet franc, Cabernet sauvignon, Chardonnay, Meritage, Merlot, Riesling, Syrah, Viognier, Zinfandel, rosé, red and white blends, port-style. *Cases:* 9,000. The late Dick Troon's name is synonymous with the genesis of southern Oregon's wine industry. The cantankerous former river guide, who first planted wine grapes on this knoll in 1972, remains so revered that posthumously he is still referred to as "Mr. Troon." Starting with a spectacular tasting room, Troon has the look of a European villa, a multibuilding complex with contemporary accoutrements. On the grounds are a wood-fired oven, five-tiered fountain, and bocce court. The

Cycle Wine County—The Applegate Trail

Description: This pedal route has it all—plenty of wineries, pastoral riding along both sides of the Applegate River, just enough climbing and options for shortcuts. And you'll finish in Jacksonville, one of Oregon's great, quaint little tourist towns. If you're not up for the entire 67 miles, skip the side trip to Plaisance Ranch (but be sure to make the drive there!). You'll climb early leaving Jacksonville, then enjoy a pleasant ride at the base of foothills in the broad Applegate Valley, where the wineries are just far enough apart to provide well-timed breaks. Reaching some of those wineries requires some modest climbing. Give yourself a full day or plan to stay over for this pedal in one of Oregon's prettiest valleys.

Wineries: South Stage Cellars, Valley View Winery, Cowhorn Vineyard, LongSword Vineyard, Jacksonville Vineyards, Devitt Winery, Academy of Wine, John Michael Champagne Cellars, Bridgeview Winery, Soloro, Vineyard, Wooldridge Creek Winery, Troon Vineyard, Schmidt Family Vineyards, Plaisance Ranch

Miles: 67

Elevation gain: 2,368

Start/Finish: South Stage Cellars, Jacksonville

- Start from South Stage Cellars and head west on OR 238, then turn south on Upper Applegate Road. Winery stops: Valley View Winery and Cowhorn Vineyard.
- Return north on Upper Applegate Road and head west on OR 238. Winery stops: LongSword Vineyard, Jacksonville Vineyards, Devitt Winery, Academy of Wine, and John Michael Champagne Cellars.
- Proceed north on North Applegate Road. Winery stops: Bridgeview Winery and Soloro Vineyard.
- Turn north on Kubli Road and then east on Slagle Creek Road. Winery stop: Wooldridge Creek Winery.
- Return west on Slagle Creek Road and continue north on Kubli Road. Winery stops: Troon Vineyard and Schmidt Family Vineyards.
- Go north on North Applegate Road, then turn south on OR 238 and continue south on Watergap Road. Winery stop: Plaisance Ranch.
- Proceed north on Williams-Murphy Road and then head east on OR 238 back to South Stage Cellars in Jacksonville.

Martins were the first in the Northwest to plant the Corsican varietal Vermentino, a full-bodied white. One of their hottest sellers is the Druid's Fluid—a red blend that, ironically, is the result of a mistake. Ask for the story.

▲ 🍷 **Soloro Vineyard** (9110 North Applegate Road; 541-862-2693). *Tasting room:* Sat. & Sun. 1–5, Apr.–Dec., and by appt. *Fee:* Complimentary. *Owners:* Tim & June Navarro. *Winemakers:* Linda Donovan & Steve Anderson. *Wines:* Grenache noir, Marsanne, Roussanne, Syrah, Viognier, red and white blends. *Cases:* 400. Catalan for "sun gold," *soloro* is an apt description for sun-drenched hills where the Navarros once raised cattle. It's also appropriate for the golden glow in the tasting room at the neighborhood's newest winery, which is laid-back and humble, friendly canine greeters included. Among its showcase wines, the estate Viognier-Marsanne blend is solid gold.

Wooldridge Creek Winery (818 Slagle Creek Road; 541-846-6364). *Tasting room:* Daily 11–5, and by appt. *Fee:* $10. *Owners:* Ted & Mary Warrick, Greg Paneitz, and Kara Olmo. *Winemakers:* Greg Paneitz & Kara Olmo. *Wines:* Cabernet sauvignon, Chardonnay, Gewürztraminer, Malbec, Tempranillo, Zinfandel, red and white blends, port-style, dessert, sparkling. *Cases:* 4,500. Former airline industry employees Ted and Mary Warrick took off on a new career path in 1978 when they bought 18 acres within view of the Applegate River. Over time, they've expanded to 56 planted acres with 12 varietals. Cheerful Adirondack chairs on the lawn and a picnic area frequented by resident wildlife are part of Wooldridge's charm. They're innovative, too: The bulk of their wine leaves in kegs—no glass bottles—for restaurants and special events.

WILLIAMS

Plaisance Ranch (16955 Water Gap Road; 541-846-7175). *Tasting room:* Daily 12–6, and by appt. *Fee:* Complimentary. *Owners:* Joe & Suzi Ginet. *Winemaker:* Joe Ginet. *Wines:* Cabernet franc, Cabernet sauvignon, Carménère, Malbec, Merlot, Mondeuse, Mourvèdre, Pinot noir, Syrah, Tempranillo, Viognier, rosé, white blend. *Cases:* 1,000. Winemaker Joe Ginet describes himself as "winemaker and cow boss," in charge of his working ranch where certified organic beef and hay are raised (Plaisance has been a working ranch since 1858). Tucked into the end of a pastoral valley and worth every mile, the converted dairy barn tasting room is described by Suzi Ginet as "more of the rustic experience." The ranch grows many varietals, but most interesting is the Mondeuse noire, a parent of Syrah that Joe's grandfather brought from Savoie, France, in 1898.

Wineries

in the Illinois Valley (Illinois Valley AVA)

Call it Willamette Valley Lite. The Illinois Valley's cool marine climate, with 60 inches of annual rain punctuated by warm and dry summer days, enables the vintners in this remote, scenic region to produce the same wines as their more renowned brethren 300 miles to the north.

Although Bridgeview Vineyard, with its Blue Moon label, has a huge following, the region remains relatively undiscovered. Foris Vineyards Winery owner Ted Gerber was only half-joking when he called one of his wines "Fly Over Red," a playful tweak at wine snobs who look down—literally—upon southern Oregon wineries from their jets as they dash between Willamette and Napa Valleys. There's only one route along the ground: US 199 southwest from Grants Pass.

SELMA

Deer Creek Vineyards (2680 Deer Creek Road; 541-597-4226). *Tasting room:* Daily 11–5; Sat. & Sun., Dec.–Mar.; and by appt. *Fee:* $6. *Owners:* John & Katherine Bryan. *Winemaker:* Linda Donovan. *Wines:* Chardonnay, Merlot, Pinot gris, Pinot noir, white blend. *Cases:* 2,200. Although Foris Winery conducts Deer Creek's crushing, all the handcrafted wines are strictly from the winery's 40 acres of vineyards. Deer Creek is distinct for its sustainable farming; no chemicals are used, and only wild yeast is allowed. The winery's sweeping views of the rugged Illinois River country—including two ponds, tasting room, and gift shop—entice and entertain.

CAVE JUNCTION

Bridgeview Vineyards & Winery (4210 Holland Loop Road; 541-592-4688). *Tasting room:* Daily 11–5. *Fee:* Complimentary. *Second loca-*

It's hard to miss Bridgeview's big, red-barn tasting room in the Applegate Valley.

Angela Mattey

tion: 16995 North Applegate Road, Grants Pass (541-846-1039), daily 11–5, May–Sept.; Sat. & Sun. 11–5, Mar.–May & Sept.–Nov. *Owners:* Bob & Lelo Kerivan. *Winemaker:* René Eichmann. *Wines:* Cabernet sauvignon, Chardonnay, Gewürztraminer, Muscat, Pinot gris, Pinot noir, Merlot, Riesling, Syrah, Tempranillo, Viognier, rosé, red blend, sparkling, dessert. *Cases:* 85,000. The Illinois Valley site is home base for Bridgeview, renowned nationally for Blue Moon Riesling in a cobalt bottle. The tasting room is in a large, red hay barn surrounded by 80 acres of vineyard. Blend easy-drinking wines with a lake and gardens, and you can see why Bridgeview is on the docket for everyone who passes through this remote neck of the woods. In 2011, the winery began offering boxes in Chardonnay, Riesling, Cabernet sauvignon, and Merlot.

▲ 🎁 **Foris Vineyards Winery** (654 Kendall Road; 541-592-3752 or 800-843-6747). *Tasting room:* Daily 11–5. *Fee:* Complimentary. *Owners:* Ted & Teresa Gerber. *Winemaker:* Bryan Wilson. *Wines:* Cabernet franc, Cabernet sauvignon, Chardonnay, Gewürztraminer, Muscotto, Pinot blanc, Pinot gris, Pinot noir, Riesling, red and white blends. *Cases:* 30,000. Oregon's southernmost winery has the top tongue-in-cheek name in the state. Fly Over Red, an intoxicating Bordeaux blend, suggests fewer fanatics are passing over southern Oregon. Foris has a well-earned reputation for very drinkable and affordable wines. Bryan also has a micro-size, under-the-radar brand called Cuckoo's Nest Cellars: Pinot gris, a dry white blend of Gewürztraminer and Viognier, a red blend, and sparkling Moscato.

Lodging

in the Grants Pass/Illinois Valley Areas

GRANTS PASS

♿ **The Lodge at Riverside** (955 SE Seventh Street; 877-955-0600 or 541-955-0600). Color us simple, but when a bright and welcoming face says, "We've been expecting you," they have our business. The Lodge at Riverside is adjacent to the OR 99 bridge on the banks of the Rogue River, sporting mature oak, pine, and aspen that turn golden in the fall. You'll find contemporary comfort in 33 oversized, renovated rooms, most with private decks made for watching the lazy stretch of the Rogue. Traffic noise is surprisingly light. The lodge has a wine reception from 4:30 to 7 nightly and sells seven or eight local wines in the lobby. $$$–$$$$

The Lodge at Riverside offers great access to southern Oregon Wine Country.

Courtesy Country House Inns

♿ 🐾 **The Riverside Inn** (986 SW Sixth Street; 800-334-4567 or 541-476-6873). The Riverside is a traditional motel on the banks of the Rogue, minutes from city center. The 63 rooms are a little worn but most have private balconies with views, some have fireplaces, and all have a homey feel. A continental breakfast of fruit, yogurt, and breads is included. The busy Hellgate Jetboats boarding docks are near. $$$

♿ **Weasku Inn** (5560 Rogue River Highway; 800-493-2758 or 541-471-8000). The "We ask you in" began in 1924 as a destination fishing lodge with canvas "tent cabins" for $1/day or $6/week. Thanks to frequent guest Zane Grey, it rose to legendary status and brought such luminary visitors as President Hoover, Gabby Hayes, Walt Disney, and Clark Gable. The latter was a regular, sometimes with wife Carole Lombard; it's said Gable spent three weeks secluded in an upstairs room after her tragic death. In the gracefully aged main lodge, charm has persisted through renovations. It's common to find guests sharing fish tales and sipping wine in the late afternoons. Check out the Discover Oregon Wine Country package deals. $$$$

History and charm are woven into a memorable stay at Weasku Inn. Courtesy Country House Inns

TAKILMA

♿ **Out'N'About Treehouse Treesort** (300 Page Creek Road; 541-592-2208). If you're looking to branch out in your overnight experiences, you'll find plenty to like about Michael & Peggy Garnier's unusual resort. Get your vacation off the ground in one of 15 lodging choices, including our favorite, the Forestree, which hugs the trunk of a Douglas fir. It's 35 feet off the ground and accessible by swinging rope bridge, has a toilet, real sink (affixed to the tree), and hoist for gear. If heights make your legs quiver, climb into traditional cabins on terra firma. Special features include a swimming pool, bathhouse, barbecue pavilion, and tree-house-building classes. $$$–$$$$

Dining

in the Grants Pass/Illinois Valley Areas

GRANTS PASS

Blondies' Bistro (226 SW G Street; 541-479-0420). Bobbi Best spent time, money, and sweat creating the kind of place you wouldn't expect in Grants Pass. Think fern bar. The bistro is wrapped in warm hues and dark wood, dramatic art, and stained concrete floor with coordinating hanging lights. Appetizers are atypical, dinners enhanced by worldly flavors and vegetarian or vegan options, but the Yummy bowl steals the show. A large wine selection shines a spotlight on regional. L/D $$–$$$

The Laughing Clam (12 SW G Street; 541-479-1110). Rock 'n' roll and good ol' grub 'n' grog—it's all at the Clam. Originally a cigar shop in the late 1880s, it's the kind of place where you can slurp oyster shooters, chow down on chowder, or hammer into a sloppy burger without worry. The menu goes beyond seafood, with a sea of sandwiches, pastabilities, and daily all-you-can eats. Sit at a communal table or a booth, or belly up to the perfect bar for a glass of Druid's Fluid. L/D $$–$$$

One Fifteen Broiler (115 NW D Street; 541-474-7115). We like this classic diner, with its martini-shaker collection and Big Apple memorabilia squeezed as snugly into the interior as its crab is stuffed into mushrooms. Hand-cut steaks reign supreme, but seafood and pasta hold their own. For many years, the Musselman family has been dishing up their secret recipes, such as creamed spinach, tiramisu, and a tasty Caesar that doesn't hold the anchovies. The wine menu is balanced, about half from Oregon and the rest regionally oriented. L (Mon.–Fri.) D closed Sun. $$$–$$$$

The (New) River's Edge (1936 Rogue River Highway; 541-479-3938). New owners, new energy, new effort. The menu remains reflective of the Pacific Rim but with noticeable improvements, including steak, rack of lamb, and pasta. The interior is still sigh-provoking with minimal clutter, clean lines, and a water wall so soothing you'll want to stay awhile. Dine on a deck overlooking the Rogue River and choose from eight Oregon reds and whites by the glass—more by the bottle. BR/L/D $$$$

Summer Jo's (2315 Upper River Road Loop; 541-476-6882). Crops destined for upcoming meals are grown at Summer Jo's, an organic farm, orchard, produce stand, events facility, and eatery outside busy Grants Pass. In the style of Alice Waters, the concept is basic: keep it simple, seasonal, and sensational. Jo's grows its ingredients, floral arrangements, and seasonings; bakes artisan bread; and creates special holiday menus. It's a bustling place. Some local wine is served and sold by the bottle for off-premises consumption. B/L/D Thurs.–Sun. $$$$

Taprock Northwest Grill (971 SE Sixth Street; 541-955-5998). Taprock Grill embraces what Oregonians and visitors consider important: local and regional ingredients, scenic views, and Northwest hospitality. The grill is a ginormous, multilevel timber-framed building with gorgeous grounds made for strolling. The parklike setting is a gift to the city from local banker Brady Adams, who spent three years and millions of dollars on it.

The intricately detailed hand-carved doors and bars, etched stainless-steel doors, mounted wildlife, and tip of the musket to Lewis and Clark give it a museum feel. Reasonably priced fare is well above average and complemented by a predominantly Oregon/Washington wine selection. Weather permitting, dine on the deck overlooking the Rogue River. B/L/D $$

Twisted Cork Wine Bar & Tapas (210 SW Sixth Street; 541-295-3094). The emphasis at casually classy Twisted Cork is on wine-friendly small plates, with the addition of wraps, flatbreads, and a pasta du jour to tempt. A serious 800-bottle wine list offers many Oregon and Washington glass pours (with a minor mention of California), and local dessert wines let you know it's all about what's under the cork. For additional fun times, check out the events page at the bar's website. L/D/HH Tues.–Sat. $$

To Do

in the Grants Pass/Illinois Valley Area

Attractions

If you're coming from Roseburg, take a few minutes to duck off I-5 to stretch your legs at the **Wolf Creek Inn** (100 Front Street, 541-866-2474). The historic stagecoach stop was built in 1885 as a luxury hotel for weary travelers; it's now a bed & breakfast and restaurant. Several of the fruit trees planted at the time are still producing. The **Applegate Trail Interpretive Center Museum** (500 Sunny Valley Loop, 541-472-8545), in Wolf Creek, offers a peek into the area's rich pioneer history, especially gold mining.

The driest way to experience the Rogue River is on one of the famed jetboats that once delivered mail into the wilderness. **Hellgate Jetboat Excursions** (541-479-7204 or 800-648-4874) offers two- to five-hour trips on the Rogue from May through September. Wildlife lovers won't want to miss the **Wildlife Images Rehabilitation & Education Center** (11845 Lower River Road, 541-476-0222) in nearby Merlin. Injured or orphaned animals from across the country are brought to recuperate; call for tours. While visiting Wildlife Images, include a stop at **Pottsville** (2400 Pleasant Valley Road, 541-476-7319), a community near Merlin that's a museum unto itself. Pottsville offers tours of its museum plus outdoor exhibits that provide a snapshot of Oregon history. Merlin is grounds for the **Haines Apple Tree**, the state's second oldest.

Wolves were wiped out in this part of Oregon a century ago, but you can see them live at the **Howling Acres Wolf Sanctuary** (555 Davidson Road, 541-846-8962) in Williams, a half-hour south of Grants Pass in the rugged Siskiyou Mountains. A captivating stop for the art-inclined is **The Glass Forge** (501 SW G Street, 541-955-0815) in Grants Pass, which fashions Venetian-style wine glasses. The **Josephine County Historical Society** (512 SW Fifth Street, 541-479-7827) operates a museum and offers tours every Tuesday through Saturday at the historic Schmidt House.

A strange experience is **The House of Mystery** (4303 Sardine Creek Left Fork Road, 541-855-1543), otherwise known as the Oregon Vortex, south of Grants Pass in Gold Hill. Just try standing upright. You don't have to be a spelunker to appreciate the **Oregon Caves National Monument** (541-592-2100), about 50 miles south of Grants Pass, but check your claustrophobia at the door. The monument has a moderately strenuous walk through a marble cave where the temperature remains a constant 41 degrees. On the way to or from the cave, visit the **Kerbyville Museum** (24195 Redwood Highway/US 199, 541-592-2076) in Kerby to get a turn-of-the-century history lesson on pioneer exhibits and Indian artifacts.

Back in Grants Pass, the **Outdoor Growers Market** (541-476-5375, Fourth and F Streets) takes place on Saturdays mid-March through Thanksgiving; it's loaded with produce, art, wood products, and crafts. Every Wednesday (June through September) is the **Market at Riverside Park** from 9 AM to 1 PM.

Recreation

Any conversation about recreation in the Grants Pass area starts with the Rogue. River rats enjoy modest day-trip thrills on stretches above and below town. The serious white-water action begins below the store and restaurant in Galice, which seems as busy as a metro airport. No fewer than two dozen guide services offer trips; a Bureau of Land Management permit is required for private trips.

There are few locals who don't hunt or fish in these parts, especially if the quarry is a trophy elk or a Rogue salmon or steelhead. **Lake Selmac**, in the Illinois Valley, is considered a top bass fishery. The Rogue is also favored for hiking. The **Rogue River Trail** follows the north side of the river and includes Zane Grey's cabin; a 2-mile trail on the south side of the river ends at Rainie Falls, where you might see salmon migrating upstream and daring kayakers migrating downstream. Another terrific hike is the **Rogue River Recreational Corridor and Greenway** (541-582-1112), which when finished will connect Grants Pass to Ashland and is geared to cycling as well.

The Rogue Valley offers a little bit of everything when it comes to golf. The two 18-hole courses are **Dutcher Creek** (4611 Upper River Road, 541-474-2188) and the semiprivate **Grants Pass Golf Club** (230 Espey Road, 541-476-0840). You can find three nine-hole courses as well. Winter generally consists of rain, but snow enthusiasts will find an outlet at the **Page Mountain Sno-Park** near Cave Junction, where Nordic skiing, snowmobiling, and sledding live in harmony.

Wine Shopping

Elegance (321 SE Sixth Street, 541-476-0570, closed Sunday) sells wine, craft beers, and gourmet foods, next to vintage jewelry, antiques, collectibles, and hundreds of lamps; its motto is, "Stuff Is Us." On the first Friday of the month, wines, sometimes beer, and apps are available for a fee. **Oregon Outpost** (147 SW G Street, 541-474-2918 closed Sunday), stocks gourmet food and wine from around the state and fills picnic baskets. Locally made gifts and wine sampling give more reason to stop.

More Information

Grants Pass Visitors and Convention Bureau, 541-476-5510, 1995 NW Vine Street, www.visitgrantspass.org

Southern Oregon Winery Association, www.sorwa.org

Josephine County Historical Society, 541-479-7827, 512 SW Fifth Street, www.josephinehistorical.org

JACKSONVILLE AREA

Over the hill from scorching Medford lies a treat, and not just because of its more moderate climes. Jacksonville oozes National Historic charm in its idyllic setting, and serves as one gateway to Applegate Valley wine country. It began as Table Rock City during the 1850s gold rush and eventually became one of the largest towns in the region. When much of the commerce moved east to Medford early in the 20th century, Jacksonville's city fathers had the foresight to recognize the value of what their predecessors built. It remains true to character today.

Wineries
in the Jacksonville Area

The Jacksonville tour begins at the end of the Applegate Trail, at the country junction of Ruch, which has a slam-dunk general store with deli. Continue on OR 238 into Jacksonville.

JACKSONVILLE

Academy of Wine (18200 Highway 238; 541-846-6817). *Tasting room:* Sat. & Sun. 2–5, and by appt. *Fee:* Complimentary. *Owner/Winemaker:* Bernard Smith. *Wines:* Cabernet franc, Cabernet sauvignon, Chardonnay, Merlot, Pinot noir. *Cases:* 400. The Academy of Wine is a tiny winery that prides itself on a simple French model of making wine "the old-fashioned way"—though it stops short of grape stomping. Bernard keeps enough grapes for 400 cases and then sells the rest to Eola Hills Wine Cellars in the Willamette Valley. The name reflects Bernard's previous career as a professor and his eagerness to teach Wine 101 to anyone interested. Wine 102 is for more dedicated drinkers.

▲ John Michael Champagne Cellars (1425 Humbug Creek Road; 541-846-0810). *Tasting room:* Fri.–Sun. 11–5, May–Dec., and by appt. *Fee:* $5. *Owners:* Michael & Becky Giudici. *Winemaker:* Michael Giudici. *Wines:* Chardonnay, Merlot, Pinot blanc, Pinot gris, Pinot noir, Zinfandel, rosé, red and white blends, sparkling, sake. *Cases:* 600. Champagne Cellars has the usual suspects when it comes to wines, but what sets it apart—way apart—is bubbly and sparkling sake. Michael Giudici learned to make sake from an elderly neighbor 40 years ago, when he was a high school student. Today, the second-oldest winery in the Applegate has some of the best views, best champagne, and the only sake. An added visual treat is Michael's glass art and Asian jewelry.

LongSword's greeting wine is the semisparkling Accolade.

M. Kim Lewis

▲ Devitt Winery (11412 Highway 238; 541-899-7511). *Tasting room:* Daily 12–5, and by appt. *Fee:* $5. *Owners:* Jim & Sue Devitt. *Winemaker:* Jim Devitt. *Wines:* Cabernet franc, Cabernet sauvignon, Chardonnay, Merlot, Shiraz, Viognier, red and white blends, dessert. *Cases:* 2,500. As with most labels bearing a tongue-in-cheek name, there's a story behind Devitt's dessert wine, When Pigs Fly (a.k.a. Le Petite Oink) is a blend of Syrah and Gewürztraminer. For years, the Devitts merely sold the grapes they grew. But 2003 brought a regional glut, leaving Jim and Sue wondering what to do with the excess. Said Jim, who had made wine in Napa Valley, "Let's make our own again!" Responded Sue, who was content with the status quo, "When pigs fly!" It's obvious who won this domestic dispute.

▲ Fly High & LongSword Vineyards (8555 Highway 238; 541-899-1746 or 800-655-3877). *Tasting room:* Daily 12–5; Sat. & Sun., Jan. *Fee:* 2 complimentary/$5. *Owners:* Maria Largaespada & Matthew Sorensen. *Winemaker:* Matthew Sorensen. *Wines:* Fly High label: Pinot gris, Tempranillo, Viognier. LongSword label: Chardonnay, Syrah, sparkling. *Cases:* 1,500. Picture a wine bar dropped into the middle of a farmer's field, and you've got the Fly High tasting room, fashioned out of an airplane hangar. LongSword is the one place in Oregon you could be imbibing on the patio and have a paraglider land in your lap—almost literally. The vineyard is a popular landing zone for locals who like to ride the thermals from Woodrat Mountain. Congenial Matthew and Maria, refugees of pharmaceutical jobs, first made sparkling wine for their son's wedding and caught the bug. The label's "long sword" is part of Largaespada's family crest.

▲ 🎁 **Fiasco Winery/Jacksonville Vineyards** (8035 Highway 238; 541-846-3022). *Tasting room:* Daily 11–5, June–Nov.; Fri.–Sun., Jan.–May. *Fee:* Complimentary. *Owners:* David & Pam Palmer. *Winemaker:* David Palmer. *Wines:* Jacksonville label: Cabernet franc, Cabernet sauvignon, Merlot, Sangiovese, Syrah, Zinfandel, red blend. Fiasco label: Cabernet sauvignon, Riesling, Sangiovese, Syrah, Zinfandel, red blends. *Cases:* 2,000 Jacksonville, 1,500 Fiasco. Jacksonville Vineyards is the main player, Fiasco the sibling label. The William Matney homestead, reputedly the oldest building in Oregon, houses the winery. The tasting room is a utilitarian yet multicultural creation, a reflection of the Palmers' years of overseas travel. Most notable is the unusual floor made of decomposed granite. A *fiasco* is a straw-covered, glass-blown bottle made for Chianti, or a term for a flawed production; you can decide the intent.

▲ 🎁 ✐ 🐾 ❖ **Valley View Winery** (1000 Upper Applegate Road; 541-899-8468). *Tasting room:* Daily 11–5. *Fee:* $5. *Owner:* Mike & Mark Wisnovsky. *Winemaker:* John F. Guerrero. *Wines:* Cabernet franc, Cabernet sauvignon, Chardonnay, Merlot, Pinot gris, Pinot noir, Syrah, Tempranillo, Viognier, red and white blends, port-style, dessert. *Cases:* 15,000. When it comes to "firsts" you don't often hear about Valley View. Yet, it was the state's first winery, founded before the Civil War and operated for a half-century by pioneer Peter Britt. Operations ceased in 1906, when Prohibition intervened, but the Wisnovsky brothers resurrected history by planting 12 acres in 1972. The tasting room opened in 1978 and John Guerrero, their longest-tenured winemaker, soon took over. The exceptional Anna Maria wines are named for the Wisnovskys' mother. New in 2012: "Wine on the River," a four-day float through Hells Canyon on the Snake River.

Cricket Hill Winery (2131 Little Applegate Road; 541-899-7264). *Tasting room:* Sat. & Sun. 12–5, May–Nov. *Fee:* $3. *Owners:* Duane & Kathy Bowman. *Winemaker:* Duane Bowman. *Wines:* Cabernet franc, Merlot, red blends. *Cases:* 300. Duane Bowman searched southern Oregon's soils for his Right Bank Bordeaux varietals. He found his ideal in Applegate Valley, where the Bowmans have operated a traditional French winery for 20 years. Duane imported vines from the famed Right Bank and found a place where, he says, "the grapes feel at home" with the sunlight and terroir. Cricket Hill is a no-frills place with big wines from extraordinary grapes.

▲ **Cowhorn Vineyard** (1665 Eastside Road; 541-899-6876). *Tasting room:* Tues.–Sun. 11–4, May–Nov., and by appt. *Fee:* $5. *Owners/Winemakers:* Bill & Barbara Steele. *Wines:* Marsanne, Roussanne, Syrah, Viognier. *Cases:* 1,600. Southern Oregon's first certified biodynamic and organic operation is more than a winery—it's a full-fledged farm. On 117 acres, the Steeles grow hazelnuts, cherries, black truffles, and grapes. They're so in tune with the land they resist the term *winemakers*. Instead, they're "assistants to the grapes"—and devoted to Old World–style Rhônes. As for the winery's name, to generate compost they fill cow's horns with organic manure, bury the horns for six months, and get rich black soil in the spring. It's common practice among biodynamic farmers—honest.

▲ **South Stage Cellars** (125 South Third Street; 541-899-9120). *Tasting room:* Sun.–Thurs. 12–7, Fri. till 9, Sat. till 8. *Fee:* $5. *Owners:* Don & Traute Moore. *Winemakers:* Joe Dobbes & Joe Wright. *Wines:* Alberino, Cabernet franc, Cabernet sauvignon, Grenache, Merlot, Muscat, Pinot gris, Pinot noir, Sauvignon blanc, Syrah, Viognier, red and white blends. *Cases:* 6,000. After a busy day of touring, there are few better places to unwind than at South Stage, especially on a Friday or Saturday night. The 1865 brick building—the first to be restored in Jacksonville—oozes ambience and relaxation. Sit around the wrought-iron tables in the Wine Garden & Patio and sample one of South Stage's 27 wines or other brands made from the Moores' 10 vineyard sites.

Umpqua Valley Wine Tasting Room (220 East California Street; 541-899-5333). *Tasting room:* Thurs.–Sat. 11–6, Sun. 11–5. *Fee:* Complimentary. *Wines:* Gewürztraminer, Pinot gris, Pinot noir, Riesling. This quaint brick shop in downtown Jacksonville is a satellite tasting room for two wineries from Elkton: Bradley and Rivers Edge. They bring Umpqua region's cooler-climate varietals—most notably Pinot—to an area known more for warm-weather wines.

Quady North (255 East California Street; 541-702-2123). *Tasting room:* Thurs.–Sun. 11–7. *Fee:* $5. *Owner/Winemaker:* Herb Quady. *Wines:* Cabernet franc, Syrah, Viognier, rosé. *Cases:* 1,000. Herb Quady worked his way up to Oregon after spending quality time at his family's California winery, Bonny Doon, and then Troon, before putting down his own roots. Quady finds cooler-climate grapes more compelling, so he sources his from high-elevation vineyards near Ashland and in the Applegate Valley. The tasting room is a small ivy-covered brick building with a bistro out front that invites lingering. Save room on your palate for exquisitely structured dessert wines.

▲ **DANCIN Vineyards** (4554 South Stage Road; 541-245-1133). *Tasting room:* Wed., Thurs., & Sun. 12–7; Fri. & Sat. 12–8. *Fee:* $5. *Owners:* Dan & Cindy Marca. *Winemaker:* Eric Weisinger. *Wines:* Chardonnay, Pinot noir, Syrah, red and white blends. *Cases:* 1,000. It's as if the Marcas carved out their own slice of the Willamette Valley and brought it to Oregon's deep south. DANCIN's northeast-facing slope means plenty of shade and even layers of fog—ideal for growing Pinot noir. Eric Weisinger likes to blend juices from estate vineyards with grapes purchased from the north. The resulting "Pot of Dew" is his biggest seller. All the wines work well with wood-fired pizzas, artisan breads, cheese plates, and homemade desserts served on-site.

Lodging

in the Jacksonville Area

Applegate River Lodge B&B (15100 Highway 238; 541-846-6690). The names of the rooms in this spectacular log lodge reflect the diverse frontier history of the valley: Gold Miner's Cabin, Cattleman, Sportsman, Indian, Loggers, Myrtle, and Vineyard. All rooms have spa tubs, decks, and treed views of the Applegate River, but there are no TVs or phones—nice! Just as appealing is the inviting stone fireplace, made for curling up with glass of wine and book. The dinner house ($$) and lounge (closed Mon. & Tues.) adjacent to the lodge has an all-Oregon wine list and is renowned for preparing such dishes as mushrooms and prawn skewers over a red oak fire. $$

Country House Inns (830 North Fifth Street; 541-899-2050). Country House Inns is actually an inn, a collection of cottages, and a B&B geared for the wine tourist. They range from the recently remodeled 32-room Wine Country Inn on the edge of town and three quaint cottages a block from downtown,

The McCully House Inn originally was the home of Jacksonville's first doctor.
Courtesy McCully House Inn

to the five-room McCully House Inn and stately 1800s Reames House three blocks distant. A fifth option is the Pine Creek Cottage, walking distance from everything, including the Britt Festival. All accommodations exude a connection to Jacksonville's gold-rush days. The Reames House, on the National Register of Historic Places, is rented as an entire unit. For more details, go to www.mc cullyhouseinn.com. $$$–$$$$

Jacksonville Inn (175 East California Street; 541-899-1900). Journey back to the gold-rush era with a stay at the Jacksonville Inn, a national landmark that combines luxury with a Civil War persona in the heart of this busy little tourist town. Take a close look at the mortar and you might see gleaming flecks of gold. The inn has eight rooms above the dining area and four honeymoon cottages a block or so away. The restaurant makes use of the state's plentiful bounty. The wine shop off the hotel lobby has around 2,000 selections in a snug room where almost all bottles are within reach; it's earned *Wine Spectator*'s Award of Excellence numerous times. $$$–$$$$

Dining

in Jacksonville

Bella Union Restaurant & Saloon (170 West California Street; 541-899-1770). A diverse menu of lite bites, soups, salads, sandwiches, and pasta make this bustling café worth the typically long wait. Dinner entrées run the gamut, but Bella Union is best known for its pizza—a 30-minute wait. More than 20 glass pours are available, about half from Oregon. Bella Union has a colorful history, including a shooting, and was named after a popular San Francisco gambling house. BR Sun. L/D/HH/LN $$

Gogi's Café Britt (235 West Main Street; 541-899-8699). Previous owner George Gogi built a solid reputation that brothers Jonah and Gabe Murphy are continuing with an added touch of pizzazz. Tagging their cuisine as homegrown

European, they actually cultivate many ingredients on two farms, in Jacksonville and Applegate. Other organic and local products are used whenever possible; their seared scallops over parsnip purée are renowned. The wine list is heavy on Oregon, but includes other regions and countries. BR/L/D Wed.–Sun. $$$$

To Do
in Jacksonville

Attractions

Given that Jacksonville is a National Historic Landmark, any touring should start with the **Southern Oregon Historical Society** (206 North Fifth Street, 541-858-1682), with its two museums and five other historic properties. The Jacksonville Museum, in what was once the county courthouse, is the historical society's centerpiece. Next door, in the old county jail, is the Children's Museum, featuring hands-on activities for the kids. For an indelible night under the stars, the Britt Festival (350 First Street, 541-773-6077) lures concertgoers for a variety of entertainment by marquee names. The season runs from mid-June to mid-September.

Recreation

Runners, walkers, and hikers will appreciate the **Jacksonville Woodland Trails**, which were created to help preserve the character of the foothills surrounding the town.

MEDFORD AREA (Rogue Valley AVA)

Legend has it that Medford was named for the "middle ford" of Bear Creek, which meanders in relative obscurity toward the Rogue River south of town. But the name also describes its role as an economic, shopping, and transportation hub on I-5, between distant cities in California to the south and Willamette Valley to the north.

Many who live in this workmanlike, semimetropolitan city do so either in spite of or because of the isolation. The city has made an effort to restore its downtown, with a modicum of success. Medford might be best known as home of Ginger Rogers, Harry & David's fruit and vegetable empire, and the Jackson & Perkins rose fortune.

Wineries
in the Medford Area

Some like it hot—and that's the major weather contribution in this country. Naturally, the wines are associated with warm-weather grapes. Although the 4,200-square-mile AVA is named for the Rogue, few of the wineries and 1,100 acres of vineyards are near the river's banks. The borders are roughly formed by the Applegate, Bear Creek, and Illinois Valleys. The climate is similar to that of the Bordeaux region of France and so the Rogue Valley AVA is known for Cabernet franc, Cabernet sauvignon, Merlot, Sauvignon blanc, Syrah, and Malbec grapes.

CENTRAL POINT

Caprice Vineyards (970 Old Stage Road; 541-499-0449). *Tasting room:* Thurs.–Mon. 11–5. *Fee:* $5. *Owners:* Jim & Jeanne Davidian. *Winemaker:* Jim Davidian. *Wines:* Cabernet sauvignon, Chardonnay, Gewürztraminer, Viognier, red blend. *Cases:* 700. Where else can you sit under a grape arbor, sip wine, and watch a pack of alpacas? The Davidians both work in the medical field, but they've carved out a growing wine sideline. Jeanne is also pretty handy at weaving, and her work with alpaca fibers is on display in the store on their ranch, about a mile north of Jacksonville. Jim still has his red wines made elsewhere, but he's now making drink-ready whites. It's a fun place to visit, especially for the unusual resident pets.

🍴 ❖ **Ledger David Cellars** (245A North Front Street; 541-664-2218). *Tasting room:* Thurs.–Mon. 12–5. *Season:* Sept.–Mar. *Fee:* $5. *Owners:* David Traul & Lena Varner. *Winemakers:* John Quinones, Linda Donovan, & Brian Denner. *Wines:* Cabernet franc, Chardonnay, Chenin blanc, Malbec, Malvasia bianca, Petit verdot, Sangiovese, Syrah, Tempranillo, Viognier. *Cases:* 2,000. Ledger David has taken over the old Madrone and Daisy Creek tasting room, next to the Rogue Creamery and Lillie Belle Farms chocolates (Daisy Creek wines will be poured until they run out). The grapes are custom crushed by some of southern Oregon's top winemakers. Look for live music Fridays in the tasting room.

GOLD HILL

▲ 🎁 ❖ **Del Rio Vineyards & Winery** (52 North River Road; 541-855-2062). *Tasting room:* Daily 11–6. *Fee:* $5. *Owners:* Lee Traynham & Rob & Jolee Wallace. *Winemaker:* Jean-Michel Jussiaume. *Wines:* Cabernet sauvignon, Chardonnay, Malbec, Merlot, Muscat, Pinot gris, Syrah, Viognier, rosé, port-style, red blends. *Cases:* 3,500. Del Rio is almost a small town unto itself. The expansive grounds are abuzz with various activities, such as tastings, weddings, birthday parties, and other communal gatherings. More than 200,000 vines make it the largest vineyard in southern Oregon—on a whopping 205 acres. The usually crowded tasting room is in a refurbished portion of the Rock Point Stage Hotel, built in 1864 and still one of the oldest structures in the area.

Folin Cellars (9200 Ramsey Road; 541-855-2018). *Tasting room:* Daily 12–5, and by appt. *Fee:* Complimentary for groups of less than eight. *Owners:* Scott, Loraine & Rob Folin. *Winemaker:* Rob Folin. *Wines:* Petit sirah, Syrah, Tempranillo, Viognier, rosé. *Cases:* 1,200. Everyone gets in on the action at this family-owned operation. Dad and Mom run the 25-acre vineyard, while son Rob makes the wine. Although Rob doesn't look a day over 21, he did a seven-year stint at Domaine Serene. Northwest in design, the stunning tasting room has a 20-foot tongue-and-groove cathedral ceiling, stained concrete floors, granite countertops, and large picture windows. One of the early believers in "no cork, no worries," Folin uses the Vino-Seal glass closures on all of its wines. A second tasting room is in Carlton (see listing under "Wineries in the Carlton Area").

SHADY COVE

Crater Lake Cellars (21882 Highway 62, Building B; 541-878-4200). *Tasting room:* Fri. & Sat. 11–5, May–Sept. *Fee:* Complimentary. *Owners:* Steve & Mary Gardner. *Winemaker:* Steve Gardner. *Wines:* Cabernet sauvignon, Chardonnay, Grenache, Merlot, Muscat, Pinot noir, Riesling, Tempranillo, Viognier, red blend, rosé, dessert. *Cases:* 1,700. You have to wander off the beaten path to find Crater Lake Cellars. In fact, it's the last winery stop on OR 62 on your way to the namesake lake. Although Crater Lake has won its share of awards, it's worth taking home a bottle or two or three, just for the beautiful labels of southern Oregon's most picturesque sites. Candy in a Bottle is one not to miss—the name speaks for the wine.

EAGLE POINT

▲ **LaBrasseur Vineyard** (2444 Cobleigh Road; 541-865-3648). *Tasting room:* Fri.–Sun. 11–5, Mar.–Dec. *Fee:* $5. *Owners:* Fred & Candy LaBrasseur, Tony & Deidra Schroeder. *Winemaker:* Fred LaBrasseur. *Wines:* Cabernet sauvignon, Cabernet franc,

Merlot, Muscat, Pinot gris, Pinot noir, Riesling, Syrah, Tempranillo, Viognier, rosé, red blend, white blend, dessert. *Cases:* 1,100. After 34 years with the Medford Fire Department, Fred LaBrasseur wanted nothing to do with a retirement rocking chair. In 2006 he began teaching himself to make wine and planted six types of grapes on 15 acres before opening a winery in 2010. Fred and Candy, along with daughter and son-in-law Deidra and Tony Schroeder, do all the vineyard work, bottling, marketing and distribution. Their goal: affordable high-quality wines, and a tasting room that makes you feel like you're with family.

▲ 🍴 🎁 🖊 🐾 ❖ **Agate Ridge Vineyard** (1098 Nick Young Road; 541-830-3050). *Tasting room:* Daily 1–5 (summer), Tues.–Sun. 11–5 (off-season). *Fee:* $3–5. *Owners:* Kinderman family. *Winemaker:* Brian Denner. *Wines:* Cabernet franc, Cabernet sauvignon, Grenache, Malbec, Marsanne, Petite sirah, Pinot gris, Pinot noir, Primitivo, Roussanne, Syrah, Sauvignon blanc, Viognier, rosé, red and white blends. *Cases:* 2,800. General manager Kim Kinderman wanted to "get out of Alabama" and settle on her slice of Pacific Northwest heaven. Along with her brother and father, Don, she discovered a 126-acre farm more than a century old and began planting lots of vines. They've rooted 17 varietals—some for limited production, others for blending. The tasting room is fashioned out of the original farmhouse; the setting, with lightning-magnet Mount McLoughlin as backdrop, is stunning.

WHITE CITY

Kriselle Cellars (2200 Pine Gate Way; 541-842-0029). *Tasting room:* Daily 11–5:30. *Fee:* $5. *Owners:* Scott & Krisell Steingraber. *Winemaker:* Scott Steingraber. *Wines:* Cabernet franc, Cabernet sauvignon, Sauvignon blanc, Tempranillo, Viognier, red and white blends. *Cases:* 3,000. Scott's California garage hobby turned into a full-time labor of love, culminating in a new winery and palatial tasting room in September 2012. Perched on a knoll surrounded by 230 acres of grapes, the grand lodge is 3,000 square feet of reclaimed materials, and stands 35 feet high, with picture windows stretching floor to ceiling. Equally appealing is the outdoor terrace with wide vineyard views. Cabernet sauvignon and Tempranillo are the signature wines.

MEDFORD

▲ 🎁 **RoxyAnn Winery** (3285 Hillcrest Road; 541-776-2315). *Tasting room:* Daily 11–6. *Fee:* Complimentary. *Owners:* Jack Day & Day-Parsons family. *Winemaker:* John Quinones. *Wines:* Merlot, Pinot gris, Syrah, Tempranillo, Viognier, red and white blends, dessert. *Cases:* 16,000. Medford has gradually enveloped RoxyAnn, but that hasn't prevented the Century Farm and Hillcrest Orchard from retaining their aura and charm. The old white barn is on the National Register of Historic Places and has been in the same family for 100 years; they've been running the winery for the past 10. The tasting room is a special place with a U-shaped bar that'll help you ignore the suburban homes springing up around the winery. Don't be surprised if you're joined by locals; RoxyAnn is a popular place on the way home from work.

▲ 🎁 🍴 🖊 🐾 ❖ **EdenVale Winery** (2310 Voorhies Road; 541-512-9463). *Tasting room:* Mon.–Sat. 11–6, Sun. 12–4. *Fee:* $5–10. *Owner:* Anne Root. *Winemaker:* Ashley Campanella. *Wines:* Chardonnay, Cabernet franc, Grenache, Malbec, Pinot noir, Syrah, Tempranillo, Viognier, rosé, red and white blends, port-style, dessert. *Cases:* 10,000. You might be inclined to look over your shoulder for Rhett and Scarlett at the Voorhies Mansion, but don't let the antebellum formality deter you. The tasting room might be dressed to the nines, but it's still down-home friendly. The winery sits on the oldest pear orchards in southern Oregon (1885), In fact, the property, owned by the Voorhies family for more than a century, is on the National Register of Historic Places. An array of well-made wines also contributes to its popularity.

Pebblestone Cellars (1642 Camp Baker Road; 541-512-1655). *Tasting room:* Thurs.–Mon. 12–5; May–Oct., Sat. & Sun., Nov.–Apr. *Fee:* $5. *Owners:* Ellis family. *Winemaker:* Dick Ellis. *Wines:* Cabernet franc, Mélange, Merlot, Pinot gris, Syrah, Viognier, rosé, red blends. *Cases:* 1,200. After more than two decades of harvesting grapes for others and making wine at their friends' site in California, Dick and Pat came north in 2002 to do their own thing. Their search for that perfect pebbly piece of vineyard ended a year later when they found 26 acres of sandy and gravelly soil between Medford and Ashland. The Ellises don't have their own winery; instead, they produce at various facilities.

TALENT

▲ 🎁 🐾 StoneRiver Vineyard (2178 Pioneer Road; 541-535-4661). *Tasting room:* Thurs.–Mon. 12–5, May–Oct.; Sat. & Sun. 12–5, Nov.–Apr. *Fee:* $5. *Owners:* Paul & Virginia Lange. *Winemaker:* Custom crushed. *Wines:* Chardonnay, Merlot, Pinot gris, Syrah, Viognier, rosé. *Cases:* 1,000. Like many of their neighbors, the Langes ran an orchard for 22 years before planting a vineyard, and eventually began custom crushing at EdenVale, RoxyAnn, and J. Scott. The Bear Creek Boutique Wineries group persuaded them to open their 1,000-square-foot tasting room in the middle of their lush vineyard. The atmosphere is laid-back, other than a raucous game or two of shuffleboard.

▲ ❖ Paschal Winery & Vineyard (1122 Suncrest Road; 541-535-7957). *Tasting room:* TBD *Fee:* TBD. *Owners:* Roy and Jill Paschal. *Winemaker:* TBD. *Wines:* Chardonnay, Melange, Merlot, Muscat, Pinot gris, Pinot noir, Syrah, Tempranillo, Viognier, red and white blends, dessert. *Cases:* 2,000. It has been a rollercoaster ride at Paschal since late 2011, when second owner Ron Tenuta died just as he was getting his balance as an Oregon winemaker. The Paschals re-bought the winery they founded from Tenuta's

Paschal Winery & Vineyard has lively events and stunning views. M. Kim Lewis

wife, Donna, and are making a go of it again. The tasting room will most likely retain much of its Mediterranean, boutique coffee shop flavor, with rugs scattered on wood floors, warm colors, and clusters of relaxed seating. At press time, the family was waiting for OLCC to issue their new license.

Trium (7112 Rapp Lane; 541-535-4015). *Tasting room:* Thurs.–Mon. 11–5:30, Apr.–Oct., and by appt. *Fee:* $5–7. *Owners:* Kurt & Laura Lotspeich. *Winemaker:* Peter Rosback. *Wines:* Cabernet franc, Cabernet sauvignon, Merlot, Pinot gris, Viognier, rosé, red blend. *Cases:* 1,000. *Trium* is Latin for "of the three"—a reference to the winery's three vineyards and the three classic Bordeaux varietals in Trium's signature blend. Cheery potted flowers and plants give texture to the ivy-covered tasting room. Trium grows high-quality fruit and trusts it to Peter Rosback of Sineann fame. The result: Trium's wines usually fare well against the competition.

Lodging
in Medford

MEDFORD

❖ **Under the Greenwood Tree B&B** (3045 Bellinger Lane; 541-776-0000). Named for a song in Shakespeare's *As You Like It*, the highly rated B&B is in close proximity to the Britt Festival in Jacksonville, the Shakespeare Festival in Ashland, and winery hopping in any direction. The rooms—D'Anjou, Comice, Bartlett, and Bosc—are named for the area's prolific pears. The farm doesn't have any greenwood trees, but 300-year-old oaks shade the youthful farmhouse, a mere 125 years old. Labeled "Best in Oregon" by *Sunset* magazine, the B&B and 10 surrounding acres include Civil War–era buildings, bicycles to borrow, and hammocks for lazing after a day of touring. $$–$$$

Dining
in the Medford Area

MEDFORD

Bambu (970 North Phoenix Road, #106; 541-608-7545). Don't let the strip-mall locale dissuade or fool you. Chef Adam and sommelier Veronica have a hot thing going: he chefs and she manages and hostesses with baby in tow. Sit at the bar and watch Asian fusion come together in the form of small and large plates, emphasis on seafood. Rockin' crab cakes, calamari, pad thai, mahi-mahi, and Thai coconut soup to die for are meant to share. They have a well-above-average selection of local wines by glass and bottle. L/D/HH $$

Café Dejeuner (1108 East Main Street; 541-857-1290). It takes some sleuthing, but Terry and Louise Swenson's wildly popular café is worth the hunt. It looks like a modest residential home with parking on the street, but step inside the cramped rooms and feel the warmth. White linens, sparkling stemware, candlelight, and Caesar salads tossed table side add a classy touch. Expect seasonal menu changes, but you'll usually find lamb osso buco, wild salmon, and pasta dishes. Most wines hail from Oregon, making going local easy. Reservations recommended, even for lunch. B/L Mon.–Fri. D Tues.–Sat. $$$–$$$$

Elements Tapas Bar & Lounge (101 East Main Street; 541-779-0135) Channel your inner Spaniard in this authentic tapas bar where plates are prepared with wine in mind. Tempt yourself with paella (the only $$$), pastry-wrapped baked Manchego, flat-out fabulous flatbreads, or the crave-worthy grapes rolled in

Rogue Creamery smoky blue and pistachios. Elements encourages sharing in this groovy, metro-chic space, and you won't be turned away even near closing time. Local vino is listed to complement or contrast your food. Of special favor is the three-glass flight of two-ounce samples—you choose the wines. L/D/HH/LN Tues.–Sat. $$

Pomodori Ristorante (1789 Steward Avenue; 541-776-6332). As you might expect, northern Italian fare is the order of the day in this cheery nook on Medford's west side. In the back you'll find a more romantic mode with candlelit glass-top tables. In the casual front, kids are welcome. Each meal is made to order, and locals rave about the linguine and jumbo shrimp. Almost all wine comes from the Applegate Valley. John Bartow and chef Jeff Lindow also like to host affordable winemaker dinners periodically. L (Tues.–Fri.) D (Tues.–Sat.) $$

Porter's Restaurant and Bar (147 North Front Street; 541-857-1910). Look for the clock tower and ivy-covered walls that hide the entry doors to the former train depot. Classic continental cuisine stars surf and turf entrées, and a few out-of-the-ordinary selections (chicken satay, veggie Thai bowl). Leave room for the "all aboard" desserts. Out back is a festive dining patio enveloped by wisteria, giving it a secret garden look. A basket of blankets and humidor provide warmth on chilly nights. At least a dozen Oregon wines by the glass and many more by the bottle are yours for the asking. D/HH/LN $$$

The Regency Grill (2300 Biddle Road; 541-770-1234). Chef Dale Flower brings a French touch to a Continental menu, which may be enjoyed indoors or out (heaters available). Look for seasonal specials that might include Northwest steelhead, Pacific bay shrimp, or spinach tortellini—all wine-friendly. About 70 percent of the wines are grown and produced in state. If you want less formal pub grub, Chadwicks fills the bill. B/L/D/BR $$

38 Central (38 North Central Avenue, #110; 541-776-0038). "Classic continental," "wine-centric cuisine," and "an upscale casual ambience" best describe 38 Central, a busy downtown fixture. Comfort food is local and seasonal, and its region of the world is well represented on its fluid wine list. The coho salmon and Carlton Farms thick-cut pork chops are highly requested L (Mon.–Fri.) D (Mon.–Sat.) BR (Sun.) HH (Mon.–Thurs.) $$$

The Wharf (827 West Jackson Street; 541-858-0200). Brent Kenyon's love of cooking and catering for friends led him to a fish house he could call his own. He's created coastal ambience with white walls and large blue fishing boats, blue-and-white checked table tops and cozy deck seating on the patio. Because he's in a residential neighborhood, Brent built an 8-foot fence for privacy and uses the driveway for seating. His fresh seafood comes from Newport and a portion is saved for retail. His chowder is so good he has to make two batches on weekends. It's a perfect place to troll for local wines, too, specifically chosen to meld with seafood. L/D Tues.–Sun. $$$

TALENT

New Sammy's Bistro (2210 South Pacific Highway; 541-535-2779). Charlene and Vern's two-person show is heel kickin', healthy portions of the usual (burgers, salmon) and unusual (quail, suckling pig). But veggies take front stage. Reservations are essential because it's so small (six tables and a few stools). Although New Sammy's is not attention seeking, *Food & Wine* ranked it among the "top 50 wine experiences." Loyal customers and greenhorns have commented that they got more than they paid for—unusual these days. L/D Wed.–Sun., Feb.–Nov. $$$

To Do

in the Medford Area

Attractions

Medford is generally not known for unique attractions. In fact, it bills itself as a cheaper place to stay while you're visiting the more expensive Ashland and Jacksonville. Still, the area has its share of famous alums, which helps explain the **Craterian Ginger Rogers Theater** (23 South Central Avenue, 541-779-3000). The theater opened in 1924 and has since become the pride of a spruced-up downtown. Rogers, who owned a ranch in nearby Shady Cove and later a home in Medford, appeared there at age 15—less than two years after it opened—and returned 67 years later.

There was a time when water-powered gristmills seemed to be everywhere. Now, there is just one—the **Butte Creek Mill** (402 Royal Avenue North, 541-826-3531) in Eagle Point. The 1872 mill churns out stone-ground flours and other grain products, with the bran and germ preserved by the grinding. The **Rogue Valley Growers and Crafters Market** (888-826-9868), offering locally grown fruits and vegetables, comes to the Medford Armory every Thursday year-round. Although it's about 85 miles from the Rogue Valley, **Crater Lake National Park** (541-594-3000) is worth veering off your favorite southern Oregon wine trail for—especially to escape the summer heat. In Oregon's only national park, the lake is a mesmerizing blue, and there is much to explore.

Recreation

Many people in Medford live for hunting, fishing, and boating on numerous lakes and streams in the region. Boat rentals are available at **Lost Creek Lake, Lake of the Woods, Fish Lake**, and **Lemolo Lake**. Fly fishermen will see giant rainbow trout cruising the depths in the half-mile-long Holy Waters of the Rogue just below Lost Creek Dam.

Medford's warm weather isn't just for river buffs. The valley might just have the best golfing in Oregon. There are no fewer than seven courses, including the renowned **Eagle Point Golf Course** (541-826-8225), 10 miles east of Medford. That course, designed by Robert Trent Jones Jr., was rated among the top 10 in the country by *Golf Week* magazine. **Centennial Golf Club** (541-773-4653), designed by PGA Tour player John Fought, was chosen the valley's best by readers of the *Medford Mail Tribune*. Medford also has three nine-hole courses: **Bear Creek Golf Course** (541-773-1822), **Stewart Meadows** (541-770-6554), and **Quail Point Golf Course** (541-857-7000).

Wine Shopping

The **Pacific Wine Club** (3588 Heathrow Way, 541-245-3334) is a warehouse and bottle shop with a new tasting room serving wine and beer daily. Among the 2,000 bottles are many Oregon, Washington, and California wines, plus imports.

More Information

Medford Chamber of Commerce, 541-779-4847, 101 East Eighth Street, www.medfordchamber.com

ASHLAND AREA

To Oregonians and Californians alike, Ashland has long been synonymous with Shakespeare. The annual festival lures tourists the world over to what has become a trendy, cultured, picturesque community in the forested foothills of the Siskiyou Mountains. But there's more to like here: a fresh environment, moderate climate, arts and parks galore, youthful energy from Southern Oregon University students, and a plethora of outdoor activities.

Ashland's two wineries are part of the Bear Creek Boutique Wineries in the Medford area, but because the two areas are so distinct, we have separated them.

Wineries
in the Ashland Area

ASHLAND

❖ **Grizzly Peak Winery** (1600 East Nevada Street; 541-482-5700). *Tasting room:* Thurs.–Sun. 12–4, May–Oct.; Sat. & Sun. 12–4, Nov.–Apr.; and by appt. *Fee:* Complimentary. *Owners:* Al & Virginia Silbowitz. *Winemaker:* Andy Swan. *Wines:* Cabernet franc, Cabernet sauvignon, Chardonnay, Malbec, Merlot, Pinot noir, Syrah, Tempranillo, red and white blends, dessert. *Cases:* 1,000. Al and Virginia had the location. Andy Swan had the winemaking skills. Together, they have formed Ashland's second winery, Grizzly Peak, which sits amid oak savanna at a staggering 2,250 feet above sea level on the flanks of—where else?—Grizzly Peak. The venture began in 2006, the tasting room opened in 2008, and the Silbowitzes are in the process of building a large winery.

▲ ✐ 🐾 ❖ **Weisinger's of Ashland** (3150 Siskiyou Boulevard; 541-488-5989). *Tasting room:* Daily 11–5, May–Oct.; Wed.–Sun. 11–5, Nov.–Apr. *Fee:* \$3–8. *Owner/Winemaker:* Eric Weisinger. *Wines:* Cabernet franc, Cabernet sauvignon, Chardonnay, Gewürztraminer, Merlot, Mescolare, Petite blanc, Petite pompadour, Syrah, Viognier, rosé, red and white blends, ruby port-style. *Cases:* 3,000. Last call before the border! Grab a glass, pull up a chair, and enjoy views of the Siskiyous from the three-tier deck at Weisinger's. It's a great place to "get the southern Oregon vibe." A completely renovated guest cottage (\$\$\$) in the vineyard comes with an outdoor hot tub, gas barbecue, full kitchen, bottle of wine, cheese and crackers, free wine tasting, and bottle discounts for guests. Lower rates in the off-season.

Lodging
in Ashland

♿ 🐾 **The Inn at Lithia Springs** (2165 West Jackson Road; 800-482-7128). In ancient times, Indians came to what they called the Common Grounds—a site of natural mineral hot springs, or healing waters. That community feeling continues at Lithia Springs, which offers European-style rooms, English cottages, and the Water Tower—a replica of a castle's corner lookout tower, sans turrets. Each accommodation has a whirlpool tub to soak away your pain after an arduous day in wine country. \$\$\$–\$\$\$\$

🍴 🍸 ♿ **The Peerless Hotel** (243 Fourth Street; 541-488-1082). Oh, the stories these brick walls could tell. The Peerless, built in 1900, made the list of 1,000 Places to See Before You Die because of its history, proximity to everything Ashland, and Old World elegance. Even the Coca-Cola sign on the side, originally painted in 1915, has been brought back to life. Depending on which room you choose, you could be thrust back 100 years to the West Indies, Hawaii, French Quarter, or an Italian garden. Living up to the hotel's standards, the Peerless restaurant serves Northwest cuisine that pairs well with wine. \$\$–\$\$\$\$

🍴 **Winchester Inn** (35 South Second Street; 541-488-1113 or 800-972-4991). All's well that begins well, the Bard might say. At the Winchester Inn, begin with a breakfast followed by a busy day of touring, the most exquisite dining in Ashland, and withdrawal to an amenity-laced room. The elegant, Victorian-style inn has an impressive 11 guest rooms and eight suites. Rates are based on the season, which revolves around the Shakespeare Festival. Few wine bars in Oregon have more choices for sipping, and the global menu includes Vietnamese cuisine. $$–$$$$

Dining
in the Ashland Area

Amuse (15 North First Street; 541-488-9000). Whisking up American/French cuisine for many years, Erik Brown and Jamie North seem to still love what they do and it shows on their plates. Four courses provide about a half-dozen selections under each, and force some tough decisions. Solution: Bring friends who like to share. A balanced wine menu includes Oregon and Washington choices. $–$$$

Greenleaf Restaurant (49 North Main Street; 541-482-2808). Homemade goodness buds in fish-and-chips, stir-frys, and vegetarian delights with Greek flair. With many organic ingredients, and gluten free, the food tastes as good as it'll make you feel. Wines by the glass are predominantly local, exception being organic Californian, have food matching in mind. Etna cherry or pear hard cider from Salem works well, too. B/L/D $$

Larks (212 East Main Street; 541-488-5558). "Excite and surprise" your palate with products from local, sustainable purveyors. Menus reflect the season and emphasize the best Oregon has to offer. Accolades go for Larks' version of Southern-fried chicken (don't pass on bacon gravy). With exceptions in a few categories, the wines are local or from Washington. Larks is located in the Ashland Springs Hotel, where select Getaway Packages include reasonable rates, movie tickets, and credit toward dinner. BR (Sat. & Sun.) L (Mon.–Fri.) D (Thurs.–Sun.) $–$$$

Liquid Assets Wine Bar (96 North Main Street; 541-482-9463). When you want to "wine down," Jim and Denise have what you need at this intimate bar and bottle shop. Consider starters, entrées, a cheese plate, or dessert—with a glass or bottle of a tried-and-true or new-to-you wine. Condensed space makes it feel homey, while the menu gives the feeling of a night off from the kitchen. Some local selections make the list. $–$$

Omar's (1380 Siskiyou Boulevard; 541-482-1281). For 21 years running, Omar's has been tagged "Ashland's Best Steaks & Seafoods" in a city-wide poll. Fresh seafood flown in almost daily, choice steaks, and careful prep are trademarks. Lunch has variety but is known for burger-mania—beef, turkey, fish, veggie, or supersize double quarter-pounders that are the best deal in town. A classic for good food and service, it serves select Oregon wines by the glass or bottle. L (Mon.–Fri.) D/LN $$$–$$$$

To Do
in Ashland

Attractions

Come any time between February and October, and chances are, tourists and locals will be holding tickets to the **Oregon Shakespeare Festival** (541-482-0446), which began in the 1930s. No theater in the nation sells more tickets for plays or performances. Not surprisingly, art in all forms is a big deal here. The **Ashland**

Independent Film Festival (541-488-3823), staged every April, entered its 12th season in 2013. It draws top indie filmmakers from across the globe to show their films at the Varsity Theatre downtown.

Oregon Stage Works (191 A Street, 541-482-2334) offers year-round performances from national and local playwrights. If light-and-breezy music or comedy is more to your taste, the **Oregon Cabaret Theatre** (541-488-2902) has been presenting a rollicking good time for a quarter-century in a refurbished Baptist church. Matinee and evening performances include a meal featuring wine or beer from the Pacific Northwest. Speaking of music, the **Ashland City Band** is the nation's oldest, playing in Lithia Park since 1876.

Locals are justifiably proud of their lush, 100-acre **Lithia Park** (59 Winburn Way, 541-488-5340), with its bandshell, hiking trails, and Japanese garden. Decades ago, Ashland had visions of becoming a destination spa town, but all that's left of that dream is **Jackson WellSprings** (2253 Highway 99 North, 541-482-3776), a hot springs with a large swimming pool and private soaking tubs. Fittingly for such a progressive community, there are three farmers' markets: **Rogue Valley Growers and Crafters Market** (541-261-0577) offers locally grown produce on Tuesday mornings in the Ashland Armory and Saturday mornings on Lithia Way and First Street; the **Lithia Artisans Market** (20 Calle Guanajuato, 541-535-3733) features music, crafts, and arts on weekends from May to October; and the **A Street Marketplace & Pavilion** (541-488-3433) is open year-round in the Railroad District. In addition, Ashland has no fewer than 15 art galleries within a reasonable walking distance downtown.

Recreation

Whatever the season, Ashland is another Oregon outdoor-recreation hot spot. **Mt. Ashland Ski Area** (541-482-2897), which sits virtually atop the Oregon-California border, receives more than 300 inches of snow per year. The **Oak Knoll Golf Club** (3700 Highway 66, 541-482-4311) offers nine modest holes for the golfer; it's the only course in town. Southern Oregon fat-tire enthusiasts revel in the exceptional mountain biking and invigorating single-track trails leading away from town.

More Information

Ashland Chamber of Commerce, 541-482-3486, 110 East Main Street, www.ashland chamber.com

9

Columbia Gorge

A WORLD OF WINES IN 40 MILES

FEW PLACES IN OREGON ARE AS SPECTACULAR as the Columbia Gorge, and nowhere is such a dramatic diversity of terrain packed into such tight geographical quarters.

The western end, which begins abruptly 20 miles from Portland, is all about clouds, mist, Douglas firs, vine maples, blackberry brambles, and close proximity to about 1.5 million predominantly progressive citizens. Just 80 miles to the east, the largely treeless horizon is decidedly rural, arid, sunny, and conservative. Along the way, the mighty Columbia River courses through three massive dams and the Cascade Range, creating sheer 4,000-foot basalt cliffs and 77 waterfalls.

Hood River is in the heart of the gorge, where two distinct climates and topographies mesh. This is the end of the line for much of western Oregon's moist marine air. High desert begins one ridgeline to the east. The result is lush, colorful valleys and fir-bathed hillsides, sunny days, and productive orchards. If there is a downside to this Eden, it is the gale-force winds that constantly buffet the gorge floor. Then again, the town has turned this nuisance into a hefty and colorful tourist economy. In the past two decades, Hood River has emerged as one of Oregon's great outdoor playgrounds. Even more recent is its emergence on the wine scene. It has also become a mecca for foodies and the locavore movement.

GETTING HERE AND AROUND

Most adventures into the Columbia Gorge start in Portland. Access is easy from **Portland International Airport**, on the city's east side. Take I-84 through the industrial zones and suburbs of east Portland to Troutdale, where the urban hubbub ends when the freeway crosses the Sandy River. Visitors from the east typically descend on the region after lengthy drives across vast wheat fields, empty sage plains, and mountains from Boise on I-84 and from Spokane on US 395.

LEFT: Cathedral Ridge Winery was named Winery of the Year by Wine Press Northwest in 2007. Courtesy Cathedral Ridge Winery

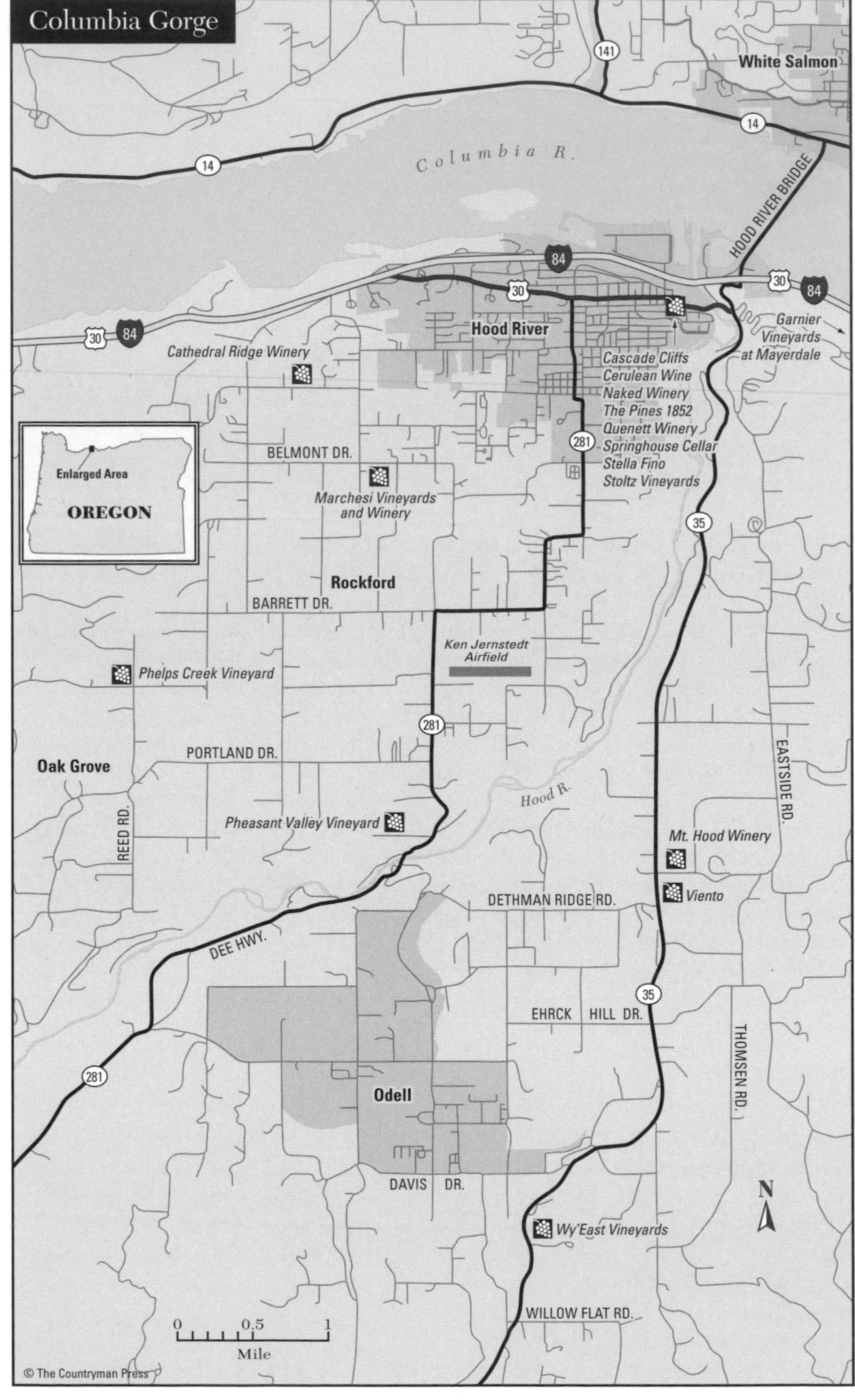
Columbia Gorge
White Salmon
Columbia R.
HOOD RIVER BRIDGE
Hood River
Cathedral Ridge Winery
Garnier Vineyards at Mayerdale
Cascade Cliffs
Cerulean Wine
Naked Winery
The Pines 1852
Quenett Winery
Springhouse Cellar
Stella Fino
Stoltz Vineyards
Enlarged Area
OREGON
BELMONT DR.
Marchesi Vineyards and Winery
Rockford
BARRETT DR.
Ken Jernstedt Airfield
Phelps Creek Vineyard
PORTLAND DR.
Oak Grove
EASTSIDE RD.
Hood R.
REED RD.
Pheasant Valley Vineyard
Mt. Hood Winery
Viento
DETHMAN RIDGE RD.
DEE HWY.
EHRCK HILL DR.
THOMSEN RD.
Odell
DAVIS DR.
N
Wy'East Vineyards
WILLOW FLAT RD.
0 0.5 1
Mile
© The Countryman Press

The Amtrak Empire Builder hugs the Columbia on the Washington side and has stops—one eastbound and one westbound daily—across the river in Wishram and Bingen. **Greyhound** has six bus arrivals daily in Hood River, three from each direction.

Wineries
in the Columbia Gorge

When spin doctors in the Columbia Gorge AVA say, "A World of Wines in Forty Miles," they aren't overdramatizing. They can legitimately claim that they grow wine grapes from A (Albarino) to Z (Zinfandel).

This phenomenon was made possible in part by a series of colossal dams that harnessed the free-flowing Columbia beginning in the Great Depression. Bonneville, The Dalles, and John Day dams changed the gorge forever. It's likely that the wine industry couldn't exist without them. Whereas once the Columbia's waters were rapidly moving and cool, now the river is a series of long, warmer lakes. The vinifera no longer endures wicked bouts of frost that came on the coattails of ferocious gorge gales.

Dramatic variances in climate mean fickle Pinot noir, Gewürztraminer, and Pinot gris are mainstays at the western end, and the burlier Syrah, Barbera, and Cabernet sauvignon thrive on the eastern side. Some vineyards were planted in the 1880s and a few remnants remain today.

HOOD RIVER

❖ **Cathedral Ridge Winery** (4200 Post Canyon Drive; 800-516-8710). *Tasting room:* Daily 11–6. *Fee:* $5. *Owner:* Robb Bell. *Winemaker:* Michael Sebastiani. *Wines:* Cabernet sauvignon, Chardonnay, Gewürztraminer, Halbtrocken, Merlot, Pinot gris, Pinot noir, Riesling, Syrah, Tempranillo, Viognier, Zinfandel, rosé, red blends. *Cases:* 5,000. Don't tell Robb Bell you can't grow Pinot noir in this AVA. He has the wine and awards to prove otherwise. Having Michael Sebastiani—a fourth-generation winemaker from a renowned family—doesn't hurt. Robb is proud to point out that all grapes for their extensive line are grown on the estate or within a 20-mile radius. Large gardens and grounds can host many events or an intimate party of two.

Marchesi Vineyards & Winery (3955 Belmont Drive; 541-386-1800). *Tasting room:* Thurs.–Mon. 11–6. *Fee:* $5. *Owners:* Franco & Sandy Marchesi. *Winemaker:* Franco Marchesi. *Wines:* Barbera, Dolcetto, Nebbiolo, Pinot gris, Pinot noir, Sangiovese, red blends. *Cases:* 2,000. Taste a sip of Italy at this up-and-coming winery. Born in Piedmont, Franco Marchesi makes wines with passion. His products are true expressions of the northern Italian varietals grown on his estate, and by friends and neighbors in the foothills. Because he's Italian, he gets a pass for calling it "Pinot grigio" in a state where it's called "Pinot gris." The tasting room is similar to an *enoteca*, brimming with Italian décor and charm.

Phelps Creek Vineyards (1850 Country Club Road; 541-386-2607). *Tasting room:* Daily 11–5. *Fee:* $5. *Owner:* Bob Morus. *Winemaker:* Rich Cushman & Alexandrine Roy. *Wines:* Chardonnay, Gewürztraminer, Merlot, Pinot noir, Syrah, rosé, red and white blends, dessert. *Cases:* 5,000. The Phelps Creek tasting room is an extension of the Hood River Golf Course parking lot, located along the valley's Fruit Loop drive and near the winery's 30-acre vineyard. Mt. Defiance Wines is Phelps's second label. The name is a reference to baseball player turned fire-and-brimstone preacher Billy Sunday, who railed against the evils of alcohol. Sunday settled in the quiet Hood River Valley in the 1920s, long before it became a hot wine region.

▲ 🎁 🍴 🖊 🐾 ❖ **Pheasant Valley Vineyard & Winery** (3890 Acree Drive; 541-387-3040). *Tasting room:* Daily 11–6, Thurs.–Mon., Feb.–Dec. (11–5 winter). *Fee:* $5. *Owners:* Scott & Gail Hagee. *Winemaker:* Randy Bonaventura & Scott Hagee. *Wines:* Cabernet sauvignon, Chardonnay, Gewürztraminer, Pinot gris, Pinot noir, Primitivo, Riesling, Syrah, Tempranillo, Zinfandel, red and white blends, rosé, blush, pear. *Cases:* 4,000. After strictly relying on certified organic pear and apple orchards for many years, a third fruit has become a charm—grapes. Organic Pinot noir and Pinot gris are grown on 17 acres and reflect the cool, moist marine air that makes its last stand here. Pheasant Valley is at the ready with an assortment of six to 15 wines typically open for tasting. The Hagees haven't forgotten their roots: They make a popular organic pear wine. They also run a three-room B&B on the property where guests are treated to complimentary wine sampling.

▲ 🍴 🖊 🐾 ❖ **Mt. Hood Winery** (2882 Van Horn Drive; 541-386-8333). *Tasting room:* Daily 11–5, Mar.–Nov. *Fee:* $5. *Owners:* Steve, Don & Libby Bickford. *Winemaker:* Rich Cushman. *Wines:* Chardonnay, Gewürztraminer, Malbec, Pinot gris, Pinot noir, Riesling, Syrah, rosé, red blend, pear, dessert. *Cases:* 2,500. Enjoy a lengthy lineup of wines under 30-foot vaulted ceilings in a Northwest-timber lodge setting with huge picture windows, or on the 3,000-square-foot patio that allows for double mountain views (Hood and Adams). The winery is best known for its Pinot noir and Pinot gris. We suggest the $10 appetizer plate accompanied by six tastes.

Viento (301 Country Club Road; 541-490-6655 or 541-386-3026). *Tasting room:* Daily 12–5. *Fee:* $5. *Owner/Winemaker:* Rich Cushman. *Wines:* Barbera, Grüner veltliner, Pinot noir, Riesling, Sangiovese, Syrah, Tempranillo, Viognier, rosé, red and white blends, dessert. *Cases:* 1,500. You frequently see Hood River native Rich Cushman listed as winemaker, but finding his Viento wines is a bit tricky. And after 28 years of making wine for others and recently pouring at the Gorge White House, he's ready to move into his own winery on Country Club Road. Regardless of where you find them, the search for his wines is definitely worth the effort. Viento is highly recognized for Riesling, made from vines planted in 1982 in Rich's own small vineyard. *Viento* is Spanish for "wind", an appropriate moniker in the gorge.

▲ 🖊 🐾 **Wy' East Vineyards** (3189 Highway 35; 541-386-1277). *Tasting room:* Daily 11–5, Apr.–Oct.; Sat. & Sun. 11–5, Feb. & Mar. *Fee:* $5. *Owners:* Dick & Christie Reed. *Winemaker:* Peter Rosback. *Wines:* Cabernet sauvignon, Chardonnay, Pinot gris, Pinot noir, Syrah, white blend, port-style. *Cases:* 2,000. The unique character of Wy' East Vineyards' Pinot noir and Pinot gris is a result of the 1,600-foot vineyard, one of the highest in Oregon. The combination of elevation and cool, blustery weather forces grapes to work extra hard, and it shows. Rosback uses these hardy grapes for his Sineann Reserve Pinot. The name "Wy' East" comes from an Anglo interpretation of the Indian name for Mount Hood, which is visible from the deck.

▲ 🖊 🐾 ❖ **Springhouse Cellar** (13 Railroad Avenue; 541-308-0700). *Tasting room:* Daily 1–5. *Fee:* $5. *Owners:* James & Lisa Matthisen. *Winemaker:* James Matthisen. *Wines:* Cabernet franc, Cabernet sauvignon, Chardonnay, Gewürztraminer, Merlot, Petite sirah, Sangiovese, Sauvignon blanc, red blends, dessert. *Cases:* 2,000. With handcrafted wines named Perpetual Merlotion, Make Cab Not War, and Peace, Love and Chardonnay . . . what's not to love? Springhouse refills sling-top bottles for takeaway, using a specifically designed spigot system that allows minimal air exposure. More wine, less packaging: James estimates the refillables have saved tens of thousands of bottles, labels, corks, and capsules. All of James's wines have medaled, but his commitment is to Sangiovese.

Wines on tap and refillable bottles make Springhouse Cellar especially eco-friendly.
Courtesy Springhouse Cellar

Quenett Winery (111 Oak Street; 541-386-2229). *Tasting room:* Thurs.–Sun. 12–5, Fri. & Sat. 12–6. *Fee:* $7. *Owners:* James & Molli Martin. *Winemakers:* James Martin & Craig Larson. *Wines:* Cabernet sauvignon, Chardonnay, Pinot gris, Sangiovese, Syrah, Viognier, Zinfandel, red blends. *Cases:* 2,200. Once the primary tasting room, this has become a second location since Quenett opened a larger facility at the Sunshine Mill in The Dalles (see chapter 10, "Eastern Oregon").

❖ **Stella Fino** (111 Second Street, Suite 200; 541-386-6150). *Tasting room:* Fri. 2–6, Sat. 12–6, Sun. 12–5. *Fee:* $5. *Owners:* Matt & Marlene Steiner. *Winemaker:* Matt Steiner. *Wines:* Barbera, Muscat, Pinot gris, Pinot noir, Sangiovese. *Cases:* 1,000. The low-key atmosphere at Stella Fino is a complement to their lively neighbors at Naked Winery across the street. Winemaker Matt Steiner sources all of his grapes from the Columbia Valley, from Walla Walla to Yakima. The result is Italian varietals that bring folks back to the inconspicuous tasting room.

Naked Winery (102 Second Street; 800-666-9303). *Tasting room:* Sun. & Tues.–Thurs. 10–7; Mon., Fri. & Sat. 10–11. *Fee:* $5. *Owners:* Barringer & Michalec families. *Winemakers:* Dave Barringer & Dave Michalec. *Wines:* Barbera, Cabernet sauvignon, Chardonnay, Meritage, Merlot, Nebbiolo, Pinot gris, Pinot noir, Riesling, Sangiovese, Syrah. *Cases:* 14,000. Changing the conversation surrounding wine from technical to sensual is Naked Winery's mission. Although technically a Washington winery, headquarters and the not-to-be-missed tasting room are in Hood River. A large, sexy lineup is poured in a city-chic yet comfortable bar with live music. Provocative back labels are great conversation starters with fellow imbibers. If you like big and oaky, try the orgasmic wines: Oh! Barbera, Oh! Nebbiolo, Oh! Meritage. Oh, yes!

Cascade Cliffs Vineyard & Winery (211 Oak Street; 541-436-4215 or 509-767-1100). *Tasting room:* Sun.–Thurs. 12–7, Fri. & Sat. 12–8. *Fee:* $5. *Owner/Winemaker:* Robert Lorkowski. *Wines:* Barbera, Cabernet sauvignon, Dolcetto, Merlot, Nebbiolo, Symphony, Syrah, Zinfandel, red blends. *Cases:* 5,000. This Washington-based winery prides itself on Barbera, but the Symphony grape makes it a standout. Developed at UC–Davis in the 1940s, Symphony is a Grenache gris and Muscat of Alexandria hybrid. Also popular is the Goat Head Red, a house blend and gorge staple.

Cycle Wine Country—The Fruit Loop

Description: Find out why the Columbia Gorge is a paradise for cyclists (except when the wind blows, which is often). Start—or finish—with a diverse collection of wineries in vibrant downtown Hood River. You'll immediately begin climbing out of the gorge into lush agricultural lands full of orchards, vineyards, and small tracts of mixed fir and pine forest. It's a gradual uphill until you reach the southernmost spot on the route, at Odell. After that, it's a breezy ride back into the gorge.

Wineries: Springhouse Cellar, Naked Winery, Quenett Winery, The Pines 1852 Tasting Room, Cerulean Wine, Cathedral Ridge Winery, Marchesi Vineyards & Winery, Phelps Creek Vineyards, Pheasant Valley Winery, Wy' East Vineyards, Viento, Mt. Hood Winery

Miles: 23

Elevation gain: 1,148

Start/Finish: Springhouse Cellar, Hood River.

- Start at Springhouse Cellar on Railroad Street and head west. Continue straight on Cascade Avenue. Winery stop: Naked Winery.
- Proceed south on Second Street, then east on Oak Street. Winery stop: Quenett Winery.
- Go west on Oak Street, then turn south on Second Street and west on State Street. Winery stop: The Pines 1852 Tasting Room.
- Head north on Third Street and west on Oak Street. Winery stop: Cerulean Wine.
- Continue straight on Cascade Avenue and south on Country Club Road, then east on Post Canyon Drive. Winery stop: Cathedral Ridge Winery.
- Proceed south on Frankton Road and west on Belmont Drive. Winery stop: Marchesi Vineyards & Winery.
- Head south on Country Club Road. Winery stop: Phelps Creek Vineyard.
- Continue east on Portland Drive, then south on Tucker Road and west on Blackburn Drive. Winery stop: Pheasant Valley Winery.
- Pedal east on Blackburn Drive, south on Tucker Road, south on Odell Highway, east on Davis Drive, north on Neal Mill Road, and then north on OR 35. Winery stops: Wy' East Vineyards and Viento.
- Turn east on Van Horn Drive. Winery stop: Mt. Hood Winery.
- Return west on Van Horn Drive and veer north on OR 35 back to Hood River.

Cerulean Wine (304 Oak Street; 503-333-9725). *Tasting room:* Mar.–Dec., Wed.–Sun. 12–6; Jan. & Feb., Fri.–Sun. 12–6. *Fee:* $5. *Owner:* Jeff Miller. *Winemaker:* Carey Kienitz. *Wines:* Barbera, Cabernet sauvignon, Chardonnay, Gewürztraminer, Grüner veltliner, Merlot, Pinot gris, Pinot noir, Tempranillo, rosé, red blend. *Cases:* 2,000. Cerulean is the story of two friends' learning the art of wine from the ground up. At first Jeff Miller and Carey Kienitz made wine for friends and family, but with growing confidence they've branched out. They specialize in classic European wines from a dry-land organic vineyard 1,000 feet above the Columbia River.

Stoltz Vineyards (514 West State Street; 541-386-8732). *Tasting room:* Sat. & Sun. 12–6, and by appt. *Fee:* $5. *Owners:* John Stoltz. *Winemaker:* Garrit Stoltz. *Wines:*

The Pines 1852 combines a tasting room and art gallery. Courtesy The Pines 1852 Tasting Room & Gallery

Chardonnay, Maria Gomes, Merlot, Pinot noir, Sauvignon blanc, red blend. *Cases:* 250. Location, location, location. The Stoltz tasting room is in the oldest house in town (1886), affectionately known as "the mansion on the hill" for its panoramic views of the Columbia River. Its wines are made from organic grapes grown in the Columbia Valley AVA in small batches, and aged in barrels—no stainless steel. Most notable is the Portuguese varietal Maria Gomes, which was grafted to gorge vines in 2008.

❖ **The Pines 1852 Tasting Room & Gallery** (202 State Street; 541-993-8301). *Tasting room:* Wed. & Sun. 12–7, Thurs. & Fri. 12–10. *Fee:* $5. *Owners:* Lonnie & Linda Wright. *Winemaker:* Peter Rosback. *Wines:* Cabernet sauvignon, Merlot, Pinot gris, Pinot noir, Syrah, Viognier, Zinfandel, red and white blends, port-style. *Cases:* 5,000. Named for a stately grove of ponderosa pines on a farm plowed out of the Oregon Territory in 1852, The Pines might be home to the state's oldest surviving vines. Photos dated 1911 show Zinfandel planted by Italian immigrant Louis Camini, who brought them from Genoa. Lonnie Wright painstakingly revived the vineyard. The tasting room/art gallery is on a corner in downtown Hood River, but the vineyard has a split personality: The line between the Columbia Gorge and Columbia Valley AVAs literally bisects the Wrights' property.

MOSIER

Garnier Vineyards at Mayerdale (8467 Highway 30 West; 541-487-2200). *Tasting room:* Fri.–Sun. 12–5, May–Sept. *Fee:* $5. *Owners:* Tom & Laura Garnier. *Winemaker:* Tom Garnier. *Wines:* Chardonnay, Merlot, Pinot noir, Sauvignon blanc, rosé, red blend, dessert. *Cases:* 1,000. The Garniers' family-owned vineyard is on the west end of a historic 300-acre estate on the Columbia River. In addition to six grape varietals first planted in 2002, they grow cherries and pears. A tasting room, set to open in spring 2013 amid orchards and vineyards, will boast views of the river and the gorge.

Lodging
in Columbia Gorge

HOOD RIVER

♿ 🐾 **Columbia Cliffs Villas** (3880 Westcliff Drive; 866-912-8366). When the economy went into free fall and the Gorge Hotel closed temporarily, the villas needed reinvention. The answer: Offer a wider range of lodging options. Columbia Cliffs choices range from European-style hotel rooms to a penthouse suite with a dining table seating 22. Private chef service is available, as well as limited room service from the bistro at White Buffalo Wines next door. $$$–$$$$

Columbia Gorge Hotel (4000 Westcliff Drive; 541-386-5566 or 800-345-1921). Built in 1904, this iconic hotel was renovated two decades later when the Columbia Gorge Highway was completed, using leftover stones from the roadway. The new owners envisioned a luxurious retreat for visitors who had navigated the gorge from the east in their Model Ts. Over the years, the hotel has hosted presidents Calvin Coolidge and Franklin Roosevelt. The hotel closed for a few years recently, but it's back in business and as opulent as ever. $$$–$$$$

Hood River Hotel (102 Oak Street; 541-386-1900 or 800-386-1859). On the National Register of Historic Places, the Hood River Hotel requires some imagination—or at least a gaze at old photos adorning the walls—to see its decorated past. The original hotel was a stately wood Victorian structure that towered above the town on a site next door. That building was demolished in 1913, leaving only an annex where the current hotel sits. Thirty-two rooms and nine suites later, it has regained its pride with rooms showcasing antique furnishings. The Cornerstone Cuisine restaurant serves breakfast and lunch daily with a twist: "happy hour" deals on mimosas and Bloody Marys from 10 to noon. $$–$$$

Inn at the Gorge (1113 Eugene Street; 541-386-4429 or 877-852-2385). A classic Queen Anne home near downtown has five guest rooms, all with private baths. The lush backyard is private and suited for quiet time. The rooms and bathrooms are a little cozy, but the three suites have kitchens. Noise from nearby traffic can be an issue, but shrubbery and trees dull the din. Hearty breakfasts go beyond the basics. $$–$$$

Lakecliff B&B (3820 Westcliff Drive; 541-386-7000). Lakecliff seems like an English country cottage tucked intimately into a Douglas fir forest—until you catch a dramatic glimpse of the Columbia through the trees from this lofty locale. Each of the four floral-themed rooms has a fireplace, private bath, and view. Enjoy breakfast on the deck and then stroll the inviting 3-acre grounds. $$$

Sakura Ridge Farm and Lodge (5601 York Hill Drive; 541-386-2636 or 877-472-5872). Want to get away from the hum of Hood River? This serene 5,000-square-foot lodge in the center of a working pear and cherry farm is on a lush bench above town, a little more than 4 miles from I-84. Three of the five bright and cheery rooms frame snow-flanked Mount Hood. Breakfast creatively incorporates organic heirloom tomatoes, berries, pears, and squash. *Sakura* is Japanese for "cherry blossom." $$$–$$$$

Seven Oaks B&B (1373 Barker Road; 541-386-7622). Situated in "The Heights" section, Seven Oaks has five tastefully decorated rooms and separate "cottage" that looks more like a converted shed—but with all the creature comforts. The main house was built in 1928 by French inventor August Guignard, and it is on the National Register. Health-conscious breakfasts include eggs from your hosts' own chickens. Retreat to the porch swing to contemplate life and the virtues of wine. Children age 10 and over are welcome. $$–$$$

Vineyard View B&B (4240 Post Canyon Drive; 541-400-9665). There's no denying Vineyard View's connection to wine, given that some rooms have views of Cathedral Ridge's vineyards. With a picture-perfect setting, romance packages, and Honeymoon Suite, the B&B is popular for weddings and families. Estate pears, plums, and Himalayan blackberries all find their way to the breakfast table. $$$

DUFUR

Balch Hotel (40 Heimrich Street; 541-467-2277). For a completely different experience, drive 40 pastoral minutes south of Hood River through agriculture fields to the stately three-story Balch Hotel, built in 1907. Jeff and Samantha Irwin have owned the hotel since 2006, taking over from previous owners who spent 18 years restoring the property. It's pure country, oozing history with rooms that reflect the region's roots. Don't come for phones or televisions; they aren't here. $$–$$$

MOSIER

🐾 **Three Sleeps Vineyard B&B** (1600 Carroll Road; 541-478-0143 or 541-490-5404). "Three sleeps" was the answer Lewis and Clark received from Indians when the explorers asked the distance to the Pacific. You might want to spend all three sleeps in this location. The views from king and queen rooms all include Dominio IV's estate vineyard, Mosier cherry orchards, and Washington's Mount Adams. Each has a private bath, patio, and entrance. Breakfast includes local fruits. Vineyard tours are available. $$$

Dining

in the Columbia Gorge

HOOD RIVER

Celilo Restaurant & Bar (16 Oak Street; 541-386-5710). Ben Stenn and Jacqueline Carey place a conscious emphasis on local organic foods, and choose the best of both from foragers' offerings each morning. Enjoy cuisine in a casual bistro setting with understated sophistication. The emphasis on handmade and sustainable is consistent down to the wooden beams, reclaimed castoffs from the Columbia River. Celilo even converts its used vegetable oil into biodiesel that powers the company car. Wines and brews are predominantly from Oregon and Washington, and the service is attentive to detail. L/D/HH $$$

Divots Clubhouse Restaurant (3605 Brookside Drive; 541-308-0304). Usually a golf course restaurant doesn't earn prime-time billing, but Divots delivers. A local favorite, Divots serves Northwest cuisine at reasonable prices and has one of the best happy hours around. And its wine list is on par for local and regional. If the weather's cooperating, dine alfresco on the flagstone patio with uninterrupted views of Mounts Adams and Hood. L/D/HH $$

Full Sail Brewing Company Tasting Room and Pub (506 Columbia Street; 541-386-2247). Take a break from vino

Take a break from vino fatigue at Full Sail Brewery in Hood River. John Baker

fatigue at one of Oregon's first microbreweries while viewing river action below. The pub-type food is above average and beer is used as an ingredient in most menu items, from sauerkraut to Imperial Stout brownies. CEO and founder Irene Firmat and her husband, executive brewmaster James Emmerson, take environmentally sound business practices seriously. Employee-owned, Full Sail pretreats all of its runoff and recycles religiously. Free tours are at 1, 2, 3, or 4 PM daily. L/D $$

Nora's Table (110 Fifth Street; 541-387-4000). Chef Kathy Watson has a little something for everyone, including vegetarians and gluten-free eaters. To nosh, Nora's international menu ranges from Peking duck drumettes to Punjabi grilled lamb tacos and naan. For more heft, "the main events" premiere a Mountain Shadow rib eye, burger, and seafood curry. Naturally there's an assortment of regional wines, but check out the farmhouse ales. L (Mon.–Fri.) D/HH $$$

Riverside (1108 East Marina Way; 541-386-4410). Riverside's first claim to fame is in its name: While some Hood River restaurants boast exceptional views, only one is actually on the Columbia. As you'd guess, there's an outdoor patio and deck for watching river traffic. Fresh and natural are the bywords for all meals, and the wine list is decidedly tipped toward Oregon—the gorge in particular. B/L/D/BR/LN $$–$$$

❖ **Stonehedge Gardens** (3405 Cascade Avenue; 541-386-3940). Mike and Shawna Caldwell have downsized their culinary energies to focus on Stonehedge, making it a magical Hood River experience. Garnished by English gardens with stone paths, fountains, and trellises, the 1898 Victorian home is divided into four distinct dining rooms—the sun porch, library, Grand Room, and Wine Cellar. A 6,000-square-foot Italian-stone outdoor patio has five levels and seats up to 200. Small wonder that Stonehedge is a coveted wedding venue and was voted Best Outdoor Dining in the Gorge by *Best Places Northwest*. On the menu: fresh, innovative cuisine with an emphasis on seafood. Plan well ahead for Saturday night reservations. D $$

3 Rivers Grill (601 Oak Street; 541-386-8883). Combine riveting views and a renovated historic house with organic, local food and an award-winning wine list, and you can see why 3 Rivers is a Hood River hot spot. The grill has as many tantalizing dishes as it has seating options. Enjoy the views from every seat in one of five dining rooms, deck, or patio. The wine list favors locals. B/L/D $$–$$$

MOSIER

Thirsty Woman Pub (904 2nd Avenue; 541-478-0199 [Big Woman] and 541-490-2022 [Little Woman]). The Little Woman is open daily and the Big Woman, which took over the former Good River Restaurant's space, opens at 5 PM (Thurs.–Sat.) The little pub dates to 1928 and has a exceptionally homey feel. Aside from "the biggest burger in town," the Thirsty Woman also claims the best French fries in the gorge. The secret: They're fried in rice oil. L (Sun.) D $$

To Do

in the Columbia Gorge

Attractions

You might want to start your journey on the east end of the gorge in The Dalles, home of the **Gorge Discovery Center** (541-296-8600). Technically it is east of the Columbia Gorge AVA, but it is full of information on geology, geography, wildlife, vegetation, and ancient cultures. Also on-site is Basalt Rock Café. To get a grand early perspective on the scenic wonders en route to wineries, take a side trip up the old **Columbia Gorge Historic Highway** (US 30) to the interpretive center in the octagon-shaped **Vista House at Crown Point**. Rising some 730 feet above the river, the Vista House is perhaps the most-photographed location in the gorge. Just east of Crown Point is spectacular **Multnomah Falls**, which plunges 620 feet from a lip directly above a historic lodge.

For relaxing diversions on unique forms of transportation, take the **Mount Hood Scenic Railroad and Dinner Train** (800-872-4661) south up the Hood River Valley. Choose from dinner, Sunday brunch, or a ride on the wild side with a murder mystery dinner show. The train ride terminates at the **Hutson Museum** (4967 Baseline Drive, 541-352-6808), located on a national historic site and full of Indian dolls, arrowheads, rocks, and taxidermy. If you prefer a watery route, the **Sternwheeler Columbia Gorge** (541-374-8427) hosts day, dinner, and charter cruises.

Hood River County has been home to the state's most prolific fruit orchards since the 1850s—hence, the **Fruit Loop** (800-366-3530). The 35-mile scenic driving tour of orchards, forests, farmlands, vineyards, wineries, dining establishments, and quintessential B&Bs starts at Hood River and finishes up the valley in the community of Mount Hood.

Recreation

Any mention of the gorge and recreation begins with windsurfing and kite-boarding. Wind is a given, especially around Hood River, where on any spring or summer day, the Columbia is awash with the bright colors of sails skimming, sweeping, and cartwheeling across the whitecaps in 40-knot breezes.

For landlubbers, bicycling has become a favored sport, whether it's a casual pedal along Old Highway 30 or a more strenuous climb up the valley along the cascading river for which the town is named. Mountain biking is excellent in the summer, but it becomes especially good in the fall after the first rains improve traction.

Although salmon numbers aren't what they once were, fishing is still a state religion, and it isn't uncommon for anglers to reel in 30-pound Chinook or feisty 10-pound wild steelhead out of the Columbia, Deschutes, and John Day Rivers as they head for spawning grounds.

For golf enthusiasts, the gorge has seven courses of varying difficulty. And just when you think you've seen it all, a new sport has arrived: stand-up paddling. Basically, all it requires is an oversize surfboard, a paddle, a wet suit, and one of those rare days when the Columbia is calm.

Wine Shopping

White Buffalo Wines (4040 Westcliff Drive, 541-386-5534 or 503-753-3134) is a blend of wine shop, tasting room, and lunch spot known for cooking from scratch; about 90 percent of the 250 wines on the shelves are from the Northwest. The **Gorge White House** (2265 Highway 35, 541-386-2828), just up the hill, pours gorge wines by the taste, glass, or bottle, and has local beers on tap. It also grows, sells, and has U-pick fruit and flowers.

Get a taste of rural history at the Gorge White House.

More Information

Hood River County Chamber of Commerce, 541-386-2000, 405 Portway Avenue, Hood River, www.hoodriver.org

Columbia Gorge Wines, 866-413-9463, www.columbiagorgewine.com

10

Eastern Oregon

HIGH, DRY, AND JUICY

WELCOME TO THE BIG EMPTY. Eastern Oregon is the antithesis of the state's rainy west. It is a land of vast sagebrush prairies, rugged mountains, harsh winters, and conservative ideology. Yet even with those attributes as anchors, you can't paint this arid region with one broad stroke of the brush.

The area around booming Bend, which straddles the Deschutes River on the eastern flank of the Cascade Range, is a vibrant, sun-drenched, and snow-kissed outdoor paradise set amid ponderosa forests. The Columbia, Umatilla, and Snake River valleys are hot, dry, and renowned for their onions, sugar beets, and wheat—though vineyards are coming on strong enough in all three to receive AVA designations. The northeast and east-central parts of Oregon are mountainous and cold, though even here a few vineyards have taken root. Also inhospitable for grapes is the south-central portion of the state, a dry and remarkably remote basin-and-range region reminiscent of Nevada's deserts.

Because nearly all of the wine produced in eastern Oregon is from the Columbia and Umatilla Valleys, our focus will be there. But the Bend/Redmond/Prineville triangle bears mention. With its vigor, money, and progressiveness, Bend is too much of a natural to be ignored by the wine industry. The town has several tasting rooms, and vineyards are popping up on the outskirts.

Although Oregon's portions of the Columbia, Walla Walla, and Snake River AVAs are immersed in the industry, most wineries are in neighboring Washington, where in the Walla Walla AVA wineries are opening like wildfire.

GETTING HERE AND AROUND

Getting anywhere in eastern Oregon requires some effort, and most definitely includes a car. The **Walla Walla (Washington) Regional Airport** has three flights a day from Seattle on Horizon Air (800-547-9308. The Columbia Valley is even farther removed from air service. Most visitors come to The Dalles and points east via Portland.

LEFT: Tuning up for impromptu music at Quenett's Sunshine Mill artisan plaza in The Dalles.

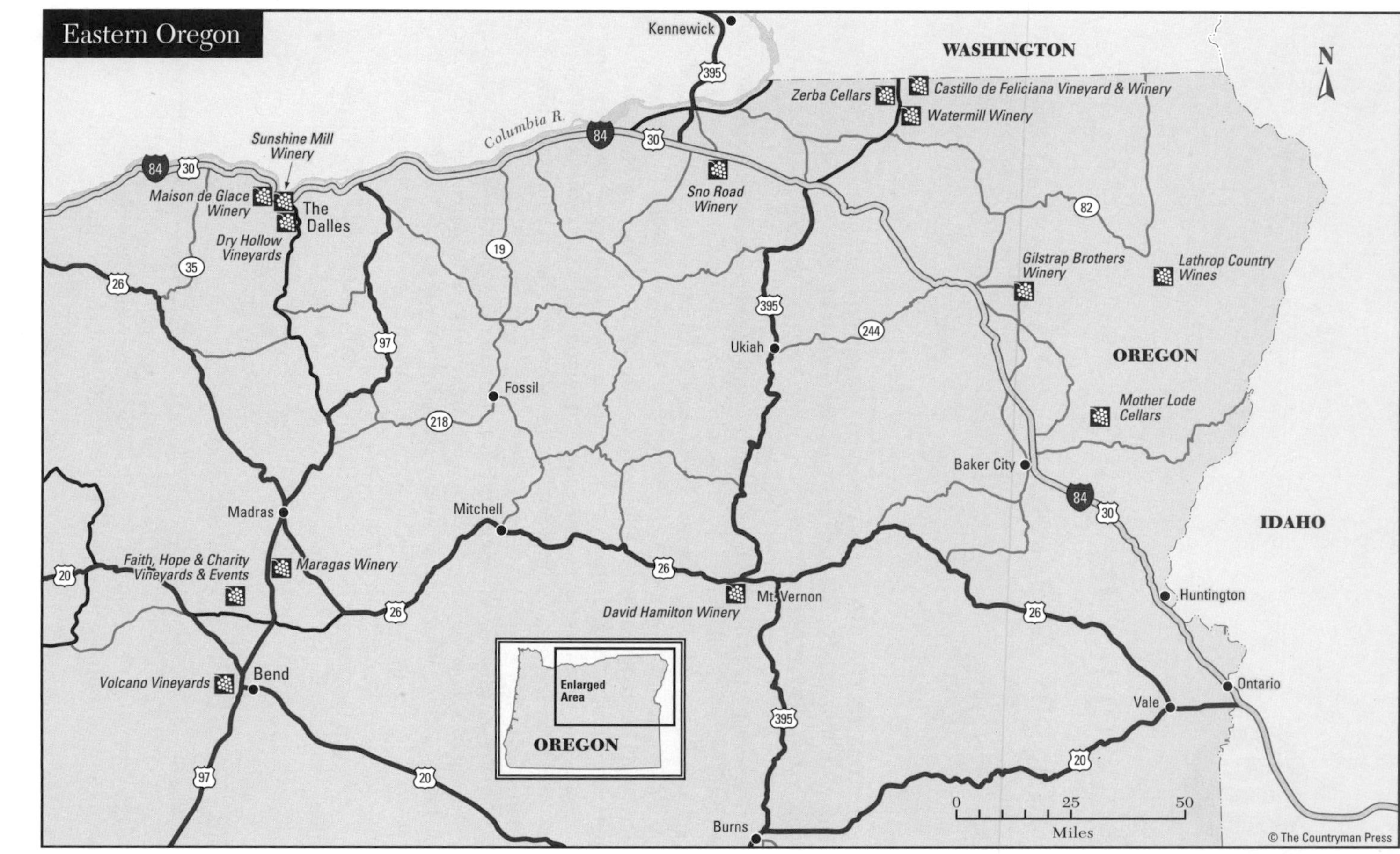
Eastern Oregon
Kennewick
WASHINGTON
N
Zerba Cellars
Castillo de Feliciana Vineyard & Winery
Watermill Winery
Columbia R.
Sunshine Mill Winery
Maison de Glace Winery
The Dalles
Dry Hollow Vineyards
Sno Road Winery
Gilstrap Brothers Winery
Lathrop Country Wines
OREGON
Mother Lode Cellars
Ukiah
Fossil
Baker City
IDAHO
Madras
Mitchell
Faith, Hope & Charity Vineyards & Events
Maragas Winery
David Hamilton Winery
Mt. Vernon
Huntington
Bend
Volcano Vineyards
Enlarged Area
OREGON
Ontario
Vale
Burns
0 25 50
Miles
84
30
395
35
26
19
97
218
244
82
20
© The Countryman Press

Getting to Bend, in central Oregon, is easier as its growth has been matched by air service to **Roberts Field** in nearby Redmond from SkyWest (800-221-1212), United Express (800-241-6522), and Allegiant Air (702-505-8888). **Greyhound** has a route on I-84 with stations in Ontario, La Grande, Pendleton, and The Dalles. Another route from Ontario goes across the heart of the state to Bend. I-84 bisects the Columbia Valley AVA, including The Dalles. Milton-Freewater is 12 miles south of Walla Walla and 26 miles north of Pendleton on OR 11.

Bend is at a crossroads in central Oregon. From Portland, the best route is to take US 26 over the Cascades to the junction of US 97 at Madras, and then head south another 42 miles. If you're arriving from the east off I-84, exit at Biggs Junction onto US 97 and continue south for 135 miles.

THE DALLES AREA (Columbia Valley AVA)

Although only 19 miles east of Hood River and similarly perched on a crescent-shaped slope overlooking the Columbia River, The Dalles is quite different than its sister city in the gorge—which helps explain the different appellations. A massive dam and industrial zone give this community of 12,500 the feel of a shipping port. People have been conducting commerce of varying sorts here for 10,000 years. Named for dangerous rapids on the Columbia, which were inundated by The Dalles Dam in 1957, the city is known for sweet cherries, salmon fishing, and the Fort Dalles Museum—Oregon's oldest history museum. The entire town is on the National Register of Historic Places.

Wineries
in The Dalles Area

Overall, the Columbia Valley AVA covers a vast high-desert area of 11 million acres, though only a fraction is in Oregon; the rest is in Washington. It is hot, dry, and seemingly vine-unfriendly.

Nevertheless, there are producing Zinfandel vines more than 100 years old. This is Oregon's driest AVA, averaging 6 to 8 inches of rain per year—less than Phoenix, Arizona—on the Columbia Plateau, meaning irrigation from the Columbia River and its tributaries is crucial. A wide variety of grapes—most notably Merlot, Syrah, Chardonnay, Pinot gris, Gewürztraminer, Semillon, Riesling, and Cabernet sauvignon—grows well here amid these sunny days and cool nights.

THE DALLES

❖ **Maison de Glace Winery** (208 Laughlin Street; 541-993-4640). *Tasting room:* Tues.–Thurs. 12–6, Fri. & Sat. 12–7, Sun. 12–3. *Fee:* $5. *Owners:* Kelley & Aaron Lee. *Winemaker:* Aaron Lee. *Wines:* Barbera, Cabernet sauvignon, Dolcetto, Lemberger, Merlot, Petit verdot, Roussanne, Syrah, Tempranillo, Zinfandel, rosé. *Cases:* 5,000. One look at Maison de Glace's label—and a little knowledge of French—provides some insight into the new winery's story. Aaron and Kelley renovated a 1909 building downtown that was once eastern Oregon's largest ice and cold-storage facility. Kelley's grandfather actually owned the business and drove the ice truck shown on the label. Opened in 2011, the tasting room in the former ice-crushing area has retained a nostalgic industrial ambience. *Maison de glace* is French for "house of ice."

❖ **Sunshine Mill Winery (Quenett Cellars)** (901 East Second Street; 541-298-8900). *Tasting room:* Daily 12–6. *Fee:* $7. *Owners:* James & Molli Martin. *Winemakers:* James Martin & Craig Larson. *Wines:* Cabernet Sauvignon, Chardonnay, Pinot Gris,

Sangiovese, Syrah, Viognier, Zinfandel, red blends. *Cases:* 2,500. Sunshine Mill is the creation of James and Molli Martin, sixth-generation residents of The Dalles. After making wine across the Columbia River at Maryhill for years, they took a condemned warehouse—all 16 grain silos included—and created a snappy urban facility. To fund it, they sold their cherry orchards and borrowed an idea from the French: selling wine in 6.3-ounce pressure-sealed plastic glasses they call Copa Di Vino. Their vision extends to an artisan plaza and gathering spot where local musicians are known to stop and drop a note or two. HH

Dry Hollow Vineyards (3401 Dry Hollow Lane; 541-296-2953). *Tasting room:* Sat. & Sun. 12–5, Feb.–Nov. *Fee:* $5. *Owner:* Eric & Bridget Bailey Nisley. *Winemaker:* Rich Cushman. *Wines:* Cabernet sauvignon, Chardonnay, Malbec, Merlot, Riesling, Sauvignon blanc, Syrah, red and white blends. *Cases:* 500. The tasting room at Dry Hollow is in an area that seems anything but dry. Visitors look out through ponderosa pines over rolling hills to thirsty Columbia River benches. The lush lawn beckons tasters outside when the wind isn't blowing. The Syrah and Merlot are estate; the rest of the grapes are from the Columbia Valley AVA. Guided walks of the 15-acre vineyard are available.

Lodging

in The Dalles Area

For exploring the Columbia Valley AVA, the lodging options can be summed up in two words: The Dalles. Fortunately, there are plenty. Many accommodations feature views of the river and dam.

THE DALLES

♿ 🐾 **Celilo Inn Motel** (3550 East Second Street; 541-769-0001). Courteous service and views are the selling point for this 46-room inn that sits on a bluff overlooking The Dalles Dam. The motel mixes modern with vintage after its complete overhaul and caters to the wine enthusiasts by serving a complimentary glass of either the house red or white. Just be sure to ask. A continental breakfast served off the lobby with uninterrupted views, patio and fire pit, fitness room, and outdoor pool are nice touches. $$–$$$

🐾 **Court Street Bed & Breakfast** (3550 East Second Street; 541-350-9850). This modest home offers a master bedroom for one or two guests, or the entire home for $200 a night. The bedroom has a private bath with clawfoot tub. Downstairs is another bed in a recreation room with a TV. A two-night stay and four-hour tour of Hood River wineries is $360. $–$$

♿ 🐾 **The Dalles Inn** (112 West Second Street; 541-296-9107 or 888-935-2378). The Dalles is a long, crescent-shaped community where you can be far from downtown, so if you like to be at the heart of it all, this is your place. The inn supplies all the basic needs, and then some. Six types of renovated suites and studios provide a decidedly upscale feel, complete with DVD players and in-room gourmet coffee service. A complimentary breakfast and outdoor pool add to the stay. $$

🍴 🐾 **Shilo Inn & Suites** (3223 Bret Clodfelter Way; 541-298-5502). Shilo Inns is a regional chain with most of its motels in Oregon. What stands out at this location is the setting on the shores of the Columbia River, with views of the dam and Pioneer Village. Many of the 112 comfortable rooms overlook the river and some have outdoor patios. An outdoor pool, spa and sauna come with the deal. $$–$$$

Dining
in The Dalles Area

THE DALLES

Baldwin Saloon (205 Court Street; 541-296-5666). Opened in 1876, the Baldwin Saloon hasn't always been a purveyor of food and spirits. The brick building one block away from downtown was once used as a steamboat-navigation office and then for coffin storage. After a renovation, oil paintings now dress the walls around mahogany booths, an 18-foot mahogany back bar, and 1870s pendulum clock. Entrées range from steaks to coquilles St. Jacques (scallops). Local wines complete the picture. L/D Mon.–Sat. $$–$$$

Clock Tower Ales (311 Union Street; 541-705-3590). The Clock Tower is just one of those fun places to unwind after work—or a day of wine touring. Located in an early Wasco County courthouse—and site of the city's last public hanging—the pub touts its Clock Tower fish burger wrapped in a pretzel bun. A range of microbrews is the claim to fame, with no fewer than 30 on tap, but a respectable stable of local wines and handcrafted ciders makes choosing a challenge. L/D Tues.–Sun. $–$$

The Windseeker Restaurant on the Port (1535 Bargeway Road; 541-298-7171). A 2013 recipient of Robert Irvine's (*Restaurant Impossible*) generous "redo," the Windseeker seems headed for solid ground on the banks of the Columbia River. Much-needed interior and menu updates have added a layer of freshness sure to please, especially if you're a fish and seafood lover. While waiting for a seat, stroll the colorful high-desert gardens surrounding the restaurant. They were created by owner Veta's late husband and are nothing short of amazing. L/D/BR $$

To Do
in The Dalles Area

Attractions

Even if you're headed east or south to sip wine, the **Columbia Gorge Discovery Center** (5000 Discovery Drive, 541-296-8600) is a required stop for an overview of everything gorge. The expansive facility includes the **Wasco County Historical Museum.** Also on-site is the **Discovery Gallery**, which captures the story of the Lewis and Clark Corps of Discovery with detailed displays and exhibits. Oregon's oldest museum has its roots in a fort built before the Civil War—the **Fort Dalles Museum** (500 West 15th Street, 541-296-4547) is in the old surgeon's quarters at the fort. It opened in 1905 and mostly features military, pioneer, and Indian artifacts. Perhaps the most significant historical event for the valley since the arrival of European settlers was the construction of **The Dalles Dam** in 1957, with an accompanying visitors center (541-296-1181).

Recreation

It isn't Hood River, and the winds aren't quite as prodigious, but The Dalles holds its own among the board- and kite-surfing crowds. And depending on the time of year, you can always count on boats full of fishermen to be stacked up on the Columbia, angling for salmon and steelhead. Bass and walleye fishing are also popular pastimes, particularly in pools where creeks meet the Columbia.

(Walla Walla AVA)

Walla Walla—it's not just about sweet onions anymore. This is one of the fastest-growing AVAs in the country in size and pride. It's only a matter of time before Oregon steals some of the thunder from its deserving Washington neighbor, where most vineyards are actually located.

For most of its modern life, this dry, mild, and windswept corner of Oregon has been all about agriculture, ranching, and cowboys. Pendleton is famous for its woolen mill, its rich underground—literally—history, and both real and wannabe cowboys letting 'er buck at the internationally renowned Pendleton Round-Up. While Pendleton is tucked into a deep valley between benches of wheat fields, Milton-Freewater has the Blue Mountains for a backdrop. It has an abiding affection for frogs, developed in the past decade as a struggling town's clever attempt to boost tourism. Thus, Milton-Freewater is now "Muddy Frogwater Country," and visitors are invited to find 40 frog statues scattered about town.

Wineries

in the Pendleton/Milton-Freewater Area

For now, there are only four wineries and more than 30 vineyards on the Oregon side of the AVA, all in and around Milton-Freewater. But that's sure to change with the rapid growth of the Walla Walla AVA.

The soil here is silt, deposited 15,000 years ago by the Missoula Floods on top of ancient lava left 15 million years ago by one of the largest volcanic eruptions in the earth's history. A final terroir factor is the constant winds, which have coated the Walla Walla Valley with a fine soil called loess. The area is blessed with endless sunshine, warm summers, crisp evenings, mild winters, and limited rainfall (13 inches annually) augmented by irrigation. Most vineyards range from 650 feet above sea level to just under 1,500 feet at the foot of the Blue Mountains. Merlot, Cabernet sauvignon, and Syrah are predominant, though the elevation and soils allow for diversity.

MILTON-FREEWATER

▲ ❖ Watermill Winery (235 East Broadway Avenue; 541-938-5575). *Tasting room:* Thurs.–Sun. 12–4. *Fee:* Complimentary. *Owner:* Brown family. *Winemaker:* Noah Fox Reed. *Wines:* Gewürztraminer, Malbec, Sauvignon blanc, Syrah, Viognier, rosé, red blend, dessert. *Cases:* 4,500. After running the highly successful Blue Mountain Cidery, tending apple orchards, and growing grapes for other wineries, the Brown family began producing their own wines in 2005. They go out of their way to make you feel comfortable in their tasting room, which is located is in a revamped warehouse that oozes history. The facility has a separate kitchen, library, and dining room suitable for gatherings of up to 30. Plan your visit around "Summer Nights on the Patio" from 5 to 9 PM every Friday in the warmer months.

Zerba Cellars (85530 Highway 11; 541-938-9463). *Tasting room:* Mon.–Sat. 12–5, Sun. 12–4. *Fee:* Complimentary. *Owners:* Cecil & Marilyn Zerba. *Winemaker:* Doug Nierman. *Wines:* Barbera, Cabernet franc, Cabernet sauvignon, Chardonnay, Malbec, Merlot, Sangiovese, Semillon, Syrah, Viognier, rosé, port-style, dessert. *Cases:* 6,000. Zerba is probably the best-known Oregon winery in the Walla Walla region, in part because of its boatloads of awards. The bulk of the wines is sourced from three LIVE-certified estate vineyards, planted at different elevations in distinctive soils. Zerba's tasting room, in a juniper cabin next to a vineyard, is a reflection of its location near the Blue Mountains. You can find Zerba wines at many highly regarded dining establishments.

▲ ✐ 🐾 ❖ **Castillo de Feliciana Vineyard & Winery** (85728 Telephone Pole Road; 541-558-3656). *Tasting room:* Fri.–Sun. 11–5, and by appt. *Owners:* Sam & Deborah Castillo. *Winemaker:* Christopher Castillo. *Wines:* Albarino, Malbec, Merlot, Pinot gris, Semillon, Tempranillo, red blends, sparkling. *Cases:* 3,200. Take a trip to southern Spain—without leaving Oregon. Castillo de Feliciana is a Spanish-style winery complete with requisite red roof and white stucco exterior. *Castillo* means "castle," which is what Sam and Deborah have emulated with their tasting room. Surrounded by vineyards that include Spanish varietals Albarino and Tempranillo, an expansive patio takes center stage, where visitors can sit and listen to tango music while fantasizing that the distant Blue Mountains are in Spain's Andalusia region. All that's missing is an ocean.

ECHO

Sno Road Winery (210 West Main Street; 541-376-0421). *Tasting room:* Wed.–Thurs. 11–-6, Fri. 11–8:30, Sat. 1–4. *Fee:* $5. *Owners:* Lloyd & Lois Piercy. *Winemaker:* Lloyd Piercy. *Wines:* Carménère, Cabernet sauvignon, Muscat canelli, Orange muscat, Petit verdot, Pinot noir, Tempranillo, Zinfandel. *Cases:* 2,000. Sno Road is a young boutique winery tucked into a pretty little Oregon Trail valley along the Umatilla River, about 20 miles west of Pendleton. The Piercys use estate grapes exclusively from their Echo West Vineyard, and have already won their share of awards. Sip away while sitting on the patio overlooking the city park.

COVE

▲ 🎁 ✐ 🐾 ❖ **Gilstrap Brothers Vineyard & Winery** (69789 Antles Lane; 541-568-4646 or 866-568-4200). *Tasting room:* Wed.–Sat. 11–4, Sun. 1-5, and by appt. *Fee:* Complimentary. *Owners:* Warren Gilstrap & Susan Olliffe. *Winemakers:* Warren & Ted Gilstrap. *Wines:* Cabernet sauvignon, Maréchal Foch, Merlot, Syrah, red blend, dessert. *Cases:* 1,600. If Californians thought their expatriates were nuts for growing grapes in the Willamette Valley, consider the Gilstraps. They believe a vineyard at 3,000 feet above sea level, on the fringes of the Blue Mountains, can produce good wine. They replaced their cherry orchard with cold-resistant French hybrids in 1993, and have eked out a living in the upper Grande Ronde Valley. The winery is about an hour's scenic drive from Pendleton on I-84 and worth it, just for the seeing-is-believing factor.

JOSEPH

✐ **Lathrop Country Wines** (9 South Main Street, #B; 541-377-0644). *Tasting room:* Tues.–Sat. 12–5, May–Dec. *Fee:* Complimentary. *Owners:* Scott & Ruby Lathrop. *Winemaker:* Scott Lathrop. *Wines:* Cabernet sauvignon, Semillon, Shiraz, red blend, fruit, port-style. *Cases:* 600. It's fitting that the Lathrops use an old system of winemaking in a part of the state that oozes pioneer history. As former cattle ranchers on an 1881 Century Farm, the Lathrops insist on getting all their grapes from family vineyards in Oregon, Washington, and California. No sulfites or chemicals are added. In 2012, Lathrop introduced Alpenfest Polka-Up Wein, from old-vine Riesling. Also produced at Lathrop are a hard cider and many varities of fruit wines.

BAKER CITY

Mother Lode Cellars (46881 Cook Road; 541-519-4640). *Tasting room:* TBA. *Fee:* TBA. *Owners:* Michael & Cathy Cook. *Winemaker:* Travis Cook. *Wines:* Pinot noir, Syrah, rosé, red blend. *Cases:* 350. Mother Lode made history by becoming the first—and only—Oregon winery in the Snake River AVA. The Cooks like a challenge: They are testing the viability of growing grapes at 3,400 feet elevation near the base of the picturesque Elkhorn Mountains, where they've planted 144 vines on 2 acres. Meanwhile, son Travis, a graduate of Oregon State University's oenology program, is making wines from grapes purchased elsewhere. Call for their temporary tasting location in Baker City.

Lodging

in the Pendleton/Milton-Freewater Area

PENDLETON

♿ 🐾 **Pendleton House Bed & Breakfast** (311 North Main Street; 541-276-8581). Don't be looking for a place to hitch your horse here. This historic six-room home is decidedly Italian Renaissance and French neoclassical, with hints of old Pendleton's Chinese presence. In the back are English gardens, which the owners readily admit seem "slightly out of place" in arid cowboy country. The same goes for the home's primary exterior color: pink. The citified rooms are spread among three floors, with a second-floor balcony overlooking downtown. Many of the fixtures are original, including the Chinese silk wallpaper. Daily wine and cheese hour is from 5 to 6. $$–$$$

🍴 🍸 ♿ **Wildhorse Resort & Casino** (72777 Highway 331; 541-278-2274 or 800-654-9453). This 100-room hotel was recently renovated to become a more appealing, if still basic, place to put up your feet. The simple rooms are in American Indian motif. On-site are a casino, golf course, RV park, teepee village, tent camping, and museum. $–$$$

Dining

in the Pendleton/Milton-Freewater Area

MILTON-FREEWATER

The Oasis @ Stateline (85698 Highway 339; 541-938-4776). People come from miles around to eat at this western roadhouse in the country. It exudes eastern Oregon cowboy ambience with its Texas hold 'em card games, thick cuts of prime rib, and platters of seafood. You might not expect to find an extensive wine list at such a place, but Oasis highlights regional producers. It also serves seasonal farm-fresh produce. Live country music on Friday and Saturday creates a festive mood, or if gambling is your style, try your luck at Keno. B/L/D/HH Tues.–Sun. $$$–$$$$

PENDLETON

Great Pacific Wine & Coffee Company (403 South Main Street; 541-276-1350). Located in the historic Masonic Lodge downtown, Great Pacific has an eclectic feel, menu, and wine selection—with an emphasis on Oregon. That goes for the brews, too. The eating area is set amid the wine racks and exudes an aura that matches the 120-year-old building's history. The menu is casual, highlighted by sandwiches, soups, gourmet salads, and specialty pizzas. Saturday bluegrass jams and live music are part of the lively atmosphere. B/L/D Mon.–Sat. $$

Hamley Steakhouse (8 SE Court Avenue; 541-278-1100). In its ornately renovated 1869 county courthouse, Hamley is actually three eateries in one: ornate western steakhouse, saloon, and comfortable café. And if steak is your taste, this is your place. Hamley only serves certified USDA prime. The filet mignon and prime rib aren't inexpensive, but they are melt-in-your-mouth delicious. The Slickfork Saloon has a magnificent mahogany back bar that reflects the area's cowboy culture, right down to the steer mounts on the wall. For breakfast or lunch, duck into the Hamley Café between the steakhouse and famous Hamley Western Store. Don't leave without walking down the circular staircase and peering into the elegant wine cellar. B/L/D/HH $$–$$$$

Stetson's House of Prime (103 SE Court Street; 541-966-1132). Stetson's is an iconic watering hole where ranchers and livestock traders have cut deals over Herculean steaks. The menu is what you'd expect: prime rib, steaks, chicken, seafood, and pasta, but the smoked beef and green beans (yes) move it up a belt notch. Servings are robust and the atmosphere is authentically western. Stetson's gets its fresh crab and salmon from Astoria on Friday and Saturday. Most of the wines are Northwest, especially big reds that go with big steaks. D $$–$$$$

To Do

in the Pendleton/Milton-Freewater Area

Attractions

Yes, this is *the* Pendleton—at least when it comes to the famous blankets and other wool products. See where it comes together at the **Pendleton Blanket Mill** (1307 SE Court Place, 541-276-6911). Six generations of the Bishop family have watched over the company, which has thrived for 100 years since it began making Indian blankets in 1909. You probably won't need a blanket at the annual **Pendleton Round-Up** (541-276-2553) at the rodeo grounds in September, unless it's to keep the dust off your chaps. The Round-Up is Carnivale meets the frontier, with rowdy crowds of 50,000 partying long into four starry nights. If you're not in town for the rodeo, stop by the **Happy Canyon Hall of Fame** (1114 SW Court Street, 541-278-0815), which is across from the rodeo grounds and open every day but Sunday. To give you an idea of the local mind-set: of the first 15 inductees, five were horses. The **Heritage Station Museum** (108 SW Frazer Avenue, 541-271-0012) offers a similar peek at area history.

Few places reveal the seamy underbelly of the American West better than **Pendleton Underground Tours** (37 SW Emigrant Avenue, 800-226-6398). To take home a piece of Pendleton's leathery cowboy persona, stop by the **Hamley Western Store** (30 SE Court Avenue, 541-278-1100)—and be sure to check out the saddlery in the back. This town isn't all about cowboys; the **Pendleton Center for the Arts** (214 North Main Street, 541-278-9201), in a historic library building, features local creativity. For a deeper look into the area's native history, you'll be impressed by the **Tamástslikt Cultural Institute** (72789 Highway 331, 541-966-9748). After picking up your obligatory frog souvenir in Milton-Freewater, you'll want to visit the popular **Blue Mountain Cidery** (235 East Broadway, 541-938-5575), best known for its award-winning handcrafted hard ciders. The cidery, one of 100 of its kind in the United States, shares a tasting room and patio bar with Watermill Winery.

You'd expect to find fresh fruits and vegetables in the heart of ag country, and yes, roadside stands are common. To find it all in one place, check out the **Pendleton Farmers' Market** (541-969-9466), every summer Friday from 4 PM to dusk in the 300 block of Main Street.

Recreation

Thanks to a mild climate, golf is almost a year-round pastime in the Umatilla and Walla Walla Valleys. The 18-hole **Milton-Freewater Municipal Golf Course** (301 Catherine, 541-938-7284) is economical and moderately challenging. The golf course at **Wildhorse**

Resort (541-276-5588) has four sets of tees, so the finesse types can play as short as 5,718 yards and the big hitters can go for 7,128.

BEND AND ELSEWHERE (Snake River AVA)

The eastern Oregon country outside of the Columbia and Umatilla Valleys is vast and varied, ranging from the ponderosa pines and high desert around Bend to the flat onion fields of Ontario, on Oregon's eastern border with southwest Idaho. The Bend /Redmond/Prineville area of central Oregon has become a premier outdoor summer and winter playground, with every type of recreation imaginable that doesn't involve an ocean. Bend is more cosmopolitan, thanks to its proximity to Mt. Bachelor Ski Resort, and more picturesque, thanks to its pines.

Wineries

in the Bend Area and Elsewhere

You can't help but root for folks who, being so attached to where they live, have brought the wine industry home with them instead of vice versa. Now that Oregon officially has a winery in the Snake River AVA, it seems the only place left without vinifera is the ultra-remote southeastern desert. But give those hardy folks time.

CULVER

▲ 🍴 🎁 🖋 ❖ **Maragas Winery** (15233 South Highway 97; 541-546-5464). *Tasting room:* Daily 11–5. *Fee:* $5. *Owners:* Doug & Gina Maragas. *Winemaker:* Doug Maragas. *Wines:* Chardonnay, Merlot, Muscat, Pinot gris, Zinfandel, red blend, dessert. *Cases:* 2,000. One look at Maragas's small vineyard along US 97 tells you something different is happening here. The organic vines are sprawled on the ground on a heat-trapping black liner—a distinctive approach. Doug's focus is on Bordeaux-style reds and a variety of whites. For fun factor, the tasting room rates high—and the large patio, with its views of Smith Rock and the Cascades, even higher. The Maragas clan has quite a tradition in vino: The first family winery was in Greece.

TERREBONNE

▲ 🖋 🐾 ❖ **Faith, Hope & Charity Vineyards & Events** (70455 NW Lower Bridge Road; 541-526-5075). *Tasting room:* Daily 12–5. *Fee:* $5. *Owners:* Roger & Sandy Grossman. *Winemakers:* Linda Donovan (hybrids) & Rick Mafit (vinifera). *Wines:* Cabernet sauvignon, Frontenac, La Crescent, Léon Millot, Maréchal Foch, Marquette, Merlot, St. Croix, Traminette, Vignoles, port. *Cases:* 500. *Ambitious* only begins to describe Roger and Sandy's new venture on 315 scenic acres. Named for each of the Three Sisters volcanoes that provide a postcard-perfect Cascade Range backdrop, they've crafted a tasting room, colorful gardens, pond, rental home, and small vineyard out of the sagebrush northwest of Redmond. Growing hybrids for premium wines, the formerly retired Grossmans are conducting a groundbreaking experiment to see what thrives in central Oregon's hot-and-cold arid climate and volcanic soils. Next up: a larger trout pond, narrow lake for athletic and boating competitions, chapel, cottages, small lots for homes, and a wildlife-watching area.

BEND

🐾 **Volcano Vineyards** (70 SW Century Boulevard, Suite 175; 541-617-1102). *Tasting room:* Wed. 12–6, Thurs. & Fri. 12–8, Sat. 2–6. *Fee:* $5. *Owners:* Scott & Liz Ratcliff. *Winemakers:* Gus Janeway & Scott Ratcliff. *Wines:* Merlot, Syrah, red and white blends. *Cases:* 1,500. Once you manage to find Volcano's location on Bend's busy west side, you're sure to enjoy your visit with the effusive Scott and crew. The tasting room is in a glorified urban storage garage, but it's a happening spot. The name might elicit images of wines produced in this highly volcanic region, and some grapes do come from local vineyards, but most are trucked from the Rogue Valley. Scott is a master of red and white blends, but be sure to taste his bubbly Magmita Sangria.

MOUNT VERNON

David Hamilton Winery (191 West Main Street; 541-932-4567). *Tasting room:* Fri.–Sun. 12–5. *Fee:* Complimentary. *Owner/Winemaker:* David Hamilton. *Wines:* Fruit. Hamilton goes for walks on the wild side—literally—to make his wines. David "the Winer" Hamilton makes wine from nearby mountain bounties: chokecherry, wild plum, elderberry, raspberry, blackberry, Oregon grape, and more. No sulfites are added to any of his wines, so drink them young. The winery is now in Mount Vernon's oldest and largest building, and also houses a bookstore with comfy couches.

Lodging
in the Bend Area and Elsewhere

SUNRIVER

Sunriver Resort (17600 Center Drive; 800-801-8765). Set in the ponderosa pines about 20 miles south of Bend, this residential neighborhood with town amenities is so sprawling and the layout so complex that it's easy to get lost—which isn't necessarily a bad thing, given the natural landscape. Accommodations at Sunriver Resort range from attractive Lodge Village guest rooms to river condos and full-fledged vacation homes. Sunriver is popular with Oregonians from the western valleys as an escape from the rain and for its plethora of attractions and activities: golf, fishing, bicycling, hiking, and shopping. $$$$

BEND

♿ 🐾 **The Riverhouse** (3075 North Business Highway 97; 541-389-3111 or 866-453-4480). Although it looks fairly ordinary from US 97 on the north end of Bend, you'll quickly grasp the appeal once inside. The Riverhouse is so named because it straddles the rocky Deschutes River, which runs briskly past the restaurant and many of the rooms. Accommodations range from simple deluxe queens to the Gilchrist Suite, with two full baths, three TVs, a spiral staircase, and huge living area. It's $10 extra to face the river, but all rooms include a breakfast buffet. $$–$$$$

🍴 🍸 ♿ 🐾 **Seventh Mountain Resort** (18575 SW Century Drive; 541-382-8711 or 877-765-1501). Towering pines surround a property between Bend and Mount Bachelor Ski Resort. The hotel has spendy luxury suites; affordable rooms are in the form of privately owned condos. Whether you want a romantic getaway or a family gathering place, Seventh Mountain has lodging to fit. Three outdoor pools with hot tubs, sauna, fitness room, skating rink, tennis, and a Mt. Bachelor shuttle will keep you busy. $$–$$$$

Dining
in the Bend Area and Elsewhere

BEND

Bend d'Vine (916 Northwest Wall Street; 541-323-3277). Enjoy small plates with a taste of Oregon wines, then finish off the afternoon or evening with a handmade truffle treat from Bend d'Vine's chocolatier. A happy-hour menu is offered every afternoon and features a sampling of meats, cheeses, and fruits. Local musicians are on the entertainment menu. L/D/HH $$

Crossings at the Riverhouse (3075 North Highway 97; 541-389-8810). Listen to the murmur of the Deschutes River from the restaurant's patio while dining on prime Angus beef (laced in one of five sauces) and sipping a bold Northwest red. Crossings recently expanded its menu to include more seafood. Lunch plates are equally tempting with tempura fish and yam fries, or a shrimp and crab Louie. *Wine Spectator*'s Award of Excellence is proudly displayed in this usually packed, upscale steakhouse. The separate wine bar has a Dine with Wine, and on the last Friday of each month during dinner a wine expert will stop by with samples. B/L/D $$$–$$$$

Deschutes Brewery Public House (1044 NW Bond Street; 541-382-9242). Take the usual pub grub and toss in unusual twist—you're sure to find the Deschutes Brewery a cut above. Of note: Elk meatballs drenched in Black Butte porter sauce, wild boar meat loaf, black bean veggie burger, and flatbread pizza dressed in Rogue Gorgonzola, Oregon pears, and arugula on dough made fresh in the on-site bakery. Even their mustard and ketchup are house-made, with an assist from the brewer. But it isn't all about beer: the pub has a decent representation of Oregon wines by the glass, too. L/D/LN $$

Jackalope Grill (750 NW Lava Road; 541-318-8435). Jackalope's intensely Northwest cuisine is local, organic, seasonal, and matched well to its wines. Chef Tim Garling and his wife, Kathy, wholeheartedly believe in sustainable food practices and put their philosophy into kitchen action. Wild game, fresh seafood, and Oregon beef headline the menu in a white-linen and good-glassware setting. A *Wine Spectator* Award of Excellence recipient and the "Inexpensive" rating means you can enjoy a select bottle of wine with dinner—and maybe order a second. D/HH $$–$$$

Pine Tavern (967 NW Brooks Street; 541-382-5581). The sturdy remains of a 200-year-old ponderosa pine tree juts through the roof in the middle of the dining room at the Pine Tavern, a Bend stalwart for more than 75 years. The food is plenty good, but everyone leaves talking about the baskets of scones with honey butter. You'll find a decent selection of Oregon wines. For the best dining, sit outside on the patio or near the windows overlooking Mirror Pond. Warning: The truffle fries are positively addictive. L/D/HH $$–$$$

REDMOND

Brickhouse (412 Southwest Sixth Street; 541-526-1782). Brickhouse's continental steakhouse cuisine isn't overly creative, but it's solid and consistent. It is known for its competent and amiable service, and it has a decent showing of Oregon wines by the glass and bottle. D/HH Tues.–Sat. $$$

To Do

in the Bend Area and Elsewhere

Attractions

Bend was built on volcanic rock, so it's no surprise that many attractions are related to the region's volatile geologic history.

The **Newberry National Volcanic Monument and Lava Lands Visitor Center** (541-593-2421) offer panoramic views of ancient lava flows and an understanding of how it all happened—and could happen again. If it's summer, walk to the end of the mile-long **Lava River Cave** (541) 383-5300), one of Oregon's longest volcanic tubes. It's always 41 degrees, so bring a jacket, and you might want to rent a lantern from the Forest Service. The **Oregon High Desert Museum** (541-382-4754), 3 miles south of Bend on US 97, covers just about everything related to central Oregon's geology, history, and wildlife. Its interpretive programs are highly educational and entertaining.

Recreation

Ask locals for their favorite outdoor recreation pastime in the Bend area and you'll need more than two hands to count the answers. Although Mount Hood loyalists might argue, the **Mt. Bachelor Ski Resort & Nordic Center** (800-829-2442), in the Cascades about 22 miles southwest of Bend, probably has the best skiing. The powder is prodigious, the runs many and varied, and the weather just right. When it isn't snowing, much of the recreation in the Bend area revolves around the Deschutes River, which is cherished for its rafting and fishing for redsides trout and steelhead.

Among the outdoor wonders, one rises above the rest. Climbers from around the globe come to test their mettle on the rugged outcroppings at **Smith Rock State Park** (541-548-7501) at Terrebonne, about 10 miles north of Redmond. Even if your legs get a little wobbly at the thought of roping up the sheer wall of the aptly named Monkey Face, pull up a lawn chair and watch the experts with binoculars or a spotting scope. Needless to say, given the climate, golf is a favored sport. There are nine public courses in the area, seven covering 18 holes; three are in Sunriver Resort and all are scenic.

Wine Shopping

For the everyday wine drinker, **Wine Styles** has stores in Redmond (249 NW Sixth Street, 541-526-0489) and Bend (1740 NW Pence Lane, 541-389-8889). For a taste of Italy in the Oregon mountains, try **The Wine Shop and Tasting Bar** (55 NW Minnesota Avenue, 541-389-2884) in Bend. The store features more than 40 wines by the glass and is distinctly European, with one out of seven bottles from Oregon. **Bend Wine Cellar** (1444 NW College Way, #8, 541-385-9258) isn't easy to find because it's underground, but the selection is extensive. **Cork Cellars** (161 East Cascade Avenue, Suite 8, 541-549-CORK) and **The Tasting Room** (161 C North Elm Street, 541-549-8730) serve the quaint mountain resort community of Sisters, about 20 miles northwest of Bend.

More Information

Milton-Freewater Chamber of Commerce, 541-938-5563, 157 South Columbia, www.mfchamber.com

The Dalles Area Chamber of Commerce, 541-296-2231, 404 West Second Street, www.thedalleschamber.com

Central Oregon Visitors Association, 888-781-7071, www.visitcentraloregon.com

Columbia Valley Winery Association, 866-360-6611, www.columbiavalleywine.com

Oregon Coast

SEA BREEZES AND WINES

BY NOW, PERHAPS ALL THIS TALK about Oregon's progressive attitudes might be getting old. But let's give credit where it's due. Not only are Oregonians forward-thinking about the land, they're pretty protective of the sea, too. Oregon had the foresight to decide that its stunning coastline—with long strips of beach punctuated by towering capes and jagged rock formations hugged tightly by US 101—belongs to everyone. The result: Every square inch of coastal beaches is public, a hard-fought right held dear by residents.

The Oregon Coast's geography doesn't change much from north to south, but its climate does. From Astoria down to Coos Bay, clouds, fog, and rain are a common theme, and even in the summer temperatures in the mid-60s are the norm.

GETTING HERE AND AROUND

There's no easy way to navigate this area, but that's part of the beauty. If one of the many twisty, winding drives through the misty Coast Range doesn't take your breath away, the intermittent views of the coastline surely will.

You can fly from Portland to Astoria and Newport: **SeaPort Airlines** (888-573-2767) offers three flights daily to Astoria and two to Newport. In addition, Coos Bay/North Bend is served twice daily by **United Express** (800-864-8331), with flights from Portland and San Francisco.

The Coast Range is bisected by 12 highways, all between 50 and 70 miles long, and all scenic. To make the wine tour from north to south, take US 30 from Portland to Astoria. Once on the coast, expect to move slowly along US 101 because of heavy traffic (especially in summer), numerous communities, and frequent cape traversals. You'll need more than a day to do justice to the 250 miles of viewing pleasure from Astoria to Bandon.

LEFT: Heceta Head might be the top photo op on Oregon's spectacular coast. John Baker

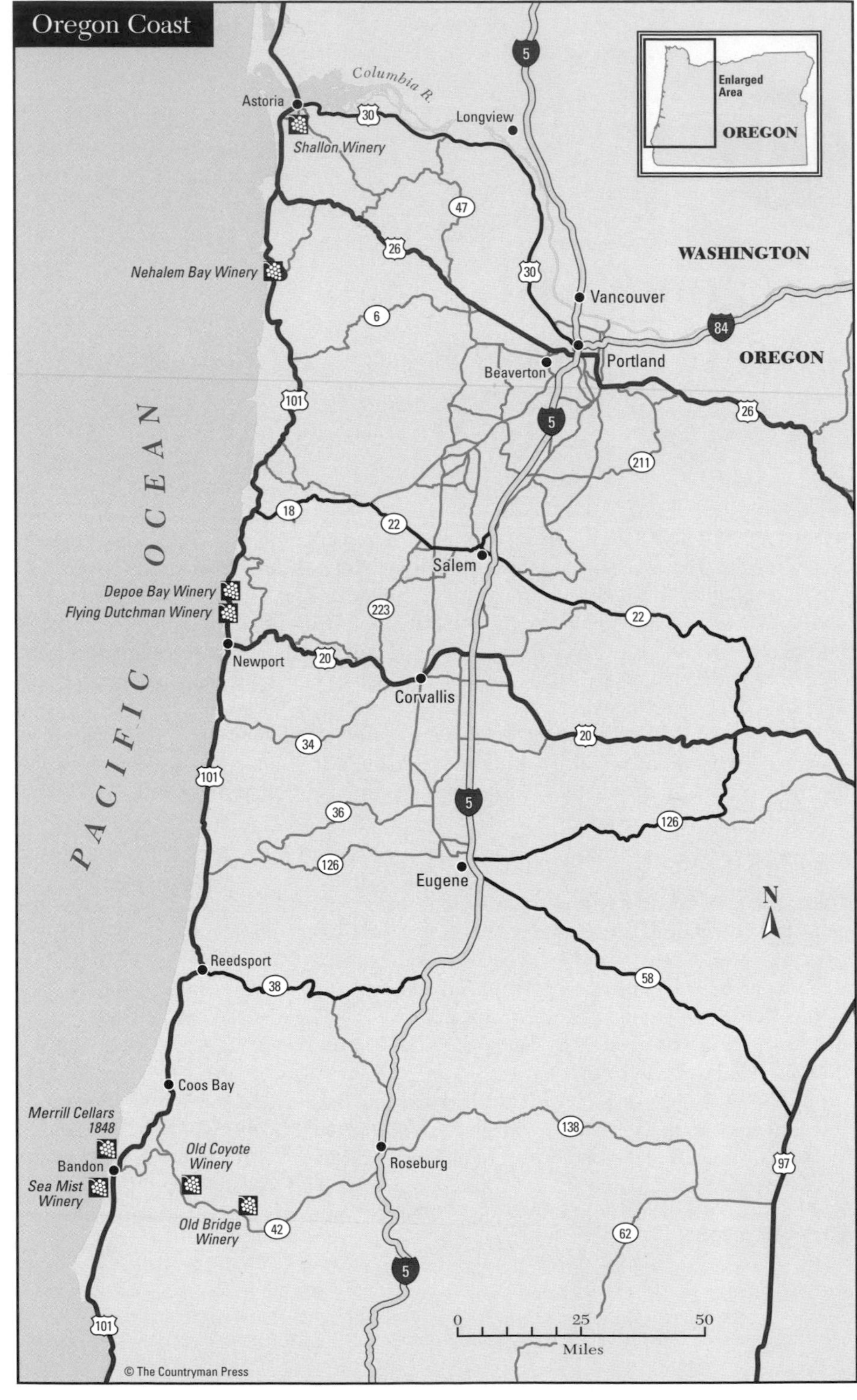
Oregon Coast
Enlarged Area
OREGON
Columbia R.
Astoria
Shallon Winery
Longview
WASHINGTON
Nehalem Bay Winery
Vancouver
Portland
Beaverton
OREGON
PACIFIC OCEAN
Salem
Depoe Bay Winery
Flying Dutchman Winery
Newport
Corvallis
Eugene
N
Reedsport
Coos Bay
Merrill Cellars 1848
Bandon
Sea Mist Winery
Old Coyote Winery
Old Bridge Winery
Roseburg
0
25
50
Miles
© The Countryman Press

Salty sea air is the key to Flying Dutchman's fermentation process. Courtesy Flying Dutchman Winery

NORTH COAST (Astoria to Lincoln City)

Oregon's north coast is rugged, wet, and windy, with old forests and towering capes separated by the estuaries of well-known salmon streams. The primary working communities are Astoria and Tillamook. Seaside and Cannon Beach are favorite vacation and weekend destinations, particularly for Portlanders.

Wineries

Along the North Coast

ASTORIA

Shallon Winery (1598 Duane Street; 503-325-5978). *Tasting room:* Daily 1–6. *Fee:* Complimentary. *Owner/Winemaker:* Paul van der Veldt. *Wines:* Whey, fruit. *Cases:* 1,000. Once a showroom for Packard cars and later a bicycle shop, Shallon's tasting room now is home to one-of-a-kind wines and an extraordinary view of the Columbia River's mouth. Van der Veldt's signature wine is a chocolate orange whey concoction that he describes as a "liquid chocolate truffle." Another uniqueness: He's been open every day for nearly three decades, holidays included.

NEHALEM

▲ ✐ ❖ Nehalem Bay Winery (34965 Highway 53; 503-368-9463 or 888-368-9463). *Tasting room:* Daily 9–6. *Fee:* Complimentary. *Owner/Winemaker:* Ray Shackelford. *Wines:* Cabernet franc, Cabernet sauvignon, Chardonnay, Gewürztraminer, Maréchal Foch, Merlot, Pinot gris, Pinot noir, Riesling, fruit. *Cases:* 5,000. Of all the claims made by Oregon's more than 400 wineries, Nehalem Bay's is the most abnormal—or should we say paranormal? The moaning, creaking, and shadowy figures going bump in the night induced a group of experts in the supernatural to come from McMinnville to check it out. The verdict: They're *heeerrre.* The living folks at Nehalem Bay are entertaining sorts as well. Nehalem Bay does a brisk business, and as far as we know, the wines are all consumed by the living. A second tasting room is open daily from 10 to 6 in Depoe Bay, 541-765-3311.

Lodging
Along the North Coast

ASTORIA

🍴 🍸 ❖ ♿ **Cannery Pier Hotel** (10 Basin Street; 503-325-4996 or 888-325-4996). When the Cannery Pier Hotel touts its location above the river, it's spot on. The swanky five-story hotel sits on a pier 600 feet above the Columbia, with magnificent oceanic views from each room. It's obvious the hotel was once a cannery, and great care was taken during renovation to ensure that its character was retained. Suites have balconies and fireplaces, but for a truly memorable stay, rent the exclusive Pilot House penthouse on the fifth floor. $$$$

CANNON BEACH

🍴 ♿ 🐾 **Arch Cape Inn & Retreat** (31970 East Ocean Lane; 800-436-2848). Start with a spectacular castle look-alike above the Pacific Ocean on a fir-bathed hillside. Then add extra touches, such as fireplaces, oversized Jacuzzi tubs, Aveda bath soaps, complimentary wine and apps, and three-course gourmet breakfast. If you like to be spoiled, this is your place. Plan on cracking crab on Saturday nights (reservations recommended). For the eco-minded, Arch Cape supports the North Coast Land Conservancy's work protecting the coast's ecological and cultural values. $$$$

NEHALEM

🍴 🍸 ♿ **Nehalem River Inn & Restaurant** (34910 Highway 53; 503-368-7708). All you need for a bucolic escape is a few miles inland on the banks of the Nehalem River. Owner Lee Vance took over in August 2012 with a vision for a more casual atmosphere and defined focus on Oregon food and wine. The inn has four comfortable rooms, two with private bathrooms. The restaurant uses organic, local produce and seafood. Although the wine list isn't extensive, it represents Oregon well. As for "casual," the dining room welcomes walk-ins. $$–$$$

Dining
Along the North Coast

ASTORIA

❖ **Bridgewater Bistro** (20 Basin Street; 503-325-6777). A prolific wine list is an extension of the charm at Bridgewater, where you'll find the regional seafood choices you'd expect at a former cannery. Views of the Columbia and the dramatic Astoria-Megler Bridge spanning the river are a treat, especially on a rare sunny day from the patio. Brunch has a splash of the unexpected with seafood cakes, prime-rib hash, and specialty French toast. An Astoria institution for three decades, Bridgewater emphasizes Oregon wines from large and small producers. L/D/BR/HH $$–$$$

❖ **Clemente's** (1198 Commercial Street; 503-325-1067). Sea-fresh, sustainable cuisine is the name of the game at Clemente's, which continues to earn regional and national accolades. Dungeness Caesar salad, Willapa Bay clams, yellowfin tuna (in season), albacore sashimi, cioppino, and award-winning chowder . . . it's a seafood lover's nirvana. On the green side, Clemente's uses rice oil for frying and reuses spent grease as biofuel. When it comes to wine, this restaurant is partial to Oregon selections. Clemente's has live music on Fridays and an art gallery. L/D Tues.–Sun. $$$–$$$$

Silver Salmon Grille (1105 Commercial Street; 503-338-6640). Owners Jeff and Laurie Martin embrace all that is Astoria: colorful history, touristy persona, and fresh seafood. Traditional seafood, pasta, and steak coexist with low-carb entrées or sandwiches and sugar-free desserts. Silver Salmon has a reasonably priced and varied (by the bottle, half bottle, or glass) wine list supplied from their temperature-controlled cellar. It also has wine under its own label, made from Columbia Valley grapes. Look for periodic wine tastings. L/D $$$–$$$$

SEASIDE

Yummy Wine Bar & Bistro Thurs.–Mon. (831 Broadway Avenue; 503-738-3100). Welcome to the hippest place in Oregon's quintessential coastal tourist town. The focus is on the wine experience, and Yummy's offers wine by taste, glass, flight, or bottle. Creative cuisine and wines come from around the world—including the Pacific Northwest—and change seasonally. Happy Hour bits and bites range from prawn quesadilla to pulled pork pasta from $4 to $7. Finish with a light Oregon berry sorbet. A retail wine shop, wines classes, wine dinners, and art gallery make it especially yummy. D/HH $$–$$$

To Do

Along the North Coast

Attractions

ASTORIA

Begin your coast tour at the end—**Fort Clatsop National Memorial** (503-861-2471), a replica of the rainy place that Lewis and Clark's Corps of Discovery called home in the winter of 1805–6. Among the features is an exhibit of the fort that the 33-member corps built. Also worth the time is the **Astoria Riverfront Trolley** (503-325-6311, May–Sept.), built in 1913. Before leaving Astoria, visit the **Columbia River Maritime Museum** (1792 Marine Drive, 503-325-2323). It has a riveting exhibit visible before you even get inside—an actual 44-foot Coast Guard boat on artificial waves, rescuing a storm-struck boater from the perilous mouth of the Columbia. Try to catch the **Astoria Sunday Market** (503-325-1010) and its flotilla of 200 vendors from 10 to 3 every Sunday from May to October.

TILLAMOOK

Down US 101 in cheese country, the **Tillamook Air Museum** (6030 Hangar Road, 503-842-1130) is almost impossible to miss because of its colossal size and 50-foot-high words AIR MUSEUM. The museum is a hangar that once housed blimps ready for Japanese submarines during World War II. Inside: a café and gift shop. To get a quick wine and cheese fix, stop at the **Blue Heron French Cheese Company** (2001 Blue Heron Drive, 503-842-8281), open daily for tastings.

Recreation

Don't drive the length of the Oregon Coast without stopping to work off some wine and cheese on one of many breathtaking hikes. The best are **Cape Lookout** and **Cascade Head**. Cape Lookout is a stunning 2-mile walk through towering Douglas firs to the tip of a narrow peninsula that juts into the Pacific south of Tillamook. Cascade Head, named for waterfalls crashing into the ocean, has three moderate trails to meadows that overlook the dramatic Pacific.

Wine Shopping

ASTORIA

Probably the most renowned wine shop on the north coast is Astoria's **The Cellar on 10th** (1004 Marine Drive, 503-325-6600). An iron spiral staircase leads you to the loaded underground wine world (4,500 bottles) and tasting bar. Weekly wine-ed classes also take place here.

CANNON BEACH

A longtime wine geek hangout is **The Wine Shack** (124 North Hemlock Street, 503-436-1100/800-787-1765) in Cannon Beach, presenting daily tastings in summer and on Saturday during the winter months. The Shack has offered a strong cadre of regional wines and hard-to-find international bottles for more than three decades. For surprisingly good in-and-out wine shopping, **Surfcrest Market** (3140 South Hemlock Street, 503-436-1189) has a sizable selection and conducts occasional tastings.

PACIFIC CITY

Once basket cases, the folks at Pacific City's lone wine shop are now merely twisted. **Twist Wine Company** (503-965-6887, 6425 Pacific Avenue) is a socially progressive tasting lounge with a flair for the zany. Twist's Basket Case wines, made in McMinnville, are Chenin Blanc, Merlot, Syrah, Cabernet sauvignon.

CENTRAL COAST (Lincoln City to Florence)

Oregon's central coast is much like the north, only it serves as playground for folks in Salem, Albany, Corvallis, and Eugene. What makes this drive spectacular is the windy highway rarely leaves sight of the ocean. Newport is an authentic harbor town with personality, and state parks come at you one after another.

Wineries

Along the Central Coast

OTTER ROCK

Depoe Bay Winery (22 South US 101; 541-765-3311). *Tasting room:* Daily 10–6. This is a second tasting room for Nehalem Bay Winery (see listing under "North Coast Wineries"). It's best known for playfulness and "Le Cave du Vin"—The Wine Cave.

Crush can be a very manual labor of love.

Courtesy Flying Dutchman Winery

Flying Dutchman Winery (915 First Street; 541-765-2553). *Tasting room:* Daily 11–6. *Fee:* 3 comp, $10/flight. *Owner/Winemaker:* Richard Cutler. *Wines:* Cabernet franc, Cabernet sauvignon, Chardonnay, Pinot noir, Syrah, fruit, dessert. *Cases:* 1,500. Flying Dutchman began as a "micro-winery" and now occupies a rocky peninsula above the churning sea waters of Devil's

Punchbowl. After grapes arrive from the Willamette, Umpqua, Applegate, and Rogue Valleys, Cutler ferments them outdoors in blustery, salty air for up to 10 days—about three times the norm—and gets the added advantage of native yeast. He believes longer fermentation and the special terroir makes for better wine. Taste for yourself in the small seaside digs.

Lodging

Along the Central Coast

NEWPORT

🍴 🍸 🎁 🐾 **Embarcadero Resort Hotel & Marina** (1000 SE Bay Boulevard; 541-265-8521). At the Embarcadero, you're in the middle of the action on Newport's lively bay front. If you want to spread out a little and have more expansive views, the Columbus on the Bay Suite offers two bedrooms and a top-floor view. A private crabbing and fishing dock, a sundries store, boat rentals, and marina offer convenient access to all the water activities that lure folks to the coast. $$–$$$$

Dining

Along the Central Coast

LINCOLN CITY

Fathom's Restaurant (4009 SW Highway 101; 541-994-1601). Tenth-floor penthouse views of the Pacific give a command performance at Fathom's, which offers a solid array of seafood, steaks, and pasta to complement the setting. Entrées with fathomable depth: linguine seafood medley, arroz bomba (Spanish risotto) loaded with prawns, mussels, cod, calamari, and clams, and Spicy Moroccan Snapper. Early-bird specials ($9.95) are a draw before 5:30. Oregon and Washington dominate the wine list, including Spanish Head's private labels of Oregon origin. B/L/D $$$$

NEWPORT

Panache (614 West Olive Street; 541-265-2929). New owner/chef Zachary Welman has taken the helm and made minor adjustments to an already stellar menu. Wild-caught fish and seafood form the base for small plates and large, and gluten-free options are now available. Our go-to pick: Smoked Fish Trio (halibut, salmon, tuna)—it's pure Pacific pleasure. Many small rooms in a renovated 1919 home afford intimate dining. The wine list is transitioning to predominantly Oregon offerings. L (except Wed.) D $$–$$$

Saffron Salmon (859 SW Bay Boulevard; 541-265-8921). Saffron Salmon is another breath of fresh sea air, with its delicate representations of fresh-caught Northwest cuisine and wines to match. Overhanging the edge of the pier on Newport's revitalized Bayfront, within yards of resident seals, this diner is a bright light for lunch and dinner. Its signature saffron salmon is prepared as entrée or sandwich and is a must order. A solid collection of Oregon wines, from Airlie to Eyrie, is meant to pair with the fare. Although it's laid-back and casual,

Dine within earshot of the ocean waves at Fathom's Restaurant, at the Inn at Spanish Head. Courtesy Inn at Spanish Head

reservations are a good idea. L/D Thurs.–Tues. (closed Nov.) $$$–$$$$

NYE BEACH

April's at Nye Beach (749 NW Third Street; 541-265-6855). Nearly two decades old and still fresh is April and Ken Wolcott's smallish (38-seat) restaurant by the sea. Don't come for Pacific views; come for the everything-from-scratch, never-deep-fried Mediterranean cuisine. Herbs, flowers, and summer produce come from the Wolcotts' 5-acre Buzzard Hill Farm. A longtime favorite for special occasions, it's a great place to celebrate life and the pursuit of the perfect wine and food pairing. A decent wave of Oregon reds and whites will help. April's closes in January and February. D Wed.–Sun. $$$–$$$$

To Do

Along the Central Coast

Attractions

NEWPORT

Two words: whale watching. Although spouts are frequently visible from the coast, you can get up close and personal from a chartered whale-watching boat out of Newport or Depoe Bay. **Marine Discovery Tours** (345 SW Bay Boulevard, 541-265-6200), on Newport's busy Bayfront, not only gets you within camera shot of whales, but your guides also explore other areas of Oregon's picturesque coastline. For a drier and less bouncy look at sea life, visit Newport's **Oregon Coast Aquarium** (2820 SE Ferry Slip Road, 541-867-3474), widely regarded as one of the nation's finest. A highlight is the walkway through glass portals where sharks and other sea creatures are visible underfoot. The nearby **Hatfield Marine Science Center** (2030 SE Marine Science Drive, 541-867-0100) is equally intriguing for the more academically oriented—young and old alike.

YACHATS

On a coast famed for lighthouses, none is more photographed than **Heceta Head Lighthouse** (92072 Highway 101 South, 866-547-3696), which is carved out of a rocky coastal bluff about 12 miles north of Florence. The still-active lighthouse, with a Fresnel lens that can be seen 21 miles out to sea, is just above the old lightkeeper's house and a reputedly haunted bed & breakfast.

FLORENCE

Sea Lion Caves (91560 Highway 101 North, 541-547-3111) is a cavernous rookery for the Stellar sea lion. A short hike and elevator ride takes you to the cave, where seals are sure to be lounging; birds, squawking; and perhaps even whales, spouting in the distance. A handy way to cover a lot of shopping in a short space is at **Old Town Florence**, a waterfront cluster of gift shops, galleries, restaurants, antiques, and myriad other stores on the Siuslaw River. And there's the **Salmonberry Naturals Organic Farmers' Market** (1845 Highway 126, 541-997-3345) every Saturday in season.

Recreation

NEWPORT

If you're an experienced boatman (or woman), rent your own seagoing craft from the **Embarcadero Resort Hotel and Marina** (1000 SE Bay Boulevard, 541-265-8521).

YACHATS

Cape Perpetua features 26 miles of hiking and biking trails—some to points overlooking the sea, some to the beach, and one to a 500-year-old Sitka spruce.

FLORENCE

A favorite beach pastime is to ply the dramatic sand hills at **Oregon Dunes National Recreation Area** (541-750-7000) in a dune buggy. **Sandland Adventures** (85336 Highway 101 South, 541-997-8087) and **Sand Dunes Frontier** (83960 Highway 101 South, 541-997-3544) have buggies for two to 10 passengers and also rent ATVs. **Aero Legends** (541-991-6139) offers 20-minute biplane rides along the coast for $130.

Golfers have numerous options on the central coast, ranging from nine-hole **Agate Beach Golf Course** (4100 Highway 101 North, 541-265-7331) in Newport and **Crestview Golf Club** (1680 Crestline Drive, 541-563-3020) in Waldport to the breathtaking 18-hole **Sandpine Golf Links** (1201 35th Street, 800-917-4653) in Florence and Oregon native Peter Jacobsen's swanky **Salishan Spa & Golf Resort** (7760 Highway 101 North, 541-764-3632) outside Gleneden Beach—one of the top courses in America.

Wine Shopping

GLENEDEN BEACH

On the grounds at Salishan Spa & Golf Resort is **Wine and Romance** (7760 Highway 101 North, 541-764-0238), a small but nifty shop where you can peruse a credible assortment of wines while watching to old movies playing on a black-and-white TV.

DEPOE BAY

If you missed tasting Nehalem Bay's wines, here's your second chance: The **Depoe Bay Winery** (22 Highway 101 South, 541-765-3311) is an outlet store for the home office up the coast. It has a "wine cave" and views of surf crashing over US 101.

NEWPORT

Swafford's Champagne Patio (1630 Highway 101 North, 541-265-3044) has more than 900 wines to pair with smoked salmon, cheeses, and other gourmet fare for your wine tour. Lunch is served from 11 to 3:30 Tuesday to Saturday, and on Thursday through Saturday, dinner begins at 5:30.

YACHATS

The Wine Place (Highway 101 and West Fourth Street, 541-547-5275) is an offbeat retail wine shop that hosts regular tastings of Oregon wines.

FLORENCE

While in Old Town Florence, check out **Incredible & Edible Oregon** (1350 Bay Street, 541-997-7018), which stocks a large selection of Oregon wines.

SOUTH COAST (Florence to Bandon)

The state's finest sand mountains are a magnet for dune-buggy enthusiasts. Farther south is the industrial port of Coos Bay/North Bend. Bandon-by-the-Sea—more commonly known as Bandon—has become a top coastal destination for its rugged beauty.

Wineries
Along the South Coast

BANDON

Merrill Cellars 1848 (220 East California Street; 541-410-0774 or 541-899-5337). *Tasting room:* Thurs.–Sat. 3–7. *Fee:* $6–8. *Owner/Winemaker:* O. Jay Merrill. *Wines:* Chardonnay, Pinot noir, Syrah, Tempranillo, Viognier, red and white blends. *Cases:* 1,000. O. Jay Merrill makes wine in southern Oregon, but his kids live in Bend and he has a home on the coast—which explains why his tasting rooms are in Bandon and Bend. Merrill specializes in Rhône varietals made from Rogue Valley grapes. His claim to fame: The most 90-plus *Wine Spectator* ratings of any Oregon winery south of the Willamette Valley. The new Bandon tasting room is in the cheese factory in Old Town.

LANGLOIS

Sea Mist Winery (86670 Croft Lake Lane; 541-347-4106). *Tasting room:* By appt. only. *Fee:* Complimentary. *Owners:* Steve & Lisa Foster. *Winemakers:* Wayne & Steve Foster. *Wines:* Cranberry. *Cases:* 1,000. At Sea Mist, it's all about doing one thing well: cranberry wines. Cranberry-blueberry. Cranberry-raspberry. Cranberry-blackberry . . . cranberry, period. Naturally fermented wines made from the abundant berry are, in a pure sense, "estate" wines. Sea Mist is located in a 20-acre bog south of Bandon, perhaps the sunniest town on the coast.

MYRTLE POINT

❖ **Old Coyote Winery** (2025 Spruce Street; 541-572-8090). *Tasting room:* By appt. only. *Fee:* Complimentary. *Owners:* Russ & Tina Barnett. *Winemaker:* Tina Barnett. *Wines:* Raspberry, cranberry. *Cases:* 100. Tina Barnett began making wine for fun after reading a how-to book. Now it's a business she can do from home. Her co-owner and husband built a stunning Old West tasting room from native maple, myrtle, and tan-oak woods. Old Coyote is open by appointment because it's difficult to find; call for directions. As for the name, Tina was undecided about her career until she saw a coyote pass in front of her, signaling her destiny.

REMOTE

Old Bridge Winery (50706 Sandy Creek; 541-572-0272). *Tasting room:* Tues.–Sun. 11–5, May–Dec. *Fee:* Complimentary. *Owners:* George & Angie Clarno. *Winemakers:* George & Janis Clarno. *Wines:* Chardonnay, Merlot, Pinot noir, Riesling, Viognier, Zinfandel, port-style, fruit, sparkling. *Cases:* 2,000. Ask George and Angie which wine is their favorite and they'll quickly answer, "The one in our hand, of course." The couple started winemaking many years ago for fun, friends, and guests who came for hunting-guide service. Finally convinced to go commercial, they became Coos County's first bonded winery; now daughter Janis has joined the winemaking fray. The fruit—blackberry, cranberry, and strawberry-rhubarb—is locally grown. Their tasting room overlooks the Sandy Creek covered bridge, once on the main road from Roseburg to the coast.

Lodging

Along the South Coast

NORTH BEND

The Mill Casino Hotel (3201 Tremont Avenue; 541-756-8800 or 800-953-4800). The Mill Casino is a shining light in the foggy coastal twin cities of Coos Bay and North Bend. Towering seven stories above the bay, many of the 92 rooms afford views. The lodge's 115 rooms reflect local Indian history. Shuttles to nearby golf courses are available; for those staying behind, the casino has marquee entertainment. $–$$

BANDON

A Bandon Inn (56131 Tom Smith Road; 541-347-4417 or 800-526-0209). A Bandon Inn is just a long three-iron away from Bandon Dunes, and exploits its proximity with abandon. The Crenshaw and Hagen rooms answer any questions about Al Greenfield's favorite pro golfers. The Top Shelf bar is for toasting birdies or forgetting bogeys. After hitting 'em straight—or not—there's no better 19th hole than the inn's huge deck with coastal views. Massages, a stocked humidor, and chartered salmon-fishing trips will help you forget those slices into unforgiving sand traps. $$$$

♿ **Lighthouse B&B** (650 Jetty Road SW; 541-347-9316). There isn't a bad view in the house—some are just more spectacular than others at this B&B on the beach across the Coquille River from Bandon's storied lighthouse. Five rooms are accented by fresh salt air and the sound of breakers. The newer Gray Whale Room literally rises to the top. The inn is only a short comb to the beach. $$$–$$$$

🍴 🍸 **The Lodge at Bandon Dunes Golf Resort** (57744 Round Lake Drive; 888-345-6008). Tee up intimate luxury in the 17-room lodge or putt over to the 39-room inn off the 18th green. Or bring your golfing team for a stay in the ultraplush four-bedroom suite situated in The Grove. If you'd like to hit one straight down the middle, go for condo-like accommodations at the Lily Pond or roomier Chrome Lake. Shuttles take you anywhere on the grounds, day or night—including the driving range, where you can hit an unlimited number of practice shots. $$$$

Dining
Along the South Coast

BANDON

Alloro Wine Bar & Restaurant (375 Second Street SE; 541-347-1850). Jeremy Buck and Lian Schmidt bring a love of Florence, Italy, to Old Town Bandon. Alloro combines local seafood, meat, berries, and produce with imported Italian goods to create high-end Tuscan-esque sensations on its regularly changing menu. Their gustoso handmade pasta is their trademark. Alloro's lengthy list of wines showcases the best of Oregon Pinot, along with a collection of Italian vino. D $$$–$$$$

To Do
Along the South Coast

Attractions

REEDSPORT

One of the best ways to understand the varied history of native tribes along the coast is at **Umpqua Discovery Center** (409 Riverfront Way, 541-271-4816), where you'll get a feel for past life near the sea. A more recent historical event was the infamous 1962 Columbus Day storm, which had wind speeds of nearly 180 mph, killed 46 people, and blew down 11 billion board feet of coastal timber. It still ranks as the worst storm in recorded Pacific Northwest history.

COOS BAY/NORTH BEND

As you're passing through to wineries at Myrtle Point, take a break at the **Coos Historical and Maritime Museum** (1220 Sherman Avenue, 541-756-6320) in North Bend. The museum provides a cultural peek into the history of the most industrial communities on the coast; construction of a new 11,000-square-foot facility on the Coos Bay waterfront just east of US 101 began in 2012. Timber was king here for a century or more, and this longtime cornerstone of western Oregon's economy comes to life at the exquisite **Shore Acres State Park** (541-888-4902), about 13 miles southwest of Coos Bay. The colorful gardens and immaculate grounds ring the former estate of Louis Simpson, one of the state's most notable timber barons.

MYRTLE POINT

The **Coos County Logging Museum** (705 Maple Street, 541-572-1014, May–Sept.), houses a wide range of logging artifacts, myrtlewood carvings, and photos. The building was constructed as a sanctuary for Mormons in 1910.

Recreation

BANDON

Only about 160 so-called "links" golf courses exist in the world, and truly one of the most stunning is **Bandon Dunes Golf Resort** (57744 Round Lake Road, 888-345-6008). Golfers from the world over travel here to challenge four courses reminiscent of those in Scotland, only with better weather.

Wine Shopping

BANDON

After playing 18 at Bandon Dunes, drop into the **Oregon Wine Tasting Room** (350 Second Street, 541-347-9081) for a taste of Oregon, California, and points beyond. **Tiffany's Wine Shop** (541-347-4438, 44 Michigan Avenue NE) inside the drugstore has more than 1,000 wines, ranging from Sea Mist's cranberry to assortments from Australia, Hungary, South Africa, and Japan.

More Information

Oregon Coast Visitors Association, 541-574-2679, 137 NE First Street, Newport, www.visittheoregoncoast.com

Oregon Coast Tourism, www.oregoncoasttourism.com

Astoria Chamber of Commerce, 503-325-6311, 111 West Marine Drive, www.oldoregon.com

Bandon Chamber of Commerce, 541-347-9616, 350 South Second Street, www.bandon.com

Coos Bay/North Bend Chamber of Commerce, 541-269-0215, 50 East Central, Coos Bay, www.oregonsbayarea.org

Florence Chamber of Commerce, 541-997-3128, 290 Highway 101, www.florencechamber.com

Lincoln City Chamber of Commerce, 541-994-3070, 4039 Logan Rd., www.lcchamber.com

Myrtle Point Chamber of Commerce, 541-572-2626, 424 Fifth St., www.myrtlepointchamber.org

Nehalem Bay Chamber of Commerce, 503-368-5100, 13015 Highway 101, www.nehalembaychamber.com

Newport Chamber of Commerce, 541-265-8801, 555 SW Coast Highway, www.newportchamber.org

Seaside Chamber of Commerce, 503-738-6391, 7 North Roosevelt, www.seasidechamber.com

Tillamook Chamber of Commerce, 503-842-2575, 3075 Highway 101 North, www.tillamookchamber.org

Yachats Chamber of Commerce, 800-929-0477, 241 Highway 101 South, www.yachats.org

Appendixes

A. FESTIVALS AND EVENTS CELEBRATING OREGON WINE

JANUARY

Oregon Truffle Festival, Eugene, Valley River Inn, 503-296-5929

First Taste Oregon, Salem, Oregon State Fairgrounds, 866-904-6165

FEBRUARY

Newport Seafood and Wine Festival, Newport, South Beach Marina Parking Lot, 800-262-7844

Portland Seafood and Wine Festival, Portland, Convention Center

Confluence Festival, Reedsport/Gardner, W. F. Jewett School, 800-247-2155

Valentine's Day: Check with your favorite winery for Valentine-themed events, dinners, and galas on and around Cupid's day.

Chardonnay runneth over at the Newport Seafood and Wine Festival.

Courtesy Newport Chamber of Commerce

MARCH

Oregon Wine, Cheese, & Pear Jubilee, Willamette Valley Vineyards, 800-344-9463

Flavors of Carlton, Carlton, Ken Wright Cellars, 503-852-4405

McMinnville Wine & Food Classic, McMinnville, Evergreen Aviation and Space Museum, 503-472-4033

Gorge Passport Weekend, Hood River, Columbia Gorge Wineries, 866-413-9463

Greatest of the Grape, Canyonville, Seven Feathers Resort and Casino, 541-673-5323

Rhapsody in the Vineyard, Corvallis, downtown, 541-754-6624

APRIL

Barrel Tours, Roseburg, Umpqua Valley Winegrowers Association, 541-672-5701

Astoria-Warrenton Crab, Seafood and Wine Festival, Astoria, 800-875-6807

Dundee Hills Passport, Dundee, various venues

Mount Angel Fine Wine and Food Festival, Mount Angel, 503-873-9979

North Willamette Wine Trail, various locations at 15 wineries starting west of Portland

Wineglass art is part of the charm at the Newport Seafood and Wine Festival.

Courtesy Newport Chamber of Commerce

Tulip Wine Down, Woodburn, Wooden Shoe Tulip Farm, 503-984-3825

Spring Beer and Wine Fest, Portland, Convention Center, 503-238-3770

MAY

Silverton Wine and Jazz Festival, Silverton, 503-873-9463

Albany Wine Walk, Albany, First Avenue, 541-928-2469

Fern Ridge Wings and Wine Festival, Domaine Meriwether Winery, 541-935-8443

Seaside Downtown Wine Walk, Seaside, 503-717-1914

Science of Wine, Ashland, ScienceWorks Hands-On Museum, 541-482-6767

Memorial Day Weekend: The onset of summer after a long winter is marked by festive celebrations that run the gamut. Anything goes: lively music, salsa dancing, barrel tastings, classes and seminars, local artisan foods paired (or not) with wine, cheeses, chocolates, nuts, meats, or chef-made cassoulet. The venues are as varied as the vintners and admission fees apply to most. Check websites for details, grab a group and a designated driver, and party hardy.

JUNE

Canby Wine and Art Festival, Canby, Clackamas County Fairgrounds, 503-266-1136

Festival of Arts and Wine, St. Benedict, Mount Angel Abbey, 503-845-3030

Hood River County Fruit Loop Wine Celebration, Hood River, 503-386-7697

Sisters Wine & Brew Festival, Sisters, 541-385-7988

JULY

Who's on Third, McMinnville, 503-472-3605

SunRiver Sunfest, The Village at SunRiver Resort, 541-385-7988

Bite & Brew of Salem, Salem, Riverfront Park

International Pinot Noir Celebration, McMinnville, 800-775-4762

Oregon Festival of Sauvignon Blanc, J. Christopher Winery, Newberg, 503-231-5094

AUGUST

Carlton's Walk in the Park, Wennerberg Park, 503-852-6572

Silverton Fine Arts Festival, Coolidge McClaine Park, 503-873-2480

Gorge Wine Celebration for Hospice, Hood River, 866-413-9463

The Bite of Oregon, Portland, Waterfront Park, 503-248-0600

Oregon State Fair Awards Ceremony & Tasting Event, Salem, 800-992-8499

Southern Oregon World of Wine, 310 East California Street, Jacksonville, 541-946-3411

SEPTEMBER

Umpqua Valley Wine, Art & Music Festival, Oakland City Park and Umpqua Community College, 541-459-1385

Taste of Harry & David, Medford

Chehalem Valley Food, Wine & Art Festival, Newberg, 503-538-2014

Oregon Brews and BBQs, McMinnville, Granary District

Labor Day Weekend: New to the famed holiday wine-weekend scene is Labor Day Weekend, an oxymoron of sorts for the industry folk. On your days off, come and watch them labor. Open houses prevail and an aura of titillation hangs in the air as wineries prepare for harvest. Admissions and festivities vary, check websites for specific details.

NOVEMBER

Holiday Food & Gift Festival, Portland, Convention Center, 888-412-5015

NW Food & Wine Festival, Portland, Memorial Coliseum, 800-422-0251

¡Salud! Wine Auction, Dundee, 503-681-1850

Thanksgiving Weekend Open Houses: A longstanding tradition in Oregon, after giving thanks and feasting with friends and family, is to get out of the house (off the video games) and do something active—like touring. And eating even more. The wineries deck their halls, barrels, and tasting rooms with new and old releases, case discounts, and specialty foods. It's the time and place to do your holiday shopping. Fri.–Sun.; tasting fees vary. Check websites for details and activities.

B. TOURING COMPANIES SERVING OREGON WINE COUNTRY

If you want to focus more on the sipping and less on the driving, give one of the many touring companies that have materialized a try. In fact, it's a good idea for many reasons. Oregon Wine Country is full of winding, challenging roads and out-of-the-way wineries. Let the experts get you there and show off their insider knowledge. You don't want to take chances with your safety or the state's strict drunk-driving laws.

PORTLAND

Beautiful Willamette Tours, 360-904-1402 or 877-868-7295

Ecotours of Oregon, 503-245-1428

Fiesta Limousine & Sunset Towncar, 503-641-8100

Grape Escape Winery Tours, 503-283-3380

Martin's Gorge Tours, 503-349-1323 or 877-290-8687

Oregon Wine Tours, 503-681-9463

Sea to Summit Tours, 503-286-9333

Wine Tours Northwest, 503-439-8687 or 800-359-1034

BEAVERTON

JMI Limousine, 503-643-6404 or 800-223-8246

Oregon Wine Tours and Tasting, 503-616-1918

My Chauffeur Wine Tour Company, 503-969-4370 or 877-692-4283

TIGARD

Eco-Wine Tours, 503-863-7777

MCMINNVILLE

Insiders Wine Tour, 503-791-0005

EUGENE

Sunshine Limousine Service, 541-543-6486

THE DALLES

Hood River Tours, 541-350-9850

ROSEBURG

Oregon Wine Country Tours, 866-946-3826

GRANTS PASS

Jules of the Valley Wine Tours, 541-973-9699

ASHLAND

Main Street Tours, 541-482-9852

C. GREAT GRAPE DESTINATIONS

Listed regionally and in touring order

2. Portland Area

TROUTDALE

❑ Edgefield Winery, 503-665-2992, www.mcmenamins.com/winery

SANDY

❑ Buddha Kat Winery, 503-668-3124, www.buddhakatwinery.com

PORTLAND

❑ Hip Chicks Do Wine, 503-234-3790, www.hipchicksdowine.com

❑ Southeast Wine Collective, 503-887-8755, www.sewinecollective.com

- ❑ Bow & Arrow, 503-367-1306, www.bowandarrowwines.com
- ❑ Division Wine Making Company, www.divisionwinemakingcompany.com
- ❑ Helioterra, 503-757-5881, www.helioterrawines.com
- ❑ Vincent, 503-740-9475, www.vincentwinecompany.com

❑ Vie de Bohème, 503-360-1233, www.viedebohemepdx.com

❑ Enso Urban Winery & Tasting Lounge, 503-683-3676, www.ensowinery.com

❑ Urban Wine Works, 503-493-1366, www.urbanwineworks.com

❑ Seven Bridges Winery, 503-203-2583, www.sevenbridgeswinery.com

❑ Boedecker Cellars, 503-288-7752, www.boedeckercellars.com

❑ HV Cellars, 541-294-8577

❑ Bodhichitta Winery & Island Mana Wines, 503-580-9463, www.bodhichittawinery.com

ALOHA

❑ Cooper Mountain Vineyards, 503-649-0027, www.coopermountainwine.com

HILLSBORO

❑ Oak Knoll Winery, 503-648-8198, www.oakknollwinery.com

❑ J. Albin Winery, 503-628-2986

BEAVERTON

❑ Ponzi Vineyards, 503-628-1227, www.ponziwines.com

3. Route 47

NORTH PLAINS

❑ Helvetia Vineyards & Winery, 503-647-7596, www.helvetiawinery.com

❑ Abbey Creek Winery, 503-389-0619, www.abbeycreekvineyard.com

FOREST GROVE

❑ Apolloni Vineyards, 503-359-3606 or 503-330-5946, www.apolloni.com

❑ Purple Cow Vineyards, 503-330-0991, www.purplecowvineyards.com

❑ Shafer Vineyard Cellars, 503-357-6604, www.shafervineyardcellars.com

❑ David Hill Winery & Vineyard, 503-992-8545, www.davidhillwinery.com

- ❏ SakéOne, 503-357-7056, www.sakeone.com
- ❏ Montinore Estate, 503-359-5012, www.montinore.com

CORNELIUS

- ❏ Ardiri Winery & Vineyards, 888-503-3330 or 503-628-6060, www.ardiriwine.com
- ❏ A Blooming Hill Vineyard, 503-992-1196, www.abloominghillvineyard.com

GASTON AREA

- ❏ Plum Hill Vineyards, 503-359-4706, www.plumhillwine.com
- ❏ Patton Valley Vineyards, 503-985-3445, www.pattonvalley.com
- ❏ Kramer Vineyards, 503-662-4545, www.kramerwine.com
- ❏ Elk Cove Vineyards, 503-985-7760, www.elkcove.com
- ❏ ADEA Wine Co./Fisher Family Cellars, 503-662-4509, www.adeawine.com

YAMHILL AREA

- ❏ WillaKenzie Estate, 503-662-3280, www.willakenzie.com
- ❏ Lenné Estate, 503-956-2256, www.lenneestate.com
- ❏ Kason Vineyards, 503-537-3070, www.kasonvineyards.com
- ❏ Zenas, 971-231-5128, www.zenaswines.com
- ❏ Stag Hollow Wines & Vineyards, 503-662-5609, www.staghollow.com

CARLTON AREA

- ❏ Cana's Feast, 503-852-0002, www.canasfeastwinery.com
- ❏ Carlton Winemakers Studio, 503-852-6100, www.winemakersstudio.com
  - ❏ Andrew Rich Vintner, 503-852-6100, www.andrewrichwines.com
  - ❏ Bachelder, 905-941-3942, www.thomasbachelder.com
  - ❏ Dukes Family Vineyards, 503-835-0620, www.dukesfamilyvineyards.com
  - ❏ Hamacher Wines, 503-852-7200, www.hamacherwines.com
  - ❏ Lazy River Vineyard, 503-662-5400, www.lazyrivervineyard.com
  - ❏ Merriman Wines, 503-852-6100, www.merrimanwines.com
  - ❏ Montebruno, 503-852-6100
  - ❏ Omero Cellars, 503-537-2638, www.omerocellars.com
  - ❏ Retour Wines, 971-237-4757, www.retourwines.com
  - ❏ Trout Lily Ranch, 503-852-6100, www.troutlilyranchpinot.com
  - ❏ Wahle Vineyards & Cellars, 503-241-3385, www.wvcellars.com
- ❏ Carlton Cellars, 503-474-8986, www.carltoncellars.com
- ❏ Cliff Creek Cellars, 503-852-0089, www.cliffcreek.com
- ❏ Troon, 503-852-3084, www.troonvineyard.com
- ❏ Noble Pig Winery, 503-474-2000, www.noblepigwine.com
- ❏ Terra Vina, 503-925-0712, www.terravinawines.com
- ❏ Barking Frog Winery, 503-702-5029, www.barkingfrogwinery.com
- ❏ Folin Cellars, 503-349-9616, www.folincellars.com

- ❑ Seven of Hearts, 971-241-6548, www.sevenofheartswine.com
- ❑ EIEIO & The Tasting Room, 503-852-6733, www.onhisfarm.com
- ❑ Ken Wright Cellars Tasting Room, 503-852-7010, www.kenwrightcellars.com
- ❑ Scott Paul Wines, 503-852-7300
- ❑ Spofford Station/Stone Griffon Vineyard, 971-237-1045, www.jlcwineryonline.com
- ❑ Scott Paul Wines, 503-852-7300, www.scottpaul.com
- ❑ Soléna, 503-662-4730, www.solenaestate.com
- ❑ Carlo & Julian Winery, 503-852-7432 or 503-550-3928, www.carloandjulian.com
- ❑ Soter Vineyards, 503-662-5600, www.sotervineyards.com
- ❑ Lemelson Vineyards, 503-852-6619, www.lemelsonvineyards.com
- ❑ Laurel Ridge Winery, 503-852-7050, www.laurelridgewinery.com
- ❑ Ghost Hill Cellars, 503-852-7347, www.ghosthillcellars.com
- ❑ Monks Gate Vineyard, 503-852-6521, www.monksgate.com
- ❑ Anne Amie Vineyards, 503-864-2991, www.anneamie.com

4. Willamette Valley North

SHERWOOD

- ❑ Raptor Ridge, 503-628-8463, www.raptoridge.com
- ❑ Alloro Vineyard, 503-625-1978, www.allorovineyard.com
- ❑ Blakeslee Vineyard Estate, 503-789-7032, www.blakesleevineyard.com
- ❑ Quailhurst, 503-936-3633, www.quailhurstwines.com
- ❑ J. K. Carriere Wines, 503-554-0721, www.jkcarriere.com

NEWBERG AREA

- ❑ VX Vineyard, 503-538-9895, www.vxvineyard.com
- ❑ August Cellars, 503-554-6766, www.augustcellars.com
    - ❑ Crowley Wines, 971-645-3547, www.crowleywines.com
    - ❑ D. P. Cellars, 503-409-9541
    - ❑ Et Fille, 503-853-5836, www.etfillewines.com
    - ❑ Laura Volkman, 503-806-4047, www.volkmanvineyards.com
    - ❑ Toluca Lane, 971-241-7728, www.tolucalane.com
- ❑ A to Z Wineworks & Rex Hill Vineyards, 503-538-0666, www.atozwineworks.com
- ❑ Dark Horse Tasting Room, 503-538-2427
    - ❑ Ferraro Cellars, 503-758-0557, www.ferrarocellar.com
    - ❑ Medici Vineyards, 503-538-9668
    - ❑ Sineann Cellars, 503-341-2698, www.sineann.com
- ❑ Ancient Cellars, 503-312-4770 or 503-437-4827, www.ancientcellars.com
- ❑ Longplay Wine, 503-489-8466, www.longplaywine.com
- ❑ Fox Farm Multi-Winery Tasting Room, 503-538-8466, www.foxfarmvineyards.com

- ❑ Hip Chicks Do Wine, 503-554-5800, www.hipchicksdowine.com
- ❑ Artisanal Wine Cellars, 503-537-2094, www.artisanalwinecellars.com
- ❑ Chehalem Wines, 503-538-4700, www.chehalemwines.com
- ❑ Anam Cara Cellars, 503-537-9160, www.anamcaracellars.com
- ❑ ROCO Winery/Cellar Door, 503-538-7625, www.rocowinery.com
- ❑ Anderson Family Vineyard, 503-554-5541, www.andersonfamilyvineyard.com
- ❑ Natalie's Estate Winery, 503-807-5008, www.nataliesestatewinery.com
- ❑ J. Christopher Wines, 503-554-9572, www.jchristopherwines.com
- ❑ Vidon Vineyard, 503-538-4092, www.vidonvineyard.com
- ❑ Lachini Vineyards, 503-864-4553, www.lachinivineyards.com
- ❑ Bergström Wines, 503-554-0468 or 503-554-0463, www.bergstromwines.com
- ❑ ArborBrook Vineyards, 503-538-0959, www.arborbrookwines.com
- ❑ Adelsheim Vineyards, 503-538-3652, www.adelsheim.com
- ❑ Ayres Vineyard, 503-538-7450, www.ayresvineyard.com
- ❑ Patricia Green Cellars, 503-554-0821, www.patriciagreencellars.com
- ❑ Beaux Frères, 503-537-1137, www.beauxfreres.com
- ❑ Whistling Ridge Vineyards, 503-554-8991, www.whistlingridgevineyards.com
- ❑ Colene Clemens Vineyards, 503-662-4687, www.coleneclemens.com
- ❑ Styring Vineyards, 503-866-6741, www.styringvineyards.com
- ❑ Redman Vineyard & Winery, 503-554-1290, www.redmanwines.com
- ❑ Trisaetum Winery, 503-538-9898, www.trisaetum.com
- ❑ Brick House Vineyards, 503-538-5136, www.brickhousewines.com
- ❑ Aramenta Cellars, 503-538-7230, www.aramentacellars.com
- ❑ Utopia Wines, 503-298-7841, www.utopiawine.com
- ❑ Penner-Ash Wine Cellars, 503-554-5545, www.pennerash.com

DUNDEE AREA

- ❑ Duck Pond Cellars, 503-538-3199 or 800-437-3213, www.duckpondcellars.com
- ❑ The Four Graces, 800-245-2950, www.thefourgraces.com
- ❑ Dobbes Family Estate, 503-538-1141 or 800-556-8143, www.joedobbeswines.com
- ❑ Ponzi Wine Bar, 503-554-1500, www.ponziwinebar.com
- ❑ Argyle Winery, 503-538-8520 x 228 or 888-427-4953, www.argylewinery.com
- ❑ Domaine Trouvère, 503-487-6370, www.domainetrouvere.com
- ❑ Zerba Cellars Tasting Room, 503-537-9463, www.zerbacellars.com
- ❑ Daedalus Cellars, 503-538-4400, www.daedaluscellars.com
- ❑ Antica Terra Wines, 503-244-1748, www.anticaterra.com
- ❑ Hawkins Cellars, 503-201-8302, www.hawkinscellars.com
- ❑ Hyland Estates, 503-554-4200, www.hylandestateswinery.com
- ❑ Thistle Wines, 503-200-4509, www.thistlewines.com

- ❑ Crumbled Rock Winery, 503-537-9682, www.crumbledrockwines.com
- ❑ Winderlea Vineyard & Winery, 503-554-5900, www.winderlea.com
- ❑ Barrel Fence Cellars, 503-538-7177, www.barrelfencecellars.com
- ❑ Maresh Red Barn, 503-537-1098, www.vineyardretreat.com
- ❑ Torii Mor, 503-538-2279, www.toriimorwinery.com
- ❑ Lange Estate Winery & Vineyards, 503-538-6476, www.langewinery.com
- ❑ Alexana Winery, 503-537-3100, www.alexanawinery.com
- ❑ Bella Vida Vineyard, 503-538-9821, www.bellavida.com
- ❑ Erath Winery, 800-539-9463, www.erath.com

DAYTON AREA

- ❑ Archery Summit, 503-864-4300, www.archerysummit.com
- ❑ De Ponte Cellars, 503-864-3698, www.depontecellars.com
- ❑ Domaine Drouhin of Oregon, 503-864-2700, www.domainedrouhin.com
- ❑ Domaine Serene, 503-864-4600, www.domaineserene.com
- ❑ Vista Hills Vineyard, 503-864-3200, www.vistahillsvineyard.com
- ❑ Winters Hill Vineyard, 503-864-4538, www.wintershillwine.com
- ❑ White Rose Wines, 503-864-2328, www.whiterosewines.com
- ❑ Red Ridge Farms/Durant Vineyards, 503-864-2000, www.redridgefarms.com
- ❑ Sokol Blosser Winery, 503-864-2282 or 800-582-6668, www.sokolblosser.com
- ❑ Stoller Family Estate, 503-864-3404, www.stollerfamilyestate.com
- ❑ Seufert Winery, 503-864-2946, www.seufertwinery.com

5. *Willamette Valley Central*

MCMINNVILLE AREA

- ❑ WineWorks Oregon, 503-472-3215, www.walnutcitywineworks.com
  - ❑ Bernard-Machado, 503-472-3215
  - ❑ Carlton Hill, 503-852-7060, www.carltonhillwines.com
  - ❑ Lundeen Wines, 503-472-4727, www.geniuslociwines.com
  - ❑ Robinson Reserve, www.robinsonreservewine.com
  - ❑ Z'ivo, www.zivowines.com
- ❑ Westrey Wine Company, 503-434-6357, www.westrey.com
- ❑ The Eyrie Vineyards, 503-472-6315 or 888-440-4970, www.eyrievineyards.com
- ❑ Remy Wines, 503-560-2003, www.remywines.com
- ❑ Dominio IV Wines, 503-474-8636, www.dominiowines.com
- ❑ Panther Creek Cellars, 503-472-8080, www.panthercreekcellars.com
- ❑ Twelve, 503-435-1212, www.twelvewine.com
- ❑ R. Stuart & Co., 503-472-4477, www.rstuartandco.com
- ❑ Willamette Valley Vineyards Wine Center, 503-883-9012, www.wvv.com

- ❑ Anthony Dell Cellars, 503-910-8874, www.anthonydellcellars.com
- ❑ Evergreen Vineyards, 503-472-9361 x4523 or 866-434-4818, www.evergreen vineyards.com
- ❑ Youngberg Hill Vineyards, 503-472-2727, www.youngberghill.com
- ❑ Coeur de Terre Vineyard, 503-472-3976, www.cdtvineyard.com
- ❑ Maysara Winery, 503-843-1234, www.maysara.com
- ❑ Yamhill Valley Vineyards, 503-843-3100, www.yamhill.com
- ❑ Hauer of the Dauen Winery, 503-868-7359
- ❑ Methven Family Vineyards, 503-868-7259, www.methvenfamilyvineyards.com

WHEATLAND

- ❑ Arcane Cellars at Wheatland Winery, 503-868-7076, www.arcanecellars.com

AMITY

- ❑ Kristin Hill Winery, 503-835-0850, www.kristinhillwinery.com
- ❑ Coelho Winery of Amity, 503-835-9305, www.coelhowinery.com
- ❑ Mia Sonatina Cellars, 503-449-0834, www.miasonatina.com

SALEM AREA

- ❑ Brooks Wines, 503-435-1278, www.brookswine.com
- ❑ Mystic Wines, 503-581-2769, www.mysticwine.com
- ❑ Stangeland Vineyards & Winery, 503-581-0355, www.stangelandwinery.com
- ❑ Witness Tree Vineyard, 503-585-7874, www.witnesstreevineyard.com
- ❑ Cristom Vineyards, 503-375-3068, www.cristomwines.com
- ❑ St. Innocent Winery, 503-378-1526, www.stinnocentwine.com
- ❑ Bethel Heights Vineyard, 503-581-2262, www.bethelheights.com
- ❑ Bryn Mawr, 503-581-4286, www.brynmawrvineyards.com
- ❑ Björnson Vineyard, 503-593-1584, www.bjornsonwine.com
- ❑ Evesham Wood Vineyard & Winery, 503-371-8478, www.eveshamwood.com
- ❑ Redhawk Vineyard & Winery, 503-362-1596, www.redhawkwine.com
- ❑ Cubanisimo Vineyards, 503-588-1763, www.cubanisimovineyards.com
- ❑ Orchard Heights Winery, 503-391-7308, www.orchardheightswinery.com
- ❑ Kathken Vineyards, 503-316-3911, www.kathkenvineyards.com
- ❑ Cherry Hill Winery, 503-623-7867, www.cherryhillwinery.com
- ❑ Firesteed Cellars, 503-623-8683, www.firesteed.com

DALLAS

- ❑ Van Duzer Vineyards, 503-623-6420 or 800-884-1927, www.vanduzer.com
- ❑ Namasté Vineyards, 503-623-4150, www.namastevineyards.com

RICKREALL

- ❑ Château Bianca, 503-623-6181, www.chateaubianca.com
- ❑ Left Coast Cellars, 503-831-4916, www.leftcoastcellars.com

❑ Johan Vineyards, 866-379-6029, www.johanvineyards.com

❑ Eola Hills Wine Cellars, 503-623-2405 or 800-291-6730, www.eolahillswinery.com

❑ Illahe Vineyards, 503-831-1248, www.illahevineyards.com

❑ Amalie Robert Vineyard, 503-882-8833, www.amalierobert.com

SALEM

❑ Honeywood Winery, 503-362-4111, www.honeywoodwinery.com

❑ Vitae Springs Vineyard, 503-588-0896 or 503-581-3411, www.vitaesprings.com

❑ Ankeny Vineyard Winery, 503-378-1498, www.ankenyvineyard.com

❑ Trinity Vineyards, 503-371-6977, www.trinityvineyards.com

TURNER

❑ Willamette Valley Vineyards, 503-588-9463, www.wvv.com

6. Willamette Valley East

WEST LINN

❑ Oswego Hills Winery, 503-655-2599, www.oswegohills.com

❑ Ribera Vineyards, 503-638-7323, www.riberavineyards.com

OREGON CITY

❑ King's Raven Winery, 503-656-6439 or 503-539-7202, www.kingsravenwine.com

❑ Christopher Bridge Cellars, 503-263-6267, www.christopherbridgewines.com

AURORA

❑ Pheasant Run Winery, 503-678-3131, www.pheasantrunwine.com

CANBY

❑ St. Josef's Winery, 503-651-3190, www.stjosefswinery.com

WOODBURN

❑ Hanson Vineyards, 503-634-2348, www.hansonvineyards.com

MOLALLA

❑ AlexEli Vineyard, 503-829-6677, www.alexeli.com

SCOTTS MILL

❑ Domaine Margelle Vineyards, 503-873-0692, www.domainemargelle.com

SILVERTON

❑ Vitis Ridge Winery, 503-873-9800, www.vitisridge.com

SUBLIMITY

❑ Silver Falls Vineyard, 503-769-5056, www.silverfallsvineyards.com

❑ Pudding River Wine Cellars, 503-365-0391, www.puddingriver.com

AUMSVILLE

❑ Piluso Vineyard & Winery, 503-749-4125, www.pilusowines.com

7. Willamette Valley South

ALBANY

❑ Springhill Cellars, 541-928-1009, www.springhillcellars.com

MONMOUTH

❑ Emerson Vineyards, 503-838-0944, www.emersonvineyards.com

❑ Airlie Winery, 503-838-6013, www.airliewinery.com

PHILOMATH

❑ Lūmos, 541-929-3519, www.lumoswine.com

❑ Cardwell Hill Winery, 541-929-9463, www.cardwellhillwine.com

❑ Harris Bridge Vineyard, 541-929-3053, www.harrisbridgevineyard.com

❑ Pheasant Court Winery/Wine Vault, 541-929-7715, www.pheasantcourtwinery.com

❑ Spindrift Cellars, 541-929-6555, www.spindriftcellars.com

CORVALLIS

❑ Nuthatch Cellars, 541-754-8483, www.nuthatchcellars.com

BELLFOUNTAIN

❑ Tyee Wine Cellars, 541-753-8754, www.tyeewine.com

SWEET HOME

❑ Marks Ridge Winery, 541-367-3292, www.marksridge.com

MONROE

❑ Benton-Lane Winery, 541-847-5792, www.benton-lane.com

JUNCTION CITY

❑ Brigadoon Wine Co., 541-998-2600, www.brigadoonwineco.com

❑ Pfeiffer Winery, 541-998-2828, www.pfeiffervineyards.com

❑ High Pass Winery, 541-998-1447, www.highpasswinery.com

CHESHIRE

❑ RainSong Vineyard, 541-998-1786, www.rainsongvineyard.com

ELMIRA

❑ LaVelle Vineyards, 541-935-9406, www.lavellevineyards.com

VENETA

❑ Domaine Meriwether, 541-935-9711, www.meriwetherwines.com

EUGENE

❑ Sarver Winery, 541-935-2979, www.sarverwinery.com

❑ Sweet Cheeks Winery, 541-349-9463, www.sweetcheekswinery.com

❑ Silvan Ridge Winery, 541-345-1945, www.silvanridge.com

❑ Noble Estate, 541-338-3007, www.nobleestatevineyard.com

❑ Territorial Vineyards & Wine Company, 541-684-9463, www.territorialvineyards.com

LORANE

❑ King Estate, 541-942-9874, www.kingestate.com

❑ Chateau Lorane, 541-942-8028, www.chateaulorane.com

COTTAGE GROVE

❑ Saginaw Vineyard, 541-942-1364, www.saginawvineyard.com

❑ Iris Vineyards, 541-942-5993, www.irisvineyards.com

8. Umpqua Region

ELKTON

- ❑ Anindor Vineyards, 541-584-2637, www.anindor.com
- ❑ Bradley Vineyards, 541-584-2888, www.bradleyvineyards.com
- ❑ Brandborg Vineyard & Winery, 541-584-2870, www.brandborgwine.com
- ❑ Rivers Edge, 541-584-2357, www.riversedgewinery.com

OAKLAND AREA

- ❑ Sienna Ridge Estate, 541-849-3300, www.siennaridgeestate.com
- ❑ MarshAnne Landing, 541-459-7998, www.marshannelanding.com
- ❑ Misty Oaks Vineyard, 541-459-3558, www.mistyoaksvineyard.com

ROSEBURG AREA

- ❑ Henry Estate Winery, 541-459-5120 or 800-782-2686, www.henryestate.com
- ❑ Reustle Prayer Rock Vineyards, 541-459-6060, www.reustlevineyards.com
- ❑ Becker Vineyard, 541-677-0288, www.beckerwine.com
- ❑ Pyrenees Vineyard & Cellars (North), 541-672-8060, www.pyreneesvineyard.com
- ❑ Glaser Estate Winery, 541-580-4867, www.glaserestatewinery.com
- ❑ TeSoAria Vineyard & Winery, 541-464-0032, www.tesoaria.com
- ❑ Melrose Vineyards, 541-672-6080, www.melrosevineyards.com
- ❑ HillCrest Vineyard & Winery, 541-673-3709, www.hillcrestvineyard.com
- ❑ Delfino Vineyards, 541-673-7575, www.delfinovineyards.com
- ❑ Chateau Nonchalant, 541-679-2394, www.chateaunonchalantvineyards.com
- ❑ Girardet Wine Cellars, 541-679-7252, www.girardetwine.com
- ❑ Abacela, 541-679-6642, www.abacela.com
- ❑ Spangler Vineyards, 541-679-9654, www.spanglervineyards.com

MYRTLE CREEK

- ❑ Pyrenees Vineyard & Cellars (South), 541-863-7797, www.pyreneesvineyard.com

WINSTON

- ❑ Wild Rose Vineyard, 541-580-5488, www.wildrosevineyard.com

9. Southern Oregon

GRANTS PASS AREA

- ❑ Red Lily Vineyards, 541-846-0601, www.redlilyvineyards.com
- ❑ Schmidt Family Vineyards, 541-846-9985, www.sfvineyards.com
- ❑ Serra Vineyards, 541-846-9223, www.serravineyards.com
- ❑ Rosella's Vineyard, 541-846-6372, www.rosellasvineyard.com
- ❑ Troon Vineyard, 541-846-9900, www.troonvineyard.com
- ❑ Soloro Vineyard, 541-862-2693, www.solorovineyard.com
- ❑ Wooldridge Creek Winery, 541-846-6364, www.wcwinery.com

WILLIAMS

- ❑ Plaisance Ranch Winery, 541-846-7175, www.plaisanceranch.com

SELMA

- ❑ Deer Creek Vineyards, 541-597-4226, www.deercreekvineyards.com

CAVE JUNCTION

- ❑ Bridgeview Vineyards & Winery, 541-592-4688, www.bridgeviewwine.com
- ❑ Foris Vineyards Winery, 541-592-3752 or 800-843-6747, www.foriswine.com

JACKSONVILLE AREA

- ❑ Academy of Wine, 541-846-6817
- ❑ John Michael Champagne Cellars, 541-846-0810, www.johnmichaelwinery.com
- ❑ Devitt Winery, 541-899-7511, www.devittwinery.com
- ❑ Fly High & LongSword Vineyard, 541-899-1746 or 800-655-3877, www.fhlv.net
- ❑ Fiasco Winery/Jacksonville Vineyards, 541-846-3022, www.jacksonvillevineyards.com
- ❑ Valley View Winery, 541-899-8468, www.valleyviewwinery.com
- ❑ Cricket Hill Winery, 541-899-7264, www.crickethillwinery.com
- ❑ Cowhorn Vineyard, 541-899-6876, www.cowhornwine.com
- ❑ South Stage Cellars, 541-899-9120, www.southstagecellars.com
- ❑ Umpqua Valley Wine Tasting Room, 541-899-5333, www.umpquatasting.com
- ❑ Quady North, 541-702-2123, www.quadynorth.com
- ❑ DANCIN Vineyards, 541-245-1133, www.dancinvineyards.com

CENTRAL POINT

- ❑ Caprice Vineyards, 541-499-0449, www.capricevineyards.com
- ❑ Ledger David Cellars, 541-664-2218, www.ledgerdavid.com

GOLD HILL

- ❑ Del Rio Vineyards & Winery, 541-855-2062, www.delriovineyards.com
- ❑ Folin Cellars, 541-855-2018, www.folincellars.com

SHADY COVE

- ❑ Crater Lake Cellars, 541-878-4200, www.craterlakecellars.com

EAGLE POINT

- ❑ LaBrasseur Vineyard, 541-865-3648, www.labrasseurvineyard.com
- ❑ Agate Ridge Vineyard, 541-830-3050, www.agateridgevineyard.com

WHITE CITY

- ❑ Kriselle Cellars, 541-842-0029, www.krisellecellars.com

MEDFORD

- ❑ RoxyAnn Winery, 541-776-2315, www.roxyann.com
- ❑ EdenVale Winery, 541-512-9463, www.edenvalleyorchards.com
- ❑ Pebblestone Cellars, 541-512-1704, www.pebblestonecellars.com

TALENT

- ❑ StoneRiver Vineyard, 541-535-4661, www.stoneriverwinery.com
- ❑ Paschal Winery & Vineyard, 541-535-7957, www.paschalwinery.com
- ❑ Trium, 541-535-4015, www.triumwines.com

ASHLAND

- ❑ Grizzly Peak Winery, 541-482-5700, www.grizzlypeakwinery.com
- ❑ Weisinger's, 541-488-5989, www.weisingers.com

10. Columbia Gorge

HOOD RIVER

- ❑ Cathedral Ridge Winery, 800-516-8710, www.cathedralridgewinery.com
- ❑ Marchesi Vineyards & Winery, 541-386-1800, www.marchesivineyards.com
- ❑ Phelps Creek Vineyards, 541-386-2607, www.phelpscreekvineyards.com
- ❑ Pheasant Valley Vineyard & Winery, 541-387-3040, www.pheasantvalleywinery.com
- ❑ Mt. Hood Winery, 541-386-8333, www.mthoodwinery.com
- ❑ Viento, 541-386-3026 or 541-490-6655, www.vientowines.com
- ❑ Wy' East Vineyards, 541-386-1277, www.wyeastvineyards.com
- ❑ Springhouse Cellar, 541-308-0700, www.springhousecellar.com
- ❑ Quenett Winery, 541-386-2229, www.sunshinemill.com
- ❑ Stella Fino, 541-386-6150, www.stellafino.com
- ❑ Naked Winery, 800-666-9303, www.nakedwinery.com
- ❑ Cascade Cliffs Vineyard & Winery, 541-436-4215 or 509-767-1100, www.cascadecliffs.com
- ❑ Cerulean Wine, 503-333-9725, www.ceruleanwine.com
- ❑ Stoltz Vineyards, 541-386-8732, www.stoltzvineyards.com
- ❑ The Pines 1852 Tasting Room & Gallery, 541-993-8301, www.thepinesvineyard.com

MOSIER

- ❑ Garnier Vineyards at Mayerdale, 541-487-2200, www.garniervineyards.com

11. Eastern Oregon & Elsewhere

THE DALLES

- ❑ Maison de Glace Winery, 541-993-4640, www.maisondeglacewinery.com
- ❑ Sunshine Mill Winery, 541-298-8900, www.sunshinemill.com
- ❑ Dry Hollow Vineyards, 541-296-2953, www.dryhollowvineyards.com

MILTON-FREEWATER

- ❑ Watermill Winery, 541-938-5575, www.watermillwinery.com
- ❑ Zerba Cellars, 541-938-9463, www.zerbacellars.com
- ❑ Castillo de Feliciana Vineyard & Winery, 541-558-3656, www.castillodefeliciana.com

ECHO

❑ Sno Road Winery, 541-376-0421, www.piercyfamilyvineyards.com

COVE

❑ Gilstrap Brothers Vineyard & Winery, 541-568-4646 or 866-568-4200, www.gilstrapbrothers.com

JOSEPH

❑ Lathrop Country Wines, 541-377-0644 or 541-432-0500

BAKER CITY

❑ Mother Lode Cellars, 541-519-4640, www.motherlodecellars.com

CULVER

❑ Maragas Winery, 541-546-5464, www.maragaswinery.com

TERREBONNE

❑ Faith, Hope & Charity Vineyards & Events, 541-526-5075, www.faithhopeandcharityevents.com

BEND

❑ Volcano Vineyards, 541-617-1102, www.volcanovineyards.com

MOUNT VERNON

❑ David Hamilton Winery, 541-932-4567, www.davidhamiltonwinery.com

12. The Oregon Coast

ASTORIA

❑ Shallon Winery, 503-325-5978, www.shallon.com

NEHALEM

❑ Nehalem Bay Winery, 503-368-9463 or 888-368-9463, www.nehalembaywinery.com

OTTER ROCK

❑ Depoe Bay Winery, 541-765-3311

❑ Flying Dutchman Winery, 541-765-2553, www.dutchmanwinery.com

BANDON

❑ Merrill Cellars 1848, 541-410-0774, www.merrillcellars.com

LANGLOIS

❑ Sea Mist Winery, 541-347-4106

MYRTLE POINT

❑ Old Coyote Winery, 541-572-8090, www.oldcoyotewinery.com

REMOTE

❑ Old Bridge Winery, 541-572-0272

D. GROCERY STORES THAT HOST REGULAR WINE TASTINGS

Bales Marketplace, Cedar Mill, West Linn, Farmington

Fred Meyer, statewide

Haggen Food & Pharmacy, Beaverton, Oregon City, Tualatin

Lamb's Thriftway, Portland, Lake Oswego, Wilsonville

Made in Oregon, statewide

Market of Choice, Eugene, Ashland, Portland, West Linn

New Seasons Markets, Portland, Beaverton, Lake Oswego, Hillsboro, Happy Valley

Ray's Food Place, statewide, excluding Portland

Roth's Fresh Markets, Willamette Valley

Stroheckers, Portland

Whole Foods Market, Portland, Hillsboro, Tigard, Bend

Zupan's Markets, Portland

Index

N

O

P

T

U

V

W

Y

Z